J. A. BALL
JULY 2012
P9-CJH-019

The Unfolding of Language

GUY DEUTSCHER

The Unfolding of Language

An Evolutionary Tour of Mankind's Greatest Invention

METROPOLITAN BOOKS
Henry Holt and Company • New York

For Janie

maṣṣar šulmim u balāṭim ina rēšiki ay ipparku

Metropolitan Books
Henry Holt and Company, LLC
Publishers since 1866
175 Fifth Avenue
New York, New York 10010

Metropolitan Books® and m® are registered
trademarks of Henry Holt and Company, LLC.

ISBN- 0-8050-7907-6
Printed in the United States of America

Contents

Icelandic
Norwegian
Swedish
Scottish Gaelic†
Irish Gaelic
English
Welsh
Cornish†
Danish
Latvian
Lithuanian
Belarussian
Frisian
Dutch
German
Polish
Ukrai
Czech
Slovakian
Breton
French
Gothic†
Slovenian
Romanian
Gaulish†
Italian
Umbrian†
Serbo-Croatian
Bulgarian
Catalan
Albanian
Mace-donian
Oscan†
Portuguese
Spanish
Greek
Lydia
MEDITERRANEAN SEA
N
NE
E
SE
S
SW
W
NW
Key to symbols
Welsh a living language
Hittite† a dead language

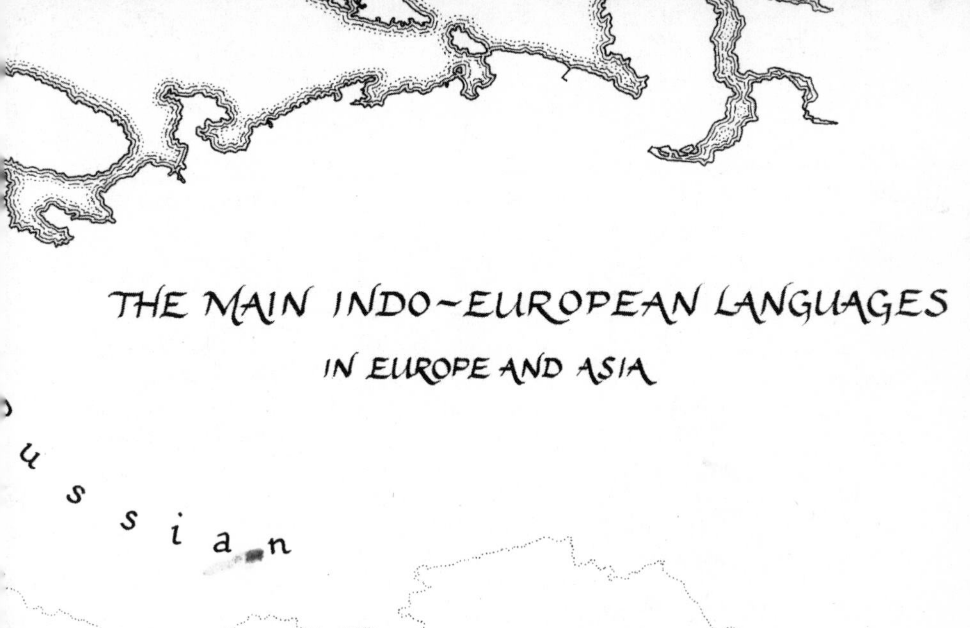
THE MAIN INDO-EUROPEAN LANGUAGES
IN EUROPE AND ASIA

Ossetic
CASPIAN SEA
Armenian
Avestan†
Kurdish
Tajiki
Tocharian†
Persian
Pashto
Punjabi
Sanskrit†
Nepali
Baluchi
Hindi
Assamese
Sindhi
Bengali
Gujarati
Oriya
Marathi
Sinhalese

THE SEMITIC LANGUAGES

IN THEIR ORIGINAL HOMELANDS

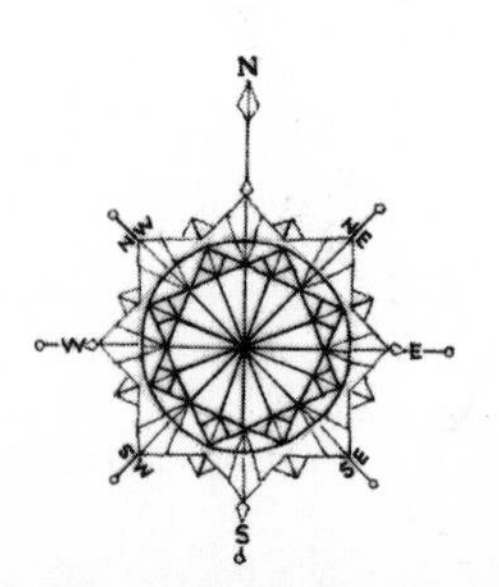

Key to symbols

Tigre a living language

Moabite† a dead language

BLACK SEA
CASPIAN SEA
Aleppo
Nineveh
Eblaite†
Ugaritic†
Assyrian†
Tehran
Aramaic
Baghdad
Damascus
AKKADIAN†
Ammonite†
Babylonian†
Moabite†
Edomite†
Arabic
Mecca
RED SEA
Mehri
Tigre
Sabaic†
GE'EZ†
Sana
Tigrinya
Soqotri
Amharic
Addis Ababa

INTRODUCTION

'This Marvellous Invention'

Of all mankind's manifold creations, language must take pride of place. Other inventions – the wheel, agriculture, sliced bread – may have transformed our material existence, but the advent of language is what made us human. Compared to language, all other inventions pale in significance, since everything we have ever achieved depends on language and originates from it. Without language, we could never have embarked on our ascent to unparalleled power over all other animals, and even over nature itself.

But language is foremost not just because it came first. In its own right it is a tool of extraordinary sophistication, yet based on an idea of ingenious simplicity: 'this marvellous invention of composing out of twenty-five or thirty sounds that infinite variety of expressions which, whilst having in themselves no likeness to what is in our mind, allow us to disclose to others its whole secret, and to make known to those who cannot penetrate it all that we imagine, and all the various stirrings of our soul'. This was how, in 1660, the renowned grammarians of the Port-Royal abbey near Versailles distilled the essence of language, and no one since has celebrated more eloquently the magnitude of its achievement. Even so, there is just one flaw in all these hymns of praise, for the homage to language's unique accomplishment conceals a simple yet critical incongruity. Language is mankind's greatest invention – except, of course, that it was never invented.

This apparent paradox is at the core of our fascination with language, and it holds many of its secrets. It is also what this book is about.

Language often seems so skilfully drafted that one can hardly imagine it as anything other than the perfected handiwork of a master craftsman. How else could this instrument make so much out of barely three dozen measly morsels of sound? In themselves, these configurations of the mouth – *p*, *f*, *b*, *v*, *t*, *d*, *k*, *g*, *sh*, *a*, *e* and so on – amount to nothing more than a few haphazard spits and splutters, random noises with no meaning, no ability to express, no power to explain. But run them through the cogs and wheels of the language machine, let it arrange them in some very special orders, and there is nothing that these meaningless streams of air cannot do: from sighing the interminable ennui of existence ('not tonight, Josephine') to unravelling the fundamental order of the universe ('every body perseveres in its state of rest, or of uniform motion in a right line, unless it is compelled to change that state by forces impressed thereon').

The most extraordinary thing about language, however, is that one doesn't have to be a Napoleon or a Newton to set its wheels in motion. The language machine allows just about everybody – from pre-modern foragers in the subtropical savannah, to post-modern philosophers in the suburban sprawl – to tie these meaningless sounds together into an infinite variety of subtle senses, and all apparently without the slightest exertion. Yet it is precisely this deceptive ease which makes language a victim of its own success, since in everyday life its triumphs are usually taken for granted. The wheels of language run so smoothly that one rarely bothers to stop and think about all the resourcefulness and expertise that must have gone into making it tick. Language conceals its art.

Often, it is only the estrangement of foreign tongues, with their many exotic and outlandish features, that brings home the wonder of language's design. One of the showiest stunts that some languages can pull off is an ability to build up words of breath-breaking length, and thus express in one word what English takes a whole sentence to say. The Turkish word *şehirlileştiremediklerimizdensiniz*, to take one example, means nothing less than 'you are one of those whom we can't turn into a town-dweller'. (In case you are wondering, this monstrosity really is one word, not merely many different words squashed together – most of its components cannot even stand up on their own.) And if that sounds like some one-off freak, then consider Sumerian, the language spoken on the banks of the Euphrates some 5,000 years ago by the people who invented writing and thus kick-started history. A

Sumerian word like *munintuma'a* ('when he had made it suitable for her') might seem rather trim compared to the Turkish colossus above. What is so impressive about it, however, is not its lengthiness, but rather the reverse: the thrifty compactness of its construction. The word is made up of different 'slots' mu–n–i–n–tum–☐–a–'a, each corresponding to a particular portion of meaning. This sleek design allows single sounds to convey useful information, and in fact even the absence of a sound has been enlisted to express something specific. If you were to ask which bit in the Sumerian word corresponds to the pronoun 'it' in the English translation 'when he had made *it* suitable for her', then the answer would have to be . . . nothing. Mind you, a very particular kind of nothing: the nothing that stands in the empty slot in the middle. The technology is so fine-tuned, then, that even a non-sound, when carefully placed in a particular position, has been invested with a specific function. Who could possibly have come up with such a nifty contraption?

My own curiosity about such questions arose when, as a boy, I first came across a strange and complex structure in a foreign language, the Latin case system. As it happened, I was not particularly put out by the idea that learning a language involved memorizing lots of fiddly new words. But this Latin set-up presented a wholly unfamiliar concept, which looked intriguing but also rather daunting. In Latin, nouns don't just have one form, but come in many different shapes and sizes. Whenever a noun is used, it must have an ending attached to it, which determines its precise role in the sentence. For instance, you use the word *cactus* when you say 'the cactus pricked me', but if you prick it, then you must remember to say *cactum* instead. When you are pricked 'by the cactus', you say *cacto*; but to pick the fruit 'of the cactus', you need to say *cacti*. And should you wish to address a cactus directly ('O cactus, how sharp are thy prickles!'), then you would have to use yet another ending, *cacte*. Each word has up to six different such 'cases',* and each case has distinct endings for singular and plural. Just to give an idea of the complexity of this system, the set of endings for the noun *cactus* is given overleaf:

*All linguistic terms used in this book are explained in the glossary beginning on page 343.

*cact-**us***	'the cactus (pricked me)'	*cact-**i***	'the cactuses (pricked me)'
*cact-**e***	'O cactus!'	*cact-**i***	'O cactuses!'
*cact-**um***	'(I pricked) the cactus'	*cact-**os***	'(I pricked) the cactuses'
*cact-**i***	'of the cactus'	*cact-**orum***	'of the cactuses'
*cact-**o***	'to the cactus'	*cact-**is***	'to the cactuses'
*cact-**o***	'by the cactus'	*cact-**is***	'by the cactuses'

And as if this were not bad enough, the endings are not the same for all nouns. There are no fewer than five different groups of nouns, each with an entirely different set of such endings. So if, for instance, you wish to talk about a prickle instead, you have to memorize a different set of endings altogether.

While struggling to learn all the Latin case endings by heart, I developed pretty strong feelings towards the subject, but I wasn't quite sure whether it was a matter more of love or of hate. On the one hand, the elegant mesh of meanings and forms made a powerful impression on me. Here was a remarkable structure, based on a simple yet inspired idea: using a little ending on the noun to determine its function in the sentence. This clever device makes Latin so concise that it can express gracefully in a few words what languages like English need longer sentences to say. On the other hand, the Latin case system also seemed both arbitrary and unnecessarily complicated. For one thing, why did there have to be so many different sets of endings for all the different groups of nouns? Why not just have one set of endings – one size to fit all? But more than anything, there was one question I could not get out of my mind: who could have dreamt up all these endings in the first place? And if they weren't invented, how else could such an elaborate system of conventions ever have arisen?

I had childish visions of the elders of ancient Rome, sitting in assembly one hot summer day and debating what the case endings should be. They first decide by vote that *-orum* is to be the plural ending of the 'genitive' case ('of the cactuses'), and then they start arguing about the plural ending for the 'dative' case ('to the cactuses'). One party opts for *-is*, but another passionately advocates *-ibus*. After heated debate, they finally agree to reach an amicable compromise. They decree that the nouns in the language will be divided into different groups, and that some nouns will have the ending *-is*, while others will take *-ibus* instead.

In the cold light of day, I somehow suspected that this wasn't really a very likely scenario. Still, I couldn't begin to imagine any plausible alternative which would explain where all these endings could have sprung from. If this intricate system of conventions had not been designed by some architect and given the go-ahead by a prehistoric assembly, then how else could it have come about?

Of course, I was not the first to be baffled by such problems. For as long as anyone can remember, the origins of language's artful construction have engaged scholars' minds and myth-makers' imaginations. In earlier centuries, the answer to all these questions was made manifest by Scripture: like everything else in heaven and earth, language *was* invented, and the identity of the inventor explained its miraculous ingenuity. Language declared the glory of God, and its accomplishment showed his handiwork.

But if language was indeed divinely conceived and revealed to Adam fully formed, then how was one to account for its many less than perfect aspects? For one thing, why should mankind speak in so many different tongues, each one boasting its own formidable selection of complexities and irregularities? The Bible, of course, has an explanation even for these flaws. God quickly came to regret the tool that he had given mankind, for language had made people powerful, too powerful, and words had given them the imagination to lust for even more power. Their ambition knew no bounds, 'and they said: go to, let us build us a city and a tower, whose top may reach unto heaven'. And so, to thwart their overweening pride, God scattered the people over the face of the earth, and confounded their languages. The messy multiplicity of languages could thus be explained as God's punishment for human hubris.

The story of the Tower of Babel is a remarkable evocation of the power of language, and is surely a premonition of the excesses that this power has made possible. Taken literally, however, neither invention by divine *fiat* nor dispersal as a punishment for human folly seems at all likely today. But has anyone ever come up with a more convincing explanation?

In the nineteenth century, when the scientific study of language began in earnest, it seemed at first as if the solution would not be long in coming. Once linguists had subjected the history of language to systematic examination, and succeeded in understanding perhaps its most surprising trait, the incessant changes that affect its words, sounds and even structures over the years, they would surely find the key to all mysteries and discover how the whole edifice of linguistic conventions could have arisen. Alas, when linguists delved into the history of the European tongues, what they began to unearth was not how complex new structures grew, but rather how the old ones had collapsed, one on top of another. Just as one example, Latin's mighty case system first fractured and then fell apart in the latter days of the language, when the endings on nouns were worn away and disappeared. A noun such as *annus*, 'year', which in classical Latin still had eight distinct endings for different cases in the singular and the plural (*annus*, *anne*, *annum*, *anni*, *anno*, *annos*, *annorum*, *annis*), ended up in the daughter language Italian with only two distinct forms intact: *anno* in the singular (with no differentiation of case) and *anni* in the plural. In another daughter language, French, the word has shrunk even further to an endingless *an*, and in the spoken language, not even the distinction between singular and plural has been maintained on the noun, since the singular *an* and the plural *ans* are usually pronounced the same way – something like {ã} (curly brackets are used here to mark approximate pronunciation).

And it is not only the descendants of Latin, and not only case systems, which have suffered such thorough disintegration. Ancient languages such as Sanskrit, Greek and Gothic flaunted not just highly complex case systems on nouns, but even more complex systems of endings on verbs, which were used to express a range of intricate nuances of meaning. But once again, most of these structures did not survive the passing of time, and fell apart in the modern descendants. It seemed that the deeper linguists dug into history, the more impressive was the make-up of words they encountered, but when they followed the movement of languages through time, the only processes that could be discerned were disintegration and collapse.

All the signs, then, seemed to point to some Golden Age lying somewhere in the twilight of prehistory (just before records began), when languages were graced with perfectly formed structures, especially with elaborate arrays of endings on words. But at some subsequent stage, and for some unknown reason, the forces of destruction were unleashed on the languages and began battering the carefully crafted edifices, wearing away all those endings. So, strangely enough, what linguists were uncovering only seemed to confirm the gist of the biblical account: God gave Adam a perfect language some 6,000 years ago, and since then, we have just been messing it up.

The depressingly one-sided nature of the changes in language left linguists in a rather desperate predicament, and gave rise to some equally desperate attempts at explanation. One influential theory contended that languages had been in the business of growing more complex structures only in the prehistoric era – that period which cannot be observed – because in those early days, nations were busy summoning all their strength for perfecting their language. As soon as a nation marched on to the stage of history, however, all its creative energy was expended on 'history-making' instead, so there was nothing left to spare for the onerous task of language-building. And thus it was that the forces of destruction attacked the nation's language, and its structures gradually cracked and fell apart.

Was this tall story really the best that linguists could come up with? Surely a more plausible scenario would be that alongside the forces of destruction in language there must also be some creative and regenerative forces at work, natural processes which can shape and renew systems of conventions. After all, it is unlikely that those forces which had originally created the pristine prehistoric structures simply ceased to operate at some random point a few millennia ago, just because someone decided to start the stopwatch of history. So the forces of creation must still be somewhere around. But where? And why are they so much more difficult to spot than the all too evident forces of destruction?

It took a long time before linguists managed to show that the forces of creation are not confined to remote prehistory, but are alive and kicking even in modern languages. In fact, it is only in recent decades that linguists have begun to appreciate the full significance of these creative forces, and have amassed enough evidence from hundreds of languages around the world to allow us a deeper understanding of their ways. At last, linguists are now able to present a clearer picture of how imposing linguistic edifices can arise, and how intricate systems of grammatical conventions can develop quite of their own accord. So today, it is finally possible to get to grips with some of the questions which for so long had seemed so intractable.

This book will set out to unveil some of language's secrets, and thereby attempt to dismantle the paradox of this great uninvented invention. Drawing on the recent discoveries of modern linguistics, I will try to expose the elusive forces of creation and thus reveal how the elaborate structure of language could have arisen. (The following chapter will describe in greater depth what 'structure' is – from meshes of endings on words to the rules of combining words into sentences – and show how it allows us to communicate unboundedly complex thoughts and ideas.) The ultimate aim, towards the end of the book, will be to embark on a fast-forward tour through the unfolding of language. Setting off from an early prehistoric age, when our ancestors only had names for some simple objects and actions, and only knew how to combine them into primitive utterances like 'bring water' or 'throw spear', we will trace the emergence of linguistic complexity and see how the extraordinary sophistication of today's languages could gradually have evolved.

At first sight, this aim may seem much too ambitious, for how can anyone presume to know what went on in prehistoric times without indulging in make-believe? The actual written records we have for any language extend at most 5,000 years into the past, and the languages that are attested by that time are by no means 'primitive'. (Just think of Sumerian, the earliest recorded language, with its cleverly designed sentence-words like *munintuma'a*, and with pretty much the full repertoire of complex features found in any language.) This means that the primitive stage that I have just referred to, and which can rather loosely be called the 'me Tarzan' stage, must lie long before records begin, deep in the prehistoric past. To make matters worse, no one even knows when complex languages first started to evolve (more on this later). So without any safe anchor in time, how can linguists ever hope to reconstruct what might have taken place in that remote period?

The crux of the answer is one of the fundamental insights of linguistics: *the present is the key to the past*. This tenet, which was borrowed from geology in the nineteenth century, bears the intimidating title 'uniformitarianism', but stands for an idea that is as simple as it is powerful: the forces that created the elaborate features of language cannot be confined to prehistory, but must be thriving even now, busy creating new structures in the languages of today. Perhaps surprisingly, then, the best way of unlocking the past is not always to peer at faded runes on ancient stones, but also to examine the languages of the present day.

All this does not mean, of course, that it is a trivial undertaking to uncover the creative forces in language even in today's languages. Nevertheless, thanks to the discoveries that linguists have made in recent years, pursuing the sources of creation has become a challenge that is worth taking up, and here, in a nutshell, is how I propose to go about it.

The first chapter will give a clearer idea of what the 'structure of language' is all about, by sneaking behind the scenes of language and surveying some of the machinery that makes it tick. Then, having focused on the object of inquiry, we can start examining the transformations that languages undergo over time. The first challenge will be to understand why languages cannot remain static, why they change so radically through the years, and how they manage to do so without causing a total collapse in communication. Once the main motives for language's perpetual restlessness have been outlined, the real business can begin – examining the processes of change themselves.

First to come under the magnifying glass will be the forces of destruction, for the devastation they wreak is perhaps the most conspicuous aspect of language's volatility. And strangely enough, it will also emerge that these forces of destruction are instrumental in understanding linguistic creation and regeneration. Above all, they will be indispensable for solving a key question: the origin of the 'raw materials' for the structure of language. Where, for instance, could the whole paraphernalia of case endings (as in the Latin *-us*, *-e*, *-orum*, *-ibus* and so on) have come from? One thing is certain: in language, as in anything else, nothing comes from nothing. Only very rarely are words 'invented' out of the blue (the English word 'blurb' is reputedly one of the exceptions). Certainly, grammatical elements were not devised at a prehistoric assembly one summer day, nor did they rise from the brew of some alchemist's cauldron. So they must have developed out of something that was already at hand. But what?

The answer may come as rather a surprise. The ultimate source of grammatical elements is nothing other than the most mundane everyday words, unassuming nouns and verbs like 'head' or 'go'. Somehow, over the course of time, plain words like these can undergo drastic surgery, and turn into quite different beings altogether: case endings, prepositions, tense markers and the like. To discover how these metamorphoses take place, we'll have to dig beneath the surface of language and expose some of its familiar aspects in an unfamiliar light. But for the moment, just to give a flavour of the sort of transformations we'll encounter, think of the verb 'go' – surely one of the plainest and most unpretentious of words. In phrases such as '*go* away!' or 'she's *going* to Basingstoke', 'go' simply denotes movement from one place to another. But now take a look at these sentences:

Is the rain ever *going to* stop?
She's *going to* think about it.

Here, 'go' has little to do with movement of any kind: the rain is not literally *going* anywhere to stop, in fact it has no plans to go anywhere at all, nor is anyone really 'going' anywhere to think. The phrase 'going to' merely indicates that the event will take place some time in the future. Indeed, 'be going to' can be replaced with 'will' in these examples, without changing the basic meaning in any way:

Will the rain ever stop?
She *will* think about it.

So what exactly is going on here? 'Go' started out in life as an entirely ordinary verb, with a straightforward meaning of movement. But somehow, the phrase 'going to' has acquired a completely different function, and has come to be used as a grammatical element, a marker of the future tense. In this role, the phrase 'going to' can even be shortened to 'gonna', at least in informal spoken language:

Is the rain ever *gonna* stop?
She's *gonna* think about it.

But if you try the same contraction when 'go' is still used in the original meaning of movement, you're gonna be disappointed. No matter how colloquial the style or how jazzy the setting, you simply cannot say 'I'm *gonna* Basingstoke'. So 'going to' seems to have developed a kind of schizophrenic existence, since on the one hand it is still used in its original 'normal' sense (she's *going to* Basingstoke), but on the other it has acquired an *alter ego*, one that has been transformed into an element of grammar. It has a different function, a different meaning, and has even acquired the possibility of a different pronunciation.

Of course, 'gonna' is only a very simple grammatical element – not much, you may feel, to write home about. But although 'gonna' may seem a rather slight example of 'the structure of language', worlds apart from grand architectures such as the Latin case system, the transformations that brought it about encapsulate many of the fundamental principles behind the creation of new grammatical elements. So when its antics have been exposed, they will lead the way to understanding how much more imposing edifices in language could have arisen.

Finally, once the principles of linguistic creation have begun to yield their secrets, and once the major forces that raise new grammatical structures have been revealed, it will be possible to synthesize all these findings into one ambitious thought-experiment, and project them on to the remote past. Towards the end of the book, I will invite you on a whistle-stop tour through the unfolding of language, starting from the primitive 'me Tarzan' stage, and ending up with the sophistication of languages in today's world.

Before we can begin, however, there are two potential objections which need to be addressed. First, why did I say nothing about what might have happened before the 'me Tarzan' stage? Why does our story have to start so 'late' in the evolution of language, when there were already words around, rather than right at the beginning, millions of years ago, when the first hominids were coming down from the trees and uttering their first grunts? The reason why we can't start any earlier is quite straightforward: the 'me Tarzan' stage is also the boundary of our knowledge. Once language already had words, it had become sufficiently similar to the present for sensible parallels to be drawn between then and now. For example, it is plausible to assume that the first ever grammatical elements arose in prehistory in much the same way as new grammatical elements develop in languages today. But it is not so easy to peer beyond the 'me Tarzan' stage, to a time when the first words were emerging, because we have neither contemporary parallels nor any other sources of evidence to go on. These days, there are no systems of communication which are in the process of evolving their first words. The closest parallel is probably the babbling of babies, but no one knows to what extent, if at all, the development of individual children's linguistic abilities recapitulates the evolution of language in the human race. And clearly, there are no early hominids around nowadays on whom linguists can test their theories. All we have are a few hand-axes and some dry bones, and these say nothing about how language began. In fact, artefacts and fossils cannot even establish with any confidence *when* language started to develop. Nothing illustrates our present state of ignorance better than the range of estimates offered for when language might have emerged – so far, researchers have managed to narrow it down to anywhere between 40,000 and 1½ million years ago.

Some linguists believe that *Homo erectus*, some 1½ million years ago, already had a language that was rather similar to what I have called the 'me Tarzan' stage. The arguments they advance are that *Homo erectus* had a relatively large brain, and used primitive but fairly standardized stone tools, and probably also controlled the use of fire. This hypothesis may be true, of course, but it may well be wide of the mark. The use of tools certainly doesn't require language: even chimpanzees use tools such as twigs to hunt termites or stones to crack nuts. What is more, chimps' handling of stones is not an instinct, but a 'culturally transmitted' activity found only among certain groups. The skill is taught by mothers to their children, and this is done without relying on anything like a human language. Of course, even the most primitive tools of *Homo erectus* (flaked stone cores called 'hand-axes') are far more sophisticated than anything used by chimpanzees, but there is still no compelling reason why these flaked stones could not have been produced without language, and transmitted from generation to generation by imitation. Brain size is equally problematic as an indication for language, because ultimately, no one has any clue about exactly how much brain is needed for how much language. Moreover, the capacity for language may have been latent in the brain for millions of years, without actually being put to use. After all, even chimpanzees, when trained by humans, can be taught to communicate in a much more sophisticated way than they ever do naturally. So even if the brain of *Homo erectus* had the capacity for something resembling human language, there is no compelling reason to assume that the capacity was ever realized. The arguments for an early date are therefore fairly shaky.

But the arguments for a late date are pretty speculative too. Most scholars believe that human language (and by this I include the 'me Tarzan' stage) could not have emerged before *Homo sapiens* (that is, anatomically modern humans) arrived on the scene, around 150,000 years ago. Some arguments for this view rely on the shape and position of the larynx, which in earlier hominids was higher than in *Homo sapiens* and in consequence did not allow them to produce the full range of sounds that we can utter. According to some researchers, hominids prior to *Homo sapiens* could not, for instance, produce the vowel *i* {ee}. But ultimately, this does not say very much, since by all accounts, et es perfectle pesseble to have a thoroughle respectable language wethout the vowel *i*. Various researchers have proposed a much more recent date for the origin of language, and connect it with a so-called 'explosion' in arts and technology between 50,000 and 40,000 years ago. At this time, one starts finding unmistakable evidence of art from Eastern Africa, such as ostrich eggshells from Kenya fashioned into disc-shaped beads with a neat hole in the middle. Somewhat later, after 40,000 years ago, European cave paintings provide even more striking signs of artistic creativity. According to some linguists, it is only when there is evidence of such symbolic artefacts (and not just functional tools) that the use of 'human language' can be inferred, for after all, the quintessential quality of language is its symbolic nature, the communication with signs that mean something only by convention, not because they really sound like the object they refer to. There are also other tantalizing clues to the capability of our ancestors at around that time. Some time before 40,000 years ago, the first human settlers reached Australia, and since they must have had to build watercraft to get there, many researchers have claimed that these early colonizers would have needed to communicate fairly elaborate instructions.

Once again, however, a note of caution should be sounded. First, a steadily growing body of evidence seems to cast doubt on the 'explosiveness' of the explosion in arts and technology, and is pushing the date of the earliest symbolic artefacts further and further backwards. For example, researchers have recently found perforated shell-beads in a South African cave which appear to be clear signs of symbolic art from around 75,000 years ago. So 'modern human behaviour', as some archaeologists have labelled it, may have dawned much earlier than the supposed date of around 50,000 years ago, and may have developed more gradually than has sometimes been assumed.

Moreover, there is no necessary link between advances in art and technology and advances in language. To take an obvious example, the technological explosion we are experiencing today was certainly not inspired by an increase in the complexity of language, nor was any advance in language responsible for the industrial revolution, or for any other technological leap during the historical period. And there is an even stronger reason for caution. If technology was always an indication of linguistic prowess, then one would expect the simplest and most technologically challenged hunter-gatherer societies to have very simple, primitive languages. The reality, however, could not be more different. Small tribes with stone-age technology speak languages with structures that sometimes make Latin and Greek seem like child's play. 'When it comes to linguistic form, Plato walks with the Macedonian swineherd, Confucius with the head-hunting savage of Assam,' as the American linguist Edward Sapir once declared. (Later on, I shall even argue that some aspects of language tend to be *more* complex in simpler societies.)

Needless to say, the lack of any reliable information about when and how speech first emerged has not prevented people from speculating. Quite the reverse – for centuries, it has been a favourite pastime of many distinguished thinkers to imagine how language first evolved in the human species. One of the most original theories was surely that of Frenchman Jean-Pierre Brisset, who in 1900 demonstrated how human language (that is to say, French) developed directly from the croaking of frogs. One day, as Brisset was observing frogs in a pond, one of them looked him straight in the eye and croaked 'coac'. After some deliberation, Brisset realized that what the frog was saying was simply an abbreviated version of the question 'quoi que tu dis?' He thus proceeded to derive the whole of language from permutations and combinations of 'coac coac'.

It must be admitted that more than a century on, standards of speculation have much improved. Researchers today can draw on advances in neurology and computer simulations to give their scenarios a more scientific bent. Nevertheless, despite such progress, the speculations remain no less speculative, as witnessed by the impressive range of theories circulating for how the first words emerged: from shouts and calls; from hand gestures and sign language; from the ability to imitate; from the ability to deceive; from grooming; from singing, dancing and rhythm; from chewing, sucking and licking; and from almost any other activity under the sun. The point is that as long as there is no evidence, all these scenarios remain 'just so' stories. They are usually fascinating, often entertaining, and sometimes even plausible – but still not much more than fantasy.

Of course, this means that our history of language must remain incomplete. But rather than lamenting what can never be known, we can explore the part that does lie within reach. Not only is it a substantial part, it is also pretty spectacular.

The second possible charge that could be raised against the plan of attack which I have outlined is potentially much more serious, and concerns the question of 'innateness': how much of language's structure is already coded in our genes? Readers who are familiar with the debate over this issue might well wonder how exploring the processes of language change squares with the view – advanced over the last few decades in the work of Noam Chomsky and the influential research programme which he has inspired – that significant elements in the structure of language are specified in our genes. Linguists of the 'innatist' school believe that some of the fundamental rules of grammar are biologically pre-wired, and that babies' brains are already equipped with a specific tool-kit for handling complex grammatical structures, so that they do not need to learn these structures when they acquire their mother-tongue.

Many people outside the field of linguistics are under the impression that there is an established consensus among linguists over the question of innateness. The reality, however, could not be more different. Let five linguists loose in a room and ask them to discuss innateness – chances are you will hear at least seven contradictory opinions, argued passionately and acrimoniously. The reason why there is so much disagreement is fairly simple: no one actually *knows* what exactly is hard-wired in the brain, and so no one really knows just how much of language is an instinct. (Usually, when something becomes known for a fact, there is little room left for fascinating controversy. There is no longer fierce debate, for instance, about whether the earth is round or flat, and whether it revolves around the sun or vice versa.) Of course, there are some basic facts about innateness that everyone agrees on, most importantly, perhaps, the remarkable ability of children to acquire any human language. Take a human baby from any part of the globe, and plonk it anywhere on earth, say in Indonesian Borneo, and within only a few years it will grow up to speak fluent and flawless Indonesian.

That this ability is unique to *human* babies is also clear. In Borneo, it is sadly still common practice to shoot female orang-utans and raise their babies as pets. These apes grow up in families, sometimes side by side with human babies of the same age, but the orang-utans never end up learning Indonesian. And despite popular myth, not even chimpanzees can learn a human language, although some chimpanzees in captivity have developed remarkable communicative skills. In the early 1980s a pygmy chimpanzee (or bonobo) called Kanzi made history by becoming the first ape to learn to communicate with humans without formal training. The baby Kanzi, born at the Language Research Center of the

Georgia State University, Atlanta, used to play by his mother's side during her training sessions, when researchers tried (rather unsuccessfully) to teach her to communicate by pointing at picture-symbols. The trainers ignored the baby because they thought he was still too young to learn, but unbeknownst to them, Kanzi was taking in more than his mother ever did, and as he grew up he went on to develop cognitive and communicative skills far surpassing any other ape before. As an adult, he is reported to be able to use over 200 different symbols, and to understand as many as 500 spoken words and even some very simple sentences. Yet although this Einstein of the chimp world has shown that apes can communicate far more intelligently than had ever been thought possible, and thus forced us to concede something of our splendid cognitive isolation, even Kanzi cannot string symbols together in anything resembling the complexity of a human language.

The human brain is unique in having the necessary hardware for mastering a human language – that much is uncontroversial. But the truism that we are innately equipped with what it takes to learn language doesn't say very much beyond just that. Certainly, it does not reveal whether the *specifics* of grammar are already coded in the genes, or whether all that is innate is a very general ground-plan of cognition. And this is what the intense and often bitter controversy is all about. Ultimately, there must be just one truth behind this great furore – after all, in theory, the facts should all be verifiable. One day, perhaps, scientists will be able to scan and interpret the activity of the brain's neurons with such accuracy that its hardware will become just as unmysterious as the shape of the earth. But please don't hold your breath, because this is likely to take a little while. Despite remarkable advances in neurology, scientists are still very far from observing directly how any piece of abstract information such as a rule of grammar might be coded in the brain, either as 'hardware' (what is pre-wired) or 'software' (what is learnt). So it cannot be over-emphasized that when linguists argue passionately about what exactly is innate, they don't base their claims on actual observations of the presence – or absence – of a certain grammatical rule in some baby's neurons. This rather obvious point should be stressed, because readers outside the field of linguistics need to form a healthy disrespect for the arguments advanced on all sides of the debate. Uncontroversial facts are few and far between, and the claims and counter-claims are based mostly on indirect inferences and on subjective feelings of what seems a more 'plausible' explanation.

The most important of these battles of plausibility has been fought on grounds that are at some remove from the course of our historical exploration. The debate is known in linguistic circles as the 'poverty of stimulus' argument, and revolves around a perennial miracle: the speech that comes out of the mouth of babes and sucklings. How is it that children manage to acquire language with apparently so little difficulty? And how much of language can children really learn on the basis of the evidence they are exposed to? Chomsky and other linguists have argued that children manage to acquire language from scanty and insufficient evidence (in other words, from 'poor stimulus'). After all, most children are not taught their mother-tongue systematically, and even more significantly, they are not exposed to 'negative evidence': their attention is rarely drawn to incorrect or ungrammatical sentences. And yet, not only do children manage to acquire the rules of their language, but there is a variety of errors that they don't seem to make to start with. Chomsky claimed that since children could never have worked out all the correct rules purely from the evidence they were exposed to, the only plausible explanation for their remarkable success is that some rules of grammar were already hard-wired in their brain, and so they never had to learn them in the first place.

Other linguists, however, have proposed very different interpretations. Many have argued that children can learn more from the evidence they are exposed to than Chomsky had originally claimed, and that children receive much more stimulus than Chomsky had admitted. Others maintain that children don't need to master many of the abstract rules that Chomsky postulated, because they can acquire a perfect knowledge of their language by learning much less abstract constructions. Finally, some linguists turn the argument on its head, and claim that the reason why children manage to learn the rules of their language from what appears to be scanty evidence is that language has evolved only those types of rules that can be inferred correctly on the basis of limited data.

The debate is still raging. But in what follows, the issue of learnability will not take centre stage, so it should be fairly easy to stay well clear of the crossfire on the front line. This psychological aspect of the 'nature versus nurture' controversy will not impinge directly on our historical exploration, so – at least until the cows come home – I will just regard the question as unresolved. (If you wish to embroil yourself in the details of the controversy, you can find suggestions for further reading in the note on page 310.) Nor will the following pages be concerned with the biological question of the make-up of our brains. Instead, the aim will be to explore how elaborate conventions of communication can develop in human society. In other words, the subject of investigation will not be biological evolution, but rather the processes that are sometimes referred to as 'cultural evolution': the gradual emergence of codes of behaviour in society, which are passed down from generation to generation.

Nonetheless, it is inevitable that the question of innateness will hover somewhere in the background, and at least in one sense, I hope that exploring the paths of cultural evolution can make a positive contribution to the debate. The processes through which new linguistic structures emerge can offer a fresh perspective on what elements can plausibly be taken as pre-wired, and in particular, they can point to those areas in the structure of language for which there is no need to invoke innateness. The idea is fairly simple: it seems implausible that specific features in the structure of language are pre-wired in the brain if they could have developed only 'recently' (say within the last 100,000 years), and if their existence can be accredited to the natural forces of change that are steering languages even today. In other words, the details of language's structure which can be put down to cultural evolution need not be coded in the genes (although the ability to learn and handle them must of course be innate). It thus seems implausible to me that the *specifics* of anything more sophisticated than the 'me Tarzan' stage, to which we'll return in Chapter 7, need to be pre-wired.

In the pages that follow, I hope to make a convincing case for this view, not by investigating the plausibility or otherwise of certain genetic mutations in earlier hominids, nor by exploring the composition of chromosomes or the chemistry of neurons, but by looking at the evidence that language itself supplies in lavish abundance – in the written records of lost civilizations and in the spoken idiom on today's streets. I invite you, therefore, to set off in pursuit of the elaborate conventions of communication, and discover how systems of sometimes breathtaking sophistication can arise through what appear to be the mundane and commonplace traits of everyday speech. But before we can begin, the object of the chase needs to be identified more clearly: the mysterious 'structure of language' – what it is, what it does, and how cleverly it goes about doing it.

I

A Castle in the Air

C'est un langage estrange que le Basque . . .
On dit qu'ils s'entendent, je n'en croy rien.

Basque is really a strange language . . .
It is said that they understand one another,
but I don't believe any of it.

Joseph Justus Scaliger (1540–1609)

Everyone knows that the words of a language, from its aardvarks to its zucchini, lend meaning to our utterances, and allow us to understand one another. And it is because foreign languages use so many strange words that we cannot understand them without years of labour. Even Joseph Scaliger, the most erudite scholar of his day, a polyglot not only fluent in Latin, Greek and most of the modern languages of Europe, but also self-taught in Hebrew, Arabic, Aramaic and Persian, still had to give up on Basque, because it used completely different words for absolutely everything. The effort of memorizing many thousands of words so overwhelms our perception of what language learning is all about that it may easily lead to the impression that knowing a language just comes down to knowing its words. Surely, if one could only recognize the meaning of each word, all one would need to do is add all these meanings up somehow, in order to grasp the sense of a whole sentence. But if this is so, and language ultimately amounts to just words, then isn't the quest for the origin of structure merely an intellectual wild goose chase?

On reflection, however, it soon becomes clear that language is much more than the sum of its words. In fact, a language with only words, and no structure to prop them up, would be a poor instrument of communication. Words may be the bricks in the language edifice, but when we want to convey subtle thoughts, involving intricate relations between different concepts, we need to combine words into proper sentences. The structure of language is what can turn a pile of word-bricks into a palace of expressions – a castle in the air.

As a simple illustration, consider the following example:

Head vizier Sultan troops the of to the his the brought

If the meaning of a sentence is nothing more than the sum of its words, then why doesn't this one amount to any substance at all, even though the meaning of each word is perfectly familiar? The reason is that there is an essential feature missing from this sentence, and exactly what that is becomes clear as soon as one takes the very same words and arranges them in a different order. Suddenly, they leap into sense:

The Sultan brought his vizier to the head of the troops.

In this arrangement, the words convey a detailed event involving various participants, and now describe not only who these participants are, but also exactly who is doing what to whom. And to remove any lingering suspicion that the choice of words by itself dictates the meaning of a sentence, consider what happens when the same words are once again juggled into a different order:

The troops brought to the Sultan the head of his vizier.

There are many well-turned aphorisms which play on exactly such word permutations: 'better to lose a moment in life than to lose life in a moment'; Mae West's 'a hard man is good to find'; or the definition of 'foreign aid' as the transfer of money 'from poor people in rich countries to rich people in poor countries'. One of my favourites is Kermit the Frog's rearrangement of a well-worn cliché: 'time's fun when you're having flies' (although note that he allows himself some poetic licence by sneaking in an additional '*s*). But most famous, perhaps, is Alice's conversation at the Mad Hatter's Tea Party:

'Then you should say what you mean,' the March Hare went on. 'I do,' Alice hastily replied; 'at least – at least I mean what I say – that's the same thing, you know.' 'Not the same thing a bit!' said the Hatter, 'Why, you might just as well say that "I see what I eat" is the same thing as "I eat what I see"!' 'You might just as well say,' added the March Hare, 'that "I like what I get" is the same thing as "I get what I like"!' 'You might just as well say,' added the Dormouse, who seemed to be talking in his sleep, 'that "I breathe when I sleep" is the same thing as "I sleep when I breathe"!'

Clearly, then, the sense of a sentence depends not only on the meaning of each word but also on the particular arrangement in which these words are joined. The choice of meaning matters, but just as much the order of the combination. (Or you might as well say that 'the choice of order matters just as much to the meaning of the combination'.)

Now a natural reaction to all this might run along the following lines: of course it matters in which arrangement words are combined, but don't we simply put the words in the *natural* order? Doesn't the order of words in the sentence simply follow the natural order of ideas? To see why things are not so simple, consider another variation on the Sultan theme, in the example below:

Sultan vizier his troops his of head their to brought.

Here we go again, I can hear you thinking. No doubt this is just another meaningless list, a jumble of words waiting to be juggled into some sensible order to create yet another meaning. But in fact – the sentence above already makes perfect sense. Or, to be more accurate, it would make perfect sense if you happened to be born in the Sultan's own city and spoke Turkish. For the string above is simply a word-for-word gloss of an entirely respectable Turkish sentence:

Padişah	*vezir-ini*	*ordu-lar-ı-nın*	*baş-ı-na*	*getirdi*
Sultan	vizier-his	troop-s-his-of	head-their-to	brought

'The Sultan brought his vizier to the head of the troops.'

Let's not bother for now with the fact that one Turkish word (like *ordularının*) can express what English conveys with various independent words, and just concentrate for a moment on the *order* in which the Turkish elements are arranged. Clearly, 'natural' is very much a matter of geography: what is perfectly natural to a Turk does not seem even remotely natural to an English speaker. An even more striking example of the discrepancy between the ordering rules of the two languages is provided by the sesquipedalian Turkish word from the previous chapter: *şehirlileştiremediklerimizdensiniz*. The gloss below gives an approximate translation of each of this word's components, in the order in which they appear. Still, the gloss looks almost as much like gobbledegook as the Turkish word itself:

şehir- li- leş- tir- eme- dik- ler- imiz-den- siniz
town-someone.from-become-cause.to-can't-whom-those-we- one.of-you.are

But now try a simple trick, and read the parts in reverse order:

you.are-one.of-we-those-whom-can't-cause.to-become-someone.from-town

This reverse order almost precisely matches the English translation. We now only have to make one slight alteration (move the 'we' two places along) to get a perfectly comprehensible English sentence: 'you are one of those whom we can't cause to become someone from town', or more idiomatically, 'you are one of those whom we can't turn into a town-dweller'. Incidentally, this almost exact mirror-image in the word order of English and Turkish has nothing to do with the direction of writing – both languages are written from left to right. So which order is 'natural'? Is it the English or the Turks who spend their lives talking back to front?

It is only to be expected that the habits of one's own language should seem utterly natural, while those of other peoples much less so – 'natural', after all, is what one is used to. But when one overcomes the biases of familiarity, it becomes clear that neither the English nor the Turkish order is any more natural than the other. Both orders are just cultural conventions, and conventions, by their very nature, can vary across time and space.

All this is not to say, of course, that the conventions of word order are completely arbitrary in every respect, and that different languages can order their words entirely at whim. In fact, in Chapter 7 I will argue that there are a few simple principles for ordering words, which are indeed 'natural', and which are common to all languages. Nevertheless, as will become clear later on, these natural principles still leave considerable scope for various choices, and there is one particular choice that languages make at some stage in their development, which can then ripple throughout their structure, and ultimately result in the mirror-image effect between English and Turkish. For the moment, however, the important thing is to note that a sentence makes sense not because its words are simply placed in some 'natural' and universally valid 'order of ideas'. Rather, the feat of transforming a pile of words into a complex coherent whole is achieved through the mediation of an elaborate system of structural conventions, which can vary greatly from language to language.

The conventions of word order are probably the oldest element in the structure of language. Chapter 7 will suggest that back in the 'me Tarzan' stage, speakers who were trying to string words together had nothing but some simple ordering principles to go on. And even in today's languages, it is fair to say that arranging the bricks in a particular order is still the most important element in the art of sentence construction. Nevertheless, word order is no longer the *only* means speakers can rely on when combining words, since languages have also developed a range of other techniques to help make the bricks stick, such as the use of various adhesives which facilitate the construction of much more complex edifices. The following pages will survey some of these other features in the structure of language – from the mortar, bolts and nails to the grand principles of design. By the end of the chapter, I hope it will be clear that searching for the origin of linguistic structure is nothing less than an attempt to discover how we acquired the ability to build bridges between minds.

A WASTE OF BREATH?

Most words we use, like 'table', 'kick', 'walk' or 'rabbit', have a simple solid meaning, so they are often called 'content words'. Of course, philosophers may dispute that anything to do with meaning is simple, not even the meaning of 'rabbit'. Over the years they have fought long and bitter wars – with thousands of pages as casualties – over the difference between 'denotation' and 'connotation', 'reference' and 'sense', 'symbol' and 'sign', and have busied themselves with such grave questions as whether, when a speaker of an exotic language points at a rabbit and says *gavagai*, he means 'rabbit' or 'undetached rabbit parts'. But in the end, surely anyone with a healthy dose of common sense will reach the conclusion that a rabbit is a rabbit is a rabbit, and there's no need to make a dog's dinner out of that.

Nevertheless, there is also a group of words in language whose meaning really is quite a lot less obvious. These are 'grammatical words' such as *a, the, of, so, that, which, or, than*. Think about it: what is the meaning of *a*, for instance? Can you point at a *the*, or close your eyes and imagine a *than*? In dictionaries and grammar books, such unassuming words appear under a variety of titles: conjunctions, prepositions, articles and so on. But there is one basic property that is common to them all: they cannot boast their own independent meaning. They don't refer to objects, actions or properties, or to any other concepts that can be imagined in their own right.

In fact, language is also populated by beings that are even humbler than grammatical words: various splinters which cannot even stand up on their own. Think of prefixes like *un-*, or suffixes (endings) like *-ly*, *-er*, *-s*. Not only do these fragments have no meaning of their own, they don't even have an independent existence, and in order to make any appearance at all, they must find other words to latch on to: *un*-like-*ly*, long-*er*, piece-*s*. In later chapters, the properties of grammatical elements will be probed in more depth, but for the moment, the profusion of such empty vessels raises an obvious question: why should language be crowded with these meaningless hangers-on in the first place? If grammatical words and elements don't add any independent meaning to the sentence, aren't they just a waste of breath, mouthfuls of airy superfluity, excess freight?

But it would be rash to start clearing the decks and chucking them all overboard just yet, for far from being redundant, grammatical elements are indispensable for keeping the hull of the sentence together. Consider, for instance, the following sentence:

This agreement is about a principle compromise,
not a principle compromise.

Not a terribly good example, you might feel, since this 'sentence' doesn't make any sense. But that is exactly my point – as all it takes is a modest grammatical fragment, the ending *-d*, and the meaningless lines become profoundly sensible.

This agreement is about a principle**d** compromise,
not a principle compromise**d**.
(A paraphrase of a statement by John Hume,
about Northern Ireland's 1998 peace accord)

So even though *-d* has no meaning to call its own, and even though it is a mere chip of a syllable, the whole sense of the sentence nevertheless pivots on it. The ending welds the two content words *principle* and *compromise* together, and determines the hierarchy between them, by marking which one is the head of the phrase, and which is only an appendage (the word that *-d* clings on to):

a $_{\text{principled}}$ compromise = a compromise $_{\text{(which is based on good principles)}}$

a principle $_{\text{compromised}}$ = a principle $_{\text{(which has been compromised)}}$

Similar examples are not hard to come by: a group of $_{\text{striking}}$dancers is quite different from a group of strikers$_{\text{dancing}}$; doing something with $_{\text{disgraceful}}$taste is certainly not the same as doing it with $_{\text{distasteful}}$grace; and to be $_{\text{uncommonly}}$lucky is a different thing altogether from being $_{\text{unluckily}}$common. So even though grammatical words and elements may not have any meaning of their own, they play a crucial role in the administration of the sentence, and help to determine the hierarchy and precise relations between content words.

The valuable role of grammatical words can become evident precisely in those genres that are traditionally parsimonious in their use, for instance, in newspaper headlines that economize on the article 'the'. The drawback of such a spare style is that it can fail to indicate the correct hierarchy of the sentence, and this can lead to such proverbial headline gaffes as 'Lawyers Give Poor Free Advice'. What the writer intended to convey here, of course, was the newsworthy information that lawyers were giving free advice to poor people (that is, 'giving *the* poor free advice'). So 'poor' was conceived as an independent participant in the sentence (the 'indirect object', to be precise). But as it happens, there can be quite another reading of the headline, where 'poor' is no longer an independent participant in the sentence, but only a hanger-on, another appendage to 'advice'. This different role transforms the meaning of the sentence into something rather less newsworthy, namely that the free advice given by lawyers is poor:

SUBJECT	VERB	INDIRECT OBJECT	OBJECT	
Lawyers	give	poor	free advice	(INTENDED MEANING)
Lawyers	give	–	poor free advice	(ALTERNATIVE INTERPRETATION)

The hierarchical organization of the sentence can create many similar pitfalls for headline compilers, in such well-known examples as 'Fund Set Up for Beating Victim's Family', or 'Juvenile Court to Try Shooting Defendant' (both of which would become unambiguous with the judicious placement of one little 'the'). Sometimes, playing on the internal structure of a sentence is also a source of deliberate puns, as in the children's joke-question: 'How do you get down from an elephant?' The answer, of course, is that 'You don't get down from an elephant. You get down from a duck!' The trick here is revealed when the role of the word 'down' in the question and the answer is represented graphically:

SUBJECT	VERB	OBJECT	FURTHER ELABORATION
(How do) you	get down	–	from an elephant?
You	get	down	from a duck!

The role of hierarchy in language is considerably more important, however, than merely a source for verbal wit or headline gaffes. In fact, the multi-tier organization of the sentence is one of the most fundamental design-features of language. Even though on the surface a sentence might seem like just a string of words in linear succession, underneath the floorboards there is a lot going on, with words hierarchically organized on different tiers. And even though we may not be consciously aware that we are speaking or listening 'on different levels', we are all keenly attuned to the tiered structure of the sentence. It was Noam Chomsky who first stressed this point by illustrating how even the simplest everyday linguistic operations, such as forming questions, are sensitive to the hierarchy of the sentence. Consider a sentence like 'the seal was eyeing a fish'. There is a simple way of turning this into a question, as any native speaker knows. If the first verb in the sentence is an auxiliary (a support-verb such as *was, has, will*), then all one has to do is move it to the front of the sentence:

- the seal was eyeing a fish.
- was the seal eyeing a fish?

Now suppose we want to turn a slightly longer sentence into a question: 'the seal that was eyeing a fish has picked a fight with a walrus'. Applying the simple rule above, we find the first auxiliary in the sentence – it happens to be 'was' again – and move that to the front:

- the seal that was eyeing a fish has picked a fight with a walrus.
- was the seal that eyeing a fish has picked a fight with a walrus?

Why did this operation produce such gibberish? The reason is that the rule outlined above was not entirely accurate. When forming a question, it's not the first auxiliary in the *sentence* that needs to be moved, but rather the first auxiliary *on the main level* of the sentence. And in this case, there is an entire phrase which is not on the main level, but only dangles as an appendage of the noun 'seal':

- the seal that was eyeing a fish has picked a fight with a walrus.

All speakers of English intuitively know that when posing a question, the appendage 'that was eyeing a fish' should be passed over in favour of the first auxiliary on the main level, in this case 'has', which should be moved to the front:

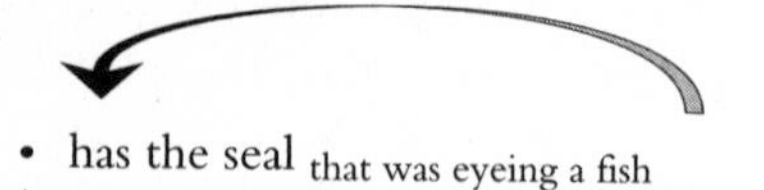

- has the seal that was eyeing a fish picked a fight with a walrus?

In linguistic parlance, the appendage 'that was eyeing a fish' is called a 'relative clause'. But no English speaker needs to sign up for a crash course in syntax to know that this phrase lies low and doesn't get involved when the sentence is rearranged to form a question. When learning the language as children, speakers have intuited that a phrase starting with 'that' or 'which' is subordinate: it doesn't participate in the real action on the main level of the sentence, and sticks to the participant it modifies. So the hierarchical structure of the sentence is not just a graphic game of subscripts, but a fundamental feature of language, which we all take into account when producing or processing sentences.

All this raises an obvious question: why design language in this way? Why not have a system where all words work on the same level? The simple answer is complexity. Later on, I will suggest that at the 'me Tarzan' stage, words were indeed combined on only one level. And as long as all that was involved were just two- or three-word sentences, this flat set-up was perfectly adequate. But when a system grows in complexity, hierarchical structure becomes a more efficient way of doing things. In a large army, for instance, chaos would prevail if the commander-in-chief had to worry about how to place each individual soldier in battle. Instead, the commander only has to think about how to arrange his divisions, the commander of each division then has to decide how to arrange his individual brigades, the commander of each brigade arranges his individual regiments, and so on. In language, a similar hierarchical principle allows us to undertake complex manoeuvres with little difficulty. Consider the following sentences, arranged in order of increasing complexity:

- The seal has picked a fight.
- The seal that was eyeing a fish has picked a fight with a walrus.
- The quarrelsome seal that was eyeing a disenchanted but rather attractive fish has picked a fight with a phlegmatic walrus.
- The quarrelsome seal that was eyeing a disenchanted but rather attractive fish that was jumping in and out of the icy water has picked a fight with a phlegmatic walrus that was innocently passing by.

The fourth sentence, running to a total of thirty-five words, is pretty complex. And yet, for a speaker of English, this sentence is immediately comprehensible, because its complexity is mitigated by the hierarchy of command. At the highest level, the first and the last sentence have the same simple structure: *The seal has picked a fight.* All the further intricacies are entirely an internal matter for the phrases headed by 'seal' and 'fight'. And even within each phrase there is an internal hierarchy of command, so that the task remains manageable at all levels:

The quarrelsome seal that was eyeing a . . . fish that was jumping in and out of the icy water

The hierarchical organization of language is thus quite an ingenious system, which allows us to perform complex tasks with remarkable ease: to produce and understand sentences with many different participants and relations, not to mention hundreds of sounds. The question of how our ancestors might have hit upon such a system will be taken up in Chapter 7.

So far, I have made various claims about the structure of 'language', but in practice, the previous examples dealt mostly with one language in particular. Nevertheless, even if the details were drawn primarily from English, the general principles are valid in all languages of the world. All languages are organized hierarchically, all languages rely on some word-order conventions, all languages use grammatical words, and almost all languages use grammatical elements such as suffixes or prefixes. But while the underlying principles are always the same, languages can differ quite radically in the details. There is considerable variation, for instance, in how the burden is divided between these strategies. Languages such as Vietnamese, Yoruba (spoken in Nigeria) and English rely heavily on word order to spell out the roles of the participants in the sentence. In English, for example, the only way of telling who shoots whom in 'the thief shot the cop' and 'the cop shot the thief' is by the word order: the subject (the one doing the shooting) comes before the object (the one being shot). But in Tamil, Warlpiri (an aboriginal language of Australia) and Russian, word order is much freer.

If not through a strict order of the participants, how can a language manage to signal who is doing what to whom? Hebrew, to take one example, uses a grammatical word for this purpose, and marks the object by putting a preposition, *et*, before it. As the example below illustrates, the participant immediately after the preposition *et* is marked as the one being swallowed:

ha-liviatan	*bala'*	***et***	*Yonah*
the-whale	swallowed	OBJECT	Jonah

'the whale swallowed Jonah'

If one wants to swap the roles (and set the story in a sushi-bar), there is no need in Hebrew to change the order of the participants. It is enough simply to move the preposition *et* to before the whale:

et	*ha-liviatan*	*bala'*		*Yonah*
OBJECT	the-whale	swallowed		Jonah

'Jonah swallowed the whale'

Japanese employs a similar method, only that instead of a **pre**position, it uses two **post**positions, which come *after* the relevant nouns. Here, the postposition *ga* marks who is doing the eating, and *o* marks what is being eaten:

Hanako	*ga*	*susi*	*o*	*tabeta*
Hanako	SUBJECT	sushi	OBJECT	ate

'Hanako ate the sushi'

Russian (like Latin) uses another strategy and instead of adding independent grammatical words, tacks endings on to the nouns themselves. In the example below, the ending *-a* on *akul**a*** 'shark' marks it as the subject, and the ending *-u* on *ryb**u*** 'fish' marks it as the object:

*akul**a***	*videla*	*ryb**u***
shark-SUBJECT	saw	fish-OBJECT

'the shark saw the fish'

Because the endings indicate the roles of the participants explicitly, changing the order of the words doesn't change the basic meaning of the sentence:

akula	*videla*	*rybu*	'the shark saw the fish'
akula	*rybu*	*videla*	
rybu	*akula*	*videla*	
rybu	*videla*	*akula*	
videla	*rybu*	*akula*	
videla	*akula*	*rybu*	

Finally, some languages manage to have a flexible word order, but still don't need to compensate for this by tagging markers on the participants themselves. Their trick is to indicate the role of the participants on the verb instead, as can be seen in the following sentences from a dialect of modern Aramaic spoken in Alqosh, a small town in northern Iraq. The only thing which signposts who is seeing whom in the two sentences below is the shape of the verb: 'saw-she-him' means that the girl sees the boy, while 'saw-he-her' reverses the roles.

ε	*brāta*	*kemxaz-yā-le*	*brona*
that	girl	saw-**she-him**	boy

'that girl saw the boy'

ε	*brāta*	*kemxāz-ē-la*	*brona*
that	girl	saw-**he-her**	boy

'the boy saw that girl'

The examples above should have given a flavour of the variety of the strategies languages have come up with to highlight the basic plot of the action. But there is more to life, of course, than who is doing what to whom, and languages have developed various tools for conveying a great deal of information far and above the rudimentary business of imparting the basic roles of the two leading protagonists. English, for instance, may rely on word order to distinguish between the subject and the object, but for marking the function of various supporting roles, as well as circumstantial evidence such as time and place, it uses both prepositions and postpositions:

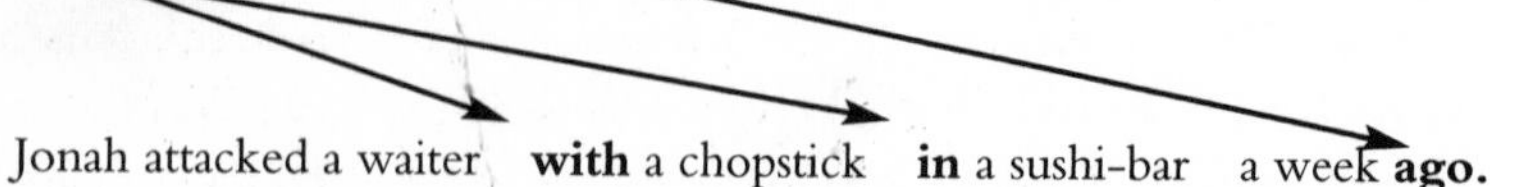

Languages have also devised a range of different forms of the verb, which can express subtle nuances of the action itself. Consider, for instance, the following variations on the theme 'the seal ate the fish'. All of the examples below have precisely the same participants, playing precisely the same roles: a seal is doing the eating and a fish is being eaten. But the sentences still vary considerably in their meaning.

The seal ate	the fish	(yesterday afternoon)
The seal will eat	the fish	(tomorrow at 9:30 sharp)
The seal had eaten	the fish	(before we managed to start filming)
The seal eats	the fish	(in our Wednesday shows, and the fish eats the seal on Thursdays)

The seal was eating	the fish	(when it spotted the walrus)
The seal would have eaten	the fish	(had the walrus not got there first)
The seal should have eaten	the fish	(but it went for the squid instead)
The seal might not have eaten	the fish	(had the fish not called it names)
The seal should eat	the fish	(said its worried aunt. It has lost weight recently.)

So even when the participants all stay the same, and even when the action remains 'eating', there is still a variety of finer nuances of the action that speakers can convey. For one thing, we can specify the time of the action ('will eat', 'ate'), and the manner in which it takes place ('eats' when it happens regularly, or 'is eating' when it happens right as we speak). We can also add our own personal perspective on what is going on, by indicating how much we know about it and what we think about it. If you say *may have eaten*, you imply that you are not sure whether it happened or not; if you say *must have eaten*, you imply you are pretty certain; saying *should eat* means you think it's a good idea; *must not eat* means you think it isn't.

All languages have the means of expressing such nuances, but again, they vary in how they go about doing it. Suppose, for instance, that you were conversing with an English seal about one of its favourite pursuits, the consumption of fish. Should you try to convey the various ins-and-outs of this activity, you would have to use independent grammatical words: *may eat, should eat, will eat.* And if you wanted to draw out even subtler nuances, you would generally use different combinations of independent grammatical words: *should have eaten, were not being eaten.* But were you to hold the same conversation with a Roman seal instead, you would have to employ another method, and rely mainly on different endings on the verb itself:

LATIN	ENGLISH
ed-*is*	*you* eat
ed-*es*	*you will* eat
ed-*ebas*	*you were* eat-*ing*
ed-*eras*	*you had* eat-*en*
ed-*eris*	*you will be* eat-*en*
ed-*ebaris*	*you were being* eat-*en*

In Latin, the *root* of the verb ('ed-') gives the basic meaning ('eat'), while the endings supply all the various nuances of the activity. As it happens, the Latin verbal system is much more complex than the forms above would suggest, since the endings on the root also vary according to who is performing the action (that is, according to the 'person'):

	I	YOU	HE/SHE/IT	WE	YOU	THEY
EAT	ed-*o*	ed-*is*	ed-*it*	ed-*imus*	ed-*itis*	ed-*unt*
WILL EAT	ed-*am*	ed-*es*	ed-*et*	ed-*emus*	ed-*etis*	ed-*ent*
WAS EATING	ed-*ebam*	ed-*ebas*	ed-*ebat*	ed-*ebamus*	ed-*ebatis*	ed-*ebant*
ATE	ed-*i*	ed-*isti*	ed-*it*	ed-*imus*	ed-*istis*	ed-*erunt*
WILL HAVE EATEN	ed-*ero*	ed-*eris*	ed-*erit*	ed-*erimus*	ed-*eritis*	ed-*erint*
WILL BE EATEN	ed-*ar*	ed-*eris*	ed-*etur*	ed-*emur*	ed-*emini*	ed-*entur*

No wonder that the Latin verb seems so off-putting to learners. As opposed to English, where the various nuances are expressed by combinations of independent words, in Latin each individual ending is a *synthesis* of different pieces of information: the person performing the action, the time it took place, as well as various other nuances. The drawback of this system is that there are so many different endings, which all have to be memorized individually. But 'synthetic' structures such as this do also have their advantages. The architects behind the Latin system made it possible to express a wide range of nuances with admirable brevity. In the form ed-*ar*, for example, a single one-syllable ending -*ar* encapsulates all the information which English has to code with the rather long-winded '*I will be* (eat)-*en*'. And by the time an English fish has managed to spit out 'I will be eaten', the seal will have polished him off three times over.

Finally, if the Latin verbal system looked uncomfortably complex, here is an example which makes Latin seem like child's play: the verbal system of the Semitic languages, such as Arabic, Aramaic and Hebrew. The architecture of the Semitic verb is one of the most imposing edifices to be seen anywhere in the world's languages, but it is founded on a concept of the sparest design: a root which consists of only consonants. The verbal root in Semitic is not a pronounceable chunk like English 'eat' or Latin 'ed-', but a group of just three consonants, like the Arabic `l-b-s`, which means 'wear', or `s-l-m`, which means 'be at peace'.

But how can a vowel-less group of three consonants ever mean anything, if it cannot even stand up on its own three legs and be pronounced unaided? The answer is that such roots do not have to be spoken by themselves, because the root is an abstract notion, which comes to life only when it is superimposed on some *templates*: patterns of (mostly) vowels, which have three empty slots for the three consonants of the root. To take one example, the Arabic template ◯*a*◯*i*◯*a* forms the past tense (in the third person 'he'), so if you want to say 'he was at peace', you just insert the root `s-l-m` ('be at peace') into that template, to get:

Root: `s-l-m`

↓ ↓ ↓

Template: ◯*a*◯*i*◯*a*

ⓢ*a*ⓛ*i*ⓜ*a* ('he was at peace')

And if you want to form the past tense of another verb, say 'wear', you take the root `l-b-s`, and insert that into the same template, to get `l`*a*`b`*i*`s`*a* ('he wore'). In order to give a sense of what these templates actually feel like for native speakers of Semitic languages, I will fill the three blank slots ◯ with the consonants of the fictitious root `s-n-g` – let's pretend, for the sake of argument, that it means 'snog' (Americans, read 'make out'). So in other words, instead of representing a template purely notionally as ◯*a*◯*i*◯*a* (PAST TENSE), I will write it as ⓢ*a*ⓝ*i*ⓖ*a* ('he snogged'). The ⓢ should thus be taken to represent the first consonant of *any* root, the ⓝ represents the second consonant, and ⓖ the third. The template ⓢ*a*ⓝ*i*ⓖ*a* is just one among many dozens in Arabic, and these express every conceivable nuance of the verb, from *ya*ⓢⓝ*a*ⓖ*u* 'he snogs', to *ta*ⓢ*ā*ⓝ*u*ⓖ 'the action of snogging each other'. The table overleaf illustrates a few more templates from Arabic, to give an idea of the complexity of the system.

	PRESENT	PAST	ONE WHO . . .	THE ACTION OF
SIMPLE	*ya*Ⓢ*ⓝ*a*ⓖu* he snogs	Ⓢ*a*ⓝ*i*ⓖ*a* he snogged	Ⓢ*ā*ⓝ*i*ⓖ one who snogs	Ⓢ*a*ⓝ*ā*ⓖ the action of snogging
CAUSATIVE	*yu*Ⓢⓝ*i*ⓖ*u* he causes to snog	*a*Ⓢⓝ*a*ⓖ*a* he caused to snog	*mu*Ⓢⓝ*i*ⓖ one who causes to snog	*i*Ⓢⓝ*ā*ⓖ the action of causing to snog

When one takes a real root, say s-l-m ('be at peace'), and inserts it into these templates, one gets forms such as:

s*a*l*i*m*a* – he was at peace

s*a*l*ā*m – 'being at peace'

*mu*sl*i*m – one who causes to be at peace
(this has developed the specific meaning of someone who submits to God, a Muslim)

*i*sl*ā*m – submitting to God, Islam

To English ears, words like *Islam, Muslim, Salām,* which have hardly any vowels in common, may sound quite dissimilar, but for speakers of Semitic languages, such words, as well as names like *Salman, Suliman, Salim, Solomon, (Ab-)salom,* are all perceived as closely related variations on a theme: the root s-l-m.

The Semitic verbal architecture may already seem pretty scary, but please fasten your seat-belt, because the cells in the table above represent only a handful of around a hundred different such nuances in Arabic. And if all that were not enough, each of these cells can actually contain up to thirteen different forms for the different persons (I, you, she, etc.). Again, merely to give the gist of what's involved, here are the forms for the different persons in just one of the cells above (the top left corner), the simple present tense.

a-snag-u	I snog
ta-snag-u	you (man) snog
ta-snag-īna	you (woman) snog
ya-snag-u	he snogs
ta-snag-u	she snogs
na-snag-u	we snog
ta-snag-āni	you two snog
ta-snag-ūna	you (three or more men) snog
ta-snag-na	you (three or more women) snog
ya-snag-āni	they (two men) snog
ta-snag-āni	they (two women) snog
ya-snag-ūna	they (three or more men) snog
ya-snag-na	they (three or more women) snog

It won't come as a surprise that the verb is the cause of some consternation for learners of Semitic languages. But since we do not need to sweat over the details, let's just sit back and reflect on the principles involved. Think for a moment about all the meticulous planning which must have gone into developing such a system – it almost defies belief that such an algebraic scheme could have been conceived in any other way except through the inspiration of a gifted designer. How else could the abstract idea of a purely consonantal root have been devised? Is it really possible that the templates that produce a whole network of nuances could have arisen of their own accord? Cracking the Semitic verb poses a serious challenge, one which will be taken up in Chapter 6.

SEXED TURNIPS AND OTHER IRREGULARITIES

The previous pages presented a few examples of both familiar and exotic structures from languages around the world. Needless to say, there is a great deal more to the structure of language than what we have seen. There are whole expanses of language that have not been mentioned, and those areas that were touched upon were only sketched in rough outlines. Nevertheless, even the few examples above should have left little room for doubt as to the sophistication of language's structure and the ingenuity of its designers.

But it would be disingenuous not to mention another side of language, a less appealing aspect that I have so far conveniently overlooked. For wherever one finds impressive edifices in language, one is also likely to find scores of imperfections, a tangle of irregularities, redundancies and idiosyncrasies that mar the picture of a perfect design. English, for example, is renowned for the irrationality of its past tense verbs. Native speakers may be blithely unaware of the chaos that reigns in the English verbal system; not so anyone who has had to learn it at school. Here is a rhyme I wrote in memory of my frustrations:

The teacher claimed it was so plain,
I only had to use my brain.
She said the past of throw was threw,
The past of grow – of course – was grew,
So flew must be the past of fly,
And now, my boy, your turn to try.
But when I trew,
I had no clue,
If mow was mew
Like know and knew
(Or is it knowed
Like snow and snowed?)

The teacher frowned at me and said
The past of feed was – plainly – fed.
Fed up, I knew then what I ned:
I took a break, and out I snoke,
She shook and quook (or quaked? or quoke?)
With raging anger out she broke:
Your ignorance you want to hide?
Tell me the past form of collide!
But how on earth should I decide
If it's collid
(Like hide and hid),
Or else – from all that I surmose,
The past of rise was simply rose,

And that of ride was surely rode,
So of collide must be collode?

Oh damn these English verbs, I thought
The whole thing absolutely stought!
Of English I have had enough,
These verbs of yours are far too tough.
Bolt upright in my chair I sat,
And said to her 'that's that' – I quat.

Another area where languages often display erratic behaviour is what linguists call 'gender', by which they don't necessarily mean distinctions based on sex, but any classification imposed on nouns according to some of their essential properties. 'Masculine' versus 'feminine' is indeed one of the most common distinctions, but many languages choose instead (or in addition) to divide nouns into 'human' versus 'non-human', or 'animate' (humans and animals) versus 'inanimate', or sometimes even 'edible' versus 'non-edible'. (Which class humans then fall into depends, of course, on local custom.)

While the idea behind such gender distinctions sounds quite sensible, the problem is that in most languages reality doesn't match up to the theory, and so it is often difficult to discern any logic behind the actual classification. The American author Mark Twain came across such a capricious classification system for the first time when he was trying to master the German language. Like most foreign learners, he was somewhat put out by the arbitrary gender of different objects, and in his book *A Tramp Abroad,* he vented his frustrations in an appendix entitled 'The Awful German Language':

> Every noun has a gender, and there is no sense or system in the distribution; so the gender of each must be learned separately and by heart. There is no other way. To do this one has to have a memory like a memorandum-book. In German, a young lady has no sex, while a turnip has. Think what overwrought reverence that shows for the turnip, and what callous disrespect for the girl. See how it looks in print – I translate this from a conversation in one of the best of the German Sunday-school books:

GRETCHEN: 'Wilhelm, where is the turnip?'
WILHELM: '*She* has gone to the kitchen.'
GRETCHEN: 'Where is the accomplished and beautiful English maiden?'
WILHELM: '*It* has gone to the opera.'

Twain could not understand why, for instance, German rain should be a 'he', a German fishwife should be an 'it', and a German fish-scale a 'she'. So after a few more pages of rant, he went on to recount the following touching 'Tale of the Fishwife and its Sad Fate', purportedly translated literally from the German:

> It is a bleak day. Hear the rain, how he pours, and the hail, how he rattles; and see the snow, how he drifts along, and of the mud, how deep he is! Ah the poor fishwife, it is stuck fast in the mire; it has dropped its basket of fishes; and its hands have been cut by the scales as it seized some of the falling creatures; and one scale has even got into its eye. And it cannot get her out. It opens its mouth to cry for help; but if any sound comes out of him, alas he is drowned by the raging of the storm. And now a tomcat has got one of the fishes and she will surely escape with him. No, she bites off a fin, she holds her in her mouth – will she swallow her? No, the fishwife's brave mother-dog deserts his puppies and rescues the fin – which he eats, himself, as his reward . . .

Twain was venting his anger at German, because German was the language he happened to be learning. But despite his protestations, there is really nothing special about German in this respect. French, for instance, with *la pluie, la grêle, la neige*, would not cut a much better figure: 'hear the rain, how she pours, and the hail, how she rattles; and see the snow, how she drifts along . . .' And if Twain had tried wrestling with Russian, Latin or a long list of other languages, he would have encountered similar idiosyncrasies. A stone, for instance, may be an 'it' in English, but it is most definitely a 'he' in German, Norwegian, Polish, Albanian, Russian or Lithuanian, and unquestionably a 'she' in French, Italian, Irish or Hebrew. Classical Greek and Akkadian (the language of Ancient Babylon and Assyria) came up with something even better, since in these languages, a stone was a 'he' or 'she' depending on one's fancy.

A comprehensive survey of all the different types of irregularities in all languages would make for a very hefty tome indeed. So I will mention just one more example of particularly eccentric behaviour, from a North American Indian language of the Kiowa family, called Jemez, spoken by about 2,000 people who live near Albuquerque in New Mexico. Jemez has an ending *-sh* which is placed on nouns in order to change their number, as can be seen below:

tyó	'a girl'	*tyó**sh***	'girls'
séé	'an eagle'	*séé**sh***	'eagles'
wéhų́	'a skeleton'	*wéhų́**sh***	'skeletons'

It seems, then, that the Jemez ending *-sh* performs exactly the same function as the English plural ending *-s*. And what could be more sensible than that? But now consider what happens when the ending *-sh* is added to a different group of nouns in Jemez:

hhú	'at least three cedars'	*hhú**sh***	'one or two cedars'
hwúúy'a	'at least three weeds'	*hwúúy'**ash***	'one or two weeds'
káápæ	'at least three tents'	*káápæ**sh***	'one or two tents'

On these nouns, the ending *-sh* has quite the reverse effect, as instead of marking plurality, it indicates a reduction in number. When it is added to nouns like weeds or trees, which tend to come in quantities, the ending *-sh* marks them as few (one or two). But how can the same ending function as a plural marker with some nouns, but as a 'paucal' marker with others? It seems that even Jemez speakers themselves were not entirely comfortable with this polarity between the two groups, so on a third set of nouns they decided to opt for the middle ground:

pá	'one, or at least three flowers'	*pá**sh***	'two flowers'
dééde	'one, or at least three shirts'	*déédesh*	'two shirts'
géésu	'one, or at least three cheeses'	*géésu**sh***	'two cheeses'

It would appear, then, that language strongly bears out Napoleon's dictum that it is but a small step from the sublime to the ridiculous. On the one hand, the designers behind the structure of language have somehow managed to erect magnificent palaces of sophistication, but for some mysterious reason they failed to clear away the piles of ramshackle irregularities and irrationalities that lie just a stone's throw away. To understand what has brought about this mix of grandeur and folly, we will have to uncover much more of the forces that shape, batter, and renovate linguistic structures. The following chapters will set out to do exactly that, and the first challenge will be to solve a simple-sounding problem: what is it that makes language change?

2

Perpetual Motion

Eppur si muove!

And yet it does move!

(Galileo Galilei, 1632)

There is a story about an Englishman, a Frenchman and a German who are debating the merits of their respective languages. The German starts by claiming: 'German is off course ze best language. It is ze language off logik and philosophy, and can communicate viz great clarity and precision even ze most complex ideas.' 'Boeff,' shrugs the Frenchman, 'but French, French, it ees ze language of lurve! In French, we can convey all ze subtletees of romance weez elegance and flair.' The Englishman ponders the matter for a while, and then says: 'Yes, chaps, that's all very well. But just think about it this way. Take the word "spoon", for instance. Now you French call it a "cuillère". And what do you Germans call it? – a "Löffel". But in English, it's simply called a "spoon". And when you stop to think about it . . . isn't that exactly what it is?'

The reason why the Englishman's argument is so outrageous, of course, is that the names we use for things bear no inherent relation to the things themselves. Names are entirely arbitrary, and this is why 'Löffel' or 'cuillère' is just as good a designation for as 'spoon'. And if you still have a lingering feeling deep down that there is something especially spoonish about  , then you should know that even in English, a spoon was not always a spoon . . .

In the fourteenth century a monumental work appeared in English, a seven-volume history of the universe called the *Polychronicon* (a translation from the Latin of a work by a Cheshire monk called Higden). Somewhere deep in volume five, the *Polychronicon* describes how the Emperor Charlemagne spent ten whole years building a wooden bridge over the Rhine. But one day, shortly before Charlemagne's death, the bridge was destroyed by such a conflagration that within three hours, 'nought oon spone' was to be seen floating above water. 'Not one spoon' . . . ? Well, the *Polychronicon* wasn't really concerned with cutlery. At that time, 'spoon' just meant a thin piece of wood, a chip, or a splinter.

Initially, it seems odd that the meaning of 'spoon' has managed to change so much over a relatively short period of time. What is more, such somersaults in meaning may appear alien to the very purpose of language, namely providing a stable system of conventions that allow coherent communication. For how can speakers reliably convey their thoughts to one another if the sense of the words they use can suddenly change? It may therefore come as even more of a surprise that the leap in meaning that 'spoon' has accomplished is by no means a rare event. When one inspects the history of a language – any language – one soon discovers that change is not the exception but the rule.

This chapter will set out to expose what drives the transformations in all areas of language, and reveal how the changes can proceed without causing severe damage to effective communication. And ultimately, the motives behind language's perpetual motion will point us on the right track for understanding the mechanisms of linguistic creation.

When one thinks of languages that are very different from one's own, one tends to imagine exotic tongues from distant corners of the globe. But strangeness can be found much closer to home, by wandering in time instead. The English language, or rather the various 'Englishes' of the last millennium, is as good a testimony as any to the chronic variability of language, and one effective way of appreciating the extent of the changes is to look at how one supposedly immutable document has mutated through the centuries. Here is a short excerpt from the Book of Genesis, which relates the story of the Flood:

English around 2000

The Lord regretted having made humankind on the earth . . . So the Lord said: 'I will wipe the human beings I have created off the face of the earth, people together with animals and reptiles and birds of the air, because I regret having made them' . . .

And God said to Noah '. . . Make yourself an ark of gopher wood . . . and cover it inside and out with pitch. For my part, I am going to bring a flood of waters on the earth, to destroy all flesh in which there is the breath of life.'

From modern, albeit literary English, let's now jump four centuries back in time, to the year 1604, when King James I, newly installed on the throne of England, and desiring to soothe the religious strife that had plagued the realm for more than a century, commissioned the best scholars in the land to produce a translation of the Bible into the English of the day. Forty-seven scholars laboured on the text for the suitably biblical period of seven years, until finally, in 1611, what has come to be known as the King James Version was published:

English around 1600 (King James Version)

It repented the Lord that he had made man on the earth . . . And the Lord said: 'I will destroy man whom I haue created from the face of the earth, both man, and beast, and the creeping thing, and the foules of the aire, for it repenteth me that I haue made them.'

And God said vnto Noah: 'Make thee an arke of gopher wood . . . and [thou] shalt pitch it within and without with pitch. And behold, I, euen I, doe bring a flood of waters vpon the earth, to destroy all flesh wherein is the breath of life.'

Because of the enduring prestige of the King James Version, its language still seems quite familiar, give or take a few thee's and thou's. But if one only ventures further back in time, to two centuries before King James commissioned his group of scholars, the going soon gets a little tougher. The first translation of the entire Bible into English was undertaken towards the end of the fourteenth century by a group of heretical scholars led by John Wycliffe, a forerunner of the Protestant Reformation who challenged the authority of the Church. Wycliffe and his associates worked on rendering the Bible into the vernacular of the day, to make the 'law of God' available to everyone who could read – an audacious undertaking for the time. Their translation finally appeared around 1390, a few years after Wycliffe's death:

English around 1400 (Wycliffe Bible)

It forthouȝt* him that he had made man in erthe. 'I shal do awey,' he seith, 'man, whom I made of nouȝt, fro the face of the erthe, fro man vnto thingis hauynge soule, fro crepynge beest vnto fowles of heuen; forsothe it othenkith me to haue maad hem.'

He seide to Noe: 'Make to thee an ark of planed trees; and with ynne and with oute thow shal diȝten it with glew. Se, I shal lede to watres of a flood vpon the erthe, and I shal slee al flehs in the which spiryt of lijf is.'

Wycliffe's may have been the first *complete* Bible to appear in English, but some parts of the Bible had been rendered into English as early as four centuries before. One of the first English translations was made at the turn of the first millennium, by Ælfric, Abbot of Eynsham. Ælfric was celebrated as the greatest prose writer of Anglo-Saxon England, but for speakers of modern English, his language might seem just a tad odd:

English around 1000 (Translation of Ælfric)

Gode ofðuhte* ða ðæt he mann geworhte ofer eorðan . . . And cwæð: 'Ic adylgie ðone man, ðe ic gesceop, fram ðære eorðan ansyne, fram ðam men oð ða nytenu, fram ðam slincendum oð ða fugelas: me ofðingð soðlice ðæt ic hi worhte.'

And God cwæð ða to Noe: 'Wyrc ðe nu ane arc of aheawenum bordum and clæmst wiðinnan and wiðutan mid tyrwan. Efne ic gebringe flodes wæteru ofer eorðan, ðæt ic ofslea eal flæsc on ðam ðe is lifes gast.'

The four passages above reveal the waywardness of the 'English language' over the last thousand years, and highlight just how thoroughly it has

* The letter ȝ corresponds to *gh* in modern orthography: *forthouȝt* = 'forthought'. At the time, it was pronounced more like the *ch* in Scottish *loch or* German *Buch*. The letter ð corresponds to *th* in modern orthography.

changed. Geoffrey Chaucer, a contemporary of Wycliffe, was keenly aware of language's mutability, and put it beautifully in his *Troilus and Criseyde*:

Ye knowe eek that in forme of speche is chaunge	(eek = also)
With-inne a thousand yeer, and wordes tho	(tho = then)
That hadden pris, now wonder nyce and straunge	(pris = value, nyce = odd)
Us thinketh hem; and yet they spake hem so,	(hem = them)
And spedde as wel in love as men now do.	(spedde = succeeded)

And as if to prove the point, Chaucer's (and Wycliffe's) English – from just over half a millennium ago – already looks 'wonder nyce and straunge'. But go back a full 'thousand yeer', and Ælfric's English is not merely strange – it sounds like double Dutch. Within a span of only about thirty generations, 'English' has undergone such a thorough overhaul that what is supposed to be one and the same language is barely recognizable. Indeed, Ælfric's language seems so entirely foreign that one might need some convincing to accept that it even has anything to do with English at all. And yet, on closer inspection, and with a word-for-word gloss into modern English, it turns out that the two 'Englishes' have a lot more in common than meets the eye:

Gode	ofthuhte	tha	thæt	he	mann	geworhte	ofer	eorthan,
to.God	*displeased*	*then*	*that*	*he*	*man*	*wrought*	*over*	*earth*

And cwæth:	Ic	adylgie	thone	man,	the	ic	ge-sceop,	fram	thære	eorthan	ansyne
and said	*I*	*destroy*	*the*	*man*	*that*	*I*	*shaped*	*from*	*the*	*earth's*	*face*

fram	tham	men	oth	tha	nytenu,	fram	tham	slincendum	oth	tha	fugelas
from	*the*	*men*	*to*	*the*	*beasts,*	*from*	*the*	*crawlers*	*to*	*the*	*fowls*

Armed with this gloss, it may become easier to accept that Ælfric's language and modern English really do represent two stages of the same language. Quite a few words are the same (*and*, *he*, *men*), and others are much of a muchness (*ofer* 'over', *fram* 'from') or at least close enough to be identifiable: *eorthan* 'earth', *geworhte* 'wrought', *cwæth* 'quoth', *fugelas* 'fowls'. Even so, the knowledge that Ælfric's language really was the

'English' of a millennium ago only makes the extent of the changes seem more baffling.

Perhaps the most surprising feature of Ælfric's English is that, like Latin, it had a complex case and gender system, so that nouns and even the definite article 'the' had an array of different forms depending on their role in the sentence and on their gender and number. Just consider how many different forms the article 'the' could assume even in the three short lines from the biblical passage above: ***thone*** man ('the man'), *fram* ***thære*** eorthan ansyne ('from the earth's face'), *fram* ***tham*** men ('from the men'), *oth* ***tha*** nytenu ('to the animals'). Add to this the fact that the genders of nouns were just as erratic as in German today ('earth' was a 'she', for instance, but a 'stone' a 'he') and you can imagine that an earlier incarnation of Mark Twain wouldn't have dared bat an eyelid at the complexity of any foreign case and gender system. To give an idea of the labyrinth of different forms in the English of Ælfric's day, the set of endings for one class of nouns is shown below:

SINGULAR			PLURAL		
thæt	*wæter-*	'the water'	*tha*	*wæter-u*	'the waters'
tham	*wæter-e*	'to the water'	*tham*	*wæter-um*	'to the waters'
thæs	*wæter-es*	'of the water'	*thara*	*wæter-a*	'of the waters'

It is the case system, perhaps more than anything else, that makes Ælfric's language appear so outlandish, whereas Wycliffe's English seems much less peculiar, largely because by 1400 the case system had almost entirely disintegrated. But while the collapse of the case system was an enormous upheaval in the history of English, it was by no means the only change. One only need compare a short phrase from the four biblical passages above to appreciate that no area of English stood still for very long:

~ 1000: *me ofthingth*(displeases) *sothlice*(soothly) *thæt*(that) *ic*(I) *hi*(them) *worhte*(made)
~ 1400: *forsothe it othenkith*(displeases) *me to haue maad hem*(them)
~ 1600: *for it repenteth me that I haue made them*
~ 2000: *because I regret having made them*

The first thing one notices is how words come and go over the centuries, with older words (like *worhte* 'wrought') dying out, and being replaced by new ones (*maad*). The expression of displeasure, for instance, seems to have been particularly moody. Ælfric uses a verb current at the time, and says *me ofthingth* ('it displeases me'), but by 1400 the verb *ofthink* had begun to sound rather dated. Wycliffe could still expect his readers to understand *it othenkith me*, but by 1600 this verb had long been forgotten, and *it repenteth me* was used in its stead. Today, the verb 'repent' is still easily recognizable, but it nevertheless seems quite out of place in this particular context. Since the seventeenth century, 'repent' has undergone a complete role reversal: what the King James translators understood by *it repenteth me* is what we would render with 'I repent (or regret) it'.

But it is not just the meaning of words that changes over time. Some of the basic features in the structure of English, such as the conventions of word order, also seem to have been rather unstable. We saw earlier that word order plays a crucial role in modern English, as it is the only means of distinguishing the subject (which comes before the verb) from the object (which comes after). But consider the order of words in Ælfric's passage: *me ofthingth* 'me displeases' (for 'it displeases me'), and *ic hi worhte* 'I them made' (for 'I made them'). Clearly, Ælfric's idea of which words should go where was different from ours.

Finally, the pronunciation of English words has also erred and strayed over the centuries, but these wanderings are only partially mirrored in the passages above, because of the conservative nature of the writing system. Only in a few cases, such as the word *ic* in Ælfric's passage, can the changes in pronunciation be glimpsed from the spelling. *Ic* is in fact one and the same word as our modern 'I', and only looks so different because its pronunciation has changed so much. In the tenth century, *ic* was pronounced something like {itch}, but by 1400 the final {tch} had disappeared, and the word came to be pronounced {ee} (as in 'bee'), and thus to be spelt as just 'I'. In the writing system, 'I' has looked the same ever since, but the actual pronunciation of 'I' has continued to meander. During the fifteenth century, there was an upheaval in the pronunciation of many English vowels, which linguists call 'The Great English Vowel Shift'. As a part of this shift, all long {ee} vowels turned into {ay} (as in modern 'day'), so by the sixteenth century, 'I' came to be pronounced {ay}. And by the eighteenth century, {ay} changed further into the modern pronunciation {eye}.

Most of the changes in pronunciation, however, are masked by the spelling. For cultural reasons that are extraneous to spoken language itself, the system of spelling we use today has remained pretty much frozen for at least 400 years, even though the pronunciation continued to drift during this time. So if one compares the King James passage with the modern translation, one could easily fall under the impression that for some reason changes in pronunciation came to an abrupt halt after 1611. But this is just an illusion. Take, for instance, the phrase 'flood of waters to destroy all flesh'. The King James translators spelt this phrase precisely as we do (or more accurately, we spell it precisely as they did). But in fact, most of the words in this phrase would have sounded quite different then. In 1611, the word *flood* rhymed with *good*; *waters* had an audible {r}, and was pronounced roughly with the vowels of modern {matters}; and the word *all* sounded like our word {owl}.

The frozen spelling system also conceals changes in pronunciation that occurred even more recently. When reading Jane Austen or George Eliot, for example, one is tempted to assume that their characters sounded just like actors in BBC costume dramas. The reality was rather different, however. In 1902, the art critic Charles Eastlake reminisced about the speech of 'old fellows' forty years before, those people born around 1800 (the generation of Darwin and Disraeli), who would have been in their teens when Jane Austen's novels first appeared. And particularly as he is referring to the genteel speech of the educated classes, their pronunciation of various words might seem rather surprising today:

> Men of mature age can remember many words which in the conversation of old fellows forty years ago would sound strangely to modern ears. They were generally much *obleeged* for a favour. They referred affectionately to their *darters*; talked of *goold* watches, or of recent visit to *Room*; mentioned that they had seen the *Dook* of Wellington in Hyde Park last *Toosday* and that he was in the habit of rising at *sivin* o'clock. They spoke of *Muntague* Square and St *Tummus's 'Ospital*. They would profess themselves to be their hostess's *'umble* servants, and to admire her collection of *chayney*, especially the vase of *Prooshian* blue.

So although the conventions of spelling might not have changed much for nearly four centuries, the peregrinations of pronunciation have carried on regardless. And it is precisely for this reason that English spelling is so infamously irrational. Just have a go at reading the following poem out aloud as quickly as you can:

> I take it you already know
> Of tough and bough and cough and dough?
> Others may stumble, but not you,
> On hiccough, thorough, lough, and through?
> Well done! And now you wish perhaps,
> To learn of less familiar traps?
> Beware of heard, a dreadful word
> That looks like beard and sounds like bird.
> And dead – it's said like bed, not bead –
> For goodness sake, don't call it 'deed'.
> Watch out for meat and great and threat
> (They rhyme with suite and straight and debt):
> A moth is not a moth in mother,
> Nor both in bother, broth in brother.
> And here is not a match for there
> Nor dear and fear for bear and pear.
> And then there's dose and rose and lose –
> Just look them up – and goose and choose,
> And cork and work and card and ward,
> And font and front, and word and sword,
> And do and go, and thwart and cart –
> Come! Come! I've hardly made a start!
>
> (From the *Manchester Guardian*, 1954)

So really, it is unfair to say that English spelling is not an accurate rendering of speech. It is – it's only that it renders the speech of the sixteenth century.

It is clear, then, that no corner of the English language has remained protected from changes: sounds, meanings and structures all seem to have suffered from a curious inability to stay still. This inconstancy of English may seem surprising and eccentric, and one might be tempted to blame it on some particular predicament of its speakers: the wanderlust of a seafaring nation, perhaps, or the unsettling effects of mint sauce. Alas, the reason is much more prosaic, as there is nothing special about English in this respect – *così fan tutte.* When one traces the records of any other language with a sufficiently long history, a similar picture unrolls. A thousand years may be 'but as yesterday when it is past' for the Psalmist, but for the German language it has allowed ample time to roam:

GERMAN ~ AD 1000

Uuanda fóre dînen ougon zênstunt zênzech iaro sint
samo so der gésterîgo dag, der feruáren ist.
Vnde so éin uuáhta.

GERMAN ~ AD 2000

Denn tausend Jahre sind in deinen Augen
wie der gestrige Tag, wenn er vergangen ist,
und wie eine Wache in der Nacht.

For a thousand years in thy sight are
but as yesterday when it is past,
and as a watch in the night.
(Psalms 90:4)

And French has not exactly sat on its hands either:

LATE LATIN ~ AD 400

Quia mille anni in oculis tuis
sicut dies hesterna
quae pertransiit
et vigilia nocturna.

FRENCH ~ AD 1200

Kar mil an devant les tuens oilz
ensement cume li jurz d'ier
chi trespassa,
e la guarde en nuit.

FRENCH ~ AD 2000

Car mille ans, à tes yeux,
sont comme le jour d'hier
quand il est passé,
et comme une veille dans la nuit.

The simple truth is that all languages change, all the time – the only static languages are dead ones.

The dramatic changes in languages will prove important, first and foremost because they will provide the major clues for how complex linguistic structures can arise. But as an added bonus, language's perpetual motion also solves another problem: the babble of Babel. It transpires that languages did not need any divine intervention in order to proliferate, for given half a chance (and sufficient time), they multiply quite happily of their own accord. Just imagine two groups living in two neighbouring villages, speaking similar varieties of one language. With the passing of time, their language undergoes constant transformations, but as long as the two communities remain in close contact, their varieties will change in tandem: innovations in one village will soon spread to the other, because of the need to communicate. Now suppose that one of the groups wanders off in search of better land, and loses all contact with the speakers of the other village. The language of the two groups will then start wandering in different directions, because there will be nothing to maintain the changes in tandem. Eventually, their varieties will have strayed so far apart that they will no longer be mutually intelligible, and so turn into different languages.

Incidentally, the decision about when to start calling such varieties different 'languages', rather than 'dialects' of the same language, often involves factors that have little to do with the actual linguistic distance between them. An American linguist once quipped that 'a language is a dialect with an army and a navy', and his point is illustrated by recent cases such as Serbian and Croatian, which before the break-up of the former Yugoslavia were regarded as dialects of one language, Serbo-Croatian, but afterwards were suddenly proclaimed to be different languages. So ultimately, the decision about whether something is a language or a dialect relies on what the speakers themselves consider it to be. But from a purely linguistic perspective, and as a rule of thumb, when two varieties of what used to be the same language are no longer mutually intelligible, they can be called different languages.

Linguistic diversity is thus a direct consequence of geographical dispersal and language's propensity to change. The biblical assertion that there was a single primordial language is not, in itself, unlikely, for it is quite possible that there was originally only one language, spoken somewhere in Eastern Africa, perhaps 100,000 years ago. But even if this were the case, the break-up of this language must have had much more prosaic reasons than God's wrath at Babel. When different groups started splitting up, going their own ways and settling across the globe, their languages changed in different ways. So the huge diversity of languages in the world today simply reflects how long languages have had to change independently of one another.

The different periods of separation between languages also explain why some languages are much more closely related than others. English, for instance, is more similar to Swedish, Icelandic, Dutch and German than it is to Polish, Albanian, Punjabi, Persian, Turkish, Yoruba (spoken in Nigeria) or Chinese:

English:	Give	us	this day	our	daily	bread
Swedish:	Giv	oss	i dag	vårt	dagliga	bröd
Icelandic:	Gef	oss	í dag	vort	daglegt	brauð
Dutch:	Geef	ons	heden	ons	dagelijks	brood
German:	Gib	uns	heute	unser	tägliches	Brot

Polish:	Chleba naszego powszedniego daj nam dzisiaj
Albanian:	Bukën tonë të përditëshme jepna neve sot
Punjabi:	Sāḍī gujar jogī roṭī aj sānūṉ dih
Persian:	Nān-e-rūzīne-ye-mārā dar īn rūz be-mā bebakhš
Turkish:	Bugün bize gündelik ekmeğimizi ver
(Mandarin) Chinese:	Wǒmen rìyòng de yìnshí jīnrì cìgěi wǒmen
Yoruba:	Fun wa li onjẹ õjọ wa loni

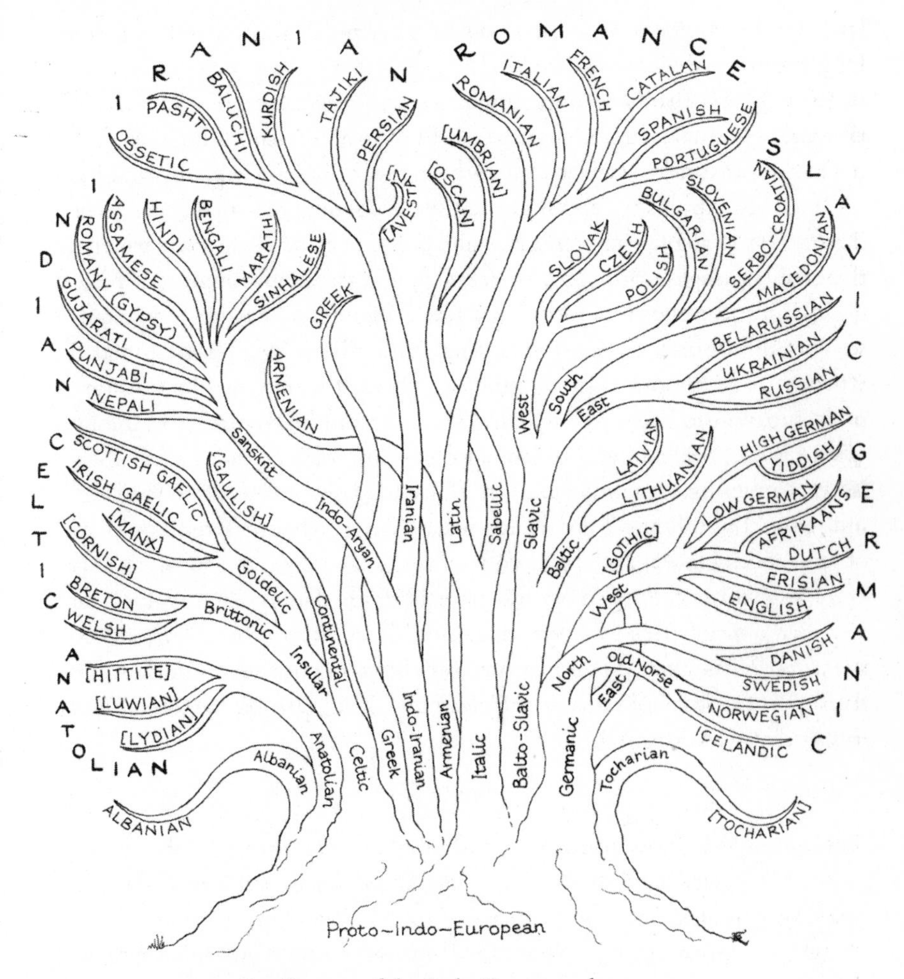

Family tree of the Indo-European languages

The reason why English, Dutch, German and the Scandinavian languages look so akin is that they all stem from one prehistoric ancestor, which linguists today call Proto-Germanic, so in fact they were all one and the same language until the beginning of the first millennium AD. (The term 'Proto' is a designation linguists use to refer to an assumed prehistoric language from which various attested descendants have sprung.) But once the Germanic tribes started spreading out from their original homelands in southern Scandinavia and along the North Sea and Baltic coasts, their speech varieties gradually began to diverge, eventually turning into different languages.

English and the Germanic languages are themselves related – more distantly – to many other languages of Europe and Asia. Ultimately, they go back to the same common ancestor as that of Italian, French, Spanish, Irish, Welsh, Russian, Lithuanian, Polish, Greek, Albanian, and even Armenian, Persian, Hindi and Punjabi. This ancestral prehistoric tongue, probably spoken around 6,000 years ago, is called by linguists Proto-Indo-European, because in the first few millennia BC the descendants of its speakers spread over an area stretching all the way from India to Europe (see map on pages vi–vii). So although it may not be immediately apparent to the naked eye, the second group of languages in the list above (Polish, Albanian, Punjabi, and Persian) are all related to English, albeit somewhat distantly, and are descended from the same forebear. But since English and Persian, for instance, must have parted company at least six millennia ago, the two languages have diverged so much that only a few basic Persian words are still immediately identifiable (for instance *pedar* 'father', *dokhtar* 'daughter' or *do* 'two'). So to the naked eye, the Persian or Albanian sentences above do not look much more similar to English than the ones from Turkish or Yoruba, which are not descended from Proto-Indo-European.

There should be little room left for doubt by now that mutability is not a secret vice of English or any other language in particular, but an epidemic of universal proportions. Nonetheless, the realization that change is a chronic condition that all languages suffer from only sharpens a fundamental question – why? Why are languages constantly on the move, and why can't they simply pull themselves together and keep still?

The first reaction might be that the answer is glaringly obvious. The world around us is changing all the time, and naturally, language has to change with it. Language needs to keep pace with new realities, new technologies and new ideas, from ploughs to laser printers, and from political-correctness to sms-texting, and that is why it always changes. This line of argument may seem appealing at first, but when one looks at the actual changes close up, the picture becomes far more complicated. Take, for instance, this short phrase from the passages quoted earlier:

~ AD 1000: *me ofthingth sothlice thæt ic hi worhte*
~ AD 2000: *I regret having made them*

What new inventions or new ideas could have been behind the differences here? Which new technology, for example, could have sparked the change in sounds from *ic* {itch} to *I* {eye}? And which new ideology is responsible for the switch in the order of the words, from 'them made' (*hi worhte*) to 'made them'?

Or let's look at the question the other way round, and consider a language not burdened with any mod cons or even with ploughs, for that matter. Mbabaram was once the language of a small Aboriginal tribe in north-east Queensland, Australia, about fifty miles south-west from Cairns. In the 1930s an anthropologist recorded a list of a few words in Mbabaram, which seemed entirely different not only from all the neighbouring languages of the region, but from all other Aboriginal languages on the Australian continent – it was as if the Mbabaram tribe had somehow been parachuted into the north Australian rainforest from some faraway place, and there was even a theory that the Mbabaram were related to the extinct Tasmanians, thousands of miles to the south. In the 1960s, when a linguist started gathering more evidence about the language from the handful of old people who still could remember it (the last person who could speak some Mbabaram died in 1972), the decidedly 'un-Australian' nature of the language at first only seemed to be confirmed. And it took some ingenuity to recognize that Mbabaram was indeed closely related to the languages of the neighbouring tribes, only that its affiliation had been entirely obscured by sweeping changes in pronunciation that the language had undergone at some stage in its history: whole syllables had been chopped off, and new vowels had sprung up, so that, just as one example, a word originally pronounced *gudaga* ended up in Mbabaram as *dog* (which by sheer coincidence happens to mean . . . 'dog').

But if a language is supposed to change only in order to keep up with ploughs and laser printers, then why should the language of a small tribe of hunter-gatherers, who have never moved beyond stone age technology, be so unstable? It appears, then, that our first 'obvious' explanation for why language keeps on changing is not so convincing after all. Even if *some* changes in language come about in order to adapt to changing realities, these constitute only a minor part of the overall transformations that languages undergo. The main bulk of changes must stem from entirely different reasons.

There is a close runner-up in the list of 'obvious' explanations for why language changes so much, and that is the issue of contact. It is easy to imagine that languages change only because their speakers come into contact with speakers of other languages or dialects, and start borrowing words and expressions from one another. This line of argument seems especially tempting in the case of English, since although English is a Germanic language, about half of its vocabulary is not of Germanic origin but borrowed from various other languages, mostly Norman French and Latin. But while contact, 'keeping up with the Joneses', so to speak, is undoubtedly the source of a great many changes, and thus a much better explanation than 'keeping up with laser printers', it still cannot be held responsible for the sweeping changes in absolutely *all* languages, even those whose speakers have had hardly any exposure to other languages. And what's more, even in the case of English, surely one of the most covetous of languages, a quick look at the changes, say from *ic* {itch} to {ee} to {ay} to {eye}, will soon reveal that many of them cannot just be put down to borrowing.

Finally, a third 'obvious' explanation for why language should change so much is that people are progressive creatures who value novelty and improvement and thus set about trying to renovate and improve language. But this idea is a complete non-starter. As we'll see in the next chapter, when people bother to think about changes, they generally portray them as a great danger to language (as well as to society, if not the whole of civilization) and condemn them as slack, slovenly or just plain wrong. If anything, the weight of censure and authority conspires to prevent language from changing. And yet, it does move!

All the obvious explanations, therefore, fall short of accounting for the sheer scale of the changes. It seems that languages need neither nudging from the Joneses nor the gadgetry of ploughs in order to be transformed, for they keep changing, even without the slightest provocation, and even in spite of people's best intentions. But if all these external reasons fail to explain the changes, then there must be something in language itself which makes it so unsteady. There must be something inherently unstable in the very way in which we communicate, some element of volatility which drives language into a state of **inner restlessness**, and gives it itchy feet. But what?

The conundrum of change has been one of the enduring puzzles in the study of language, and it preoccupied linguists throughout the nineteenth century and the first half of the twentieth. But only in the last few decades have linguists finally managed to make significant progress in cracking it. Like any respectable whodunit, the mystery of change turned out to have three main elements: a suspect – *who* is really behind the changes? a motive – *why* should whoever is doing it be doing it? and finally the toughest question of all, the get-away – how do the perpetrators get away with these changes, without causing devastating damage to communication?

Tracking down the suspect may at first seem a rather difficult mission, since it's quite hard to think of anyone who is really trying to change language. (Are you?) But the identification turns out to be fairly straightforward, since although no one *in particular* is changing language, it is in fact all of us who bring about the changes, even if we never wish to. There are a great number of things that people bring about without ever intending to. Just think of traffic jams. Nobody has ever set out on their daily commute with the express purpose of creating one, and yet each driver contributes to the congestion by adding one more car to an overcrowded road.

But unintended changes don't always have to be harmful. Imagine two public buildings with an overgrown field lying directly between them. The only road connecting the buildings winds its way lengthily around the field, so people who have to walk from one building to the other start crossing the field as a short-cut. The first person to do so tries to make his way through the long grass, and people who come afterwards find the track which the first person has made the most inviting way through, because some grass and bracken have already been trodden down. As more and more people cross the field, more and more vegetation is trampled, so that eventually the track turns into a nice clear footpath. The point is that no one in particular created this footpath, and no one in particular even intended to. The path did not emerge from some project of landscape design, but from the accumulated spontaneous actions of the short-cutters, who were each following their own selfish motives in taking the easiest and quickest route.

Changes in language come about in a rather similar fashion, through the accumulation of unintended actions. These actions must stem from entirely selfish motives, not from any conscious design to transform language. But what could these motives be? This is a rather more involved question, and doing justice to it will occupy us in the next few chapters. But in essence, the motives for change can be encapsulated in the triad *economy*, *expressiveness* and *analogy*.

Economy refers to the tendency to save effort, and is behind the short-cuts speakers often take in pronunciation. As we shall see in the following chapter, when these short-cuts accumulate, they can create new sounds, just like the new footpath cutting through the field. *Expressiveness* relates to speakers' attempts to achieve greater effect for their utterances and extend their range of meaning. One area where we are particularly expressive is in saying 'no'. A plain 'no' is often deemed too weak to convey the depth of our unenthusiasm, so to make sure the right effect is achieved, we beef up 'no' to 'not at all', 'not a bit', 'no way', 'by no means', 'not in a million years', and so on. But as we shall see later on, the results of this hyperbole can often be self-defeating, since the repetition of emphatic phrases can cause an inflationary process that devalues their currency.

The third motive for change, *analogy*, is shorthand for the mind's craving for order, the instinctive need of speakers to find regularity in language. The effects of analogy are most conspicuous in the errors of young children, as in 'I goed' or 'two foots', which are simply attempts to introduce regularity to areas of the language that happen to be quite disorganized. Many such 'errors' are corrected as children grow up, but some innovations do catch on. In the past, for example, there were many more irregular plural nouns in English: one *bōc* (book), many *bēc*; one *hand*, two *hend*; one *eye*, two *eyn*; one *cow*, many *kine*. But gradually, 'errors' like 'hands' crept in by analogy on the regular *-s* plural pattern. So *bēc* was replaced by the 'incorrect' *bokes* (*books*) during the thirteenth century, *eyn* was replaced by *eyes* in the fourteenth century, *kine* by *cows* in the sixteenth.

The following chapters will take a much closer look at the different motives for change, and explore their effects on language in much greater depth. Economy and expressiveness will feature first, and the third part of the triad, analogy, will be the subject of Chapter 6. But for the moment, and even without going into all the details, the reasons for language's chronic inner restlessness should be beginning to come into focus. Different forces, powered by different motives, keep pulling and pushing language in different directions, and in such a complex system, these constant thrusts ensure that the whole never stays still.

Having formed an idea of both the suspect and the motives, we are left with the third and trickiest part of the whodunit: how do speakers ever let language get away with it? Why are changes not brought up short and stopped in their tracks? At first sight, there seem to be all the reasons in the world why society should never let the changes through. After all, the primary purpose of language is to allow effective communication, a flow of ideas and information between minds. And since the names we use for things are just arbitrary conventions (a spade would be just as good a name for a spoon as a spoon would be for a spade), the only way to achieve coherent communication is if the system of conventions is agreed upon and adhered to by everyone. So if the rules and regulations of language can keep on changing all the time, surely its very purpose is under threat. English, for instance, has changed almost beyond recognition within less than thirty generations, but how could this mutation have proceeded without causing a breakdown in communication along the way?

One only needs to think about the effects of change on other complex systems to grasp the severity of the threat. Just imagine what it would be like to drive, if the Highway Code kept on changing while you were on the road. There is a story I once heard in Norway about what happened a few decades ago, when the traffic system in neighbouring Sweden underwent a complete reorganization. Originally the Swedes drove on the left, but since all surrounding countries drove on the right, the government decided that Sweden must keep up with the times. The switch-over was set for one day in 1967, and a massive publicity campaign was launched to inform drivers about the impending change. But as the deadline drew nearer, the government grew nervous, fearing that chaos would ensue on the first few days after the change. So, the story goes, it was hurriedly decided to revise the plans and take a softly-softly approach. In the first week, only lorries and buses would drive on the right, and everyone else would still drive on the left . . .

Whether apocryphal or not, the implications of this story are clear. Evidently, speakers cannot all switch over from one form to another at exactly the same moment, so how is it that fatal crashes don't ensue? If the rules of the communication system are allowed to keep on changing, why are there no serious misunderstandings at the time when the changes are taking place? Take the change in the verb 'repent', which 'flipped' its meaning, so that when a seventeenth-century speaker said *it repenteth me*, what he really meant was not 'it repents me', but rather 'I repent it'. How could this change of direction proceed without causing accidents along the way?

At first, one might imagine that such a strange flip was only possible because 'repent' is a fairly rare word, used in restricted contexts. Perhaps there were no complete write-offs because the change occurred on some small deserted country lane, but surely such a change of direction would be unthinkable on a busy motorway. It may therefore come as a surprise that several other verbs underwent a similar flip in English, including the verb 'like', which by anyone's standards is not a small country lane. Suppose one wants to translate into modern English the following fifteenth-century sentence: 'This is my loved son that liketh me.' The obvious translation would run on the lines of 'this is my beloved son who likes me'. But that would be quite the wrong way round, since what the sentence actually meant was 'this is my beloved son, whom I like'. Originally the verb 'like' was not a weaker synonym for 'love', but rather meant 'to please' or 'to be pleasing to', so the phrase 'he liketh me' meant 'he is pleasing to me', or in the modern sense of 'like': 'I like him'. This older meaning of 'like' was still frequently used by Shakespeare at the turn of the seventeenth century:

HOST: The music likes you not?
JULIA: You mistake; the musician likes me not.
(*The Two Gentlemen of Verona*)

Translated into modern English, this would mean:

HOST: Don't you like the music?
JULIA: You're wrong, I don't like the musician.

But today the older sense seems entirely alien. At some stage, and in broad daylight, the verb 'like' – surely one of the more common and crucial verbs in the English language – flipped from one sense to the other, apparently without creating a whole series of real-life trouser-role comedies about who really likes whom.

An even more puzzling example concerns the transformation of the verb 'resent'. In 1677, for instance, Isaac Barrow, Newton's teacher and predecessor in Cambridge, wrote in one of his sermons: 'Should we not be monstrously ingratefull if we did not deeply resent such kindness?' And in the following century, a certain Bishop Warburton wrote in a letter to a friend: 'I was sure that this instance of his friendship to you would ever be warmly resented by you.' Contrary to first impression, however, these are not anachronistic attempts at Wildean wit, for neither of these authors intended any irony. In their day, the verb 'resent' simply had a different meaning, and could do the work of our modern 'appreciate' or 'feel grateful for' – exactly the opposite of its sense today. So somehow, the verb managed to make a U-turn in its meaning, again with no evidence of things going haywire along the way.

The meaning of words is not the only area of language where such changes could be expected to throw spanners in the workings of communication, for sweeping transformations in pronunciation should surely be equally obstructive. Imagine, for instance, a change in sounds that systematically turns every *p* in its path into an *f*. Even assuming that there was a thoroughly good motive for such a change (let's not worry for now about what that motive might be), can one really imagine that such a transformation would ever be allowed to pass the censors and catch on in English? Does it seem likely that in fifty years' time, respectable people will start throwing farties, go on ficnics in the fark, and will in all seriousness say things like 'could you flease fass the feas'? Surely, such a change would never be tolerated, since otherwise, how would anyone be able to tell the difference between *pork* and *fork*, *please* and *fleas*, 'The Duke shot a *pheasant*' and 'The Duke shot a *peasant*'?

But as unlikely as it may seem, this very change from *p* to *f* has already occurred, not in some exotic tribal tongue, but in English itself, albeit in the fairly distant past. Take a look at the following list of English words, and their counterparts in Danish, Italian and French:

ENGLISH	DANISH	ITALIAN	FRENCH
father	**f**ader	**p**adre	**p**ère
fish	**f**isk	**p**esce	**p**êch(er) {**p**oisson}
foot	**f**od	**p**iede	**p**ied
for	**f**or	**p**er	**p**our
few	**f**å	**p**oco	**p**eu
first	**f**ørst	**p**rimo	**p**remier

The words in each row are clearly 'cognates' (they derive from the same root in the prehistoric ancestor of all four languages, Proto-Indo-European) so any differences in pronunciation between them must stem from sound changes that occurred in the histories of the individual languages. And while a few other changes are evident, one difference sticks out in particular: wherever Italian and French have a *p*, English and Danish have an *f* instead. By comparing such cognates from all the attested daughter languages of Proto-Indo-European, linguists have worked out that *all* the words above originally began with a *p*: 'fish', for instance, was **peisk* or **pisk* in Proto-Indo-European, and 'foot' was **ped*. (The asterisk is a conventional way to mark words that are not attested in actual documents, but reconstructed on the basis of comparisons between the daughter languages.) And while Italian and French still retain the initial pristine *p*, in the history of English and Danish (and, in fact, of all the other Germanic languages), the *p*'s have somehow wandered into *f*'s.

As far back as 200 years ago, linguists discovered that a change from *p* to *f* must have occurred in Germanic, but for almost a century and a half they could not grasp *how* such a change could ever get under way. After all, why should this transformation be any more feasible in prehistoric times than in the present day? In an effort to discover how such changes could proceed, linguists tried to scan the historical records for clues. The Germanic change of *p* to *f* lay lost in prehistory, of course, so obviously it could not be observed directly. But even when linguists looked for evidence from sound changes that occurred during the historical period, they found to their chagrin that for some reason the changes could never be observed in progress. All that could be made out from the records was a stage before a certain change had started, and a stage some generations later, after the change was completed. The records never seemed to illuminate the elusive process in between, when the transformations were actually taking place.

The linguists of the nineteenth century devised a brilliant theory to explain their way out of this predicament, and to account for why they failed to catch those sound changes in the act. Trying to observe sound changes, they claimed, was like trying to observe a tree growing: the progress of change is so slow that the naked eye can only detect it by comparing the language at two distant points in time. Speakers started off with a proper *p*, and then over generations – so the theory ran – the sound inched towards something just a bit closer to an *f*, and then a little closer still, until, a century or more later, the sound finally reached a real *f*. In 1933, Leonard Bloomfield, the leading American linguist of the time, summed up this view with confidence: 'The process of linguistic change has never been directly observed,' he assured his readers. 'Such an observation, with our present facilities, is inconceivable.' The theory was doubly attractive, since at a stroke it managed to explain not only why linguists were failing to observe changes in progress, but also how the changes were allowed to proceed in the first place. Because the changes happen slowly and imperceptibly, speakers do not get confused by them, and in fact, they don't even notice them, and so no one tries to stop them in their tracks.

As ingenious as the theory was, it had only one slight drawback: it had little foothold in reality. While vowels may be able to slide continuously from one into another, with consonants like *p* and *f* this idea makes no sense, for where are all the phantom sounds that are supposed to exist somewhere in between the two? Even granted that the combination *pf* could be claimed as a milestone half-way between *p* and *f*, then how should the sound which is two-thirds of the way be pronounced? And if such a mysterious fluffy sound does exist, why is it that one never finds it around in any language today? There are plenty of languages with a *p*, a fair few with an *f*, but why is it that one doesn't find languages which just at the moment happen to have a sound that is five-sixths of the way in between?

It is easy to poke fun at the theory of gradual sound change, but for decades no one managed to come up with a better alternative. Until, that is, it turned out that the solution had been lying right under everybody's noses all along. Of course it is possible to observe the changes in progress – one just needs to know where to look. Only in the 1960s did linguists finally realize that in order to observe the elusive changes in action they should not delve into ancient records, but go out on to the streets and listen to what is happening in the here and now. And once linguists finally started to take in what was going on around them, the answer was not long in coming.

Consider again the change from *p* to *f*, which seems so implausible today. If I predicted that in fifty years' time signs will read 'fick-fockets will be frosecuted', one would, quite rightly, greet this prediction with disbelief. But now let's test out a different forecast: suppose I suggested that in fifty years' time *th* will turn into *f*, so that people will say 'it's going to funder on Fursday, I fink'. Would you treat that prediction with the same incredulity? In all probability, you wouldn't, and the reason why not is the solution to the mystery of how change is ever allowed to proceed in language.

If you are familiar with the way English is spoken in Britain, you will know that even today, some people say *fink* and *Fursday*. These pronunciations are already a feature of English, or at least of some people's English. And because they are already a part of the established variation, it is much easier to imagine how such pronunciations might one day become the norm: they will simply become more and more common, and eventually take over. The key to the mystery of change, then, is **variation**. Language is not a monolithic rigid entity, but a flexible fuzzy system, with an enormous amount of 'synchronic' variation (that is, variation at any given point in time). There is variation between the speech of people from different areas, of different ages, different sexes, different classes, different professions. The same person may even use different forms depending on the circumstances: 'fink' to mates in the pub, but 'think' to the boss at work. And it is through variation that changes in language proceed, for what really changes with time is the frequencies of the competing forms. So if, at some future date, English moves from *th* to *f*, this will not be after a long period during which the sound *th* gradually creeps closer and closer to an *f*. It will simply be because more and more people will say *f* instead of *th*, until in the end *th* will become so rare that people will just forget about it.

Indeed, if we were able to nip back in time and roam the streets of a Germanic village, say sometime around 400 BC, just when *p* was changing to *f*, we would undoubtedly hear the two pronunciations side by side. Older and more genteel people might say 'pisk' (fish), but young and trendy folk would say 'fisk'. In all probability, we would also hear the older generation fuming about the careless and vulgar pronunciation of the young. But if we stuck around for a generation or two, we would gradually hear fewer and fewer people saying 'pisk', and more and more saying 'fisk', until eventually, no one would have a clue what a 'pisk' was.

This answer to how changes manage to proceed in language may seem quite cheeky. Not to put too fine a point on it, I am claiming that people can cope with the chaos of change over the years (that is, with 'diachronic variation'), simply because they can cope with the even greater chaos of synchronic variation, the diversity at any one point in time. The ability to deal with synchronic variation is an essential part of our knowledge of language. We can cope not only with 'Thursday' and 'Fursday', but also with '*ee*ther' and '*ey*ether', 'dreamed' and 'dreamt', 'shedule' and 'skedule', 'am I not?' and 'aren't I?' and thousands of other variations in sounds, meanings and structures. When it comes to language, we are all incredibly good drivers – all of us have been trained to race in the streets of Naples, and this is why we don't crash head-on into one another all the time.

If you doubt that your own driving skills really merit this flattery, think of the following simple case. Suppose you see two elderly ladies coming out of the theatre, and from their animated conversation you catch the word 'wicked!' Of course, you would automatically assume that the ladies thoroughly disapproved of the performance. But if behind the two ladies there were two teenage girls, and one said to the other 'wicked!' you would probably interpret her mood very differently. In a hundred years' time, when the original meaning of 'wicked' has all but been forgotten, people may wonder how it was ever possible for a word meaning 'evil' to change its sense to 'wonderful' so quickly. But for us who are in the midst of it, the variation does not seem to cause too much angst. We judge the meaning by drawing information from the context, from what we know about the speaker and from what we infer about their intentions. And more often than not, we get it right. Sometimes, the contradictory meanings even rub shoulders for centuries: a word like 'fast', which started off meaning something like 'secure', or 'not moving at all', later developed the contrary sense 'moving quickly'. Both meanings have survived until this very day, but we still manage to get along all right, apparently without too many serious mishaps.

This is not to say that there never are any head-on collisions. Take this report of a crash caused by a recent change in the pronunciation of vowels by some younger speakers of British English. The following conversation was recently overheard in a university cafeteria. A student came to the canteen and asked for 'a *cake*'. 'Wha' sor'a *cike* d'yer want, love?' replied the dinner lady at the counter. The student looked rather at a loss, and repeated: 'No, just a *cake*, a *cake*! A *caka-cala* . . .'

But although such prangs do occur, they seem to be remarkably rare given the actual chaos on the roads, and this is a tribute to our skills in coping with variation. Exactly the same skills must have allowed speakers in the past to cope with those changes that in retrospect seem so improbable. Recall the flipped verb 'like', for instance. To modern ears the change from 'it likes me' to 'I like it' seems unlikely, but from the perspective of the seventeenth century it was just another case of synchronic variation. Shakespeare may have used 'like' in the older sense ('the musician *likes* me not'), but in fact, he also uses 'like' in the modern – flipped – meaning. In *Othello*, for instance, the musicians are told: 'the general so *likes* your music, that he desires you, for love's sake, to make no more noise with it.' Listeners in Shakespeare's time must have employed the same skills to work out the question of who likes whom, as we do to decide the meaning of 'wicked' or 'fast'. As the seventeenth century progressed, however, the older sense of 'like' became rarer, and eventually disappeared altogether. Because we are no longer used to coping with this particular instance of variation, the change in meaning looks like a dangerous swerve on a busy motorway. But for the speakers then, the gradual petering out of the old meaning would have barely been noticeable.

The verb 'resent' is a similar case in point, since what seems today an about-turn in its meaning felt like nothing of the sort for speakers in the seventeenth century. At the time, 'resent' could mean either 'take with a good feeling', or 'take with a bad feeling', or more accurately, it could mean take with *any* feeling, as the following examples from letters of Charles I illustrate:

> The misfortune of our forces in the north we know is resented as sadly by you. (1644)

> Let the army know that we highly resent this their expression [of loyalty] to us. (1647)

And although those were especially turbulent times in England, there is no evidence that the flexibility in the meaning of 'resent' contributed significantly to the miseries of the period, or to Charles's unhappy end. Later, however, as the seventeenth century drew to a close, the positive sense of 'resent' gradually faded away. While speakers at the time would hardly have noticed it, nearly four centuries on this creates the appearance of a complete U-turn.

The most important discovery we have made so far is that language is in a perpetual state of flux. While no one in particular seems to be going about changing it, a few deep-rooted motives that drive all of us (economy, expressiveness, analogy) create powerful forces of change and ensure that sounds, meanings and even structures are always on the move. And while our capacity to accommodate synchronic variation means that we are often hardly aware that one form is usurping another, changes can proceed so quickly that after just a few centuries a language can hardly recognize itself when leafing through the old family albums.

So far, the processes of change may have appeared somewhat chaotic. Not only does everything change, but these changes seem to proceed in random and unpredictable directions, as if anything could turn into anything else, entirely at whim. The word 'resent' took a U-turn from a positive meaning to a negative one, but the word 'wicked' is now lurching in exactly the opposite direction, from a negative to a positive sense. Similar examples of the haphazard nature of change are not hard to come by. The word 'adder', for instance, started out in life as 'nadder' and shed its initial *n* some time in the fourteenth century (when the phrase 'a nadder' was misheard as 'an adder'). But the word 'nick-name' turned in exactly the opposite direction: having started out as an '*eke*-name', it picked up an *n* through a similar misinterpretation ('an eke-name', meaning an 'also-name' was misheard as 'a nick-name'). Changes in the past tense of English verbs don't seem to follow a very reliable compass either: *help*, for instance, started out with an irregular past tense *healp*, but took on a regular form *helped*. The verb *dive*, on the other hand, started with a regular past tense *dived*, but is nowadays taking a plunge in the other direction, and turning into an irregular *dove*. All these apparently shambolic developments may give the impression that there is as much logic to the course of language change as there is to the vagaries of fashion. Hemlines go up and down, but it would be hopeless to look for any sense behind the fluctuations.

Nevertheless, despite the apparent bedlam, there is also a very different face to language change: though this be madness, yet there is method in't. On closer inspection, it turns out that amid the chaos of random vacillations, a distinct element of regularity can be discerned in language's motion. The following chapters will reveal how language after language, in wave after wave, drifts along the same channels of change, and in exactly the same direction. To take one example, the sound change from *p* to *f*, which blew over the prehistoric settlements of the Germanic tribes, appears to have made its presence felt not only in Germanic, but in dozens of other languages across the globe. A change in the opposite direction, however, from *f* to *p*, is practically unheard of.

In what follows, our focus will stay almost exclusively on these regular and recurrent paths of change, and rarely veer towards the sporadic and more unpredictable types. The rationale is fairly straightforward: the clues to how linguistic structures rise and fall will be found not in chaos but in order, within those predictable and systematic aspects of change. Of course, the random elements will always be there somewhere, buzzing around in the background. But they can just be ignored as white noise, and need not distract us from enjoying the music.

3

The Forces of Destruction

Leofan men, gecnawað þæt soð is:
ðeos worold is on ofste, and hit nealæcð þam ende,
and þy hit is on worolde aa
swa leng swa wyrse . . .

Beloved men, know that this is the truth:
This world is in haste, and it approaches its end,
and therefore always in the world
The longer (it is), the worse (it gets) . . .

Wulfstan, Archbishop of York (died AD 1023)

The world has been hastening towards its imminent end for as long as anyone cares to remember, and language with it. Not only does language always change, but if one is to believe the authorities, it always changes for the worse. 'Tongues, like governments, have a natural tendency to degeneration,' declared Samuel Johnson in the introduction to his *Dictionary of the English Language*.

The critics of the English language today are divided on the question of who is to blame for its current ills: the headline-hungry press, sound-biting politicians, or the slovenly habits of the young. But they are all united by the conviction that English is in a parlous state. What a falling-off was there, from the English of even just two generations ago, in the good old days when – as a reviewer in the *Times Literary Supplement* recently reminisced – 'a mistake was a mistake and not a sign of free expression'.

That may be so, but it was not quite the opinion of the 'authorities' in those good old days. In 1946, for instance, George Orwell (about whom it was once said that he could not blow his nose without moralizing on conditions in the handkerchief industry) wrote in the journal *Horizon*: 'most people who bother with the matter at all would admit that the English language is in a bad way'. A bad way compared of course to the language of previous generations, which was purer and more correct than the English of his own time. Perhaps, but had Orwell consulted his predecessors, he would have encountered different sentiments. In 1848, a century before Orwell's article, the renowned linguist August Schleicher dismissed the English of his day as the most 'ground-down' of all the Germanic languages. English only showed 'how rapidly the language of a nation important both in history and literature can sink', and it was improbable that 'from such language-ruins the whole edifice will be raised anew'. Instead, he added gloomily, the language is likely to 'sink into mono-syllabicity'.

Or take this chilling prediction of impending doom: 'The greatest improprieties . . . are to be found among people of fashion; many pronunciations, which thirty or forty years ago were confined to the vulgar, are gradually gaining ground; and if something [is] not done to stop this growing evil . . . English is likely to become a mere jargon.' Everyone has read such sentiments expressed in countless letters to broadsheet editors, so there is nothing especially surprising about this particular one, except, perhaps, that it was written some threescore years and ten before Schleicher's proclamation, in 1780, by one Thomas Sheridan (actor, advocate of correct elocution, and father of the playwright Richard Brinsley Sheridan). What Sheridan found most galling was that the decline of English was of such recent origin, since according to him, only seventy years earlier, 'during the reign of Queen Anne [1702–14] . . . it is probable that English was . . . spoken in its highest state of perfection'.

Really? The cognoscenti at the time would have begged to differ. Very much during Queen Anne's reign, Jonathan Swift embarked on what would go down in posterity as one of the most astoundingly bigoted rants in the distinguished history of that genre. His 1712 'Proposal for Correcting, Improving and Ascertaining the English Tongue' starts with the following fanfare: 'I do here, in the Name of all the Learned and Polite Persons of the Nation, complain . . . that our Language is extremely imperfect; that its daily Improvements are by no means in proportion to its daily Corruptions . . .' and that's only the beginning.

So the English of today is not what it used to be, but then again, it never was. What is more, English is not in any way unusual in attracting all this disapprobation, for other languages have been put in the dock just as often. Take modern German, for instance, which by common consent is a mere shadow of its former glory two centuries ago, in the Golden Age of Goethe and Schiller. That may well be, but during Goethe's lifetime those in the know were of a rather different opinion. In 1819, the fairy-tale compiler and linguist Jacob Grimm compared the language of his day to that of previous centuries, and lamented that 'six hundred years ago, every common peasant knew – that is to say practised daily – perfections and niceties of the German language of which the best language-teachers nowadays can no longer even dream'.

The French have been at it too, corrupting their language on the one hand and complaining about it on the other. Anyone who is anyone can tell you that French is now going to the dogs. Until not so long ago, that illustrious institution the Académie Française wielded its authority to protect the language from the vagaries of change, but alas, scholars these days seem to be losing their clout, and so French is being attacked on all fronts, by the tainted norms of mass media and the degenerate speech habits of the decadent young. As the writer Serge Koster explains in impeccable prose, the language is paying a high price for this 'altération qui se mue en altérité' ('alteration which turns into alterity'). The new changes, he laments, are 'corrupting a system of grammar which was constructed throughout the centuries, and which has stayed almost stable since the eighteenth century'.

But has it really? One need only consult the opinions of the guardians of the language in the allegedly happy and stable centuries past. In a session of the Académie Française in November 1843, an argument erupted between two distinguished Victors, the philosopher and educationalist Victor Cousin and the novelist Victor Hugo. The discussion began with a somewhat arcane debate on the merits and demerits of writing double consonants, but it soon developed into a heated exchange about the state of the language in general, with Cousin proclaiming that the recent changes French was undergoing were nothing but decay. When Hugo questioned his reasoning, Cousin replied that he even knew exactly when the rot began. 'The decay of the French language,' he declared, 'started in 1789,' to which Hugo famously retorted: 'À quelle heure, s'il vous plaît?'

Gaston Paris, a contemporary of Cousin and Hugo, and one of the leading French linguists of the nineteenth century, would certainly have agreed with Cousin that the language of their time was inferior to that of previous generations. But he had a very different opinion as to when the decline actually started, for according to him the very birth of the French language was mired in decay. French had emerged from Vulgar Latin, the language of the illiterate masses, who according to Paris had 'gradually lost the proper and instinctive sense of the laws of the language that they spoke, and let it be corrupted in their mouth, following the vagaries of the time, new needs, whims, and errors'. In consequence, he argued, the newborn language was 'inferior in beauty and logic to the language which preceded it'. Paris was of course referring to that truth universally acknowledged, that French could never hope to live up to the beauty of its classical Latin forebear, which had reached the highest peaks of purity in the Golden Age of Virgil and Cicero.

Universally acknowledged? Well, almost. There would have been at least one voice of dissent, as Cicero, for one, did not exactly feel that he was living in the heyday of Latin. Far from it – he was sure that the Latin of his time was not what it had once been, and that standards were slipping. In a tome on the art of oratory from 46 BC, which he dedicated to his friend Brutus, Cicero compared the speech of public figures of the day with that of a century before, and concluded that 'practically everyone . . . in those days spoke correctly. But the lapse of time has certainly had a deteriorating effect in this respect.'

Taking it from the authorities, then, it seems a miracle that language did not degenerate into the grunts of apes long ago. And how is it, you may ask, that so many sages have failed to spot one glaringly obvious point, namely that if language has so far managed to survive for millennia, it is rather unlikely to cave in just in the next few years or so? Well, one answer is given by the Viennese critic Hans Weigel, who asserted in 1974 that 'every age claims that its language is more endangered and threatened by decay than ever before. In our time, however, language really *is* endangered and threatened by decay as never before . . .'

So there you have it. There must be some very strong reasons why so many intelligent people should believe something that is so patently irrational: that language is always changing for the worse, and that it is even teetering on the brink of collapse. But what is it exactly that dazzles these scholars and makes them see only decay? Of course, one could write it all off as merely the consequence of some deep-rooted conservatism, a general harking back to bygone better days. 'The longer, the worse', as Archbishop Wulfstan so pithily put it – just as people were more polite in one's youth, the weather was nicer, and the apples tasted better, so was language more refined and less abused.

But it would be rather unfair to blame it all on irrational nostalgia, since there is a much more serious reason why so many people think that language is constantly decaying. This reason is quite simply that . . . decay is indeed a pervasive type of change in language, and what is more, it is the aspect of change that is by far the most easily observable to the naked eye. The forces of destruction almost seem to leap out of the pages of practically any language's history, but the contrary processes, the productive forces of renewal and creation, are much more difficult to spot – so difficult, in fact, that it is only in the last few decades that linguists have fully grasped their significance and have made real headway in understanding them. Ironically, the reason why the creative forces in language were so elusive is that they lie surprisingly close to their bugbear, the forces of destruction. And as destruction is so conspicuous, it is no wonder that decay has monopolized scholars' attention and dominated the perception of language change for so long.

The following chapters will try to shed light on the slow forge and working-house of linguistic creation. But since creation and destruction will turn out to be closely related, the route to understanding creation must lead through the alleyways of destruction. This chapter, therefore, will take a closer look at the effects of destruction on all areas of language, from sounds and meanings to most corners of its structure. The aim will be to take stock of the damages caused by these destructive forces, discover the reasons for their ferocity, and explain the ubiquity of disintegration and decay.

IRREGULAR FLOWERS, OR THE DILEMMA OF THE NINETEENTH CENTURY

It sometimes happens that a trivial experience sticks in one's mind and sparks off deep reflections and musings that go far beyond its actual significance. For me, one such experience was learning about the irregularity of flowers.

While grappling with the complexity of the Latin case system, I remember one instance in particular which set off a whole chain of intriguing thoughts, but also some serious doubts. Recall that Latin has five different groups of nouns, called 'declensions', each with a different set of case endings. But as if memorizing not just one, but five different sets were not bad enough, some of the these declensions are beset by various irregularities, and the third declension is particularly vexing in this respect. 'With the Third Declension, the high and austere order of Imperial Rome seemed to lose grip a little,' as Dorothy L. Sayers once observed. For some reason, 'the rot always seemed to set in at the Third Anything'. The 'official' set of endings for the third declension looks as follows (for simplicity, only the singular forms are printed here):

NOMINATIVE	*consul*	'the consul (saw me)'
ACCUSATIVE	*consul-em*	'(I saw) the consul'
GENITIVE	*consul-is*	'of the consul'
DATIVE	*consul-i*	'to the consul'
ABLATIVE	*consul-e*	'by the consul'

Now, the noun *flos* 'flower' belongs to the third declension, so according to the rules it should have had the following forms in the different cases: *flos*, *flosem*, *flosis*, *flosi*, *flose*. But in practice, the actual forms are *flos*, and then *florem*, *floris*, *flori*, *flore*. Instead of the expected *s*, all the cases except the nominative *flos* introduce a most irregular *r*. In itself, of course, the irregularity of *flos* was hardly an earth-shattering revelation, only another example of an irrational complication that makes life gratuitously difficult. Indeed, the *flos*-*floris* affair might have stayed at just that, had I not stumbled on a little footnote, which tried to excuse such irregularities by blaming them on a simple historical process. Originally, as it turned out, Latin flowers were perfectly regular, and so the forms were indeed *flos*, *flosem*, *flosis*, just as one would expect. But early on in the history of Latin, some time between the sixth and fourth centuries BC, a sound change took place, in which every (undoubled) *s* between two vowels turned into an *r*. In itself, this was an entirely regular change, and happened systematically to all eligible candidates. But as a result, an irregularity wormed its way into words like *flos*. The *s* in *flosem*, *flosis* and so on turned into *r*, because it was between two vowels, whereas the *s* in *flos* remained an *s*, because it was not. (Incidentally, the consequences of this Latin change from *s* to *r* can still be felt in English, not only in the borrowed word 'flower', but also in various pairs which are borrowed from different derivations of the same Latin noun. *Just* and *jurisdiction*, for instance, both go back to the Latin root *jus* 'justice', but in *justus* 'just', the *s* remained unaltered, whereas in *jurisdictio* 'administration of justice', the *s* of the genitive case *jusis* was caught between two vowels, so it changed to *juris*. The same applies to *rustic* and *rural*, both from the noun *rus* 'country'.)

So the irregular flowers were actually the result of a simple sound change. But what of it? To all intents and purposes, the explanation for how the Latin *s*-*r* irregularity crept into nouns like *flos* was just a simple solution for a simple problem, and not even a particularly crucial one at that. Nevertheless, for me the *flos*-*floris* affair was a revelation, since it showed that even irregularities, those apparently arbitrary nuisances, are not entirely arbitrary after all. Even the infamous exceptions, it seemed, succumb to some kind of logical explanation. If one could explain *flos* and *floris*, then surely one should be able to discover the reason behind other exceptions too, and the *flos*-*floris* pair even pointed to where one should start searching for the clues. What looks messy and irregular at one point in time can appear perfectly logical when traced through history.

The prospect of historical treasure-hunts seemed exciting, but there was also a darker and deeply troubling aspect to all this. There was no doubt that the explanation for *flos* and *floris* was right – after all, it relies on evidence from attested documents. Nor was there any reason to query similar historical explanations given for other exceptions, since individually they all made perfect sense. Nonetheless, when added up, the individual explanations combined to make a picture that was highly suspect. Take any irregularity (like *flos*-*floris*), and if you only trace it back far enough, it seems, it will turn out to have developed because of some change to an originally regular pattern (*flos-flosis*). And if this is so, then the further back one digs in time, the more regular a language should be. According to this logic, then, there must have been some Golden Age of perfection somewhere deep in the past, when languages could boast a flawless structure unblemished by irregularity. But if language really did enjoy these halcyon days some time before history began, then why did things start clouding over later on? Why does change always appear to muddle and destroy, rather than build and create? And if the changes only mess things up, then how did languages ever reach their Golden Age in the first place?

As it turns out, I was not the first to be troubled by such questions. My brush with irregular flowers can be said to re-enact the major dilemma of linguistics in the nineteenth century. The explanation for how the irregularity in *flos* and *floris* arose may be only a minor footnote in the great roll of achievements of nineteenth-century linguists, but its spirit nevertheless symbolizes the triumphs of that age. And yet the same *flos-floris* also epitomizes the depressing nature of the changes that emerged at the time, a one-sided picture of decay and disintegration. No wonder, then, that linguists throughout the nineteenth century and even well into the twentieth were preoccupied by destruction's grim grip on language. To start with, where did all this destructive energy come from? The answer to this question turned out to be not too difficult to find: fairly early on, it became clear that the forces of destruction draw their inexhaustible resources from one age-old human habit . . .

The Elders of Idleford

There is a long-forgotten fairy tale about the village elders of Idleford, who were always concerned with the welfare of their kinfolk, and in particular, with how they could spare them any unnecessary effort. One day, the young John Lazeley, who was the first village lad to go to university, came back to Idleford with an irresistible suggestion. 'I have learnt,' he informed the elders, 'that when we pronounce the sound *k*, we block the flow of air for a split second, by raising our tongue against the back of the palate, and then immediately lowering it again to let the air through. And I have just had a flash of inspiration: isn't it a complete waste of energy to raise the tongue all the way up to the palate, only in order to bring it all the way down again? Why not just raise the tongue half-way instead, and so save ourselves a great deal of effort?' The elders were delighted by this suggestion, and a motion was approved unanimously. The herald informed all Idlefordians that from now on they only need raise their tongues half-way up to the palate when they said *k*. And since that day, Idlefordians started pronouncing *k* as *ch* (the sound one hears in Scottish *loch*, or German *Bach*), as this is what you get when you raise the tongue only half-way up to the back of the palate. Of course, all the Idlefordians were over the moon, since they now had so much more energy to spare, which could be expended on thinking about how to save even more effort. And thus it was that only a few months later, the village doctor, Doolittle, who had always excelled in anatomy, came up with an even niftier suggestion. 'Life has much improved since we started raising the tongue only half-way,' he informed the elders. 'But just think about it like this: wouldn't it be even easier if we didn't bother with the tongue at all? For if instead of raising it half-way up to produce a *ch*, we only slightly constrained the air in what is known in my profession as the "glottis", just a little further down the vocal tract, we would get the sound *h* instead. This sound is not so very different from *ch*, but takes *so* much less energy to produce, since we don't have to go to all the effort of moving that big and heavy tongue.' With great enthusiasm, the elders approved Doolittle's revised pronunciation, and since then Idlefordians started saying *h* instead of *ch*.

The story would have ended there, were it not for a distinguished octogenarian called Percy Lounger, who some years later rose up in the assembly and announced: 'Friends, no one would deny that we are much better off now than in the days of my youth, when we all had to bother with the inconvenience of waggling the tongue for every word with a *k* in it. But you know, I have been giving the matter some thought over the last few decades, and yesterday, a much better idea sprang to mind. Constraining the glottis is all very well, but why even bother with that, when there is something much easier we could do? Wouldn't it be much better simply . . . to do nothing at all?' Needless to say, the suggestion immediately appealed and caught on. And since that day, Idlefordians pronounce not *k*, not *ch*, not even *h*, but just nothing at all. So if you happen to pass by a village one day, and someone invites you in for a nice 'up of 'offee and 'oo'ies . . . you know you are in Idleford.

Unfortunately this story never made its way into the collection of the Brothers Grimm, perhaps because it seems just too improbable, even for a fairy-tale. But in fact, there are rather more Idlefords around than you might imagine, and not just in legend. Have you ever wondered, for example, why in Italian *caldo* means not 'cold' but 'hot'? As it happens, it is not the Italians who are to blame for this mismatch, but rather the English, who turn out to be of good Idlefordian stock. Italian *caldo* and English *hot* both go back to similar roots that started with *k-* in the prehistoric ancestor language. *Caldo* ultimately comes from the Proto-Indo-European **kel* 'warm', and English *hot* goes back to the Proto-Indo-European root **kai* 'burn'. But whereas the forebears of the Italians didn't alter the shape of their **kel* too much, the ancestors of the English happily followed good effort-saving principles. As can be seen in the diagram below, the *k* of **kai* was weakened to *ch*, and then further to *h*. And since in many varieties of English, the *h* of *hot* has been dropped, so that only *'ot* remains, it's clear that the Idlefordian principle has been followed to completion:

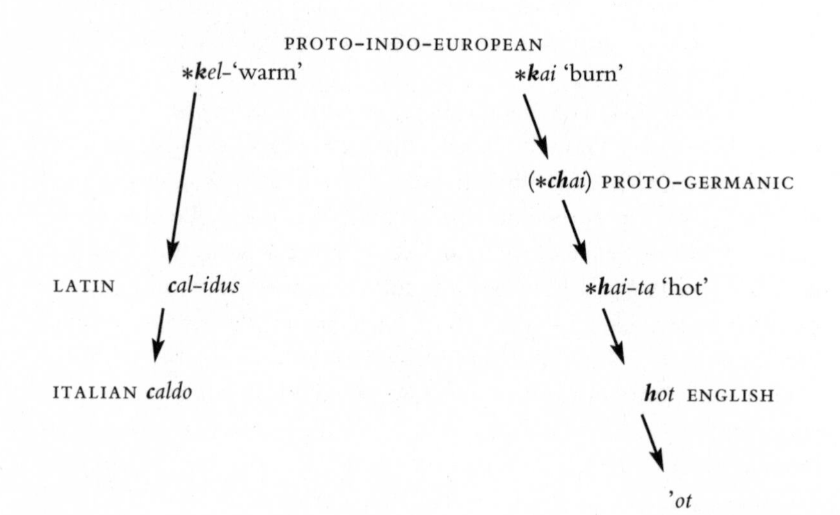

The weakening from $k \rightarrow ch \rightarrow h$ is part of a wider array of changes that took place in Proto-Germanic, probably starting sometime around 500 BC. And the scholar who expounded these changes methodically for the first time was none other than Jacob Grimm, in his groundbreaking 1822 history of the Germanic languages. So although 'The Elders of Idleford' never made it into Grimm's collection of fairy-tales, it certainly made it into his linguistic discoveries – and with a bang. The description of this series of changes, which soon came to be known as 'Grimm's law', was one of the most important milestones in the development of linguistics, and set off a new era of scientific discoveries.

The Brothers Grimm: Jacob, on the right (1785–1863), and Wilhelm

The precise details of these changes are quite complex, and there is no need to go into all of them here. But in essence, Grimm's law describes a wholesale erosion of sounds that took place in the Germanic branch of Indo-European. Six (out of the nine) changes are shown below.

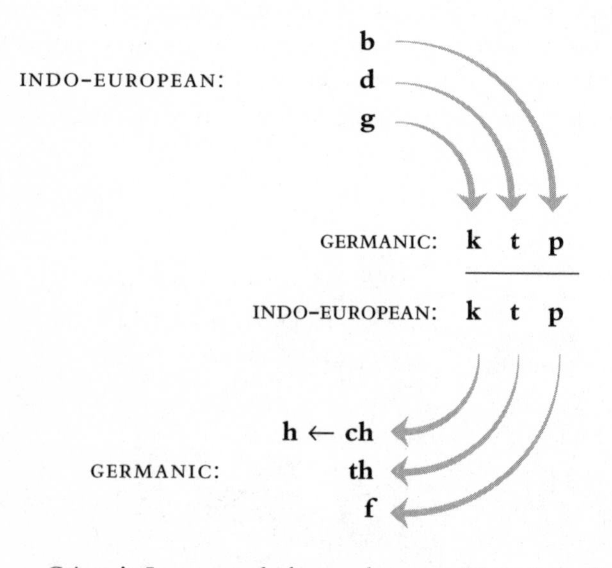

Grimm's Law: sound changes between Proto-Indo-European and Proto-Germanic

The bottom end of the diagram is by now quite familiar, since two of these changes have already featured earlier (the change from *k* → *ch* → *h* in this chapter, and the change from *p* → *f*, as in *pisk* and *fisk*, in the previous chapter). In fact, all the three changes at the bottom of the diagram are of a similar nature, since in all of them, a consonant called a 'stop' (where the air is blocked completely for a split second by the tongue or the lips) is weakened to the equivalent 'fricative' (where the tongue or lips don't block the air completely but let out a small stream that makes a sound through friction).

The changes at the top (*g* → *k*, *d* → *t*, *b* → *p*) also represent a kind of weakening, but here effort is spared for the vocal cords. The sounds *g*, *d* and *b* are called 'voiced' consonants, because when we produce them, the vocal cords start vibrating at the same time as the air is released from its temporary blockage, or just a split second before. The sounds *k*, *t* and *p* are called 'voiceless' consonants, because they are produced without the additional vibration of the vocal cords, but with the tongue or lips blocking the air in exactly the same way as in *g*, *d* and *b*. (You can check out the difference by pronouncing each of the pairs while whispering. You will hear that the distinction between the voiced and voiceless sounds almost disappears.) Of course, vibrating the vocal cords is an additional effort that can sometimes be spared, and so a voiced *g* turned into a voiceless *k*, and similarly, *d* turned to *t*, and *b* to *p*.

Grimm's law explains why the relation between English words and their cognates in non-Germanic Indo-European languages is not always immediately apparent to the untrained eye. English *cold*, for instance, is related to Italian *gelato* 'frozen' rather than to its false friend *caldo* 'hot'. And there are many other such surprising 'twins', cognates such as *grain* and *corn*, which may look rather different to the casual observer, but nevertheless come via different routes from exactly the same Proto-Indo-European root. The reason why English has many such pairs is that more than a millennium after Grimm's changes had taken their course, English started borrowing heavily from Latin and French, and thus developed a two-tier vocabulary of home-grown and borrowed words. *Corn* is the native English sibling, which underwent the *g* → *k* change some time after 500 BC, whereas *grain* was borrowed from French much later on, and so bypassed this change. As the table overleaf illustrates, there are many other such separated twins in English, such as ***dent***(*al*) and ***tooth***; ***can***(*ine*) and ***hound***; ***pater***(*nal*) and ***father***. Sometimes the siblings have gone such separate ways that upon meeting up they would hardly give each other a second glance. This is the case with the borrowed *part*(*ridge*) and the native ****. (The Greeks, who are the ultimate source of the loanword *partridge*, presumably gave it this name because of the loud whirring sound it makes when suddenly flushed out.)

	HOME GROWN		BORROWED LATER
***Indo-European**	***Germanic**	**English**	**Latin/Greek > English**
	k* → (*ch*) → *h		
kerd	*hert*	*heart*	*kardia* (Greek) > 'cardiac'
kwon	*hund*	*hound*	*canis* (Latin) > 'canine'
	***k* → *ch* (→ *h*) → nothing**		
nok^{w}*t*	*nacht*	*ni~~gh~~t*	*noctis* (Latin) > 'nocturnal'
lewkto	*leucht*	*li~~gh~~t*	*lucis* (Latin) > 'Luci-fer' (light-bearing)
	p* → *f		
plōw	*flōw*	*flow*	*pluere* 'rain' (Latin) > 'pluvial'
pōd	*fōt*	*foot*	*pedis* (Latin) > 'pedestrian'
pr̥tu	*furd*	*ford*	*portus* 'harbour' (Latin) > 'port'
	g* → *k		
gr̥no	*kurn*	*corn*	*granum* (Latin) > 'grain'
werg	*werk*	*work*	*érgon* (Greek) > 'ergonomic', 'energy'
gel	*kal-d*	*cold*	*gelu* 'frost' (Latin) > 'gelato', 'gelatine'
	d* → *t		
dekm̥	*tehun*	*ten*	*decem* (Latin) > 'decimal'
dont	*tanth*	*tooth*	*dentis* (Latin) > 'dental'

The systematic nature of Grimm's changes made a profound impression on his contemporaries, and transformed the understanding of the nature of language. The weakening of *k* to *ch*, *p* to *f* and so on was not a coincidence that cropped up in just a few random words, but a regular change that affected all eligible words in the language at the time. This regularity enabled linguists towards the end of the nineteenth century to develop their resounding battle cry: 'sound changes admit no exceptions!' and encouraged them to view the changes as 'sound laws' that could be studied scientifically, like the laws of the natural world. Moreover, the changes were not a collection of random events which, by a stroke of luck, all happened to take place at the same time. Rather, they were intimately bound up with one another, in a chain of cause and effect, so that when *b* eroded to *p*, the original *p* sound itself shifted ground and eroded further to an *f*, presumably in order to hinder misunderstandings on a large scale. The interlinked nature of Grimm's changes thus revealed language as a system which maintains its integrity even when its individual elements are radically transformed – a system where *tout se tient* 'everything holds together'. Indeed, it is difficult to exaggerate the influence that Grimm's systematic correspondences exercised on the subsequent development of linguistics.

All this being said, there is no escaping the fact that Grimm's law describes changes that all follow somewhat discreditable Idlefordian principles, and derive from the inclination to save effort. They all represent weakening of sounds. Grimm himself, who believed that these changes were a peculiarity of Germanic, was obviously slightly embarrassed by the linguistic high jinks of his Teutonic forebears. 'In some sense,' he wrote in 1848, 'this change of sounds seems to me a barbarism and degeneration from which quieter people have refrained.' Still, he tried to put a brave face on the matter, and suggested that the changes must also have something to do with 'the Germans' mighty progress and urge for freedom which . . . was to lead to the transformation of Europe'.

But Grimm need not have worried, because there was nothing terribly special about his Germanic ancestors in this respect. In fact, the principles of erosion that underlie Grimm's law are universal, and many of the particular changes in Germanic, such as the weakening of *p* to *f*, can be observed in dozens of languages around the world. Take Japanese, for instance. Whereas a pre-ninth-century Samurai whose honour had been compromised would commit a *para-kiri* (*para* 'belly', *kiru* 'cut'), his descendants a few generations later would remember the honourable deed of their ancestor as *fara-kiri*. Now, as it happens, the change from *p* to *f* is a part of a longer chain of weakening: *p* → *f* → *h*, an exact parallel to the path of Idlefordian erosion *k* → *ch* → *h*. The Japanese followed this route assiduously, so that after the seventeenth century, new generations of compromised warriors have all been committing *hara-kiri*.

What is more, the Idlefordians do not even have a monopoly on all labour-saving inventions, since various other techniques have been perfected in other corners of the globe. In the sleepy Italian seaside village of Santa Siesta del Farniente, a different, but no less effective method was devised. Village legend has it that one day, when a certain

Signora Pigrizia Poltrone was sitting on her *balcone* enjoying a post-prandial yawn and relishing the thought of a long afternoon nap, she was suddenly struck by a brilliant brainwave. That evening, she explained her idea to the whole village: 'Take the word for "night",' she said, 'which we pronounce *no**ct**e*. Isn't it a waste of effort to have to spit out two different sounds like *c* and *t* so close to each other? Why not just pronounce two of the same, and say *no**tt**e* instead? Or take *so**mn**o* ("sleep"), wouldn't it be so much easier to say *so**nn**o*?' The idea appealed so much that the inhabitants of the village set about trying to find other candidates: *se**pt**e* ('seven') turned into *se**tt**e*, *ma**ks**imo* ('maximum') became *ma**ss**imo*, *pi**ct**oresco* ended up as *pi**tt**oresco*.

There are many other types of linguistic labour-saving devices, but ultimately they are all variations on the same theme, and follow the principle of least effort: 'pronounce as little as you can get away with'. When it comes to language, we are all bone-idle, and especially in rapid speech, we tend to expend only the minimal amount of energy on pronunciation, just enough to make sure that the listener gets the intended meaning. As a result, sounds can be weakened over time, and they can sometimes even drop off altogether. So if you take a word or phrase and follow it through the years, chances are you will see it getting shorter and shorter, with sounds and even whole syllables falling by the wayside.

The beginning of a word or phrase is easily shed, as in the French 'je ne sais pas', which often ends up pronounced {shepa}, or the equivalent English 'I do not know', which is frequently stripped to {dunno}. But sounds can be gouged out from the middle of a word with almost equal ease, as witnessed by the fate of the Old English *hlaf-weard* 'loaf-ward(en)' or 'bread keeper'. *Hlaf-weard*, with its two words and three syllables, was shortened to *hlaford*, thence to *laferd*, then *lowerd*, until it finally ended up as our impoverished modern *lord*, with just one halfpenny-syllable to his name.

Usually, however, what bears the brunt of the forces of erosion is the end of words. Speakers tend to run out of steam by the time they get to the end, and are also more likely to assume that the hearer will have got the gist of the word by then, so they don't bother with pronouncing the end as distinctly as the beginning, thus leaving the final syllable the most exposed. In modern English, for example, words like *disturbed* or *loved* are written with *-ed* at the end, although they are pronounced {disturbd}, {lovd}. The reason for the extra *-e* is that such words were originally pronounced {disturbèd}, {lovèd} with an audible vowel at the end. At the beginning of the eighteenth century the shortened pronunciation was still rather new-fangled, and as such attracted the wrath of Jonathan Swift. In his splenetic rant of 1712, Swift had this to say about pronunciations such as *lov'd* and *rebuk't*, rather than the correct *lovèd* and *rebukèd*: 'By leaving out a Vowel to save a Syllable, we form so jarring a Sound, and so difficult to utter, that I have often wondred how it could ever obtain . . . This perpetual Disposition to shorten our Words, by retrenching the Vowels, is nothing else but a tendency to lapse into the Barbarity of those *Northern* Nations from whom we are descended.' Nevertheless, Swift's contemporaries do not seem to have been too bothered by these sagacious words, and the final vowel petered out, so that today you would have to be pretty disturbed to say disturbèd.

Swift may have been scandalized by the loss of a vowel from the end of words, but in fact, the disappearance of *just* one vowel is a fairly light casualty. Consider, for instance, what happened to the portly Latin phrase *persica malus* 'Persian apple', with its five juicy vowels and seven luscious consonants. It ended up in French as a word of just one vowel and two consonants: first, the whole second word was dropped altogether, leaving *persica*. Then the vowel *i* disappeared to give *persca*, which was further shortened to *pesca*, then to *pesche*, and finally *pêche*, ending up on English palates as a rather shrivelled 'peach'.

In fact, when it comes to shedding syllables, French is a prime example. In modern French, there are three different words that are pronounced the same way, as a rather bare and paltry {oo}: *ou*, *où*, and *août*. The first two have relatively moderate histories in terms of shrinking: *ou* 'or' comes from Latin *aut*, pronounced {out}, and here only one vowel and one consonant have disappeared. *Où* 'where' comes from Latin *ubi*, and once again, it has only lost one vowel and one consonant. But the third {oo}, the month of *août*, comes from no less a forebear than the Latin *Augustus*. Here, four consonants and three vowels have vanished without trace. At first sight, it might seem remarkable that the august *Augustus* could have ended up as a mere {oo}, but in French hands, there is nothing to it. Take *Augustus*, which by late Latin had already been shortened to *Agustus*; then drop the last syllable to get *Agust*. By the twelfth century, the *g* had also eroded away to leave {aoost}. The *s* was next in line for the chop, so the word came to be pronounced {aoot} and spelt *août*. Later, {aoot} was shortened to {oot}; and finally, the *t* was ditched . . . *et voilà, le mois d'août.*

The French may have perfected the techniques for shrinking sounds, but they are by no means the only connoisseurs in that art. I once discovered this the hard way, when during a semester at a university in Denmark I joined the university choir, which specialized in singing nineteenth-century Danish romantic songs. These songs were a great help in learning the language, but there was one particular song which I just couldn't spit out at the required speed – my tongue simply didn't keep time with the lyrics. The reason for the difficulty was that this song was written in a dialect from the island of Funen, which even the most benevolent of observers would have to describe as consonantally challenged. The standard variety of modern Danish has already managed to divest itself of many of the consonants that unduly burdened earlier stages of the language, but this dialect somehow succeeded in disposing of even those precious few consonants that standard Danish has hung on to. So in a desperate attempt not to stick out, I vaguely tried to blabber, while all around me, the other members of the choir – otherwise entirely sensible people – were producing bucket-loads of *'e 'a 'o 'a 'e 'å 'a 'e 'æ 'e*'s in public, apparently without any hint of embarrassment. The last line of the song, for example, went like this:

de hele æ' fo'a're e'er å a' de' æ' mey

The standard Danish orthography of the same line can give an idea of the consonants that once used to be there:

*de**t** hele e**r** fo**r**a**nd**ret e**ll**er o**g** a**t** de**t** e**r** mi**g***
the whole is changed or also that it is me
'everything has changed, or perhaps it is (just) me'

While the Funen dialect has dropped most of its cumbersome consonants, in other languages the disposal can affect mostly the vowels.

Some languages are notorious for being rather consonant-heavy, and often the reason is drastic vowel loss. As a sort of comic relief during the war in the former Yugoslavia, an email (based on an article in the satirical magazine *The Onion*) circulated with the following report:

CLINTON SENDS VOWELS TO FORMER YUGOSLAVIA

City of Sjlbvdnzv and Island of Krk to be First Recipients

> Before an emergency joint session of Congress yesterday, President Clinton announced plans to deploy over 75,000 vowels to the war-torn countries of Ex-Yugoslavia. The deployment, the largest of its kind in US history, will provide the region with the critically needed letters A, E, I, O and U, and is hoped to render countless names more pronounceable. 'For six years, we have stood by while names like Ygrjvslmv, Tzlynhr and Glrm have been abused by millions around the world,' Clinton said. 'Today, we must stand up and say "enough is enough!"' The deployment is set for early next week, with the Adriatic port city of Sjlbvdnzv and the island of Krk being projected to be the first recipients. Two transport planes, each carrying over 500 boxes of E's, will fly from Andrews Air Force Base across the Atlantic, and airdrop the letters over the worst affected areas. The citizens of the stricken towns are eagerly awaiting the vowels. 'My God. I do not think that we can last another day,' Trszg Grzdnvc, 44, said. 'I have six children and none of them has a name I can pronounce.' Sjlbvdnzv resident, Grg Hmphrs, added: 'With just a few vowels, I could be George Humphries. This is my dream.' The airdrop represents the biggest deployment of any letter to a foreign country since 1984. During the summer of that year, the US shipped 92,000 consonants to Chad to provide relief to the city of Ouaouaoua.

As is so often the case, however, the reality is better than any fiction. The Czech phrase for 'stick (your) finger down (your) throat' is, very appropriately, *strč prst skrz krk*.

The assorted examples of weakening and loss may so far have amounted to not much more than a miscellany of curiosities, and their disreputable appearance is only exacerbated by the dubious motive that underlies them: the human proclivity towards laziness. But do not be misled by the triviality of it all. Trifling as these 'forces of destruction' may appear, their effects on structures can be catastrophic and annihilating, for over time, erosion is a force without rival, a ruthless enemy which can obliterate the mightiest of edifices, leaving only a rubble of irregularities in its wake.

The devastation that erosion metes out is perhaps most conspicuous with case-systems, which of all monumental structures seem to be most vulnerable. The fate of the case-system in the Indo-European languages is a good example. The prehistoric ancestor, Proto-Indo-European, had eight distinct cases, but only Sanskrit retained the full system, whereas in all the other daughter languages, erosion had started taking its toll even before the earliest records began. In Classical Latin, for instance, the eight distinct cases had already been knocked down to just six, and in practice, no single Latin noun had more than five distinct case endings in the singular. In the second declension, for instance, the dative and the ablative cases fused, leaving the noun with the following forms (in the singular):

NOMINATIVE	*ann-us*	'the year$_{\text{SUBJECT}}$'
VOCATIVE	*ann-e*	'O year!'
GENITIVE	*ann-ī*	'of the year'
ACCUSATIVE	*ann-um*	'the year$_{\text{OBJECT}}$'
DATIVE/ABLATIVE	*ann-ō*	'to/by the year'

But even these five different endings didn't hold out for long. The *-um* of the accusative was first shortened to *-u*, and then further to a laxer *-o*; the long *-ō* of the dative and ablative also weakened to a short *-o*; and the rare vocative coalesced with the nominative. So by around AD 300, only three distinct endings remained:

NOMINATIVE	*ann-us*
VOCATIVE	*ann-us*
GENITIVE	*ann-i*
ACCUSATIVE	*ann-o*
DATIVE/ABLATIVE	*ann-o*

And a few hundred years later, by the time of the earliest records in the Romance languages, only two forms had survived: nominative *ann-os*, and *ann-o* for everything else. Later on, even that difference was eliminated. In Spanish, the final *-s* of the nominative dropped off to give *año* in all cases, and in French, the whole final syllable disappeared, giving just *an* in all forms. So not much more than a millennium after Cicero, the majestic Latin case system had been entirely wiped out of existence.

An even earlier casualty was the case system in the Germanic branch of Indo-European, which already by the third century AD had lost four of the original eight cases of Proto-Indo-European. By the time of Old English, in the tenth century, nouns were left with at most three distinct case endings in the singular and three in the plural:

	SINGULAR		PLURAL	
NOMINATIVE/ACCUSATIVE	*stān*	'stone'	*stān-as*	'stones'
DATIVE	*stān-e*	'to stone'	*stān-um*	'to stones'
GENITIVE	*stān-es*	'of stone'	*stān-a*	'of stones'

But not even this reduced system succeeded in standing up to the onslaughts of erosion for very long, as soon after the tenth century, the final syllables were weakened and the whole edifice started to collapse. By the fifteenth century, the system was in tatters, and only the forms ending with an *s* remained in any way distinct:

	SINGULAR	PLURAL
NOMINATIVE/ACCUSATIVE	*stōn*	*stōn-es* (all cases)
DATIVE	*stōn*	
GENITIVE	*stōn-es*	

It is this depleted system that has survived in modern English, which can only boast two distinct endings, *stone* and *stone+s* (the latter written in three different ways, *stone**s***, *stone**'s*** and *stone**s'***, in a vain attempt to talk up the number of different forms).

Moreover, even if case systems are the most conspicuous victim of erosion, they are not the only monumental structures to fall prey to it. Verbal systems are almost as vulnerable, as can be seen from the table below, which gives the different forms of one English verb in three stages during the history of the language. Over the centuries, erosion has hacked away at the final syllables, and the result speaks for itself:

	~1200	~1600	~1800
Present:			
I	her-*e*	hear	hear
thou (by 1800 'you')	her-*est*	hear-*est*	hear
he	her-*eth*	hear-*eth*	hear-*s*
Subjunctive:			
he	her-*e*	hear	hear
they	her-*en*	hear	hear
Infinitive:	her-*en*	hear	hear
Imperative:			
you (singular)	her-*e*!	hear!	hear!
you (plural)	her-*eth*!	hear!	hear!
Past:			
I	herd-*e*	heard	heard
thou	herd-*est*	heard-*est*	heard
he	herd-*e*	heard	heard
they	herd-*en*	heard	heard

Even when the forces of erosion don't obliterate a structure entirely, they can still mess things up and create irregularities in forms that were once perfectly regular. The verb 'make' is one example, since its irregular past tense 'made' is only a fairly recent mishap. In the thirteenth century, 'make' was still a well-behaved regular verb, and had a past tense with the ending *-ed*. But clearly, the form 'maked' felt too broad in the beam, and so speakers stopped bothering with pronouncing the bit in the middle. At first, the slim-line 'made' coexisted peacefully with the older 'maked', so that Chaucer could still use either to suit his whim and rhyme:

The hye god, whan he hadde Adam **maked**,	(hye = high)
And saugh him al allone, bely-naked,	(saugh = saw)
God of his grete goodnesse syde than,	(syde than = said then)
Lat us now make an helpe unto this man	
Lyk to hymself; and thanne he **made** him Eve.	(lyk = like, thanne = then)

The Merchant's Tale (*Canterbury Tales*, *c.*1390)

But in the fifteenth century, 'maked' gradually sank into oblivion, thus creating the irregular pair 'make-made' we use today.

A more extreme example of how the forces of erosion can dishevel an elegant structure is the fate of some verbs in the Semitic languages. In Chapter 1, I mentioned the architecture of the Semitic verb, with its design of purely consonantal roots and vowel templates. There, the system was shown from its best angle, but when one gets down to examining the individual languages close up, the picture appears less flattering. Biblical Hebrew, for instance, is sometimes said to have so many irregularities as to warrant scepticism in the existence of the Almighty. But in fact, the faults in the system are very much of this world, and can mostly be put down to simple and by now familiar effort-saving changes. Consider, for example, the lot of the Hebrew root n-p-l 'fall', which has the following forms in the past and the future tense: n*a*p*a*l ('he fell') and *yi*np*o*l ('he will fall'). Or rather, I should say that these forms are what the verb *ought* to have looked like, for in reality, all it took was two commonplace effort-saving changes to cast the verb into irregularity:

ORIGINAL FORM	EFFORT-SAVING CHANGE	LATER FORM
*yi*np*o*l ('he will fall')	np → pp	*yi*pp*o*l
n*a*p*a*l ('he fell')	p → f	n*a*f*a*l

The first effort-saving change to visit the ancient Israelites was the 'Santa Siesta' principle of assimilation, whereby *n* sounds assimilated to the following consonant, and so the future tense *yi*np*o*l 'he will fall' became *yi*pp*o*l. Centuries later, the common weakening of *p* to *f* did not pass over the *p*'s of the Hebrews either, and all undoubled *p*'s after a vowel were weakened to *f*, thus turning the past tense n*a*p*a*l to n*a*f*a*l. Once the storm of change subsides, the two tenses of the verb 'fall', nafal and *yi*ppol, emerge from their tents and shake the dust off their weary consonants, but find that they can hardly recognize each other any more as two variations on the root n-p-l. Only two of the simplest effort-saving changes were required in order to blow up such confusion that the only thing left in common between the two forms nafal and *yi*ppol is the last root consonant l.

Had I unknown phrases
Sayings that are strange
Novel, untried words
Free of repetition
Not transmitted sayings
Spoken by the ancestors.
I wring out my body for what it holds,
Sifting through all my words;
For what has been said is just repetition,
What has been said has been said . . .

The Complaints of Khakheperre-seneb, Ancient Egyptian poem
(Middle Kingdom, nineteenth century BC)

Just as relentlessly as the wind and the rain, the forces of erosion wear and tear away at the linguistic landscape. Whatever hideaway of the language one peers into, one discovers the same scene of dereliction. Sounds are gradually weakened, words 'slip, slide, perish . . .', structures become dilapidated and fall apart. Optimists might hold out some hope that at least one area of language, the meaning of words, would remain a safe haven protected from the battering of erosion. After all, why should the meaning of words ever become weaker, if there is no gain to be had from the process? Clearly, the economic benefits of short-cuts in pronunciation don't apply in this case, since a word like 'catastrophe', for instance, would hardly become any easier to pronounce if it meant something less catastrophic.

Alas, it seems that meaning is just as prone to attrition as sounds. And ironically, the decay in meaning seems to be set off not by any indolent desire to save effort, but rather by almost the precise opposite: the wish to enhance expressiveness. Speakers sometimes go to great lengths to intensify the effect of their utterances in order to lend their speech more force and emphasis, and in doing so they tend to go for words with ever more muscular meanings. In the short term, this method may achieve the intended result, but in the long run, the strategy is self-defeating, simply because it is inflationary. Over-familiarity inevitably weakens the force of the meaning. As the Egyptian poet recognized almost 4,000 years ago, tried words lose their novelty and power – 'What has been said has been said.'

Self-appointed guardians of the English language are in the habit of complaining that words like 'catastrophe' are used so flippantly today that their meanings are being debased, and with them the English language as a whole. What they mean by 'debasement' is that when 'catastrophe' is no longer used only for real catastrophes (but is applied to bad concerts or non-matching clothes), it loses its distinctiveness and the original force of its meaning, and in consequence, they complain, the language loses expressive power. Purists in other languages have similar complaints. French critics, for example, turn up their noses at the modern use of excessive intensifiers such as *extra-*, *super-*, *hyper-*, instead of the simpler and more sedate *très*, and claim that the overkill leads to redundancy that debases the language.

In one sense, the purists have a point, since their factual description of the process is spot-on: the strength of meaning of a particular word depends on its distinctiveness, so the more often we hear a word, and in less discriminating contexts, the less powerful the impression it makes. When certain intensifiers are used more and more often, it is only natural that an inflationary process will ensue, resulting in attrition of meaning.

Where the custodians of good usage err, however, is in assuming that this process is something new and menacing, caused by the corrupting influence of the headline-hungry mass media, or the fashionable frivolity of the young. For the erosion of meaning is as old as the hills and as common as the dales. The French purists of today need only examine the history of their own language to see that there is nothing new under the sun, as the current fate of *extra*, *super* and *hyper* mirrors exactly what happened to similar intensifiers in previous centuries, such as the negative marker *pas*. Today, *pas* may belong to the most dignified and elegantly understated style that no purist would ever dream of criticizing, but this wasn't always so. A thousand years ago, the original negation marker in French was just *ne*. This mere shrug of syllable, however, was not deemed emphatic enough to convey the full extent of Gallic unenthusiasm, so various novel and imaginative intensifiers began to be added, to make sure that a 'no' was really taken for a 'no'. *Pas*, which meant 'step', was just one of them, and was used in expressions like 'I'm not going a step'. But there were many others to play with, such as *point* 'dot', *gote* 'drop', *amende* 'almond', *areste* 'fish-bone', *eschalope* 'pea-pod' or *mie* 'crumb':

altrement	*ne*	*m'amerat*	*il*	***mie***
otherwise	not	me will love	he	crumb

'otherwise he won't love me a crumb' (that is, 'he won't love me at all')

(*La Chanson de Roland, c.* AD 1090)

One can imagine how purists in the twelfth century would have frowned upon phrases like 'he won't love me a crumb' or 'I don't care one pea-pod' as unnecessarily flamboyant and debasing exaggerations. But even if they did, their censure had little effect, and these gaudy intensifiers became more common. By the sixteenth century, *pas* and *point* had displaced most of the other variants, and had become so frequent that they lost much of their original force. In the end, they came to be seen as a necessary part of saying a simple 'no'. By the time of modern French, only one of them, *pas*, remained in regular use, and it has no fishbone of emphatic force left in it. It simply means 'no'.

If you are tempted to think that this tale only reflects Gallic hyperbole, you may be surprised to know that the English negative marker 'not' is the result of exactly the same process. The original negation marker in English was *ne*, as in French. The modern word 'not' started out as a full-bodied *ne-a-wiht* 'not-ever-thing', or in other words 'nothing-whatsoever'. This phrase was added to the simple 'no', in order to create an emphatic 'no way', 'not a jot' type of 'no'. By the tenth century, *ne-a-wiht* had already contracted to just *nawiht*, but it still retained its former meaning, so that a phrase like *ic ne seo nawiht* still meant 'I not see nothing whatsoever'.

Later on, however, as this emphatic type of 'no' started being used more and more often, attrition set in. In form, *nawiht* was reduced to *nawt*, and alongside this erosion of sounds, there was also an inflationary weakening of meaning. By the thirteenth century, a manual for female recluses called the *Ancrene Wisse* ('Guide for Anchoresses') already uses the formerly emphatic combination *ne . . . nawt* in nearly half of all 'no' statements, thus showing that *ne . . . nawt* was no longer as emphatic as it had once been. And later on, the *ne . . . nawt* combination became even more common, so that *I ne see nawt* lost all pretence of emphasis, and came to mean just 'I don't see'. Together with this attrition in meaning, the form *nawt* (sometimes also spelt *nowt* or *nought*) was eroded further to *not*, and to cap it all, the original negation marker *ne* started being dropped from the pair, to leave only *I see not*. 'Not' is thus a prime example of both material and social decline. It started as a paunchy *ne-a-wiht* 'nothing whatsoever', a word rich in length and weighty in meaning, but its form was reduced to *not* (or even just *n't*), and its meaning eroded to the plainest of no's.

Today, a similar change seems to be in the making with the phrase 'at all', albeit in questions rather than in negative statements. When one goes to a shop or a supermarket in Britain these days, one is often asked something like 'would you like a bag, at all?' or even just 'a bag, at all?' The phrase has become so common, in fact, that many people just don't notice it. But why 'at all'? Surely, whether one wants a bag or not is one of the least momentous decisions one has to make in life, so why not simply say 'would you like a bag?' The answer must be that we are witnessing a change in the making, where what started out as an emphatic intensifier, meaning something like 'would you like anything whatsoever?', is now going down the path of attrition, losing that emphasis, and becoming just a kind of extended question marker. Presumably, what lies behind 'would you like a bag at all' is a polite intensifier of the kind: 'Do you have even the slightest desire to receive a bag from me? . . . and if so, of course I shall be more than delighted to give you one.' But with repeated use, 'at all' is losing its distinctiveness and becoming conventionalized as a marker of a polite question. And it's possible that if this trend continues, 'at all' will turn into a general question marker (rather like the French *est-ce que*, only stuck on to the end of a question rather than the beginning), and that in tandem, the phrase will also be phonetically reduced, perhaps initially to *tall*. So maybe in a century or two, dialogues like this one won't be tall unusual:

– Would you like a bag tall?
– Yes, please. Actually, could you give me two tall?
– Of course, Madam, plastic or paper tall?
– Paper will do, unless you have those strong ones with handles tall?

All in all, then, the changes in meaning do not do much to lift the crepuscular gloom that hangs over sounds and structures. True, it may be reassuring that even changes in meaning are not always entirely erratic, and seem to follow repeated tendencies and well-trodden paths. But in what direction? – attrition and decay. The changes in meaning thus add up to a thoroughly bleak picture of what the transformations in language are all about: disintegration of sounds, structures and meanings.

For many years, the seemingly terminal decline of language was not only a source of chagrin for linguists, it also posed a serious threat to the whole enterprise of understanding the history of language. This threat was what I called the problem of irregular flowers, and it epitomizes the dilemma of the nineteenth century. On the one hand, that epoch witnessed extraordinary triumphs which revolutionized the understanding of language's history and thus of language itself. But on the other hand, the picture that emerged of the nature of the changes raised deep misgivings, since the processes that were being discovered all seemed to lead to a depressing dead-end. For if the forces of change are always hell-bent on destruction, but never on creation, then how could they ever have produced all those magnificent structures in the first place?

The challenge posed by this problem preoccupied some of the great minds of the nineteenth century, and produced various and sometimes rather desperate responses. Our main goal in the rest of this chapter will be to discover how linguists tried to find their way out of this predicament, and assess how successful they were in their attempts. But it would be unfair to pass judgement on these scholars without first devoting a few pages to the magnitude of their achievements. To do justice to their endeavours, it is necessary first to form an idea of the intellectual climate of the age, and to consider the revolution in the study of language that began in that remarkable century.

THE NEPTUNE OF LINGUISTICS

Before the nineteenth century, musing about the history of languages and the relationships between them was the pastime of dilettanti, who often had rather rusty axes to grind. In 1690, for instance, a certain Père Louis Thomassin wrote in all seriousness that French and Hebrew were so close to each other that 'one may truthfully say that, basically, they are no other than one and the same language'. Even as late as 1765, well into the enlightened eighteenth century, the article on 'language' in Diderot's respected *Encyclopédie* affirmed that French was closely related to Hebrew. The linguists of the time were thus not much more advanced than the Madame from Versailles, who was overheard by Voltaire as saying: 'What a dreadful pity that the bother at the Tower of Babel should have got language all mixed up; but for that, everyone would always have spoken French.'

But within a century the scene had changed beyond recognition, and linguistics was catapulted into a scientific discipline that could boast astounding achievements. The revolution was ignited at the end of the eighteenth century, by the discovery of a genuine, but surprising, linguistic relationship. Sanskrit, the ancient language of India, turned out to be closely related to the classical European languages Latin and Greek. The British orientalist Sir William Jones reported this discovery to the Asiatic Society of Calcutta in February 1786, in words that were to become legendary in the history of linguistics:

> The Sanscrit language, whatever be its antiquity, is of a wonderful structure; more perfect than the Greek, more copious than the Latin, and more exquisitely refined than either, yet bearing to both of them a stronger affinity, both in the roots of verbs, and in the forms of grammar, than could possibly have been produced by accident; so strong, indeed, that no philologer could examine them all three, without believing them to have sprung from some common source, which, perhaps, no longer exists.

Sir William Jones (1746–1794)

This revelation kicked off a century of advances. Step by step, linguists started piecing together a detailed picture of the kinship relations between languages, and discovered that most European languages (except a handful like Basque, Hungarian, Finnish and Estonian) were related to one another, and even to some languages of India and Persia, through one common prehistoric ancestor (see the 'family tree' on page 57). For the first time, linguists went beyond impressionistic comparisons of words that sounded more or less alike, to establishing *systematic* correspondences between cognate words in the different languages. These regular correspondences revealed not only the precise family relations between languages, but also something far more important, namely that language change is not always erratic and whimsical, but often follows general rules, and is thus amenable to scientific study. The regularity of the changes that were being uncovered even allowed linguists to reconstruct the prehistoric ancestor of the Indo-European languages (which they called Proto-Indo-European) and to get an idea of what this language must have sounded like, even though it was spoken at least 6,000 years ago.

Year by year, more pieces of the puzzle were falling into place, apparent exceptions to the rules were being eliminated, and the contours of the prehistoric ancestor language were being sketched more accurately. It was as if, within less than a century, linguistics had made the leap from idle star-gazing to the sophisticated science of astronomy, with its detailed telescopic observations of distant planets and an understanding of the forces that determine their movements. So sophisticated had linguists become, in fact, that less than a century after William Jones's seminal lecture another breakthrough was made which can justly be considered the linguistic equivalent to the celebrated discovery of the planet Neptune in our solar system.

Many people know that the existence and location of Neptune were hypothesized by the mathematician John Couch Adams in 1843, on the basis of peculiarities in the movement of another planet, Uranus. Following his predictions of where this planet should be found, astronomers eventually managed to spot the elusive Neptune in the sky. Fewer people know of an equally extraordinary coup in the study of language, made three decades later by a Swiss whizz-kid called Ferdinand de Saussure, probably the cleverest of linguists before or since.

By the 1870s, linguists already had a number of remarkable discoveries under their belts, and had gained a deep understanding of how the consonants in different Indo-European languages corresponded to one another. Grimm's law was a notable example, as it explained how the Germanic languages differed systematically from the other branches of Indo-European. But there were many other advances, which allowed linguists to reconstruct a picture of what the consonant system of the ancestor language must have looked like. The *vowel* system of Proto-Indo-European, however, remained a mystery, which persistently defied the scholars of the day. The mesh of different vowels in the daughter languages was so fiendishly tangled that no one could begin to make head or tail of it. There seemed to be no sensible system behind the distribution of vowels in the different branches of the family, and no one could come up with anything like a Grimm's law that would explain the correspondences.

All this changed, however, when in 1878 a young student from Geneva set his mind to the problem. At the implausible age of twenty-one, Ferdinand de Saussure proposed a revolutionary theory which in one stroke transformed the impenetrable complexity of the distribution

Ferdinand de Saussure (1857–1913)

of vowels in the daughter languages into a system of almost incredible simplicity. He argued that although verbs showed a perplexing variety of vowels in the attested languages, all verbs in the ancestor language had just one core vowel: *e*. According to his hypothesis, verbal roots in Proto-Indo-European looked like **sek* 'cut', **bher* 'bear', **bhewg* 'flee', **deyk* 'show'. (In the following discussion, I will not continue to put asterisks before hypothesized Proto-Indo-European roots, as it should be clear that they are reconstructed and not attested.) In some verbs, this core vowel *e* hung on in the daughter languages, so for instance *bher* ends up in English as 'bear', and *sek* turns up in Latin as *sec* (from which English gets *dissect*, *secateurs*, *sector*).

So far so good. But there were also less well-behaved verbs, such as Saussure's conjectured *bhewg*, which didn't show the expected *e* in the attested languages, and turned up instead with a *u*. In Latin, which consistently changed Proto-Indo-European *bh* to *f*, the root appears as *fug* (hence English *fugitive*). How did Saussure account for these more troublesome cases? He claimed that the change in vowels could be blamed on a few 'rogue sounds', such as *w* and *y*, which originally appeared immediately after the core vowel *e* in the Proto-Indo-European root. His hypothesized root *bhewg* turns up in the daughter languages with a *u* instead of an *e*, because the sequence *ew* contracted to just *u*, or in other words, because the rogue sound *w* 'coloured' the *e* into *u*.

There was, however, one last group of verbs which posed much more serious problems, as they turned up with an awkward *a* in the attested languages. One example that Saussure mentioned was the root *pā* or *pās* 'protect', which is found in Sanskrit *pātar* 'protector' or Latin *pāstor* 'shepherd'. Roots like *pās* did not show the expected core vowel *e* in *any* of their attested forms, but on the other hand, they also did not show any evidence of a 'rogue sound' like *w*, which could be held responsible for colouring the vowel. How were they to be explained away? Saussure conjured up a daring hypothesis. Once upon a time, he argued, verbs like *pās* did indeed have a rogue sound after the core vowel *e*, and this sound was responsible for 'colouring' the vowel from *e* to *a*. But at a later stage, and after it had wreaked all this havoc, the rogue sound disappeared from the scene. If one were to use the symbol X to represent this elusive rogue sound, then Saussure's claim was that *pās* originated as a regular root *pe*X*s*, but that some time in prehistory X coloured the vowel *e* into an *a*, so *pe*X*s* became *pa*X*s*. Much later on (but still well before the earliest records), the rogue X was itself worn away because of some other effort-saving changes, and the sequence *a*X contracted into *ā*, so *pa*X*s* turned to *pās*. Schematically, then, the whole development can be represented as *pe*X*s* → *pa*X*s* → *pās*.

Needless to say, this overview of Saussure's theory is somewhat simplified. Saussure himself needed no fewer than three hundred densely argued pages for the detailed exposition of the system. Nevertheless, the essential idea behind his hypothesis could not have been simpler, as in one fell swoop it reduced the extreme complexity of the whole vowel system into just one core vowel in all roots. The brilliance of Saussure's theory was immediately and almost universally applauded. But for a long time, his ideas were considered by many as not much more than an eccentric game of abstract symbols. After all, Saussure never tried to guess what the mysterious rogue X could have sounded like, as it was enough for him simply to postulate that *something* must have been there. But one contemporary of Saussure's, the Danish linguist Hermann Möller, was not content with leaving it at just that, and hypothesized what the rogue X must originally have sounded like. He claimed that the sound was a 'guttural' (or 'laryngeal') consonant, one of the deep-throated *h*-like sounds that can still be heard today in the Semitic language Arabic, for instance in the word *Baḥrain*. Still, even this more specific suggestion didn't bring the 'laryngeal theory' into the mainstream of linguistics, since there was no evidence for any laryngeal sounds in even one of the attested daughter languages of Proto-Indo-European. At least, not at the time.

Meanwhile, however, worlds apart from the scholarly preoccupations of European linguists, a little village in central Turkey called Boğazköy ('mountain-path village') was attracting increasing interest from travellers and adventurers. The reason for the excitement was the ruins of an enormous ancient city lying high above the village, set in spectacular mountain scenery. After various travellers had returned with sketches of rock-engravings and other tantalizing finds, a French archaeologist started digging there in 1893 and soon found a few clay tablets, written in the cuneiform script.

The cuneiform ('wedge-form') script is a writing system that was invented 5,000 years ago by the Sumerians, and appropriated by the Akkadians (otherwise known as Babylonians and Assyrians), whose language will take centre stage in Chapter 6. By the second millennium BC, cuneiform writing had come to be widely used over the whole Ancient Near East. Since the cuneiform script had been largely deciphered by the end of the nineteenth century, linguists were able to read the signs on the tablets from Boğazköy without too much difficulty. The only hitch was that the texts made no sense whatsoever. The language in which they were written was neither Akkadian, nor in fact anything else they could recognize, and so more than a decade passed without any real progress in deciphering them.

But then, in 1906, a German archaeological expedition unearthed thousands more cuneiform tablets from the ruins, and among these there were a few tablets in a familiar language. These few tablets were obviously relics of extensive diplomatic correspondence (including letters to the Egyptian Pharaohs) which were written in Akkadian, the *lingua franca* of the age. The information gleaned from these diplomatic texts was sufficient to reveal that the ruined city was called Hattusa, the seat of the Hittite kings, and the capital of a mighty ancient empire. All the same, the language of these Hittite emperors did not seem to

Aerial view of Hattusa today

An artist's impression of Hattusa in its heyday

resemble anything familiar, so the meaning of the texts, as well as the family affiliation of the language, remained a mystery.

Nearly another decade followed without any breakthrough, until the Czech linguist Bedrich Hrozný laid his hands on the tablets and set about the task of cracking their enigmatic language. As Hrozný was sifting through the texts, he began to entertain a suspicion that Hittite might actually be related to the Indo-European languages. At first the idea seemed to stretch all credibility, since had Hittite been related to Indo-European, then surely it would have been decoded much earlier. Nonetheless, Hrozný was coming across things that seemed unlikely to be dismissed as sheer coincidence. One of the first sentences he managed to make sense of was this:

. . . NINDA-*an ettsa-tteni* *watar-ma eku-tteni*

A hand-copy of a Hittite cuneiform tablet (with instructions to Palace officials) containing the phrase deciphered by Hrozny (underlined)

Hrozný knew that the Hittites must have borrowed the cuneiform script from the Akkadians, who often used one sign to stand for a whole word. Since the script had already been deciphered, Hrozný recognized NINDA as the word-sign for 'bread' (and assumed that -*an* must have been some ending). Now in a sentence with 'bread' there is a particular verb one would expect to encounter, and as it happened, the word *ettsa-tteni*, which appeared just after NINDA, looked suspiciously like the prime candidate in various Indo-

European languages: Old High German *ettsan*, Latin *edere*, Old English *etan*, Modern English *eat*. Was it really possible that *ettsa* was the Hittite verb for 'eat', with an ending *-tteni*? Of course, the resemblance might just be a coincidence, but then again, what about the next word, *watar* (assuming that *-ma* was just another ending)? If the first two words had something to do with eating bread, then it doesn't require a great leap of the imagination to guess what *watar* might mean. Hrozný then considered the final word *eku-tteni*, and concluded that if *ettsa-tteni* was the verb 'eat' with an ending *-tteni*, then *eku-tteni* had to be another verb with the same ending. And since *eku-tteni* comes just after *watar*, then it wasn't difficult to put two and two together and work out what the verb *eku* might be. Hrozný thus decided that the whole sentence must have been about eating bread and drinking water. From verbal endings in other Indo-European languages (such as Sanskrit *-thana*), he deduced that the ending *-tteni* was the second person plural ('ye'), and so he came to the conclusion that the meaning of the sentence must be 'you will eat bread, you will drink water'. As Hrozný went on to decipher more such passages, his intuition about the Indo-European nature of Hittite was becoming more than just a hopeful suspicion, and so in December 1915 he finally announced his discovery to the world. The language of the texts from Hattusa, which had defied scholars' wits for more than two decades, was thoroughly Indo-European, and the main reason why it had taken so long to work this out was that Hittite was nearly a thousand years older than the earliest known texts in the sister languages such as Greek and Latin.

In the following years, as more of the texts were being deciphered, Hrozný's analysis was confirmed beyond all possible doubt. But this was only the beginning, for in 1927 a young Polish linguist, Jerzy Kuryłowicz, revealed to the world that Hittite provided the sort of evidence about the vowel system of Indo-European that no one had even dared dream about. It was an 'almost unbelievable accident', he wrote, but Hittite appeared to have retained one of the rogue sounds which Saussure had hypothesized. Hittite was so much older than the other attested Indo-European languages (some of its texts dated from the seventeenth century BC) that it still contained a certain consonant, transcribed as *ḫ*, which – lo and behold – appeared in the very places where Saussure had expected one of the rogue sounds to turn up. Take the root 'protect', for instance, which appeared as *pās* in the other languages, but which according to Saussure must earlier have been *pa*X*s* (and ultimately have started out as a regular *pe*X*s*). In the Hittite texts, this root showed up with an additional consonant precisely where Saussure expected an X – it was written *paḫs*. What Saussure had deduced purely on the basis of formal correspondences between the other Indo-European languages was dug up more than thirty years later from the Anatolian earth, scratched on clay.

Unfortunately, Saussure never lived to see his hypothesis confirmed. He died in 1913 at the age of fifty-six, before Hittite had been deciphered. But what a triumph, to round off a remarkable century of discovery. The laryngeals turned out to be the Neptune of linguistics. Their discovery, decades after their existence had been hypothesized, was the best retrospective proof for the achievements that linguists had made since William Jones's seminal lecture on Sanskrit. After centuries of groping in the dark, linguists had at last found the way to a scientific examination of language. Language was finally yielding its secrets, and at a staggering rate.

'HISTORY, THAT ENEMY OF LANGUAGE'

And yet all the triumphs only seemed to accentuate the same basic dilemma. As systematic as the changes may have been, what linguists were uncovering turned out to be a picture of systematic *destruction*. Mighty structures had collapsed one after another, perfectly regular systems in the ancestor language had given rise to latter-day chaos in the daughter languages, regularities had made way for scores of irregularities. Was the brand-new science of linguistics condemned to be a sort of prolonged post-mortem? The linguist who expressed the problem most poignantly was undoubtedly August Schleicher, whose theories about 'language-building' and 'history-making' were mentioned in the introduction. There is every reason to expect, Schleicher wrote in 1850, that languages should progress and develop more and more perfect structures during their history, but alas . . .

> at first sight we observe precisely the opposite. The further back we can follow a language, the more perfect we find it. Latin, for example, is richer in forms than the living Romance languages. The living languages of India that stem from Sanskrit have sunk even deeper from the high level of linguistic perfection of their ancestor. In historical times, as we know from experience, languages as such go backwards.

Not only was this picture of decay depressing for Schleicher, it also posed a serious threat to the enterprise of understanding the workings of language. The threat is the dilemma of 'irregular flowers': if the processes of change only destroy, then how could the ancient languages have developed their structures in the first place? And if the processes of change in prehistory were of a very different and more constructive nature, then what could possibly have caused such a shameful reversal of direction? Schleicher's own solution to these questions combined the ideas of Grimm and the linguist Wilhelm von Humboldt with Hegelian philosophy into a grand scheme that captivated the imagination of his contemporaries. 'Languages,' he declared, 'are natural organisms which emerged independently of man's will, grew and developed according to certain rules, and in turn become old and die; they also possess that series of symptoms which one is accustomed to understand as "life".'

So, like any other living organisms, languages have an early period of growth, followed by a period of decay. And the turning-point between these two periods lies exactly at the 'dawn of history'. As Schleicher explains, 'precisely the fact that we find language already fully constructed by the first dawn of history provides the proof that language-building actually takes place before history. History and language-building are two opposing activities of the human spirit.' In prehistoric times, according to Schleicher, a nation was busy constructing its language, and 'only when a nation has perfected its language, may it make its entrance into history'. But upon entering the stage of history a radical change of direction has to take place, since from now on the energy of a people is invested in history-making instead. So once history, 'that enemy of language', gets under way, language begins to fall apart and decay.

It is hard not to be impressed by the nerve, ingenuity and above all elegance of Schleicher's theory. Not only does he put his finger on the problem, but he also offers an answer that manages to solve at one stroke all the difficulties he was facing. In his theory, the observable period coincides precisely with the stage of decay in language, whereas the phase of building coincides precisely with the period that is impossible to observe (as it lies before the 'dawn of history', that is, before records begin). Schleicher had thus come up with a perfect explanation for why the only thing linguists ever managed to observe was decay.

Of course, the ingenuity doesn't make Schleicher's theory any less absurd. His mélange of romantic philosophy may be very much a product of its time, but to us it seems rather off the wall. In fact, even by the end of the nineteenth century, the opposition to Schleicher's ideas became more vocal, when linguists started pointing out that language is *not* a living organism, but a system of conventions used by society in order to communicate. As one frustrated scholar put it later on, 'languages are historical creations, not vegetables'. And since people must have communicated with one another in roughly the same way before and after the 'dawn of history', there is no reason why the forces that changed language in prehistoric times should be so different from those operating throughout history, and even today.

But if Schleicher got it all wrong, and the forces of change stayed the same before and after history began, then how can one explain away the Golden Age of perfection? Why is it that only destruction and disintegration could be observed during the historical period? Where are the forces of creation lurking?

The first of these two problems, the alleged perfection of prehistoric languages, was much easier to tackle, since on closer inspection the Golden Age of perfection turned out to be an optical illusion caused by one small but critical oversight. Recall that the idea of a past age of perfection stemmed from simple but apparently compelling logic: the attested languages are riddled with irregularities (such as *flos-floris*), but when such irregularities are pursued into the past, they can usually be traced or at least reconstructed to a more regular pattern from which they sprang (*flos-flosis*). The clear implication, then, is that the further back in time one goes, the more regular languages should become. Unassailable logic, surely? Well, there is one snag in this line of reasoning, and to identify it, let's consider another simple example, this time from English. Take a look at the final consonant in the following two forms of the verb 'choose': I *chose*-they *chose*. But what is there to note here? Both forms have exactly the same consonant, and so there is no irregularity to be accounted for.

And that's precisely the point. One would never feel the need to justify the sound here, or look for any explanations for it, let alone dream up an irregularity behind this well-behaved pair. But as it happens, there are records from earlier stages of English which reveal that in the past 'choose' was not quite the pillar of uprightness it is today. In fact, 'choose' has quite a doubtful history, since the corresponding two forms in Old English were *ceas* ('I chose') but *curon* ('they chose'). It turns out that English 'choose' was rather riotous in its youth, and only acquired a mantle of respectability in later stages of English, when the irregularity in *ceas-curon* was ironed out. But we only know about this juvenile delinquency because we happen to have records from the right period. If the written history of English happened to start at 1200, say, rather than around 800, there would never be any reason to suspect that 'choose' had such a chequered history.

The asymmetry between English 'choose' and Latin *flos* illustrates the problems in our methods of reconstruction. The history of 'choose' is an exact reversal of the Latin flower-pair *flos-floris*, which started out respectably regular as *flos-flosis*, and acquired its notoriety only in later life. But whereas it wouldn't be difficult even without historical records to reconstruct from the irregular pattern *flos-floris* a well-behaved ancestor *flos-flosis*, going in the other direction is an entirely different matter. The pair *chose-chose* would never give us cause to reconstruct an irregular ancestor *ceas-curon* if we didn't happen to possess past records.

All this goes to show that even if our methods of reconstruction are very powerful, they are by necessity seriously skewed, because they often allow us to reconstruct past order from present chaos, but rarely the reverse. Past irregularities are like footprints on a sand dune. Once a breeze has blown them over, there is often no way of telling that they had ever been there. So while it is true that the particular irregularities of present-day languages may all have been less irregular in the distant past, there is also a different side to this story, and one that our reconstructions simply cannot capture. Prehistoric languages must have had scores of irregularities, but these must have vanished without trace. So the image of a flawless language spoken some time in prehistory turns out to have been mainly a mirage. In reality, there never was a Golden Age of perfection.

Dispelling the illusion of a regular past may have settled a part of the dilemma of the nineteenth century. But this was by far the easier part, and it still leaves the more serious conundrum, the apparent absence of linguistic creation during history. Why is it that structures only seemed to crumble in the observable period? If Schleicher was on the wrong track, then alongside the ubiquitous forces of destruction there must also be forces that create new structures in language, and these must have been active throughout history, and should be creating new structures even today. But if so, then where are they, and why are they so difficult to spot?

As we shall see in the following chapters, the reason why the forces of creation eluded linguists for so long is that they lie so close to the forces of destruction, and so destruction was blocking the view. Far from being irreconcilable foes, it will soon transpire that creation and destruction in language are very much akin. The following chapter will argue that the link between these apparent opposites hinges on one main element, which at first glance may seem rather surprising. The element in question is metaphor.

4

A Reef of Dead Metaphors

In Antonio Skármeta's *Burning Patience* (the novel on which the film *Il Postino* was based), the Chilean poet Pablo Neruda tries to explain to the young postman Mario what poetry is all about:

> 'Metaphors, I said!'
> 'What's that?'
> The poet placed his hand on the boy's shoulder.
> 'To be more or less imprecise, we could say that it is a way of describing something by comparing it to something else.'
> 'Give me an example.'
> Neruda looked at his watch and sighed.
> 'Well, when you say the sky is weeping, what do you mean?'
> 'That's easy – that it's raining.'
> 'So, you see, that's a metaphor.'

Mario desperately wants to become a poet himself, but he fails to come up with any metaphors of his own. So Neruda tries to give him a helping hand:

> 'You are now going to walk along the beach to the bay and as you observe the movement of the sea, you are going to invent metaphors.'
> 'Give me an example!'
> 'Listen to this poem: 'Here on the Island, the sea, so much sea. It spills over from time to time. It says yes, then no, then no. It says yes, in blue, in foam, in a gallop. It says no, then no. It cannot be still. My name is sea, it repeats, striking a stone but not convincing it. Then with the seven green tongues, of seven green tigers, over seven green seas, it

caresses it, kisses it, wets it, and pounds on its chest, repeating its own name.''

He paused with an air of satisfaction.

'What do you think?'

'It's weird.'

'Weird? You certainly are a severe critic.'

'No, Sir. The poem wasn't weird. What was weird was the way I felt when you recited it . . . How can I explain it to you? When you recited that poem, the words went from over there to over here.'

'Like the sea, then!'

'Yes, they moved just like the sea.'

'That's the rhythm.'

'And I felt weird because with all the movement, I got dizzy.'

'You got dizzy?'

'Of course, I was like a boat tossing upon your words.'

The poet's eyelids rose slowly.

'Like a boat tossing upon my words.'

'Uh-huh.'

'You know what you just did, Mario?'

'No, what?'

'You invented a metaphor.'

Skármeta here portrays the conventional image of metaphor as the 'language of poetry', the summit of the poetic imagination. On a flight of inspiration, the poet carries a concept away from its natural environment into an entirely different realm. Mario's chance metaphor, which links the unrelated worlds of words and the sea, may not be the most striking of poetic images, but in the hands of more inspired poets the impact of uprooting a concept from its natural environment can be arrestingly evocative – just think of Yeats's closing lines from his poem 'He Wishes for the Cloths of Heaven': 'I have spread my dreams under your feet; Tread softly because you tread on my dreams.'

As the quintessence of poetic genius, metaphor may at first seem entirely irrelevant to the history of ordinary day-to-day language. For what could this elixir of artistic inspiration possibly have to do with the evolution of mundane communication? But in fact there is also an entirely different side to metaphor, far-flung from the poetic imagination.

Removal van in Athens

Removal vans in Athens, like the one in the picture above, don't bear the word ΜΕΤΑΦΟΡΕΣ (METAFORES) on their back end because they are advertising courses in creative writing. The reason is much more prosaic, and is simply that *meta-phora* is Greek for 'carry across' (*meta* = 'across', *phor* = 'carry'). Or to use the Latin equivalent, *meta-phor* just means *trans-fer*.

And one certainly does not have to be an aspiring poet in order to transfer concepts from one linguistic domain to another. Even in the most commonplace discourse, it is hardly possible to venture a few steps without treading on dozens of metaphors. For metaphors are everywhere, not only in language, but also in our mind. Far from being a rare spark of poetic genius, the marvellous gift of a precious few, metaphor is an indispensable element in the thought-processes of every one of us. As will soon become apparent, we use metaphors not because of any literary leanings or artistic ambitions, but quite simply because metaphor is the chief mechanism through which we can describe and even grasp abstraction.

This chapter will expose the role of metaphor in the making of linguistic structures, by tracing a stream of metaphors that runs right through language and flows from the concrete to the abstract. In this constant surge, the simplest and sturdiest of words are swept along, one after another, and carried towards abstract meanings. As these words drift downstream, they are bleached of their original vitality and turn into pale lifeless terms for abstract concepts – the substance from which the structure of language is formed. And when at last the river sinks into the sea, these spent metaphors are deposited, layer after layer, and so the structure of language grows, as a reef of dead metaphors.

TREADING ON METAPHORS

If these high-flown claims about the ubiquity of metaphor sound rather far-fetched, then consider the following paragraph:

> At the cabinet meeting, ground-breaking plans were put forward by the minister for tough new legislation to curb the power of the unions. It was clear that the unions would never go along with these suggestions, and the conflict erupted as soon as news of the plan was leaked to the press. At the trade-union conference, the minister encountered a frosty reception. He tried to get across the idea that the excessive power of the unions was holding back economic growth. He said that while productivity had sunk in recent years, salaries were rising. But his comments were drowned by angry heckling. Any semblance of politeness collapsed when the General Secretary confronted the minister head on, saying that he was not on top of the facts, and that his figures were riddled with inaccuracies. The unions were not asking for any rise in salaries, he argued, they only wanted to avoid further cuts in real terms, by ensuring that salaries remain in line with inflation.

This report can be accused of many things, but certainly not of being poetically inspired. If anything, its flat journalese feels only marginally less boring than a shopping list or a telephone directory. And yet this paragraph is jam-packed with metaphors. The first sentence alone contains no fewer than four different ones:

> At the cabinet meeting, *ground-breaking* plans were *put forward* by the minister for *tough* new legislation to *curb* the power of the unions.

Literally, 'ground-breaking' is something you do with a shovel, not with a plan. And 'tough' is really an attribute of materials like fabrics, metals or meat. A steak, for instance, can be tough when it is not easily chewed, but by no stretch of the imagination was the legislation really meant to be masticated. 'Tough' here has been transported out of its original environment in the physical world of materials, and carried across to the abstract domain of ideas. And in just the same way, the plans for new legislation were never actually 'put forward' by the minister, as this is yet another metaphor, where the physical act of pushing something is presented as an image for 'suggesting'. *Curbing* the power of the unions is also metaphorical, since a curb is literally the piece of metal put in horses' mouths to control their movement, but not even this minister was planning to rein in union members with bridles.

The rest of the passage is also laden with metaphors, which are italicized in the paragraph below. As you run through it once again, bear in mind that what really *erupts* is a volcano, not conflicts; what really *leaks* is water, not information; trees *grow*, not the economy; ships *sink*, not productivity; people *drown*, not comments; buildings *collapse*, not semblances of politeness. Most importantly, note that all the metaphors here flow in one direction, from the concrete to the abstract. In every one of them, concrete terms have been transferred from their original habitat to more abstract domains.

> At the cabinet meeting, *ground-breaking* plans were *put forward* by the minister for *tough* new legislation to *curb* the power of the unions. It was *clear* that the unions would never *go along* with these suggestions, and the conflict *erupted* as soon as news of the plan was *leaked* to the press. At the trade-union conference, the minister encountered a *frosty* reception. He tried to *get across* the idea that the excessive power of the unions was *holding back* economic *growth*. He said that while productivity had *sunk* in recent years, salaries were *rising*. But his comments were *drowned* by angry heckling. Any semblance of politeness *collapsed* when the General Secretary *confronted* the minister *head on*, saying that the minister was not *on top of* the facts, and that his figures were *riddled* with inaccuracies. The

unions were not even asking for any *rise* in salaries, he argued, they only wanted to avoid further *cuts* in real terms, by ensuring that salaries remain *in line* with inflation.

In India there is a sect of Jainist monks called the Shvetambara, who always carry a broom and sweep the ground before them as they walk, lest they accidentally tread on some insects and squash them. If one were to show the same consideration towards metaphors in language, one would require much more than a broom. One would need to levitate, or take a vow of eternal silence, for it transpires that even the most tedious prose is teeming with metaphors.

Still, there is plainly a huge difference between the humdrum metaphors in this passage and the evocative images of Yeats or Neruda. Poetic metaphors can be stunning, but in this news report one barely even notices the metaphors, unless they are specifically pointed out. So why don't we react to 'tough legislation' in the same way as to 'treading on dreams'? The answer, in a word, is familiarity. The reason why we don't trip up on any of the metaphors in this passage is that they have all been recycled many times before. 'Tough' may once have been a glamorous newcomer in the domain of ideas, but it is now so often used in this abstract sphere that it has been entirely assimilated, so that a conscious effort is required to remember that 'tough' is not a native of the region, but an immigrant from the world of materials. With 'curb', the process of naturalization is even more advanced, since these days one is much more likely to hear about someone curbing the power of the unions than curbing the movement of a horse. What was once a vibrant metaphor has thus asserted itself as the usual meaning of this verb, and the literal sense is hardly remembered.

In literary studies, metaphors which have become commonplace and have lost their evocative power are dismissed as 'dead metaphors', and in the passage above all the metaphors are thoroughly and irremediably dead. They have come to be used so often in their metaphorical abstract sense that all semblance of their former vitality has been lost and they have firmly established themselves as the stock-in-trade of ordinary language.

But there is more to familiarity than individual acquaintance, for most metaphors in ordinary language are also familiar on a much deeper level. Suppose, for instance, that during an election campaign you read in a newspaper that 'critics derided the new election manifesto as nothing more than a soufflé of promises'. This phrase is clearly metaphorical, since by anyone's standards a soufflé is properly made of egg whites, not of promises. But although you may never have heard this particular metaphor before, it is still unlikely to strike you as a great poetic coup, or as something entirely out of the ordinary. The reason must be that 'soufflé of promises' belongs to a larger context which *is* familiar. You will certainly have encountered many similar images that use food terms to describe abstract ideas, thoughts, and emotions. People speak of troubles *brewing*, anger *simmering*, resentment *boiling*, fanaticism *fermenting*, employees *seething* (literally: 'boiling') with discontent. People *chew* over new suggestions and *digest* new information; the masses *swallow* whatever lies the newspapers *feed* them; students *regurgitate* facts at the examination; children *gobble up* the latest Harry Potter book; fans *devour* reports of their idols' private lives. We can have *sweet* dreams, *bitter* hatreds, *sour* relations, or *half-baked* ideas; and all this can give some *food for thought*. So there is a well-established link in our mind between the two domains, which unites all the individual images into a broader conceptual metaphor: 'ideas are food'. And thus when we hear a phrase like 'soufflé of promises', the image does not sound so surprising, because it fits neatly into this familiar frame.

Needless to say, such 'conceptual metaphors', mappings of one domain on to the other, are not confined to food and ideas. They have been shown to pervade not only everyday language, but our whole perception of the world. One example that can illustrate how deeply such conceptual mappings are engrained in both language and mind is the image 'more is up, less is down'. In the news report above, there were three different images that derived from that overarching metaphor: 'economic growth', 'productivity had sunk', and 'salaries were rising'. But there is a variety of other expressions that fit into the same image: 'sterling is up against the dollar'; 'they're down to their last supplies'; 'turn up the heating'; 'this engine has very low power'; 'the population will peak, but there will be a drop in consumer spending'; 'his self-esteem plummeted'. The number of examples can rise without difficulty, and this shows that we consistently think of more complex or abstract notions (such as self-esteem or the economy) in terms of the simpler spatial directions, up and down.

At this point, one may protest that 'sterling is up against the dollar' is surely not just a figure of speech. After all, isn't it possible to see in practice when sterling goes up or down, by looking at the daily chart in the newspaper? And when the central heating needs to be 'turned up', this often does involve pushing a knob upwards. So how can all this be dismissed as a mere metaphor? But try thinking about it this way: why are graphs plotted to show that more is up and less is down? In theory, there is no particular reason why graphs shouldn't be drawn with 'down' meaning 'more', and 'up' meaning 'less', just like the two charts below:

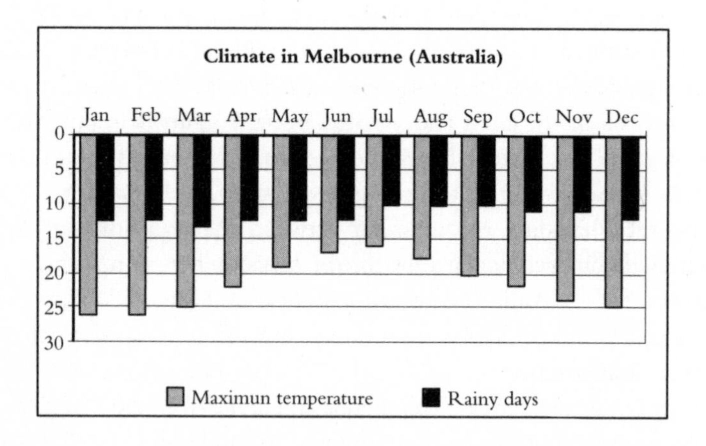

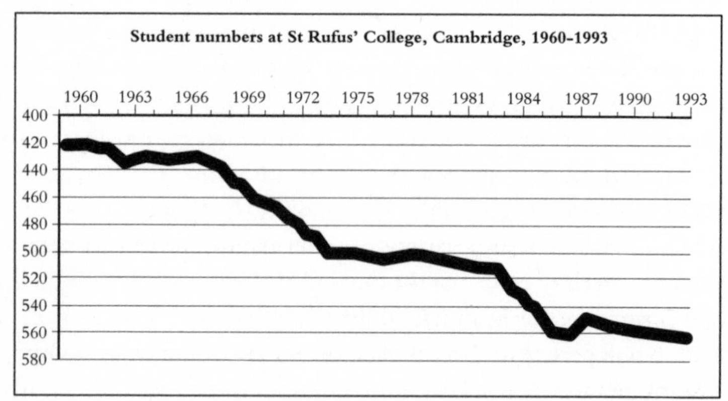

These two diagrams may look pretty odd, but there is nothing wrong with them from a logical point of view. They only appear so strange because they go against the pervasive 'more is up' convention. And in the same way, there would be nothing mechanically unnatural about a control panel where 'turning up' the heating would require pushing a knob down. So the conceptual metaphor 'more is up' has taken over much more than just language, and has become so deeply entrenched in our minds that it even influences how we plot graphs and design control panels. In these, as in countless other examples, the image has gained an independent existence, and through our cultural artefacts, it even shapes the world around us.

Of course, all this does not mean that the image 'more is up' is *wholly* arbitrary. When water is poured into a bottle, for instance, the more water there is, the higher its level. And if apples are piled up in the larder, the more apples, the higher the pile. So the image 'more is up' is clearly rooted in real life and based on experience. Nevertheless, in language, the image has gone far beyond this original basis. The Admissions Tutor may boast that 'student numbers at St Rufus are up', but nothing really becomes higher in the college when more students are admitted, just as nothing really becomes lower when the temperature is 'down'. 'Up' and 'down' here are merely metaphors, albeit thoroughly dead ones.

MONSIEUR JOURDAIN: I'm in love with a lady of great quality, and I wish that you would help me write something to her in a little note that I will let fall at her feet . . .

PHILOSOPHY MASTER: Is it verse that you wish to write her?

M.J: No, no. No verse.

PH.M: Do you want only prose?

M.J: No, I don't want either prose or verse.

PH.M: It must be one or the other.

M.J: Why?

PH.M: Because, sir, there is no other way to express oneself than with prose or verse.

M.J: There is nothing but prose or verse?

PH.M: No, sir, everything that is not prose is verse, and everything that is not verse is prose.

M.J: And when one speaks, what is that then?

PH.M: Prose.

M.J: What! When I say, 'Nicole, bring me my slippers, and give me my nightcap,' that's prose?

PH.M: Yes, Sir.

M.J: By my faith! For more than forty years I have been speaking prose without knowing anything about it.

(Molière, *Le Bourgeois Gentilhomme*, Act II)

Like Monsieur Jourdain, who all his life has been speaking prose without knowing it, we all speak and think in metaphors. In ordinary language, we trample on the relics of metaphors all the time, and hardly even pay them a moment's thought.

But in unearthing these metaphors we have only begun to scratch the surface of language, since up to now, all the metaphors have been dug up from very shallow linguistic strata. The metaphors so far may be barely noticeable to the casual onlooker, but with some conscious effort their original meaning is at least still recognizable. If one only pauses to think about these images, one is aware that it's really a steak that is tough, not legislation, or that what really rises is water, not unemployment. Scratch a bit deeper, however, and you will find hundreds of metaphors that are no longer even identifiable remains, but merely dried-up skeletons whose original literal meanings have long been lost, and are only recoverable from yellowing historical dictionaries. Take the following sentence, for instance, and try to detect the metaphors it contains:

> Sarah was thrilled to discover that the assessment board had decided to make her barmy rival redundant, after she suggested that he had made sarcastic insinuations about his employers.

Unless you happen to be an enthusiastic etymologist, you should find it difficult to spot many metaphors here. Nevertheless, almost every word in this sentence was once a thriving image. If one puts the flesh back on these dry bones, and restores them to their original vitality, the result will be something like this:

> Sarah was pierced to un-cover that the sitting-by plank had cut off to make her full-of-froth person-from-the-river overflowing, after she carried-under that he had made flesh-tearing twistings about those who fold him.

Barmy as the sentence may now seem, it simply shows the origin of the words in the previous one. The word 'thrill', for example, goes back to an Old English verb *thyrlian*, which originally meant 'pierce' (and incidentally, is related to the word *nos-thyrl*, 'nostril', or 'nose-hole'). The current sense of 'thrill' must have started out as a metaphor with some shock value. 'I'm thrilled to bits' (literally 'I'm pierced to bits') must have been a graphic equivalent of today's 'it's killing' or 'smashing'. But as the image became familiar and established, the metaphor was bleached of its vitality and died, and eventually the original sense fell by the wayside, so that today, 'thrill' is only a skeleton that betrays no trace of its metaphoric origin. The other words in the sentence above have comparable histories:

- 'Dis-cover' initially meant 'remove the cover from'. In the seventeenth century, it could still be used in this physical sense: 'if the house be discovered by tempest, the tenant must in convenient time repaire it.'
- 'Assessment' comes ultimately from Latin *assidere* 'to sit by'. (In the law courts, the *assessor* was an aid who 'sat by' the judge.)
- 'Board' originally meant 'plank', and is not as skeletal as the other metaphors here, since it can still be used in the concrete sense today.
- 'Decide' comes ultimately from Latin *de-caedere* 'cut off'.
- 'Barmy' originally meant 'full of barm' (that is, 'froth' or 'yeast').
- 'Rival' comes from Latin *rivalis*, meaning someone who shares the same river. From there, the word came to mean someone who shares (or competes for) the same mistress (that is, *rival* in love), and from there, to *rival* more generally.
- 'Redundant' also comes from Latin, where it literally meant 'overflowing' (from *unda* 'wave').
- 'Suggest' comes from Latin *sub-gerere*, 'carry under'.
- 'Sarcastic' comes from Greek 'flesh tearing' (*sárx* – flesh), and is related to the word *sarcophagus* (literally 'flesh eating').
- 'Insinuation' comes originally from Latin *sinus* 'curve'.
- 'Employ' comes ultimately from Latin *plicare* 'to fold'.

The words in the sentence above are by no means isolated examples. Browse through any historical dictionary and you will find thousands of such dry bones. Nor is there anything terribly unusual about English in this respect. If English can boast anything exceptional, it is only that so much of its abstract vocabulary was borrowed from French and Latin, so in many cases, the concrete-to-abstract transfer did not happen on home turf, but before the words were borrowed. But similar metaphors are found in languages all over the world. As one example from the list above, consider the verb 'decide', which in English derives from a Latin verb meaning 'cut off'. At first this image may seem unusual, but in fact, the physical activities of cutting or separating seem to be the source of the concept of 'deciding' in many languages, even those which did not borrow from Latin so heavily, if indeed at all. The German *ent-scheiden*, for instance, comes from *scheiden* 'separate'; Ancient Greek *diaireô* literally means 'to take one from another' or 'cleave in twain', but was also used to mean 'decide'; the Swahili phrase *-kata shauri* 'decide' literally means 'cut matter'; the Basque *erabaki* 'decide' literally means 'to make (someone) cut' (from the verb *ebaki* 'cut'), the Indonesian *memutuskan* 'decide' derives from the stem *putus* 'severed'; in Endo, a Nilo-Saharan language of Kenya, the verb *til* 'cut' is also used for 'decide'; and the same goes for ancient Akkadian *parāsum*, biblical Hebrew *gazar*, and Chinese *jué*. Similar images are found in many other languages across the world. So even though other languages may have fewer Latinisms than English, they still closet just as many skeletons in their cupboards.

Chiedi al rio perché gemente
dalla balza ov'ebbe vita
corre al mar, che a sé l'invita,
e nel mar sen va a morir.

Ask the stream why, groaning,
from the slope where it was born,
it runs into the sea that lures it
and in the sea it goes to die.

L'elisir d'amore (Librettist: Felice Romani)

At first, the ubiquity of metaphors even in the plainest of speech may seem perplexing, and their persistent one-way course even more so. Why is it that when one only scratches a bit, most abstract words turn out to have concrete origins? Why should the surge of metaphors always flow from concrete to abstract, and so rarely in the other direction? Why do we say about legislation that it is 'tough', but not about a steak that it is 'severe'?

The answer to these questions is quite straightforward. Imagine for a moment that the metaphor 'tough' was not at our disposal, and that some alternatives for describing 'tough legislation' had to be found. Except for 'severe', what options are there? We could say that the legislation was 'inflexible', 'strict', 'repressive', 'oppressive', 'firm', 'stern', 'stringent', 'unyielding', 'unbending', 'harsh', and so on. But there's the rub – none of these alternatives would help dodge a metaphor, since, just like 'tough', all these tough-talking terms originally derive from the physical world. They all set out in life in the domain of materials. Some, like 'unbending', 'firm', 'unyielding' or 'inflexible', still betray traces of their old selves – think of 'flexing your muscles', for instance. But even the other options, those that are no longer recognizable, are skeletons of what once were full-blooded metaphors from the world of materials. 'Oppressive', for instance, comes from 'press against' (*opprimere* in Latin); 'stringent' is derived from 'bind tight' (*stringere*), while 'harsh' (from Middle English *harsk*) originally meant 'hard and rough to the touch'.

The truth of the matter is that we simply have no choice but to use concrete-to-abstract metaphors. And when one stops to think about it, this is not even so surprising, since after all, if not from the physical world, where else could terms for abstract concepts come from? One thing is certain, nothing can come from nothing. The mind cannot just manufacture words for abstract concepts out of thin air – all it can do is adapt what is already available. And what's at hand are simple physical concepts: objects one can point at (like 'head' or 'tree') and physical actions (like 'cut' or 'run').

A simple experiment suffices to demonstrate that there is no way of getting round a concrete-to-abstract metaphor. Try choosing at random a few of the most abstract of abstractions you can imagine, and then tracing their ultimate origin. As long as their pedigree is known, chances are they will go back to some simple words from the physical world. The word 'abstract' itself is one such example, for what could be more abstract than that? Today 'abstract' may be the fare of philosophers, a word used to refer to concepts that are removed from physical reality. But the origins of 'abstract' are much more earthly, as 'abstract' comes from a Latin verb which simply meant 'draw away' (*abstrahere*).

Another good candidate for the 'what can be more abstract than that?' competition is the concept of 'understanding', which after all takes place entirely within the fiction of the mind; one cannot see it, hear it, or touch it. Now, suppose your language did not have a word to describe 'understanding', how would you go about expressing the concept? If you are short of inspiration, try looking at some of the metaphors that English speakers use today as synonyms: we talk of *grasping* the sense, *catching* the meaning, *getting* the point, *following* an explanation, *cottoning on to* an idea, *seeing* the difficulty. Are you *with* me? And it's not just the more colourful synonyms that go back to simple physical origins, for even the basic words for 'understanding' derive from similar sources. The verb 'understand' itself may be a brittle old skeleton by now, but its origin is still obvious: *under-stand* originally must have meant something like 'step under', perhaps rather like the image in the phrase 'get to the bottom of'. Its close synonym 'comprehend' is also a skeletal metaphor from the physical world, and originally comes from 'seize' (Latin *prehendere*).

One could pick hundreds of other examples of abstract concepts, and the result would always be the same. They can't help but go back to some terms from the physical world. Quite simply, then, metaphors flow from the concrete to the abstract because we *need* them to. The only way we have of expanding our expressive range to encompass abstract concepts is to draw on concrete terms.

Chapter 2 mentioned a triad of motives for language's inner restlessness: economy, expressiveness and analogy. In previous chapters, expressiveness has featured only in a rather narrow role of adding emphasis, for instance when bolstering a simple 'no'. But the examples above are beginning to reveal that expressiveness goes much deeper than merely shoring up refusals. Speakers feel the need to express novel and abstract ideas, or to convey already existing concepts in fresh and original ways, and there is generally only one outlet for this expressive urge: adapting existing means – concrete concepts – to new ends. The cognitive mechanism that allows us to draw links between different domains is analogy (to which we shall return later on, in Chapter 6). But while analogy is what allows us to think in metaphors in the first place, what lures the stream of metaphors down towards abstraction is nothing other than our need to extend our range of expression. This expressive urge also drives us to use the same images again and again, but through such over-use the metaphors are bleached of their original vitality and eventually fade and die.

TO HAVE AND TO HOLD

We have probed deep enough by now to realize that metaphor is much more than just a frill on the edges of language. The sheer density of metaphors even in the most listless prose may be surprising, but the real extent of metaphor's involvement in ordinary language is only just beginning to surface. All the metaphors mentioned so far, from 'redundant' to 'insinuations' and from 'stringent' to 'sarcasm', appear to be at a remove from simple quotidian language, and may thus give the impression that metaphorical thinking is confined to an elevated level of sophisticated discourse, and that plain speech would have neither the need nor the inclination for metaphor. So it may seem all the more startling that far from being rare, metaphor is as rife in the plainest day-to-day chit-chat as it is in the most highfaluting prose.

Take the verb 'have', for instance. By anyone's standards, 'have' is not some fancy optional extra, but an indispensable component of the hard-core of language. We 'have' hands and legs and eyes, we 'have' relatives and friends, we 'have' clothes and houses, we 'have' dandruff and the flu, and it's difficult to imagine having even the simplest conversation without having 'having' at the tip of one's tongue. And yet, even though 'have' is the bread-and-butter of the vernacular, it is nevertheless a fairly abstract notion, quite unlike physical activities such as 'kicking' something or 'putting' it somewhere. Think about it this way: what do you actually *do* when you 'have' something? (Not much, probably, if what you 'have' is a third-cousin-twice-removed in Oklahoma with whom you've lost all contact.) Now, suppose for a moment that there was no word around to describe 'having' something. How would you go about expressing the notion?

As it happens, this question is by no means academic, because many languages today (most, in fact) don't have a verb that corresponds to the

English 'have', and so they use other ways of expressing possession. To see some of the alternatives they come up with, consider the following examples:

Russian (Slavic branch, Indo-European family)
U menja kniga
at me book
'the book (is) at me' (= I have a book)

Turkish (Turkic, Altaic)
Ben-de bir kitap var
me-on a book is
'a book is on me' (= I have a book)

Irish (Celtic, Indo-European)
tá leabhar agam
is book at.me
'the book is at me' (= I have a book)

Russian, Turkish and Irish all opt for the strategy of using physical proximity as a metaphor for the notion of possession. They take one of the possible physical manifestations of 'having something', namely the thing being *near*, *on* or *at* you, and use this simpler physical state of affairs as an image for the more general abstract notion of possession. This image is extremely common across the languages of the world, and it often turns up also in more elaborate forms. Here are a few variations on the theme 'position is possession':

Akkadian (Semitic, Afro-Asiatic, spoken in ancient Mesopotamia)
ṣibûtum ina qāti-ja
wish in hand-my
'a wish (was) in my hand' (= I had a wish)

So (Kuliak, Nilo-Saharan, spoken in Uganda)
mek Auca eo-a kusin
aren't Auca home-in clothes
'Clothes aren't in Auca's home' (= Auca has no clothes)

Mupun (Chadic, Afro-Asiatic, spoken in Nigeria)
war *kə* *siwol*
she with money
'she (is) with money' (= she has money)

At first sight, such metaphors may seem quaint and perhaps even rather poetic. But on reflection, it should be clear that similar images are used in ordinary English. Think of phrases like 'a man with a lot of money', which really means the same as 'a man who *has* a lot of money', or the phrase 'it's in the bag', which means it's a dead cert that you *have* it.

In addition to physical proximity, there are also various other sources speakers can draw on to express the notion of 'having' something. The languages below all use another common image, that of 'target' or 'goal'. The idea here is that if something is intended *for* you, or destined *to* you, it is yours:

Quechua (Quechuan (American-Indian), as spoken in Bolivia)
waska *tiya-pu-wa-n*
rope exist-for-me-it
'a rope is for me' (= I have a rope)

Breton (Celtic, Indo-European, spoken in Brittany)
ur *velo* *c'hlas* *am* *eus*
a bike blue to.me is
'a blue bike is to me' (= I have a blue bike)

Tamil (Dravidian, spoken in India and Sri Lanka)
enakku *oro* *nalla* *naay* *irukkiratu*
to me a good dog is
'to me is a good dog' (= I have a good dog)

It seems, then, that even a language without an actual 'have' verb at its disposal need not feel unduly disadvantaged in expressing acquisitiveness, since there are plenty of other means for conveying the notion of possession. Even so, what if a language did want to acquire a proper 'have' verb – where would it go shopping for it? As it happens, there is no need to speculate about prehistoric thought-processes, since even today the origins of the verb 'have' in many languages are still transparent:

Spanish (Romance, Indo-European)
Tenemos *muchos* *libros*
'we hold many books' (= we have many books)

Dullay (Cushitic, Afro-Asiatic, spoken in Ethiopia)
lő'ó *an-sheega*
cow I-carry
'I carry a cow' (= I have a cow)

Waata (Cushitic, Afro-Asiatic, spoken in Kenya)
ani *mín* *k'awa*
I house seize
'I seize a house' (= I have a house)

Nama (Khoisan, spoken in Namibia)
kxoep ke *'autosa* *'uu hââ*
man car took
'the man took a car' (= the man has a car)

The images here are simple: what one holds or carries or seizes is used to convey what one 'has'. And in fact, English does the same thing with the verb 'get' in sentences like 'the man's *got* a car', which means the same as 'the man *has* a car'. So like Waata and Nama, English takes a verb of taking, and uses it as a metaphor for possession: 'what one has *got*, one *has*'. And if you are still unpersuaded, and are inclined to discount the expression 'he's got' as just a sloppy substitute for the more respectable 'have', then you might like to know that the origin of 'have' itself is as grasping as all the rest. 'Have' ultimately derives from a Proto-Indo-European root **kap*, which meant 'seize'. The original sense of **kap* survives in the Latin root *cap* 'seize', which found its way into English in the borrowed words 'capture' (as well as in 'captive', 'caption', 'capable', 'recipe', 'occupy', and even 'catch'). The reason why the English home-grown 'have' looks so different from its forebear **kap* is simply Grimm's law, the series of sound changes in Germanic mentioned in the previous chapter, in which *k* was weakened to *h*, and *p* to *f*, thus turning **kap* into **haf*. So while 'capture' and 'have' look rather un-identical, they are in fact a pair of separated twins, deriving from the same source, **kap* 'seize'.

It seems, then, that there are numerous highways and byways that languages can take in order to express the notion of possession. But whatever the means, whether with a transitive verb like *take*, *seize* or *hold*, or with an image of physical proximity, there is no avoiding a metaphor from the physical world. The details may vary from language to language, but the idea is always the same: take one simple physical situation that is characteristic of 'having' something, and use it as an image for the abstract notion of possession more generally. Of course, 'have' is just a single word out of the rich lexicon of everyday communication, and it could be argued that one molehill does not make a mountain. But the role of metaphor in creating 'have' is by no means unusual – it is symptomatic of countless other run-of-the-mill words, even those from the most unpretentious vocabulary and the most plodding discourse. Indeed, as the novelist Jean Paul once said, language is nothing but a 'dictionary of faded metaphors'. While in poetry, metaphors which have expired through over-use are dismissed as faded clichés, ordinary language is not so prodigal. The death of metaphors in no way detracts from their usefulness, as they simply add more means to our vocabulary.

But this is not all. In the following pages, I will argue that not even Jean Paul's radical characterization can do justice to the pivotal role of metaphor in language. It turns out that metaphor is not only a chief supplier to our store of words, it also provides the raw materials for the structure of language itself.

SPACE-TIME

The *Encyclopaedia Britannica* begins its article on the concept of 'space-time' in Einstein's theory of relativity with the following declaration:

> Space-time. In physical science, single concept that recognizes the union of space and time, posited by Albert Einstein in the theories of relativity (1905, 1915). Common intuition previously supposed no connection between space and time . . .

But is it really true that 'common intuition' did not spot the connection before Einstein? Physicists may not have identified the relation between space and time in their theories until a century ago, but everyday language proves that 'common intuition' has in fact recognized this link for many thousands of years (even if not exactly in Einstein's sense). For in language – any language – no two domains are more intimately linked than space and time. Even if we are not always aware of it, we invariably speak of time in terms of space, and this reflects the fact that we *think* of time in terms of space. Consider some of the simplest words we use to describe spatial relations: prepositions such as *in*, *at*, *by*, *from*, *to*, *behind*, *within*, *through*. The examples below should suffice to show that all these spatial terms function just as well in the domain of temporal relations:

SPACE	TIME
from London *to* Paris	*from* Monday *to* Friday
in England	*in* January, *in* time of war
at the door	*at* noon
the king rode *before* the army	*before* the battle started
they are a mile *behind* us	they are an hour *behind* us
sit *by* the window	arrive *by* tomorrow
the shop *after* the post-office	the hours *after* darkness
within the prison	*within* a year
through the jungle	*through* the month
outside Africa	*outside* office hours
around the fire	*around* lunchtime
about the neighbourhood	*about* midnight

The list could easily be lengthened, and the correspondences are by no means coincidental. What's more, if the same experiment were to be repeated with spatial concepts in any other language, the result would be the same, as there is no known language where spatial terms are not also used to describe temporal relations. Language thus demonstrates that long before physicists, common intuition had already spotted the relation between space and time, and the nature of this intuited link is none other than metaphor. All the prepositions above originally denoted spatial terms, and all of them were metaphorically extended into the domain of time.

The link between space and time is another example of conceptual mappings between two domains (just like food and ideas). The movement nearly always goes in one direction, from space to time, since time is an abstract concept that can only be grasped by being visualized as something more tangible. So we think of time as a line in space, with 'now' as 'here', the past as the part 'behind' us, and the future stretching out 'in front' of us. A period of time (like a year) can thus be seen as a segment of this line, and this enables us to talk of being *in* it, going *through* it, and so on.

This link between space and time is so entrenched in our cognition that it is extremely difficult to extricate ourselves from it, and appreciate that time cannot literally be 'long' or 'short' (unlike sticks or pieces of string), nor can time literally 'pass' (unlike a train). Time cannot even 'go forwards' and 'backwards' any more than it goes sideways, diagonally or downwards. Time doesn't actually go anywhere at all. Since the images here are so deeply rooted, it might seem strange to lump them together with the kind of poetic metaphors from the beginning of the chapter. The connection between space and time is so instinctive, and the metaphoric meaning so thoroughly naturalized in its new domain, that we need to make a considerable effort to register that even entirely functional prepositions like 'to', 'from', or 'in' could ever be used metaphorically. And yet, even if 'from Monday' and 'treading on dreams' seem worlds apart, in essence they are still two instances of the same mechanism: the carrying of a concept away from its original environment into a different sphere.

But this is still not the last of it, since metaphor does not just dally with a few spatial prepositions here and there. It will soon emerge that metaphor is endemic within the structure of language, and that the flow from space to time is in fact only a part of a much more widespread drift.

Outside of a dog, a book is a man's best friend.
Inside of a dog, it's too dark to read.
(Groucho Marx)

For British readers, Groucho's pun requires a double-take, since it pivots on a meaning of the phrase 'outside of' that is not current in Britain. In the past, using 'outside of' to mean 'except for' was frowned upon even in America, as witnessed by the censure of an American manual of good usage from 1859: '*Outside* . . . is frequently used by writers in newspapers in a sense not known to the language: . . . "outside of the Secretary of War" for "no one but that official".' Nevertheless, if one takes precedents into account, the criticism looks rather misplaced, for the change of 'outside of' from the spatial relation 'on the outer side of' to the logical relation of exclusion precisely parallels the development of more respectable synonyms such as '*besides* the Secretary', '*except for* the Secretary', or 'no one *but* that official'. All of these started out in life as simple spatial terms:

- *But* comes from Old English *be-utan* 'by the outside'.
- *Except* comes from Latin *ex-cipere* 'out-take'.
- *Excluding* comes from *ex-cludere* 'out-shut'.
- *Besides* and *aside from* still clearly betray their spatial origin.
- *Apart* (*from*) comes from French *à part*, literally 'to the side'.
- *Without* was originally the counterpart to *within* and meant 'outside', as in the hymn 'there is a green hill far away, without a city wall', or in the instruction to Noah to cover the ark 'within and without with pitch' (see p. 47).

It seems, then, that spatial terms are not only the sources of temporal concepts, but also lurk behind other complex notions such as logical exclusion. The flow from space to time is thus only one part of a much more far-reaching drift, from space to many other abstract domains. The change from 'outside' to 'except' is just one example, but we only have to return to the spatial prepositions 'from', 'through', 'at', and so on, to find other comparable translocations. As shown below, many of these spatial terms have not only acquired a temporal meaning, but have also drifted to even more abstract realms and are used to describe causes and reasons:

Space	**Time**	**Cause or Reason**
from London	*from* today	he shivers *from* cold
about the town	*about* midnight	this election is *about* the economy
through the jungle	*through* the month	*through* your stupidity
out of Africa	*out of* term	*out of* despair
at the door	*at* noon	*at* my request
by the window	*by* tomorrow	*by* your authority

Like most of the metaphors already encountered, the images here are ultimately grounded in experience. Think of a sentence like 'the travellers got typhoid *from* the contaminated water'. The physical origin of the disease is also its cause: the disease started *because* of the water, but it also came – physically – *from* it. But in generalizing the metaphor we have unshackled the image from that basis in experience, and can now talk freely about one thing coming 'from' another, 'out of' another, or happening 'through' another, to express abstract chains of cause and event.

The flow from space to abstract domains is by no means restricted to prepositions, however, and can reach even the most unexpected areas of language's structure. One good example is 'pointing words' (or 'demonstratives' in linguistic terminology) such as the English 'that', which are used to point at an object and single it out. If one sees a shirt in a shop window, for instance, one might point at it and say 'I like that.' Now at first, it might seem that the action of pointing would be unlikely ever to become a metaphor, for what could be the point of 'pointing metaphorically' at a shirt, or at anything else for that matter? But consider the following marital exchange: 'Darling, do you have any idea where my blue Marks and Spencer's shirt is, you know, the one with the button missing from the cuff?' 'Oh, I chucked *that* away ages ago, it was so scruffy!' It would be difficult to pretend that the word 'that' does any real physical pointing here – you cannot point at a shirt that's no longer there. What the word 'that' does in this context is 'point' at the previous mention of this shirt in the conversation. The act of pointing has thus been transferred from the domain of physical space into the abstract 'space of conversation', to refer to previously mentioned participants (something that linguists call 'anaphora'). 'Pointing metaphorically', therefore, is both extremely common in language, and has all the point in the world to it, for it helps to maintain coherence over long stretches of discourse, and allows us to refer to people and objects concisely and efficiently. Just imagine how protracted the ensuing domestic exchange would become, if instead of simply saying, 'But *that* was my favourite shirt, I got *that* from my grandmother for my graduation . . .' you had to repeat 'the blue Marks and Spencer's shirt with the button missing from the cuff' over and over again. Quite simply, then, pointing metaphorically allows us to get to the point.

One could (and people do) write thousand-page monographs on the flow of meaning from space into abstract domains, describing every twist and turn it takes in language after language. But it's not necessary to rake through all the details in order to get the wider view of the linguistic landscape, and to appreciate that the surge of metaphors from the domain of space makes its presence felt everywhere in language, and even seeps into the deepest foundations of its structure.

So far, in tracking the course of metaphoric abstraction, I have ended the discussion of each section with the refrain 'but this is not all'. At this stage, however, it may seem difficult to continue in this vein. If, as I have suggested, metaphors have drifted from the domain of space into absolutely everywhere in language, then what more is there left to chart? And yet, one crucial aspect of the process remains to be discovered, for we still have not traced the stream to its ultimate source.

AT THE BACK OF SPACE

So far, spatial relations such as 'in', 'through' or 'behind' have featured as the source of metaphoric extension into the abstract domains of time, cause, and so on. But are spatial terms the ultimate source of this flow? After all, spatial relations already entail some degree of abstraction, since they are not things of substance that can directly be observed. (You cannot point at a 'through', for instance, any more than you can directly observe an 'in'.) So might words for spatial terms in fact develop from something even simpler and more solid? And if so, then from what? By this stage, we are beginning to run out of places to look, but the following examples from Ewe, a language spoken in Togo and Ghana, can point us in the right direction:

Ewe (Kwa, Niger-Congo)

i. *épé* ***megbé*** *fá*
his back is.cold
'his back is cold'

ii. *é-le* *xɔ-á* ***megbé***
he-is house-the back
'he is back of the house'

iii. *é-ku* *le* *é-**megbé***
he-died was his-back
'he died back (= after) him'

iv. *é-tsí* ***megbé***
he-remains back
'he remains backward (= retarded)'

These examples illustrate four stages of the flow towards abstraction, the last three of which should by now be thoroughly familiar, as they go from space ('behind') to time ('after'), and from there, to the abstract domain of mental faculties. But Ewe shows that the spatial term 'behind' is itself a product of metaphor, and reveals the ultimate origin of the word *megbé*: a solid noun, part of the human body.

The parts of the body are the closest and most immediate things in our physical environment, and are thus most deeply imprinted in our cognition, so it is no wonder that body-parts are the sources of terms for all kinds of more abstract concepts in so many languages. English 'back', for instance, took almost exactly the same route as Ewe *megbé*, for 'back' is the back-bone of the prepositional phrase 'at the back of', which simply means 'behind'. Moreover, just as in Ewe, 'back' proceeded even further towards abstraction, and can also be used as a temporal relation ('she died a few years back'), or even as the description of a mental condition ('backward'). So the development from 'back' to 'after' or 'behind' is not just a peculiar feature of some tropical languages, it is a part of a universal march of limbs and ligaments towards abstraction.

Here is another example from a different language, drawing on a different part of the body:

Modern Hebrew (Semitic, Afro-Asiatic)

i. ***pney*** *ha-yeled*
face (of) the-child
'the face of the child'

ii. *hi omedet* *li-**pney*** *ha-bayit*
she stands to-**face** (of) the-house
'she stands to the face of (= in front of) the house'

iii. *hi barḥa* *li-**pney*** *ha-milḥama*
she fled to-**face** (of) the-war
'she fled to the face of (= prior to) the war'

iv. *hi barḥa* *mi-**pney*** *še-hitḥila* *ha-milḥama*
she fled from-**face** that-started the-war
'she fled from the face (= because) the war started'

And if the progress from 'face' to 'in front of' sounds rather laboured, then it might help to bear in mind that the English phrase 'in front of' comes from precisely the same source. The original meaning of the noun 'front' was simply 'brow' or 'forehead', as can still be seen in Shakespeare's line 'Grim-visag'd war hath smooth'd his wrinkled front'. But through a natural metaphor, what is 'at one's forehead' was transferred to what is 'in front', and the change was so successful in English that the original sense of 'front' has all but been forgotten.

There is hardly any part of the body which has not been enlisted as a metaphor for spatial and more abstract concepts, as the following examples illustrate.

'belly' → 'middle', Albanian (Indo-European)
në bark të *javës*
in belly-the week (= the middle of the week)

'intestines' → 'inside', Hungarian (Finno-Ugric, Uralic)
bel-ügy-minisztérium
intestines-affairs-ministry (= ministry of interior affairs)

'heart' → 'in', Nahuatl (Aztec, Uto-Aztecan (American-Indian), spoken in Mexico)
huēi *āltepētl* *i-yōllò-co*
big town its-heart-in (= in the big town)

'hand' → 'next to', Hebrew (Semitic, Afro-Asiatic)
le-yad *ha-bayit*
to-hand.of the-house (= next to the house)

'breast' → 'in front of', Welsh (Celtic, Indo-European)
ger fy mron
near my breast (= in front of me)

'lip' → 'along', Albanian (Indo-European)
buzë-s së detit
lip-by the sea (= along the seaside)

'heel' → 'after' → 'because of', Hebrew (Semitic, Afro-Asiatic)
be-iqvot ha-mašber
in-heels.of the-crisis (= after/because of the crisis)

'head' → 'in front of' → 'prior to', English (Germanic, Indo-European)
he is a mile a-head of us
he is an hour a-head of us

'mouth' → 'in front of', Mursi (Nilo-Saharan, spoken in Ethiopia)
dori tutuo
house mouth.of
'mouth of the house' (= in front of the house)

'back' → 'above', Mixtec (Oto-Manguean (American-Indian), spoken in Mexico)
saà ndéčé siki itú
bird fly back cornfield
'the bird flies over the cornfield'

Incidentally, some of these metaphors, such as from 'mouth' to 'in front of' or from 'back' to 'above', may appear somewhat contorted. Why should Mixtec speakers, for instance, say 'a bird is flying back the cornfield' when they mean 'over' the field rather than 'behind' it? But of course, it is not just humans that have body parts that can serve as metaphors, and some languages rely on what linguists call the 'zoomorphic model'. When we free ourselves from our anthropocentric prejudices, and think of four-legged animals instead, then it becomes clear why 'mouth' or 'head' can be mapped to 'in front', why 'back' can become 'above', and 'belly' 'underneath'.

This chapter began with a view of metaphor as an ornamental figure of poetic art, but as we probed more deeply, the picture changed beyond recognition. Metaphors turned up everywhere, dead or alive, hiding behind even the plainest words of ordinary language. It transpired that metaphor is an essential tool of thought, an indispensable conceptual mechanism which allows us to think of abstract notions in terms of simpler concrete things. It is, in fact, the only way we have of dealing with abstraction. The desire to communicate abstract concepts is thus behind a relentless surge from the concrete to the abstract: from parts of the body to spatial relations, from physical proximity to possession, from seizing to understanding. There is practically no patch of language that this surge does not reach, no plot that it does not irrigate.

The last few examples of this flow towards abstraction, where parts of the body are used to describe spatial relations, may not seem so different from the metaphors on display earlier on. Certainly, the principle is the same: simple concepts – here, parts of the body from 'head' to 'heel' and from 'breast' to 'intestines' – are swept out of their original environment and carried into the domain of spatial relations. Compared to some of the metaphors from the beginning of the chapter (such as the shift from 'pierced' to 'thrilled', say, or from 'flesh-tearing' to 'sarcastic'), the shift in meaning from 'back' to 'behind' or from 'lip' to 'along' does not even seem so dramatic.

In one crucial sense, however, these body-part examples are different from everything else we have seen so far, since the metaphors here have somehow breached the border between 'content words' and 'grammatical elements'. Recall that content words are the solid bricks of language, nouns and verbs like 'head', 'back', 'go' or 'give', whereas grammatical elements such as prepositions, auxiliaries or conjunctions are only the mortar, the adhesives that help to bind the content words into meaningful sentences. But let's take another look at what these body-part metaphors have achieved. Their starting point was sturdy nouns like 'back' or 'head' – entirely normal content words. Yet after what seems only a modest metaphorical leap, these body-parts find themselves transformed into grammatical elements. Through metaphor, therefore, these solid nouns have somehow crossed the boundary between content and structure, and turned into prepositions. It appears that metaphor not only alters the meaning of *existing* grammatical elements, but through its ability to transform content into structure, metaphor is also involved in creating those grammatical elements in the first place.

So finally, the flow of metaphors towards abstraction is beginning to reveal how life and death in language are entwined. Whereas in poetry metaphors turn into empty clichés once they die of over-use, in everyday language dead metaphors are the alluvium from which grammatical structures emerge. Like a reef, which grows from layer upon layer of dead coral skeletons, new structures in language can rise from the layers of dead metaphors deposited by the flow towards abstraction.

How this metamorphosis from content to structure is achieved in practice will be the subject of the following chapter. For this, we shall take a short break from our normal transmission, and go live to the George Orwell Centre at the London South Bank, where a conference in honour of Orwell's centenary is now in full swing. This year, the delegates are discussing 'The State of the Language', so let's join them in the main auditorium, where the afternoon session is about to begin.

5

The Forces of Creation

A conference room. The conference logo **Language, Whither?** *is draped on the wall behind the speaker. At one end of the table sits the chairman, a distinguished columnist. Next to him, a young academic is fiddling with the projector and arranging his first slide:*

> 'Let us put our trust in the eternal spirit,
> which destroys and annihilates only because it
> is the perpetual creative source of all life.
> The urge for destruction is,
> at the same time, a creative urge!'
>
> *Mikhail Alexandrovich Bakunin, 1842*

The chairman glances uneasily at the screen behind him, but assumes an air of official optimism as he rises to introduce the speaker.

CHAIRMAN: Ladies and gentlemen, welcome to the afternoon session of the George Orwell Centenary Conference, dedicated to debating a passionate concern of that great author: the state of the language – whither it is heading, and how it was ever let hither. I trust you all took full advantage of the luncheon break to repair your spirits after the doom and gloom of this morning's session. For I believe we shall all need our wits about us as we attend to the speaker this afternoon, who, as you may well have gathered, is promising to play something of the devil's advocate. Without further ado, then, it gives me great pleasure to introduce our guest speaker, Chris de Troy. Dr de Troy's theories, I am led to believe, have recently been making waves throughout the academic community and further afield. His recent book [*hastily rifling through his notes*], *Bakunian Linguistics: Toward a Dialectic of Categorical Deconstruction*, has established him as a leading expert in the field of . . . um, his field. He will talk to us today about 'Creation through Destruction'.

DR DE TROY: Cheers. I can only hope I won't live up to your diabolical expectations . . . but if you are fearing a rather different 'take' on language, I certainly won't let you down. As I was listening to the speakers this morning discussing the sorry state of the language, and lamenting its destruction and decay, I was wondering how to find a polite way to begin my talk. But to be frank, the only phrase which sprang to mind was: 'Guys, you've got it all wrong. You're completely missing the point.' Because, you see, without these much maligned forces of destruction, language would never have developed in the first place. Without what you write off as so much decay, we wouldn't have got much beyond grunts and groans. I'd even go so far as to say that if Mikhail Bakunin had only directed his zeal to the study of language, rather than to permanent revolution, he would have gone down in history as a thinker of extraordinary insight, way ahead of his time. Because as far as language is concerned, Bakunin is spot on: the forces that create grammatical structures in language are nothing other than the by-products of destruction.

The main thrust of my argument is fairly simple: the starting point, which I take it we can all agree on, is that grammatical elements don't just appear out of thin air. And if things like prepositions, case endings or tense markers were not consciously invented, they must have developed from something that's already there. But from what? Now, it's hardly breaking news that grammatical elements such as prepositions originate ultimately from normal nouns and verbs like 'back' or 'go' – didn't we hear only this morning someone complaining about the invasion of Americanisms like 'back of', which is displacing the preposition 'behind'? And I won't be spilling the beans if I also tell you that metaphor provides the raw materials for grammatical elements. What might come as more of a surprise, though, is *how* exactly the transformations from content to grammar proceed. What is responsible for turning nouns and verbs into grammatical elements? And here, I think, is where the Bakunian theory can offer a real breakthrough, since the point I'll be pressing home today is that the builders of new grammatical structures are none other than the forces of destruction that were vilified so enthusiastically in this morning's session.

I realize that this claim may seem far-fetched, so what I'd like to do now is give a few actual examples of how the transformations work on the ground. The first example is fairly simple, and involves the English verb 'go'. I'll try to demonstrate how the forces of destruction took hold of 'going to', a phrase that was simple, solid and set in its ways, and turned it into something entirely different, a grammatical element marking the future tense. And once we have deconstructed 'going to', I'll move on to some fancier grammatical structures, like the French verbal system and the case system of Latin, and show that even these are really just the result of destruction.

Next slide, please. Have a look at these two English sentences:

Are you **going to** the concert this evening? No, I'm **gonna** stay at home.

Let's suppress – a least for a moment – any hang-ups we might have about correct and incorrect usage, and just consider the transformation that 'going to' has undergone. In the first sentence, 'going' is still a completely normal verb, but in the second, no one is actually going anywhere – quite the opposite – someone is planning to stay put. So 'gonna' in the second sentence has lost its status as a verb of movement, and functions as a mere grammatical element, a future marker very similar to the auxiliaries 'will' or 'shall'. Somehow, 'going to' has managed to turn itself into part of the structure of language. This transformation may seem strange at first, but I'm going to argue that what's behind it is nothing other than metaphor and the much maligned erosion in meaning and sounds. You only need to compare the two sentences to see that metaphor must have had something to do with it, because the first 'going to' deals with movement in space, but the second refers to time. Erosion of meaning has had a hand in the process too, since the first 'going to' has a full meaning all of its own, but the second has lost its independent meaning, so that 'gonna' no longer denotes a separate action. And finally, erosion in sounds was clearly involved, because whereas the first 'going to' has hung on to its original complete form – no one would say 'are you *gonna* the concert' – the second 'going to' has been pared down to 'gonna'.

A member of the Royal Society for the Protection of the English Language, who this morning had presented a loving obituary for the pronoun 'whom', can hold back no longer.

RSPEL MEMBER: But surely, Dr de Troy, you are not claiming that 'going to' changed into a structural element merely because of a simple metaphor and some rather sloppy pronunciation? I can't see how metaphor or erosion could have actually transformed the verb into an auxiliary, and tipped it over from one syntactic category to another, from an ordinary content word into a grammatical marker.

DE TROY: Well, rather than philosophizing about this on an empty stomach, why don't we first munch through some detail, and have a look at what actually happened to 'going to' over the last few centuries? Because we'll be in a much better position to argue about what caused this transformation once we've reviewed the history of this phrase . . .

RSPEL MEMBER: Fire away, then.

DE TROY: OK. As you would expect, 'going to' originally meant 'walking' or 'travelling' somewhere: 'going to London', 'going to the market', and the like. The phrase 'going to *do* something' seems to have made its entrance only in the fifteenth century. One of the earliest examples is found in an appeal sent to parliament in 1439 by the burghers of Scropton in Derbyshire, who were trying to secure the arrest of a runaway called John Forman. In their petition, they allege that Forman had previously been lawfully arrested for 'diverse grete and notable causes and offenses', and dispatched under guard to the nearby Castle of Tutbury. But on the way the convoy was ambushed by Robin Hood style guerrillas, and this is how the worthy burghers describe what happened next:

as they were **goynge to bringe** hym there . . . cometh one Piers Venables . . . with many othere unknowen, in manere of Werre, Riote, Route, and Insurrection arraied, with force and armes, and . . . toke awey the saide John Forman fro theym.

Examples like this one make it pretty clear that 'going to do something' started out simply as a kind of shorthand for 'going *somewhere, in order* to do something'. 'Going' meant walking somewhere, and 'to' just marked the intention to do something. The Sheriff and his minions were actually walking to Tutbury, with the aim of bringing Forman there, and it was *en route* that they were ambushed.

But in the following decades, 'going to' slowly starts sliding down the long slippery slope towards abstraction. About forty years later, in 1482, we find another example of 'going to' followed by a verb, which is perhaps the first sign that things are really on the move. This example comes from one of the earliest books ever printed in English, the *Revelations of St Nicholas to a Monk of Evesham*. The story relates a monk's journey through purgatory, and his meeting with various people who recount their sufferings. One chapter tells how Saint Margaret intervened on behalf of the tormented soul of a sinful woman, who in a large convoy

was **goyng to be broughte** into helle for the synne and onleful [unlawful] lustys of her body.

During the procession to hell, the woman is so cruelly afflicted by devils and wicked spirits, and her cries are so anguished, that lo, a great light shines from on high: Saint Margaret appears, takes pity on the poor soul, and saves her.

RSPEL MEMBER: But I really do not see how this example is different from your previous one. Surely, the phrase 'going to' here still refers to the physical act of going – didn't you say just now that the woman was *moving* in a procession on the way to hell?

DE TROY: Sure, but if you look carefully, you'll see that the emphasis here is on something else. The passive form of the verb, 'to be brought', shifts the focus away from any intention on the part of the woman – after all, she can't really have been intending to go to hell, can she? So the physical movement mainly serves to highlight the more abstract implication: the fact that the woman will soon be brought into hell and made to suffer for her sins.

RSPEL MEMBER: That all sounds rather impressionistic to me.

DE TROY: It has to be, because the actual situation involves both the physical aspect of moving and the abstract dimension of time. But that in itself is illuminating, since in the metaphors of everyday language, the shift from concrete to abstract usually has some basis in experience, and here you have exactly that basis: the woman is moving – albeit rather unwillingly – towards her suffering, and this means that she's about to suffer.

A journalist from the front row, who has been assiduously taking notes, now butts in.

JOURNALIST: But I thought that an image only becomes a true metaphor when it flies away from that basis in experience and is used in a new environment.

DE TROY: Actually, this is exactly what happens to 'going to' later on. But if you examine its history closely, you'll see that it never really 'flew away' – it was more like a slow *creeping* away from that basis in experience. For at least a century after the *Revelations*, not much seemed to change, except that 'going to' appeared a bit more frequently with the abstract sense in the foreground. On the whole, though, the phrase still held tightly on to the sense of physical movement. Even in Shakespeare's plays, from the end of the sixteenth century, 'going to' is still used only when actual movement is involved, as you can see in this example from *The Two Gentlemen of Verona*:

> DUKE: Sir Valentine, whither away so fast?
> VALENTINE: Please it your Grace, there is a messenger that stays to bear my letters to my friends, and I am **going to deliver** them.

JOURNALIST: So when do things finally hurry up and get a move on?

DE TROY: Only during the seventeenth century. The sense of future in 'going to' comes increasingly to the fore, while the physical movement remains somewhere in the background. Take this example from a play called *Women Pleased*, written by John Fletcher in 1620. I think you'd all agree that 'going' is not quite the activity at the forefront of Penurio's mind:

PENURIO: Pray ye take me with ye.

THIRD GENTLEMAN: To supper do'st thou meane?

PENURIO: To any thing that has the smell of meat in't: tell me true, Gentlemen, are not you three now **going to be** sinfull . . . ? I have found your faces, and see whore written in your eyes.

RSPEL MEMBER: Yes . . . but isn't this still rather vague? After all, even here there is actual movement involved.

DE TROY: Sure. But only a little later, we start finding cases where the metaphor really has taken wings. Look at this next example from 1642. In April of that year, Charles I was prevented from entering Hull and its big arms depot, or 'magazine'. A few weeks later, he summoned the gentry of Yorkshire, and tried to rally them to his cause by whingeing on about how he was being betrayed left right and centre:

To be short, You see that My Magazine **is going to** be taken from Me, being My Own proper Goods, directly against My will; the Militia, against Law and My Consent, **is going to** be put in execution . . . All this considered, none can blame Me to apprehend Dangers.

JOURNALIST: Well yes, I suppose the arms depot couldn't really have been wandering off anywhere.

DE TROY: Nor is this example just some isolated quirk of royal speech. There are a few other examples of a similar nature from around that time, and we even have an explicit remark made by a contemporary linguist to prove it. In a manual from 1646, Joshua Poole describes 'going to' as a 'sign of the future':

'. . . going to' is the signe of the Participle of the future, as . . . 'I am . . . going to read'.

So by the middle of the seventeenth century we are no longer dealing with vague impressions. We have pretty clear evidence that 'going to' can be used as a future marker without any residue of the original meaning of movement.

JOURNALIST: And is that the end of the story?

DE TROY: In one sense, yes, since 'going to' was certainly an established future marker by the mid-seventeenth century. But to tell the whole story you'd have mention that at the time, 'going to' was still much less common than in modern English, and there were some contexts in which it had not yet appeared. It's only in the nineteenth and twentieth centuries that the future marker 'going to' really takes off.

JOURNALIST: And what about the eroded form 'gonna'?

DE TROY: Unfortunately, it's difficult to say for sure when that first cropped up, since the written sources don't tend to reflect such 'substandard' pronunciation. The earliest recorded examples seem to come from Scotland, from around the beginning of the nineteenth century. In 1806, the poet Alexander Douglas wrote: 'Now Willie lad, I'm ganna gie You twa or three directions.' The earliest 'gonna' quoted by the *Oxford English Dictionary*, though, is from American English, in 1913, a whole century later. And the jazz song 'I ain't gonna give nobody none o' this jelly roll' from 1919 is another early example. But it's quite difficult to tell how long the pronunciation had been around before it made its literary debut.

RSPEL MEMBER: Dr de Troy, you have taken us on a fascinating historical perambulation, and told a touching tale of gentle changes in meaning. But I am still waiting for an answer to my original question: how exactly was an ordinary verb like 'going to' transformed into an auxiliary, a mere element of grammar? So far, we have not heard a single word about the real chemistry of changes from one syntactic category to another. When precisely did 'go' decide to stop being a content word and turn into a grammatical element, and how did this metamorphosis actually happen?

DE TROY: But don't you see – that's exactly why I went into the history of 'going to' in such detail. It was to show you that there was no dramatic volte-face, no sudden leap over the border between content and structure. There was no Berlin wall, no passport-control, not even a checkpoint between content words and grammatical elements. When you take a closer look at what happened to 'going to' in real life, all you'll find is a peaceful story of very gradual erosion in meaning, followed by erosion of sounds.

RSPEL MEMBER: But you are not alleging, are you, that there is no difference between content words and grammatical elements?

DE TROY: No, but what I'm trying to get at is that words don't walk around wearing different designer T-shirts with labels like 'Content Word' or 'Grammatical Element'. It's true that we distinguish between 'content' and 'grammar' when we talk *about* a language, but when you stop to think about it, the only valid reason for drawing the distinction in the first place is meaning: we call some words 'content words' because they have an independent meaning, and we call other words 'grammatical words' because they don't. So in fact, all that was needed to push the phrase 'going to' from the camp of 'content words' to 'grammatical words' was the erosion of its original meaning as an independent action.

JOURNALIST: Still, I don't see why you can't put your finger on when exactly this change happened. Why can't you say when it flipped from having an independent meaning to not having it any more?

DE TROY: Because having an independent meaning or not is not always a simple matter of black or white. Of course, a word like 'tree' has a simple meaning all of its own, whereas a word like 'which' is devoid of almost any independent meaning. When you consider these two extremes, the difference between the camps seems clear enough. But when you really get down to it and look closer, you'll find there's a considerable grey area in between. To take just one example, think of prepositions like 'under' or 'with'. They may not have an independent meaning like 'tree', but are they really as empty as 'which'? And it's the same with 'going to'. The reason why I wanted to run through its history in such detail was to show you that it never suddenly changed from black to white. It went through subtle shades of grey, depending on background, foreground, intention, implication.

JOURNALIST: I just don't get what 'intention' or 'implication' have to do with the question of having an independent meaning.

DE TROY: Quite a lot, actually. Here is a slightly absurd example, which might help to drive the point home. I don't know if you've ever heard the story about the two Jewish merchants in Poland who bump into one another at the train station in Warsaw one morning. Both are competitors in the same trade, so they eye each other suspiciously, and one of them asks: 'So where are you travelling today?' 'To Łódz,' comes the cautious answer. 'To Łódz, eh?' the first says sceptically. 'I know very well that you are only telling me that to make me think that you are *actually* going to Krakow. But – I happen to know that you really *are* going to Łódz . . .' And after a little pause he adds: 'So tell me: why are you trying to deceive me?'

You see, in real life, the actual meaning of what you say is often more than the literal sense of the words. What you say may not be exactly what you imply. How the hearer interprets what you said may not be exactly what you think you implied, and so on. In the joke, this is all brought to absurd extremes. But when we were arguing earlier about what exactly people *meant* when they said 'going to', we faced the same problem: we had to consider the context, the intention, what was in the foreground, what was in the background. The gist of the tale of 'going to' was that the original literal meaning gradually faded into the background, and the abstract sense came more and more to the fore. But it was never the case that 'going to' was transformed overnight from having the meaning of movement to being rid of it altogether.

You could of course take one particular point, and just decide to call that *the* moment when 'going to' hopped across the border between content and structure. You could argue, for example, that this happened when 'going to' was first used in a context where movement was really no longer possible, say when Charles's magazine was 'going to be taken away'. But if you look at the history as a whole, it becomes clear that this choice would be somewhat arbitrary, because there never was a cataclysmic break at that or any other point. Charles's 'going to' was just one step in a long and gradual process, brought about by a particular combination of metaphor and erosion in both meaning and sounds.

CHAIRMAN: I'd like to pose a rather different question, if I may. Suppose one accepts your analysis that all that is involved here is a 'particular combination', as you have just said, of metaphor and erosion. But isn't this particular combination – how shall I put it – rather too particular? It is quite remarkable that metaphor and erosion in meaning should join forces in just the right way, and that the erosion of sounds should know when to clock in at just the right time. Such a coincidence seems almost too good to be true, don't you think?

DE TROY: I know what you mean, but if you think that 'gonna' is a fluke, then maybe you'd like to explain why it is that exactly the same fluke somehow repeats itself in dozens of languages across the world. Just look at these examples:

French: *je vais dire*
'I'm going to say'

Basque: *kanta-tze-ra noa*
sing-ing-to I.go ('I'm going to sing')

Tamil: *Kumaar oru viiṭu kaṭṭa·p pookiṟaaṉ*
Kumar a house to.build he.goes ('Kumar is going to build a house')

Zulu: *Ba-ya-ku-fika*
they-go-to-arrive ('they are going to arrive')

CHAIRMAN: Now it is beginning to sound more like a conspiracy.

DE TROY: I bet Bakunin would have had something to say about the bourgeoisie's paranoia of conspiracies during the last stages of capitalist decline. But seriously, there's nothing especially mysterious about this 'particular combination' of metaphor and erosion. What happens to the 'going' verbs in all these languages is the result of two common motives that are *always* behind the scenes: the desire to enhance our expressive range on the one hand, and laziness on the other. The flow towards abstraction is a consequence of this expressive urge: even if a language already has a future marker, speakers will always seek fresher ways of emphasizing that something is really going to happen. For example, they may want to stress that something will happen very soon indeed. Just think of the promise

'I'm going to do it right away' – doesn't it sound much more promising than a mere 'I'll do it'?

CHAIRMAN: But how does the erosion of sounds know when to start?

DE TROY: It doesn't. It carries on regardless, and keeps on trying to hack away at everything all the time. But some constructions are more susceptible to it, while others are more resistant. So what happened to 'going to' was really just a consequence of its hackneyed use in its new domain. As long as 'going to' retained its independent meaning, it had a much stronger resistance, and this is why no one says 'I'm gonna bed'. But once 'going to' lost its independent content, it became much more exposed, because it was now used more often, in more predictable circumstances, and with far less stress. So naturally, the temptation to take short-cuts in pronunciations grew, and the risk of misunderstanding decreased. In such conditions, the phrase was more prone to erosion than ever before, and so it's not surprising that the bleached future sense was shortened to 'gonna'.

JOURNALIST: So would you say that 'go' turns into a future marker so often because it's the most obvious source for the abstract concept of 'future'?

DE TROY: 'Go' is certainly one obvious source, but by no means the only one. The notion of future attracts metaphors from all kinds of places. You can imagine it as a kind of 'functional sink' into which different sources converge. Just think of the English future marker 'will'. No one today would dare raise an eyebrow at such a thoroughly respectable grammatical marker, but originally 'will' was an entirely normal verb that simply meant 'want to' or 'desire'.

JOURNALIST: Do you mean as in 'unwilling' and 'as you will'?

DE TROY: Precisely, or as in the marriage vow of the Anglican church. Although hardly a bride or groom realizes it today, the original sense of the promise 'I will' was simply 'I want to' love, honour, cherish, and so on. But when one *wants* to do something, it often implies that one jolly well *will*. So 'will' underwent a process rather like 'going to', and eventually ended up as a future auxiliary. And again, there's nothing peculiarly English about this development. The same path of change was traversed by languages all over the world. The Swahili verb *taka* 'want', for instance, ended up as the future marker *ta*, and the same thing happened to the Greek verb *thélei*.

CHAIRMAN: Dr de Troy, I must admit that I am quite taken with your account of 'going to'. But there is something else that is troubling me. You have explained how the grammatical marker 'gonna' emerged as a result of erosion, and made a good case for your thesis on 'creation through destruction'. But with all due respect, the substandard 'gonna' is hardly 'the structure of language', is it? It is just one grammatical marker, and quite a trifling one at that. Do you really expect us to believe these 'forces of destruction' can also produce the truly majestic architectures of language?

DE TROY: Well, Rome wasn't destroyed in a day, you know. I see your point that 'gonna' seems like a kind of 'baby structure', but what I'm trying to get at is that the same forces that created 'gonna' can also create much more impressive structures. Actually, I was just about to mention another example, the French verbal system. Now I'm sure you don't need to be reminded of the complex conjugation of the French verb, with its dozens of different endings, so I don't want to worry about the details here. But just to make the point that it doesn't suffer from lack of complexity, I've put the main tenses of the verb *aimer*, 'love', on a slide, and I think you will agree that we are no longer dealing with 'baby structure'.

	PRESENT	IMPERFECT	CONDITIONAL	SUBJUNCTIVE	PAST HISTORIC	FUTURE
je (I)	aim-*e*	aim-*ais*	aim-*erais*	aim-*e*	aim-*ai*	aim-*erai*
tu (you)	aim-*es*	aim-*ais*	aim-*erais*	aim-*es*	aim-*as*	aim-*eras*
il (he)	aim-*e*	aim-*ait*	aim-*erait*	aim-*e*	aim-*a*	aim-*era*
nous (we)	aim-*ons*	aim-*ions*	aim-*erions*	aim-*ions*	aim-*âmes*	aim-*erons*
vous (you)	aim-*ez*	aim-*iez*	aim-*eriez*	aim-*iez*	aim-*âtes*	aim-*erez*
ils (they)	aim-*ent*	aim-*aient*	aim-*eraient*	aim-*ent*	aim-*èrent*	aim-*eront*

CHAIRMAN: This is certainly no 'gonna'. But you are not implying, are you, that destruction could have given rise to such an edifice?

DE TROY: I am, actually. But I don't want to bore you here with the history of each and every ending, so as an illustration, I'd like to look at the endings of just one of these columns: the future tense. The next slide shows the future endings of *aimer* again, and next to them, I've put a different set of endings, those of the present tense of *avoir*, 'have'.

*j'aimer**ai***	I will love	*j'**ai***	I have
*tu aimer**as***	you will love	*tu **as***	you have
*il aimer**a***	he will love	*il **a***	he has
*nous aimer**ons***	we will love	*nous av**ons***	we have
*vous aimer**ez***	you will love	*vous av**ez***	you have
*ils aimer**ont***	they will love	*ils **ont***	they have

JOURNALIST: Even I can spot the resemblance, if that's what you're getting at. But do you mean that the future in French developed from the verb 'have'? If anything, I'd guess that 'have' should have something to do with the past: *j'ai aimé* – 'I have loved'.

DE TROY: That's right: 'have' found its way into various constructions, and sure enough, the past tense *j'ai aimé* is one of them. But there was also another construction with 'have', which took quite a different course. In Late Latin, the forebear of French, the verb *habere* 'have' could be used to express obligation, just as in English 'I *have to* do something'. So *amare habeo* meant 'I have to love', *amare habes* meant 'you have to love', as you can see here:

LATE LATIN

amare	*habe-o*	I	have to love
amare	*habe-s*	you	have to love
amare	*habe-t*	she	has to love
amare	*habe-mus*	we	have to love
amare	*habe-tis*	you	have to love
amare	*hab-ent*	they	have to love

RSPEL MEMBER: Are you proposing that 'I have to love' changed into 'I will love'? In my experience, no one starts loving someone simply because they have to.

DE TROY: No, well, maybe 'love' is not the best example . . . But here is a much better one, from a situation where what one has to do really is very close to what one *will* do. On the next slide, you can see a short extract from a document written by the Holy Inquisition in the Year of Our Lord 715. The inquisitors were called in to investigate an ownership dispute between the bishops of Siena and Arezzo, and their report mentions the testimony of a priest who piously told them how one of the parties in the dispute, a Lombard duke called Warnefrit, had tried to pressure him into lying under interrogation:

The Duke Warnefrit asked me:

si	*interrogatus*	*fueris,*	*quomodo*	*dicere*	*habes?*
if	questioned	you.will.be	what	to.say	you.have?

'If you are questioned, what will you say?'

I responded:

si	*interrogatus*	*fuero,*	*ueritatem*	*dicere*	*habeo*
if	questioned	I.will.be	truth	to.say	I.have

'If I am questioned, I will (/have to) say the truth.'

In the smug response of the priest – *ueritatem dicere habeo* 'truth to.say I.have' – we can see a perfect example of that basis in experience, where 'have to' and 'will' are practically one and the same. If one 'has to' tell the truth to the Inquisition, it is pretty damn likely that one 'will'. But what makes this exchange even more revealing is the Duke's question in the previous sentence. There, the sense of obligation has entirely faded away: when the Duke asks *quomodo dicere habes*, literally 'what to.say you.have', the last thing on his mind is what morality dictates – after all, he came in order to convince the priest *not* to tell the truth. So the meaning of obligation has entirely disappeared here – the Duke uses the *dicere habes* construction only to ask what the priest *will* say to the Inquisitors.

RSPEL MEMBER: I see that this is turning into yet another tale of gentle changes in meaning. But if I understood you correctly earlier on, what you promised to show was how those verbal *endings* emerged.

DE TROY: I was just getting to it. When the 'have to' construction was increasingly used with this bleached future meaning, something else happened: its form underwent substantial reduction. The first unmistakable sign of change appears in the writings of a guy called Fredegar. Not much is known about him, except that he lived in the seventh century, in what today would be France, and that he wrote a long rambling history of the Frankish kingdoms. Poor old Fredegar hasn't had a very good press. The *Encyclopaedia Britannica*, no less, dismisses his *Chronicle of the Frankish Kingdoms* as 'written in barbarous Latin and excessively dull'.

RSPEL MEMBER: Oh dear, that's all we need . . .

DE TROY: But you see, it's precisely this so-called 'barbarism' that gives us the first glimpse of the new reduced form of 'have to' in the Romance languages. In one of his numerous digressions, Fredegar describes a battle between the Byzantine Emperor Justinian and the Persian king Kavadh, which was fought around a border town called Daras. Fredegar offers a quaint explanation for how Daras got its name. Having defeated the Persians, Justinian had Kavadh brought to him in fetters, and demanded that he cede large territories. But Kavadh wouldn't hear of it. He kept saying *non dabo* ('I won't give'), and Justinian kept answering *daras* ('you will give'). And according to Fredegar, the town Daras was founded on the precise spot where the argument took place.

CHAIRMAN: As I'm sure you know, Dr de Troy, *daras* is not the correct Latin for 'you will give'. It should be *dabis*.

DE TROY: But that's exactly the point. Although Fredegar was writing in Latin, in this instance he chose a word from his 'barbarous' vernacular to explain the town's name. *Daras* is in fact the first recorded example of the future tense in the Romance languages: it's the contraction of the phrase *dare habes* 'to.give you.have'.

JOURNALIST: Do you mean that the whole phrase *dare habes* was reduced to just *daras*? That's pretty drastic, isn't it?

DE TROY: Not as drastic as the month *Augustus*, which ended up as a mere 'oo'. *Daras* is a fairly mild reduction compared to that, wouldn't you say?

JOURNALIST: But isn't something else going on here? We started off with two words, *dare habes*, but somehow they coalesced into one!

DE TROY: Sure, but there's nothing very unusual about that either. The same happens with 'going to' and 'gonna', or words like 'gotta' or 'gimme' – and if this register is beneath you, then what about 'don't', 'let's', 'o'clock'? In fluent speech we don't pause between words, and the sounds just run into one another. Just think how difficult it is to work out in a foreign language where one word ends and the next begins. When you don't know where the borders are meant to be, it is often impossible to hear them, because they are not really there in the sounds themselves.

RSPEL MEMBER: The way people mumble these days, I can hardly even hear the borders in English . . .

DE TROY: I'll pass on that one. But the point is that in a language we understand, the identity of words as individual entities is maintained because they appear in different combinations – a word like 'going' does not have to be followed by 'to', since there are many other options that could come after it: 'going away', 'going from', 'going out', and so on. But when two words such as 'going to' or *dare habes* appear together extremely frequently, the border between them can lose its relevance, so that when the phrase is worn down, the two words fuse into one. So really, there's nothing particularly mysterious about *habes* merging with the preceding verb and turning into an ending. And the other future endings arose in just the same way. I can think of no better illustration of 'creation through destruction':

	LATE LATIN →	(POSSIBLE → MIDDLE STAGE)	OLD → FRENCH	MODERN FRENCH (PRONUNCIATION)
(I will love)	*amare* ***habeo***	*amar-**ayo***	*aimer**ai***	*emre*
(you . . .)	*amare* ***habes***	*amar-**ays***	*aimer**as***	*emra*
(he . . .)	*amare* ***habet***	*amar-**ayt***	*aimer**a***	*emra*
(we . . .)	*amare* ***habemus***	*amar-**aymus***	*aimer**ons***	*emrõ*
(you . . .)	*amare* ***habetis***	*amar-**aytis***	*aimer**ez***	*emre*
(they . . .)	*amare* ***habent***	*amar-**awnt***	*aimer**ont***	*emrõ*

JOURNALIST: And is this how the endings in all the other tenses of French developed?

DE TROY: In principle, yes. They didn't all come from the verb 'have', of course, but the basic mechanism must have been the same.

CHAIRMAN: Far be it from me to nit-pick, but isn't there a slight hitch to your argument? You seem to be implying that the different endings all developed from auxiliary verbs such as 'have'. But doesn't your theory presuppose that *some* verbs already had personal endings to start with? After all, the only reason why we ended up with so many future endings is that there were so many different person endings on the verb 'have' in the first place. In other words, the endings on one verb created the endings on the other. But where did the original endings on 'have' itself come from?

DE TROY: You are absolutely right – 'have' must have got these markers from somewhere. The actual origin of the endings on the French 'have' lies too far back in prehistory to tell us anything in detail. But if you want to get an idea of what the ultimate source must have been, then you don't need to delve thousands of years into the past. You can stay with the present, and even with the same language.

CHAIRMAN: I must confess I don't see how modern French can help here.

DE TROY: Then let's try a little exercise in creative history. Imagine, for a moment, that the course of colonialism had gone rather differently, and that in the year 2000, a few enterprising missionaries from the Vatican in Nairobi had managed to set foot for the first time in the impenetrable forests by the river Seine, deep in the unexplored reaches of the European subcontinent. The missionaries try to make contact with the ferocious tribes that roam those dark forests, and after the first attempt ends rather stickily with one of them in the stew-pot – *flambé dans son jus* – they finally succeed in establishing cordial relations with the natives. Obviously, since the savages don't speak a word of Swahili, they can't understand the New Testament in the original. So the missionaries decide they had better make a translation into Frãsé, which is what the natives call their lingo. And to facilitate the task, the missionaries start by writing a grammar of Frãsé. Now, in describing the forms of the verb *em* ('love') in the present tense, the missionaries come up with a table looking more or less like this, showing the prefixes on the verb for the different persons:

mwa	***jem***	I love
twa	***tem***	you love
lwi	***ilem***	he loves
el	***elem***	she loves
. . .		

JOURNALIST: It looks like Turkish to me.

DE TROY: Of course it *looks* odd, because it's written as it sounds in the spoken language, rather than in the standard and highly archaizing French orthography. Does the following look less strange?

Moi, j'aime
Toi, tu aimes
Lui, il aime
Elle, elle aime
. . .

RSPEL MEMBER: Of course it does, but here, the pronouns *tu*, *il*, *elle* are clearly presented as independent words, while your funny phonetic rendering pretended they were part of the verb.

DE TROY: No, I'm afraid the pretension is entirely on the part of the archaizing written language, which shows the state of affairs centuries ago, not today. In the spoken language, the pronouns are in advance stages of merging with the verb: in phrases like *Jean, il aime* ('John, he loves'), or *lui, il aime* ('him, he loves'), the pronoun *il* has entirely lost the ability to stand on its own. So if French had never been written down, our missionaries would have had every reason to assume that these 'pronouns' were simply prefixes on the verb. They would hear the third person singular marker as a prefix *il-*, or even just *i-* when the verb begins with a consonant, as in *i-fe* 'he does'. Of course, the pronouns of modern Frãsé are turning into prefixes, not endings. But in a language where the pronouns usually come after the verb, such pronouns would turn into endings instead.

CHAIRMAN: Dr de Troy, I am sure no one here present would wish to dispute that your examples are impressive. And I, for one, am certainly beginning to warm to your theory that destruction can create complex new structures. Still, everything you have told us so far has to do with verbs: person endings emerging from eroded pronouns, and tense markers emerging from auxiliaries. But we haven't heard a single word on the majestic architectures that surround nouns. Are you trying to imply that it was just erosion that carved out the whole Latin case system, for instance?

DE TROY: I am, but the problem with working out the details of the Latin case system is that it's so old – it was inherited from the Proto-Indo-European ancestor language, and must have emerged at the very least 6,000 years ago. Still, even if the details are obscure, the principles are fairly clear, especially since similar developments can be observed in other languages in more recent times. Take Hungarian, for instance, a language renowned for its large number of cases. Luckily, some of these cases only emerged during the last millennium, so we can catch them in the act. Here is a modern Hungarian phrase containing two instances of the case ending *-ra*, which means 'to' or 'onto':

Hungarian (21st century):

*Fehérvár**ra***	*menő*	*hadi*	*út**ra***
Fehérvár-**to**	going	military	road-**onto**

'onto the military road going to Fehérvár'

But let's jump back a thousand years, and look at the same phrase in a text from the eleventh century:

Hungarian (11th century):

Feheuuaru	***rea***	*meneh*	*hodu*	*utu*	***rea***
Fehérvár	**to**	going	military	road	**onto**

'onto the military road going to Fehérvár'

You can see that the modern case ending *-ra* started out as an independent word, a postposition *rea*, which performed the same function as a preposition like 'to', only that it came after the noun rather than before it. And this is by no means an isolated case – there are examples in lots of other languages of such postpositions eroding and fusing with the noun to become case-endings.

CHAIRMAN: Yes, but what about Latin? Could the whole case system really have emerged in this way, from postpositions?

DE TROY: It must have done. One of the few case endings that still betrays something of its origin is the ablative plural ending *-ibus*, as in *consul-ibus* 'by the consuls'. This *-ibus* probably contains traces of an Proto-Indo-European postposition **bhi*, which is related to what ended up in English as the preposition *by*. But all this is highly speculative, of course, because we are dealing with such a distant time.

CHAIRMAN: Fair enough. But isn't there another problem which you have not mentioned? In Latin, not all nouns have the same case endings. Different nouns have different sets, and that makes the whole system so much more elaborate. But if, as you claim, those case endings all came from postpositions, then shouldn't all nouns have had exactly the same endings?

DE TROY: Actually, it's quite likely that in the earliest stages of Proto-Indo-European, there really was just one set of endings for all nouns – one size to fit all, as it were. But what made the system so much more complex was . . . none other than the forces of erosion. The postpositions fused with the nouns to become case endings, but the erosion did not stop at that. In the process of reduction, the case endings also merged with the final syllable of the nouns, and this is ultimately what produced so much variety. The actual details of this development are terribly fiddly, but here's just one example. Look at the dative case endings of these two different 'declensions' of Latin nouns:

SECOND DECLENSION	THIRD DECLENSION
lupō	*pedī*
('to the wolf')	('to the foot')

Although the two declension endings -*ī* and -*ō* look quite different, there are good reasons to think that they go back to just one ending in Proto-Indo-European: -*ei*. What made this ending diverge into -*ī* and -*ō* are different paths of erosion and fusion, depending on the sound at the end of the respective words. When -*ei* was added to nouns that ended in a consonant, like *ped* 'foot', the resulting form *pedei* was simply weakened to *pedī*. But when -*ei* was added to nouns that ended with the vowel -*o*, such as *lupo* 'wolf', the erosion took a different course. The original form *lupoei* was first reduced to *lupōi*, the form found in the most ancient Latin texts, and later on, the final *i* was dropped, to leave just *lupō*. So in fact, what's rather grandly called the 'second declension' is nothing other than those nouns that originally ended in the vowel -*o*, and the 'third declension' is just those nouns that originally ended in a consonant.

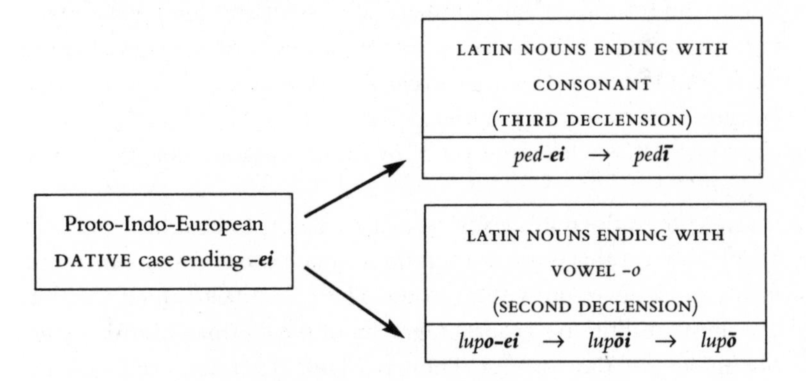

JOURNALIST: So this huge mesh of forms in the Latin case system was created by erosion? You're saying that the forces which later brought down the whole system are in fact the same ones that created it in the first place?

DE TROY: Exactly. You see, it's just one downhill slope. First erosion creates the case endings by fusing postpositions with the noun, and later on, erosion rubs them away again:

NOUN + Postposition ↘ NOUN-case ending ↘ Noun

JOURNALIST: Sorry for being a bit slow on the uptake, but there's something that's still bothering me. If erosion is behind it all, and if even the birth of new endings is really just a part of the same process of reduction, then how come words don't just get shorter and shorter and shorter all the time, until they dissolve completely?

DE TROY: That's a very good question. In fact, the great nineteenth-century linguist August Schleicher was troubled by exactly the same problem: seeing erosion all around, he concluded gloomily that in the future we will all end up communicating in monosyllabic grunts. But there was just one little thing he forgot. You see, you only have to add one more arrow to the diagram, going from the end back to the beginning, and it turns into a cycle. It's true that erosion makes words shorter and shorter, but speakers also start stringing two words together again, for instance by putting a new postposition after the noun. And then the whole cycle can start afresh when the new postpositions fuse with the noun.

JOURNALIST: But what's the point of stringing words together? Why bother?

DE TROY: Often the point is just to make a point, to be more emphatic. Think about it this way: you can do so much more with many words than you can ever do with just one. There's actually a nice anecdote that illustrates this in the autobiography of the German historian Golo Mann, son of the novelist Thomas Mann. In 1923, when he was fourteen, Golo was invited to stay with a school-friend over the Christmas holidays. This was no ordinary school-friend, though, but the son of a certain Count Lichnowsky, a high-ranking diplomat. Golo had never been taught formal manners by his parents, so his stay in the Lichnowskys' ancestral castle was marred by a few social solecisms. The most embarrassing incident occurred right at the end of his stay, when the boy tried to thank the Count formally for his hospitality. This is how he describes the occasion: 'I knew I had to say thank you, but how? A few years later, I would have managed it correctly: "May I thank you for your generous hospitality, for all the unforgettable experiences . . ."' and so on and so forth. But instead of gushing lengthily as etiquette would have it, the young Golo merely offered his hand to the Count, and tried to put as much emotion and gravity as he could muster into just two words: *vielen Dank* ('many thanks'). Of course, this attempt fell rather flat, and the Count's answer came prompt and cold: *Bitte sehr* ('that's all right').

RSPEL MEMBER: Oh the good old days when at least some people stood on ceremony.

DE TROY: You'd be surprised, but the reason I'm telling you all this is that ordinary language operates according to very similar principles even today. There's only so much you can do with a single word. You can spit it out with passion and intone it with gravity, but there's a limit to the amount of emphasis you can invest in it this way. So what do you do if you want to add more weight? You add more words. You combine them, pile them up into longer phrases. And just to show you that this isn't only about diplomatic politeness, here is a very proletarian example. What do you think 'on the day of on the day of this day' might mean?

RSPEL MEMBER: It sounds alarmingly like one of your dialectical deconstructions.

DE TROY: Oh, I'm afraid it's really something much more prosaic. Let's see what you make of the history of the French word for 'today'. Once upon a time, in the days before records of Latin began, there must have been a phrase *hoc die*, which meant '(on) this day'. By the time of attested Latin, this phrase had eroded and fused into one word, *hodie* 'today'. Later on, in Old French, *hodie* was ground down into a meagre *hui*, but the French soon found that they couldn't utter this paltry syllable with enough emphasis, so they piled up more words, and started saying *au jour d'hui*, literally 'on the day of this-day'. But with repeated use, this became a set phrase, and so it fused into one word again: *aujourd'hui*. And nowadays in colloquial French, the same cycle is beginning all over again. A mere *aujourd'hui* is not deemed to have sufficient presence, and so to emphasize it, the French have started saying *au jour d'aujourd'hui* – literally 'on the day of on-the-day-of-this-day'. As you can imagine, this usage is frowned upon by purists, but things have now sunk so low that you can find the phrase in practically any French dictionary, even if still labelled 'colloquial'.

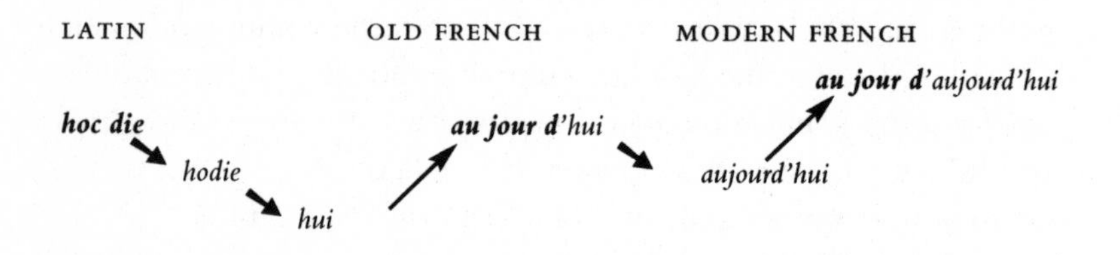

JOURNALIST: Ils sont fous ces Romains . . .

DE TROY: Maybe, but such cycles are not just a Gallic idiosyncracy. Take an English phrase like 'up above', and you'll discover a no less hyperbolic history. Old English *ufan* meant 'on up' – it was the locative case of the preposition *uf* 'up'. But this little *ufan* was not considered nearly sturdy enough, so it was reinforced by another preposition, *be* 'by', to give a beefier *be-ufan* 'by on up'. But before long, *be-ufan* was assaulted by the forces of erosion, and ended up as a mere *bufan*. Naturally, the syllabically-challenged *bufan* had to be pumped up again, this time by the preposition *an* 'on', to give *an-bufan* 'on by on up'. Later on, *anbufan* was ground down by erosion, and – to cut a long story short – ended up as the modest *above*. But it seems that a mere *above* doesn't soar nearly high enough nowadays, so we sometimes feel the need to reinforce it with 'up', to give *up above* – literally 'up on by on up'.

Let's see, how am I doing for time?

The Chairman looks at his watch and gives a rather terminal glance.

DE TROY: OK, I suppose I'd better start rounding things off. Now, I know you might say that silly little examples like 'up above' or *au jour d'aujourd'hui* are rather marginal. But the principles that they represent are by no means confined to the fringe of language. They are thoroughly mainstream. We can see similar cycles, for instance, with postpositions that first merge with the noun to become case endings, are then chiselled away altogether, and then a new round of postpositions can begin the process all over again. And ditto with auxiliaries, which are squashed on to the verb to become tense endings, then drop off completely, only to make place for a new wave of fusions.

So perhaps the easiest way of understanding these cycles of piling up, fusion and erosion is to imagine the forces that work on language as a kind of tireless compressing machine. Erosion keeps pounding at words, making them shorter and shorter. But shortened words are piled up into longer expressions, and the same forces of erosion then hack away at the pile, fuse the words and condense them into a more compact word once more. And so a new cycle begins all over again.

To return to my original theme of creation and destruction, what I tried to show was that erosion can bring about changes that are very different from the 'decay' that attracted so much criticism this morning. Erosion is not only a negative influence on language, which tears away and rips apart existing structures. In combination with the piling up of words, erosion is also a regenerative force that constantly creates new and leaner structures from overweight multi-word phrases. Erosion is a highly useful compacting mechanism which allows us to convey ideas faster and more efficiently. Erosion checks the excesses of expressiveness, just as expressiveness repairs the excesses of erosion.

JOURNALIST: Well, all this is beginning to make sense. But if it's all so straightforward, then I can't help wondering why it took linguists so long to cotton on to the idea. Didn't people like Schleicher know the examples you have just mentioned?

DE TROY: The funny thing is that they must have known about at least some of these examples, but they simply failed to grasp their significance, because they were so blinded by their admiration of the classical languages. Actually, there were a few linguists who were on the right track quite early on. Hermann Paul, for example, wrote as early as 1880 in perfect Bakunian spirit: 'That which one calls construction comes about only through decay, and that which one calls decay, is just the further continuation of this process.' But for most linguists, this didn't really sink in until much later. Even as late as 1933, Leonard Bloomfield, who was by all accounts a giant in the field, could write something that now appears astonishing in its short-sightedness: 'Merging of two words into one is excessively rare; the best-known instance is the origin of the future tense-forms in the Romance languages, from phrases of infinitives plus "have": Latin *amare habeo* "I have to . . . love" > French *aimerai* "I shall love" . . . This development must have taken place under very unusual conditions.'

JOURNALIST: And did it?

DE TROY: About as unusual as rain in Wales. If you want, I can give you countless examples, from any language under the clouds.

CHAIRMAN: Ahem, I don't want to put a dampener on things, but my watch tells me that we are beginning to run a little late. So unless there are very strong objections, I think we had better adjourn.

RSPEL MEMBER: But I still haven't had a full answer to the question I raised in the beginning, about the change between syntactic categories!

CHAIRMAN: I am terribly sorry, but I'm afraid we really do have to stick to the schedule. Of course, this does not mean that the discussion cannot be continued informally over the coffee-break. I am sure we could all do with some liquid refreshment to mull over the many mergers of words and acquisitions of endings we have been bombarded with this afternoon. But for the moment, I think all that remains is to thank Dr de Troy for unleashing his destructive powers on us today.

A round of polite applause.

Unfortunately, the ensuing discussion about syntactic categories cannot be transmitted during prime time, but interested viewers can follow it in Appendix A: Flipping Categories, on page 277.

6

Craving for Order

After the heated session in the conference room, welcome back to the studio. Having listened in on de Troy's disquisition on the merits of destruction, I must admit that it's hard to fault his argument that much of creation in language is just a by-product of erosion. If there is anything to quibble with, it is only with the ringing overtones of completeness. By trumpeting the forces of destruction, and boasting how much they can achieve, de Troy may have given the impression that erosion can account for *all* the elaborate structures in language. But here I beg to differ. Even though the forces of destruction can explain an enormous amount, they cannot account for everything. And some of the structures that erosion alone cannot explain happen to be among the most dazzling architectures found in the world's languages.

One striking example is an edifice which I mentioned in Chapter 1, the verbal system of the Semitic languages. You may recall that the root of a Semitic verb is not a pronounceable string of consonants and vowels, like English 'twist' or 'turn', but an abstract entity which consists excusively of consonants. Roots such as Arabic s-l-m 'be at peace' or Hebrew š-b-t 'rest' (*š* stands for the sound *sh*) come to life only when they are inserted into a 'template': a sequence of sounds with empty slots for the three root-consonants. The Hebrew template ◯*a*◯*a*◯, for instance, expresses the past tense (in the third person 'he'), so when the root š-b-t is superimposed on this template, it yields š*a*b*a*t 'he rested' (hence 'Sabbath' – the day on which 'He rested'). When the same root is inserted into other templates, it generates various other nuances of the verb. In the template ◯*o*◯*e*◯, for example, the root creates the form š*o*b*e*t 'he rests'; the template *hu*◯◯*e*◯*ta* yields *hu*šb*e*t*a* 'she was made to rest', and the template *na*◯◯*i*◯ gives *na*šb*i*t 'we will cause to rest' or 'we will bring to a standstill' (typically said by striking workers). These are just a handful of simple examples, but as I mentioned earlier, there are many dozens of such templates, through which the Semitic languages can express every conceivable nuance of the verb.

But isn't it possible that the forces of erosion alone could have created such a system? After all, haven't we just seen that the wear and tear of erosion can create finely laced structures like the French verbal system, with its criss-crossing of endings for different persons, tenses and other nuances? Why couldn't a structure like the Semitic verb have developed in much the same way? The fact is that while erosion can create endings – reams and reams of them – the structure on display here is of an entirely different order. What makes the Semitic verbal architecture so special is not so much the sheer bulk of the templates, but rather the remarkable idea behind their design, the system of tri-consonantal roots and prefabricated vowel templates. There is just no way that erosion on its own could ever have come up with such an abstract algebraic scheme, a conceptual design of roots that cannot even be pronounced, but which are superimposed on vowel templates to produce every conceivable nuance of the verb. In fact, if there is anything in language which still seems to cry out for a conscious invention, this is surely it. For if it was not invented, how could people ever have stumbled across such an unusual idea?

And yet, there is an alternative explanation. We do not have to call on a *deus ex machina* to account for the origin of designs such as the Semitic verbal system, nor is there any need to discern the guiding hand of an architect in their construction. The following pages will try to show that it is within our grasp to understand how abstract linguistic designs could have arisen of their own accord. But if there is to be any chance of success in this enterprise, then we cannot pin all our hopes on erosion alone. We have to call on another essential element, one which the previous chapters have rather neglected.

Chapter 2 mentioned a triad of motives for language's inner restlessness: economy, expressiveness and analogy. So far, however, only the first two of these motives have received much attention: economy, which causes the erosion in sounds, and expressiveness, which results in the inflationary erosion in meaning and drives the flow of metaphors from the concrete to the abstract. The role of analogy was acknowledged only summarily (in Chapter 4), as the cognitive mechanism behind our ability to find similarities between different domains, that is, our capacity for metaphorical thinking. Nevertheless, to understand how abstract designs can emerge in language, what will prove critical is exactly this overlooked third part of the triad, analogy, or the mind's craving for order.

This chapter thus sets out to redress the balance, and explore the power of analogy. Analogy will soon emerge as the main element of 'invention' in the course of language's evolution. Nonetheless, this type of invention does not spring from the design of any architect, nor does it follow any careful plan. The element of invention comes from thousands of spontaneous attempts by generation upon generation of order-craving minds to make sense of the chaotic world around them. And as we shall see, the force of such spontaneous innovations can sometimes accumulate to create imposing linguistic structures. By exploring the role of analogy in language change, we will also complete the survey of the central mechanisms of linguistic creation, and will thus be on course for our ultimate goal, projecting our findings onto the distant past in order to discover how the full complexity of language could gradually have evolved.

TO THINK IS TO FORGET A DIFFERENCE

In his story 'Funes the Memorious', the Argentinian writer Jorge Luis Borges tells of a man called Funes, who lost consciousness when he was thrown off a horse and after regaining it found that he couldn't forget anything he had ever seen or heard. 'He remembered the shapes of the clouds in the south at dawn on the 30th of April of 1882, and he could compare them in his recollection with the marbled grain in the design of a leather-bound book which he had seen only once . . .' But it is because of this unusual gift that Funes is incapable of any real thought – he is simply drowning in detail:

> It was not only difficult for him to understand that the generic term *dog* embraced so many unlike specimens of differing sizes and different forms; he was disturbed by the fact that a dog at 3.14 (seen in profile) should have the same name as the dog at 3.15 (seen from the front) . . . I suspect that he was not very capable of thought. To think is to forget a difference, to

generalize, to abstract. In the overly replete world of Funes, there were nothing but details, almost contiguous details.

Borges understood that the ability to pick out patterns, to draw analogies between unequal yet similar things, in short, to 'forget a difference', is at the very core of our intelligence. And the process of mastering a language is a good illustration of the role of analogy in enabling us to cope with an overwhelming amount of detail. As anyone who has tried to learn a foreign language will remember, the more order and regularity that can be picked out, the fewer the forms that need to be memorized individually. (An old German proverb says that keeping order is a crutch for those who are too lazy to search for things . . .) Were it not possible to extract any recurrent patterns from the mass of new information to be absorbed, our minds would simply be swamped by detail.

The ability to pick out patterns is not only crucial when learning a foreign language, it is just as vital to young children grappling with their mother-tongue. Babies do not imbibe their language with their mother's milk, they have to work out the whole darned system for themselves, and the mass of information they have to take in is mind-blowing. The burden becomes lighter, however, the more recurrent patterns they can identify. So it's no wonder that children act on the assumption that as much as possible in language should follow simple regular rules, hence cute errors such as 'I goed', 'my twoth birthday', 'foots', and so on. These mistakes are nothing other than perfectly sensible attempts to introduce order to corners of the language which happen to be quite messy and irregular. Sometimes, children even manage to outwit language's most basic principle of the arbitrary sign. Not content with the idea that words mean something only by convention, they find meaningful patterns in the most random of words. An oft-cited case is that of a toddling clever-clogs, who, when presented with a fork with only three prongs, studied it intently and quite naturally pronounced it to be a 'threek'.

Fork and threek

As they grow up, children gradually come to learn which areas of their language do not abide by regular rules, so that most of the errors are corrected: 'twoth' is replaced by 'second', 'foots' and 'mouses' by 'feet' and 'mice', and so on. All the same, if such errors do persist beyond childhood, they can sometimes gain ground, and ultimately overtake some well-established forms. I mentioned in Chapter 2, for instance, that the nouns *eye* and *cow* originally had irregular plurals *eyn* and *kine*. But at some stage, the 'errors' *eyes* and *cows* caught on, and eventually usurped the original forms.

While the most ear-catching mistakes are certainly those made by young children, analogical innovations can also come from grown-ups. Here is one recent example which is much more likely to have originated from the speech of teenagers than toddlers, but which is nonetheless based on very similar analogical principles. Some time in the early 1960s a new coinage made its way into British English, and quickly gained currency after featuring in the Beatles' film *A Hard Day's Night*. In one scene, a pompous advertising agent mistakes George Harrison for a 'focus group' participant, and asks for his opinion on some new designs of shirt:

AGENT: Now, you'll like these . . . They're 'fab' and all the other pimply hyperboles.

GEORGE: I wouldn't be seen dead in them. They're dead grotty.

AGENT: Grotty?

GEORGE: Yeah, grotesque.

AGENT: (to secretary) Make a note of that word . . . I think it's rather touching really.

So the adjective 'grotty' began as a groovy abbreviation of 'grotesque', a simple case of laid-back effort-saving. But at this point in the story the order-craving mind begins to make its presence felt. As the dialogue shows, the relation of 'grotty' to its forebear 'grotesque' was initially still transparent to all who used it. But before too long, the connection with 'grotesque' was forgotten and 'grotty' set itself up in its own right, as a word meaning 'dirty' or 'shabby'. And as it happens, the new word 'grotty' fitted neatly into a simple regular pattern in the language, whereby many English nouns give rise to adjectives through adding on the ending *-y*:

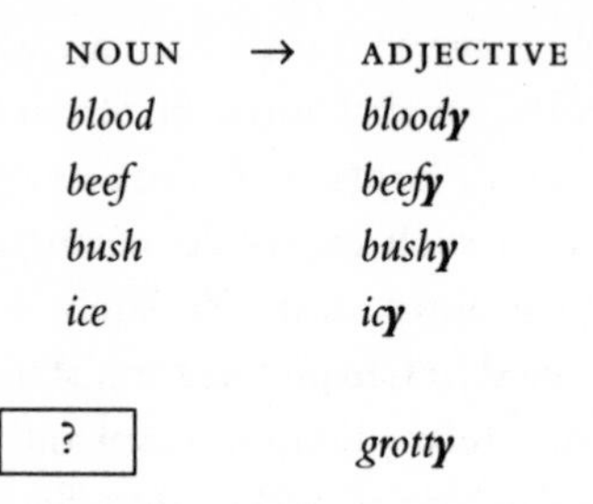

NOUN →	ADJECTIVE
blood	*blood**y***
beef	*beef**y***
bush	*bush**y***
ice	*ic**y***
?	*grott**y***

So some time around the early 70s, speakers made the following entirely reasonable inference: if adjectives like *blood**y*** and *beef**y*** are related to the nouns *blood* and *beef*, then what could the noun corresponding to the adjective *grott**y*** be, except . . .

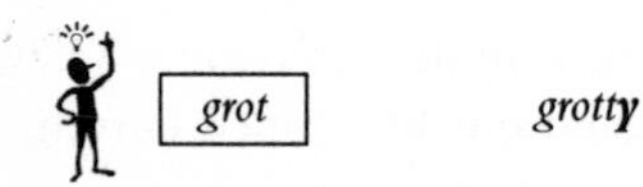

And thus the noun 'grot' was born, meaning something like 'dirt' or 'rubbish'. This new coinage seems to have been popularized by a BBC television series of the late 70s, in which a character called Reginald Perrin makes a fortune from a chain of shops called 'Grot' that sell goods with 'terminally built-in obsolescence'.

Linguists call the type of analogy that produced 'grot' 'back formation', because in terms of historical accuracy, it actually went backwards. Unlike 'bloody', for instance, which indeed had the noun 'blood' as its forebear, 'grotty' began life as an abbreviation of another adjective, 'grotesque'. (Of course, if one were to trace the ancestry of 'grotty' itself much further back, it would emerge that the adjective from which it sprang, 'grotesque' ultimately does go back to a noun, but a different one, *grotto*, meaning 'cave'. As far as 'grot' is concerned, however, this early history is beside the point.) From a historical perspective, then, 'grotty' did not owe its existence to a noun 'grot', and the analogy that produced 'grot' was incorrect. But the speakers who made this inference couldn't give two hoots about the historical perspective. All they did was recognize a pattern (NOUN+*y* → ADJECTIVE) and apply it, albeit in reverse, to a new adjective that seemed to fit, thereby making the adjective conform to the regular pattern.

Such an analogical back formation may seem rather strained at first, but inferences of this kind are extremely common, and the history of English provides dozens of other examples. The noun 'greed', for instance, emerged in the seventeenth century through exactly the same type of back formation, when speakers 'incorrectly' applied the pattern NOUN+*y* → ADJECTIVE to the adjective 'greedy', which did not have a noun counterpart at the time. New verbs can also emerge through such analogical innovations, when common patterns are applied in reverse. The pattern VERB+*or* → NOUN, for instance, creates many nouns from verbs: 'visit-or' (from 'visit'), 'govern-or' (from 'govern'), 'vend-or', 'survey-or', and so on. But in the eighteenth century the pattern was incorrectly applied backwards to the nouns 'editor' and 'legislator' (both of which came from Latin nouns), to create the new verbs 'edit' and 'legislate'. Who knows, perhaps at some stage in the future, similar back formations will make writers 'auth books', medics 'doct patients', and ships 'anch in harbour'.

Other back formations produced the English singular nouns 'cherry' and 'pea'. 'Cherry' comes from Old Northern French *cherise*, a word which happened to end with an *s* sound although it wasn't plural – just like 'cheese' today. In the fourteenth century, some speakers falsely assumed that *cherise* was an instance of the common pattern NOUN+S → PLURAL, so they applied this pattern in reverse, and produced the singular form 'cherry'. This must initially have sounded just as 'wrong' to educated speakers as 'one chee' would to us today. 'Pea' had a similar history, as it derives from an earlier singular 'pease' (which still survives in the set phrase 'pease-pudding'). But around 1600 'pease' was misinterpreted as a plural, and so 'pea' emerged as the singular form. Such back formations continue even now, as illustrated by the child who was overheard complaining that there was only 'one Weetabick' left in the packet.

All this goes to show that the course of change is determined not only by 'blind' effort-saving forces, heedless of all but the phonetic environment, but also by the craving for order of generation upon generation of speakers. The mind is constantly on the lookout for any signs of recurrent patterns, because the more regularity it can recognize, the easier its task of coping with the mass of linguistic detail it has to absorb. When the mind picks out a recurrent pattern, it naturally tries to extend it to whatever seems to fit. And since speakers rarely know (nor care) about earlier stages of the language, they can happily extend a pattern even to those forms which never had anything to do with it in the first place.

The birth of 'grot' was the outcome of one extremely simple sequence of effort-saving and analogy: a hip abbreviation followed by an extension of the pattern (NOUN+*y* → ADJECTIVE) to the 'inappropriate' 'grotty'. And it may require a considerable stretch of the imagination to believe that such a simple cycle could have anything to do with the creation of abstract linguistic designs, let alone highly sophisticated ones. And yet the following pages will argue that a series of similar cycles is capable of great feats. In particular, the interplay between erosion and analogy is what must have been behind the development of the Semitic verbal system.

Before delving into the verbal system of the Semitic languages, a few words about their cultural history are in place. The Semitic languages have a written history spanning more than 4,500 years. The original heartland of the Semites seems to have been the Arabian peninsula, whence Semitic-speaking tribes spread in different waves into large areas of the Near East and North Africa (see map on pages viii–ix).

The oldest known member of the language family is **Akkadian**, which is attested from around 2500 BC, and is thus one of the earliest written languages of all. (Only Sumerian and Ancient Egyptian can beat that record.) Akkadian was spoken in Mesopotamia, the land 'between the rivers', the Euphrates and the Tigris, in an area roughly corresponding to today's Iraq. The name of the language derives from the city of Akkade, founded in the twenty-third century BC as the imperial capital of the first 'world conqueror', King Sargon. Later on, after 2000 BC, Akkadian diverged into two main varieties, Babylonian in the south of Mesopotamia and Assyrian in the north, both of which were to become the languages of powerful empires. Speakers of Akkadian (both Babylonian and Assyrian) dominated the political and cultural horizon of the Near East up until the sixth century BC. Their political star may have waxed and waned, but for a good part of 2,000 years, Mesopotamian emperors, from Sargon in the third millennium BC to Sennacherib and Nebuchadnezzar in the first, would lay claim to the title 'King of the Universe', ruling over the 'the four corners (of the earth)'. More stable than the power of the sword, however, was the cultural hegemony of Mesopotamia over the whole region. The Akkadian language shaped the dominant canon for much of the Near East in religion, the arts, science and law, and was used as a *lingua franca*, the means of diplomatic correspondence. Petty governors of provincial

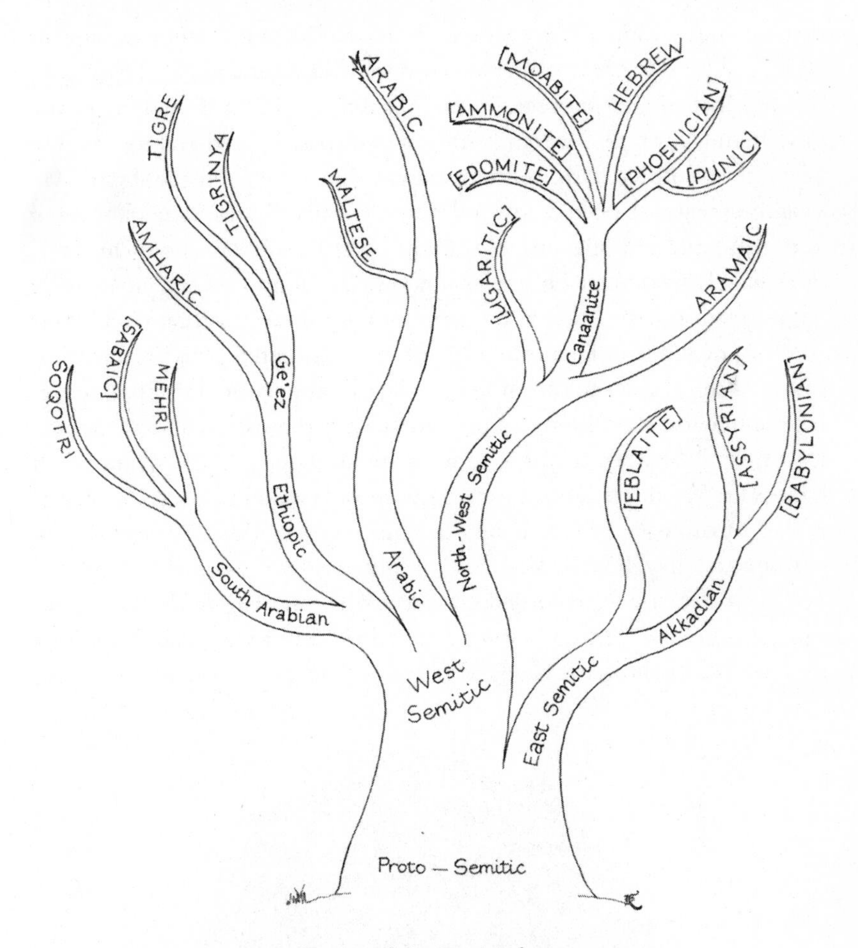

Family tree of the Semitic languages

Canaanite outposts, mighty Anatolian kings, and even Egyptian Pharaohs wrote to one another in Akkadian. Languages across the Near East also borrowed many scientific and cultural terms from Akkadian, a few of which may even be recognized by English speakers today. The Jewish expression *mazel tov* 'good luck', for example, is based on the Hebrew word *mazal* 'luck', which was borrowed from the Akkadian astrological term *mazzaltu* 'position (of a star)'.

But after nearly 2,000 years of cultural supremacy, the political demise of Assyria and Babylon in the sixth century BC ushered in an age of rapid decline, and within a few centuries both the Akkadian language and its writing system fell into oblivion. Hundreds of thousands of clay tablets, the product of two thousand years of civilization, lay forgotten in the desert sands for two more millennia, to be rediscovered and deciphered only in the nineteenth century. Since then, an almost unbelievable wealth of texts has been recovered from the soil of Iraq and neighbouring countries, and has opened up a unique perspective on one of history's greatest civilizations. The texts encompass almost every imaginable genre, from poetry (such as the Epic of Gilgamesh) to legal documents (such as the Code of Hammurabi), not to mention religious incantations, histories, royal inscriptions of heroic deeds, diplomatic correspondence, monolingual and multilingual dictionaries, mathematical and astronomical texts, medical treatises, and a seemingly endless quantity of administrative documents. One of the most revealing genres, however, is that of ordinary private letters dealing with quotidian subjects, from commercial haggling to domestic disputes. Here, as one example, is perhaps the first ever recorded endeavour to calm family tensions. This short missive was written in the twenty-third century BC, and shows that on some issues, little has changed in more than 4,000 years:

A letter from the Old Akkadian period,
twenty-third century BC

enma Babi ana Šārtim	This is what Babi says to Shartum:
aṣeḫḫammi	I'm very worried.
ana mīnim atti u Ibbi-ilum	Why do you and Ibbi-ilum
in bītim taṣa''alā	quarrel at home?
ištēniš šibā	Live with one other!
šamnam šūbilim	Send me (sesame) oil!

The other languages of the Semitic family are attested from a much later period. The next in line is the Canaanite branch of Semitic, which includes Hebrew and other closely related varieties such as Phoenician, Moabite and Ammonite. Some time in the second millennium BC, the Canaanites developed the first ever writing system for the common man, the alphabet. (Which group among them was the first to do so is still a moot point.) **Hebrew** was spoken by the Judeans and Israelites until the last few centuries BC, when it was displaced by Aramaic, but it survived as the religious and literary language of the Jews, and was revived in the twentieth century as the language of modern Israel. **Phoenician** was the language of the seafaring people of the Lebanese coastal cities Tyre, Sidon and Byblos. The entrepreneurial spirit of the Phoenicians is responsible, among other things, for the exportation of the Canaanite alphabet to the Greeks, and for the word 'Bible'. (The Greeks called papyrus-paper 'Byblos', because that was the city from which they imported this commodity. The word then assumed the sense of 'book', and thence 'The Book'.) The Phoenicians also founded various trading colonies in Europe and North Africa, one of which was Carthage (*Kart-ḥadasht* or 'Newtown' in the Punic dialect of Phoenician).

Another sibling in the Semitic family, **Aramaic**, has its roots in today's Syria. During the first millennium BC, Aramaic speakers spread across a much wider area, so that Aramaic eventually became the street-lingo in Palestine and even in Assyria and Babylon. In the sixth century BC, after the fall of Babylon, Aramaic even became the official language of the Achaemenid (Persian) empire. Some parts of the Old Testament, such as the Book of Daniel, are written mostly in Aramaic, and a later dialect, Syriac, became the vehicle of important Christian literature and exegesis. Varieties of Aramaic are still spoken in some towns and villages of Syria and Northern Iraq today.

Some famous speakers of Semitic languages. Clockwise from top left: Sargon of Akkade, the first 'World Emperor', twenty-third century BC (spoke Akkadian); King Solomon of Judah, tenth century BC (spoke Hebrew) and the Queen of Sheba (probably spoke South Arabian); Hannibal, Carthaginian general, 247–182 BC (spoke Punic, a dialect of Phoenician); Khalil Gibran, Lebanese-American poet, 1883–1931 (spoke Arabic); Emperor Haile Selassie of Ethiopia, 1892–1975 (spoke Amharic)

Classical **Arabic** is attested from a much later period, and is the language of the Qur'an (seventh century AD). Many words in European languages, especially those to do with science, medicine and mathematics were borrowed from Arabic. Notable examples are the words 'cipher' and 'zero', which through different routes both derive ultimately from the same Arabic word *ṣifr*, meaning 'nothing' (*ṣ* stands for the sound *ts*). The word 'algebra' is also a loan from Arabic *al jabr* 'the setting-together (of broken things)'. With the expansion of Islam, Arabic spread from the

Arabian peninsula to large parts of the Near East and North Africa, and is today spoken by around 150 million people.

Finally, on the southern tip of the Arabian peninsula, there are Semitic languages quite different from Arabic, which belong to another branch of the family. These are the **South Arabian** languages, one of which was spoken in the Kingdom of Saba (biblical Sheba). Speakers of South Arabian languages also emigrated to Africa by crossing the narrow straits between the Red Sea and the Indian Ocean, eventually giving rise to the Semitic languages of Ethiopia, such as Amharic and Tigré.

A MYSTERY IN FIVE PARTS

One might well imagine that with such a lineage – longer than that of any other language family – it would be a straightforward matter to discover how the Semitic verbal system came into being. Surely, all that one would need do is look carefully at written records from the last forty-five centuries, and observe 'in the act' how the verbal system gradually evolved. Alas, the reality is far less tractable, for when the Semitic languages stepped on to the stage of history in the third millennium BC, the characteristic traits of their verbal system, the consonantal roots and the abstract design of the vowel templates, were already fully in place. So although history dawned so early for the Semitic languages, the birth of their verbal system is nevertheless hidden deep in prehistoric darkness.

This does not mean, however, that all hope need be abandoned just yet. If we are prepared to settle for something less than absolute historical certainty, then the situation improves considerably, for we are lucky enough to have various fossilized relics embedded in the crevices of Semitic languages which can give vital clues as to earlier periods in the life of their verbal system. So by identifying these remnants and piecing them together, we can get a pretty good idea, at least in principle, of how the whole edifice could have arisen.

I invite you, therefore, on a historical mystery tour which will take us from Africa to Northern Europe, and from the present to as far back as eight millennia ago. The prize will be an understanding of how a system could have emerged which perhaps of all linguistic structures comes closest to defying the claim that language was never 'invented'. In order to reach this goal, we will rely on five major clues from the Semitic languages, as well as from languages closer to home. The first clue, the 'Quirk Vowel', will reveal the simple origins of the Semitic verb, and suggest that once upon a time the prehistoric ancestor of the Semitic languages must have had completely 'normal' verbal roots, pronounceable words containing both consonants and vowels. The second clue, 'Mutant Vowels and Hollow Verbs', will suggest that the first step which this ancient ancestor may have taken towards the root-and-template system was the change of just one vowel inside the root. With the third clue, 'Geese, Guests, and German Cardinals', we will draw on parallels from English and German in order to discover what may have caused this vowel mutation inside the root. The fourth clue, 'Revolving, Revolutions, and Revolutionizing', will suggest how verbs with exactly three consonants could have risen to dominance in Semitic. And finally, the last clue, 'Syncope and the Liberation of Consonants', will expose the cycles of erosion and analogy which must have hatched some of the vowel templates, and in so doing created the concept of a purely consonantal root.

But before setting off, a word of warning. As complex structures go, the Semitic verbal system is not easily out-complicated. So trying to uncover its origin does not make for light bedtime reading. The developments involved here are – to put it mildly – tricky, and getting to grips with them is not for the fatigued or faint-hearted. So if you wish, you can safely skip the rest of this chapter and jump straight to the next. But if you do stick with me, and go where many philologists fear to tread, the reward will be the satisfaction of cracking one of the hardest nuts in language.

CLUE I: 'THE QUIRK VOWEL'

In the complex systems of language, there is hardly any area that is entirely devoid of blots and blemishes, and the Semitic verb is no exception. For learners these irregularities can be a nightmare, but for linguists bent on uncovering the origin of the system they can be a godsend, as they can lead to dark undisturbed corners littered with ancient linguistic fossils, and thus provide vital clues to the earliest days of the verbal system. Perhaps the most conspicuous of all these irregularities is the 'quirk vowel', which at first sight seems to mar the clean lines of the verbal system. The language which gives the best idea of what this quirk vowel is about is the oldest sibling in the Semitic family, Ancient Akkadian.

Earlier on, I mentioned that the root of Semitic verbs contains only consonants, and that the vowels only belong to the templates that determine the verb's various nuances. Here are a few simple templates from Akkadian, where, as before, the fictional root ⓢ-ⓝ-ⓖ is used (with the fictional meaning 'snog') to stand for the three consonants of *any* root. The italicized sounds belong to the templates themselves:

aⓢⓝ*u*ⓖ	SIMPLE PAST:	'I snogged'
aⓢⓢ*a*ⓝ*i*ⓖ	PASSIVE PAST:	'I was snogged'
ušaⓢⓝaⓖ	CAUSATIVE FUTURE:	'I will cause to snog'
uⓢ*a*ⓝⓝ*a*ⓖ	INTENSIVE FUTURE:	'I will snog intensely'
ⓢ*a*ⓝⓖ*um*	VERBAL ADJECTIVE:	'(a) snogged (person)'

The table above looks neat and orderly, a perfect model of the abstract architecture one has been led to expect by all the brochures. But once on location, one doesn't need to search too hard to spot the first cracks in the walls. In particular, while it is generally true that the vowels in the Semitic verb are only there to determine the nuance, there is a verbal form which seems to flout this rule. In the table above, the first cell is shaded, because as it stands, the past tense template *a*ⓢⓝ*u*ⓖ only tells a part of the truth. To be more precise, I should have mentioned that while some roots indeed go with the template *a*ⓢⓝ*u*ⓖ in the past tense, there are also other roots that for the same nuance choose a different template, *a*ⓢⓝ*i*ⓖ, with an *i* between the consonants instead of a *u*. Two examples are shown below:

ROOT		SIMPLE PAST		
k-t-m	('cover')	*a*ⓢⓝ*u*ⓖ	*a*kt*u*m	('I covered')
p-t-l	('twist')	*a*ⓢⓝ*i*ⓖ	*a*pt*i*l	('I twisted')

At first sight, there doesn't seem to be anything especially untoward in the variation between *a*ⓢⓝ*u*ⓖ and *a*ⓢⓝ*i*ⓖ. After all, the entire template system is based on the use of different vowels between the root consonants, so one more vowel change seems neither here nor there. But the variation between *u* and *i* in the past tense is something of quite a different nature from the abstract design of the other templates. In the other templates, a change of vowel is used to make some grammatical distinction and mark a particular nuance such as tense or person. The variation here, however, does not play any grammatical role, since the change between the vowels *u* and *i* does not mark any different nuance of meaning: it doesn't change the tense, nor does it mark the verb as passive, intensive, or anything of the kind. The choice of vowel here is entirely arbitrary, and when you learn the language, you simply have to memorize which root goes with which vowel in the simple past, just as you have to memorize the gender of every French or German noun.

This arbitrary vowel in the past tense of all Akkadian verbs is what I have called the 'quirk vowel'. But what is such a random vowel doing in the middle of the root-and-template system, where vowels are only meant to mark the grammatical nuance? It is tempting to write off the quirk vowel as just a silly irregularity, whose only purpose is to mess things up and make life unnecessarily difficult for learners. But it turns out that there is much more to the quirk vowel than meets the eye. There is every reason to assume, in fact, that the quirk vowel is an extremely old feature, whose unruliness contains critical clues to the origin of the whole Semitic verbal system.

The first reason to suspect that the quirk vowel is a very old fixture in the system is its location. The quirk vowel does not crop up in fancy nuances such as 'I will cause to snog' or 'I was made to snog intensely'. Rather, it appears in the most basic and common nuance: the simple past 'I snogged'. And when linguists discover a situation where the simplest forms behave erratically, while more elaborate ones are better behaved, their suspicion is soon aroused, because the simplest and most common words are often those that have managed to cling on to ancient traits that have disappeared elsewhere in the language.

A good example of just that type of conservatism is provided by one particular English verb. In earlier stages of English, all verbs maintained a distinction between singular and plural in the past tense: he 'herde' but they 'herden' (see Chapter 3, page 94). In modern English this distinction has long been levelled out, so that verbs nowadays only have one form: he/they 'heard'. There is, however, a single but notable exception. Perhaps the most common verb of all, the ubiquitous 'be', has clung on to this long forgotten distinction, and it still shows a difference between 'he *was*' and 'they *were*'.

The reason why such frequent words can sometimes cling on to outmoded traits that have long been shed elsewhere in the language is their extreme familiarity. The most common words are heard so often that they can quickly become indelibly imprinted in the minds of new generations of learners, and thus withstand even drastic overhauls in the rest of the language. So when a certain trait is found only in the simplest and most common words or forms, there are good reasons to believe that this trait is a survivor from olden times. And since the quirk vowel in Semitic appears in the simplest and most common of the nuances, there is already fertile ground for suspicion that some very old feature is hidden behind the façade of irregularity.

What is more, it turns out that the quirk vowel is not just a whim of Akkadian, but that it crops up in other Semitic languages too. Consider the two corresponding verbs in Arabic:

k-t-m	('cover')	*a*kt***u***m
f-t-l	('twist')	*a*ft***i***l*

Arabic is not a descendant of Akkadian but a sister language (see tree on page 179), and thus could not have inherited the quirk vowel from Akkadian. This suggests that the quirk vowel is a feature with a very long pedigree, and that it was already in place in Proto-Semitic, before the Semitic languages had started diverging from one another, at the very least 5,000 years ago.

Still, even if the quirk vowel turns out not to be a random quirk after

*Arabic has weakened the original Semitic *p*'s into *f*'s, following a well-trodden path which has also been traversed by the Germanic languages (Grimm's law from Chapter 3). This is why the equivalent to the Akkadian root p-t-l appears in Arabic as f-t-l. What makes Arabic somewhat unusual, however, is the thoroughness of the change. Absolutely all the *p*'s in the language were weakened to *f*'s – no *p* was left unturned – so that Arabic is one of the few languages in the world which lacks the sound *p* altogether.

all, but a very ancient feature, how does it help us in our quest? Let us invent a simple thought experiment, and suppose for a moment that the only form of the Semitic verb that was known was this simple past tense with the quirk vowel. If we didn't know a thing about any of the other templates, and only had Akkadian forms like *aktum* or *aptil* to go on, would there be any reason to suppose that the Semitic verb was anything out of the ordinary? And would there be any grounds for suspecting that roots were made up only of consonants? Not at all. If the only evidence available was the simple past tense, the most convincing analysis would surely be that the verb *a-ktum* 'I covered' is made up of the root *ktum*, and a prefix *a-* ('I'), and that the verb *a-ptil* 'I twisted' is similarly made of *a-* and the root *ptil*. Just as vowels are a part of the root in English verbs like *stab*, *step* or *spit*, the most obvious explanation for the forms *a-ktum* and *a-ptil* would be that the vowels *u* and *i* belong to the roots *ktum* and *ptil*.

In fact, it wouldn't even be too difficult to draw up an explanation for how the prefix *a-* came to join forces with the root in forms like *a-ktum* or *a-ptil*. One could simply say that *a-* must have come from a pronoun which eroded and fused with the verb, just like the pronouns of colloquial French from the previous chapter, which coalesced with the verb to become prefixes: *je* + *aime* → *jem*. The Semitic forms could thus be explained along the same lines: an original pronoun 'I', which comparative evidence suggests started out as *ana*, was reduced to just *a* and fused with the verb:

ana	+	*ktum*	→	*aktum*
I		cover		I-covered
ana	+	*ptil*	→	*aptil*
I		twist		I-twisted

In short, if the only verbal form around in Semitic were the simple past tense, then there would really be nothing at all unusual about its design, nor about the 'quirk vowel' it contained. The most obvious explanation would simply be that this vowel had always been a part of roots like *ktum* or *ptil*.

By now, the aim of this thought experiment is perhaps becoming clearer. Since we know the 'quirk vowel' is such an ancient feature, the most likely explanation for why it is there is that it is a relic from a much earlier stage of the language, a time *before* the root-and-template system had started to develop. In other words, the best explanation for how the quirk vowel got to be there is that it was there all along. It must have been there even before the design of the consonantal root was dreamt of, when the ancestor language had roots which looked like *ktum* or *ptil*. Now, when a root is a pronounceable string of sounds like this, it is sometimes called a 'stem', so to avoid confusion, I will use the term 'ancient stems' from now on to refer to the roots in the prehistoric period, which still contained both consonants and vowels.

To sum up then, the distant ancestor of the Semitic languages must have had a fairly 'normal' verbal system, with stems like *ktum* or *ptil*. The irregular quirk vowel is simply a relic from that distant age – it is the original vowel of these ancient stems. At a later stage of the language, however, and in a way which remains for us to determine, the verbal system somehow underwent a complete transformation, through which those ancient stems gave way to the purely consonantal roots. The more elaborate templates in Semitic derive from that later stage, when the vowel of the ancient stem had been all but eliminated (remaining only in the simple past) and had given way to the abstract design of the purely consonantal root. So, for example, in the nuance 'I will snog intensely', only one template *u*ⓢ*a*ⓝⓝ*a*ⓖ is used with all roots, regardless of the 'quirk vowel' in the simple past.

From the point of view of the mature root-and-template system, therefore, the quirk vowel may look like an unmotivated irregularity, one that only detracts from the clean beauty of the architecture. But the quirk vowel allows us to peer back into the murk of prehistory, to a time before the consonantal root was even conceived. The simple past was such a common form that it acted as shelter, and managed to protect the quirk vowel from the drastic overhaul of the rest of the system.

CLUE 2: MUTANT VOWELS AND HOLLOW VERBS

What could have transformed the ancient stems, those pronounceable chunks with both consonants and vowels, into the abstract algebraic system of purely consonantal roots? Fortunately, there are some other relics strewn around the Semitic verb which give us clues about the early days of its evolution, and suggest that the thousand-mile march towards the root-and-template system may have started as early as eight millennia ago, with just one small step. A single 'mutation' may have developed in the vowel of the ancient stem, and assumed the function of a tense distinction, rather like in the English verbs *sit-sat* or *drink-drank*.

To uncover the traces of this early vowel mutation, we have to go scavenging among irregularities again, this time among verbs with an irregular number of consonants. I mentioned earlier that roots in the Semitic languages generally comprise three consonants. The qualifier 'generally' was necessary, because there are some roots, such as m-t 'die', which fall short of this regular pattern and have only two consonants. These verbs are sometimes called 'hollow', because what would have been their middle consonant is empty.

Now, in the simple past tense of Akkadian, these hollow verbs misbehave only mildly. Just like normal verbs like *a-ktum* or *a-ptil*, the hollow verbs show the quirk vowel *u* or *i* in the simple past, and so they deviate only in that they have one fewer consonant: *a-mūt* 'I died'; *a-nīk* 'I had sex'; *a-ṣīḥ* 'I laughed' (the hollow verbs tend to belong to the most basic level of vocabulary). When one moves to the future tense, however, one finds that the hollow verbs begin to misbehave much more wildly. The regular verbs form their future tense with an elaborate template (*a*-ⓢ*a*ⓝⓝ*a*ⓖ), but the hollow verbs have a much simpler future pattern: they simply change their 'quirk vowel' to *a*:

PAST		FUTURE	
a-mūt	('I died')	*a-māt*	('I will die')
a-ṣīḥ	('I laughed')	*a-ṣāḥ*	('I will laugh')

The behaviour of the hollow verbs in the future tense can be called ***a*-mutation:** the vowel of the ancient stem (*i* or *u*) changes to *a*. This behaviour is quite similar to that of English pairs like *sit-sat*, *spit-spat*, or *drink-drank*, only that in English it is of course in the *past* tense that the vowel changes to *a*.

At first sight, the hollow verbs may seem like just another eccentricity in the elegant architecture of the Semitic verb. Instead of conforming to the proper template for the future tense, the only thing they deign to do is change their single vowel to *a*. But these irregularities should not be dismissed too lightly, since there are once again good reasons to believe that the *a*-mutation is an extremely old pattern, a relic from the first steps that the ancestor of the Semitic languages was taking in developing the root-and-template system.

There are various clues within the Semitic languages themselves which suggest the extreme antiquity of the *a*-mutation, but perhaps the most compelling evidence comes from languages further afield. The Semitic languages are distantly related to some language families in Africa, including the Berber languages of Morocco and the Cushitic languages of Ethiopia and Somalia. Semitic, Berber and Cushitic are members of what scholars nowadays call the Afro-Asiatic language family. No one can say for sure when the Semitic branch of Afro-Asiatic started diverging from the Cushitic branch, but based on the linguistic distance between the languages, linguists believe that it must have been at the very least 8,000 years ago. While none of the other Afro-Asiatic languages has a root-and-template system like that of Semitic, many of them do show a suspiciously familiar vowel mutation between the tenses. In the Cushitic language Somali, for example, one comes across forms like these:

Somali (Cushitic, Afro-Asiatic)

imid	'I came'	*imādd*	'I (will) come'
īl	'I was in place	*āl*	'I am (/will be) in place'
iqīn	'I knew	*aqān*	'I (will) know'

In fact, using the evidence from such verbs in various Cushitic languages, linguists have come to the conclusion that in the ancestor language of Cushitic (and perhaps of other Afro-Asiatic branches) there was a vowel mutation from *u* or *i* in the past tense to *a* in the present/future tense. So it would seem that the *a*-mutation goes back even beyond the earliest stratum of Semitic, to a time before Proto-Semitic started diverging from Proto-Cushitic, probably at least 8,000 years ago.

The evidence thus suggests that the *a*-mutation is an extremely old pattern. But if this is so, then why is this mutation only found in a few exceptional hollow verbs? Why is it that the regular verbs form their future tense with an entirely different pattern (the template *a*-ⓢ*a*ⓝⓝ*a*ⓖ)? The most plausible explanation seems to be that the *a*-mutation was originally much more widespread, and was also the fashion among the normal three-consonant verbs. So, for example, the future tense of the verb *a-ktum* 'I covered' would simply have been *a-ktam*. But at a later stage, the *a*-mutation was displaced by the more elaborate future template (as a part of the general overhaul the system underwent with the development of the mature root-and-template system). The few Akkadian verbs that still show the *a*-mutation are just the last survivors, those which managed to hold out against the new template most obstinately. So even if from the later perspective of the mature Semitic system the *a*-mutation may look like nothing more than an unmotivated and rather embarrassing irregularity, the *a*-mutation was probably around long before the other templates had even been thought of.

Let's now put together everything we have uncovered so far: some time in the prehistoric period, the ancestor of the Semitic languages must have started out with 'normal' verbs, with sturdy stems like *mūt*, *nīk*, *ktum* or *ptil*, which had both consonants and vowels to their name. The first step in the evolution of the root-and-template design may have been taken as early as 8,000 years ago, when, for some strange reason, a vowel mutation emerged in the future tense: the vowel of the ancient stem changed to *a*:

ANCIENT STEM	SIMPLE PAST	SIMPLE FUTURE
ktum ('cover')	*a-ktum* ('I covered')	*a-kt**a**m* ('I will cover')
mūt ('die')	*a-mūt* ('I died')	*a-m**ā**t* ('I will die')
ptil ('twist')	*a-ptil* ('I twisted')	*a-pt**a**l* ('I will twist')

In itself, this mutation pattern may not seem such a huge leap forward. Nevertheless, the *a*-mutation is a defining moment in the evolution of the Semitic verbal design, since the kernel of a new concept has been formed, from which the notion of the consonantal root will later spring: the idea that a verb can keep the same consonants, but change the vowels between them to mark nuances like tense.

Now this is all very well, of course, but suggesting that the first step was the emergence of one vowel mutation still doesn't say anything about *how* this first step could ever have been taken. What could have galvanized the change of vowel in the future tense from *i* or *u* to *a*? The next clue will help us tackle exactly this question.

CLUE 3: GEESE, GUESTS AND GERMAN CARDINALS

The clues so far have relied mostly on evidence from within the Semitic language family, but in order to understand how the *a*-mutation could have developed, the best clues actually come from parallels much closer to home. Are there any familiar languages which have a pattern similar to the *a*-mutation? The first example that springs to mind, of course, is those English verbs like *sit-sat, drink-drank*, or German ones like *trinken-tranken*. Unfortunately, however, the origin of the vowel mutation in the Germanic verbs is also pretty obscure, as it goes back to the deepest strata of Proto-Indo-European. But we shouldn't give up on Germanic just yet, because there happens to be another pattern of vowel mutation in the Germanic languages, whose origin is more recent and thus better understood. Consider the following pairs:

ENGLISH	GERMAN	
goose – geese	*Gast – Gäste*	('guest – guests')
man – men	*Hals – Hälse*	('neck – necks')
tooth – teeth	*Nacht – Nächte*	('night – nights')
foot – feet	*Fuss – Füsse*	('foot – feet')

At first, messing around with a bunch of badly behaved Germanic nouns may seem rather a detour from the quest for the origins of the Semitic verb. Nevertheless, I promise that wandering through the thickets of Germanic philology will soon bring us to where we want to be. For whether in Germanic or Semitic, whether in nouns or verbs, our goal is to understand how a vowel mutation with a *grammatical* function can emerge. And once we have worked out how one vowel mutation has come to mark one grammatical function in one family, it will become much easier to grasp how another vowel mutation could have come to mark a different grammatical function in another family.

To see how the vowel mutation developed in the Germanic nouns, it is easier to start off with German rather than with English. Comparative evidence suggests that initially, there was nothing unusual about the noun *gast* ('guest'), and that its plural was simply **gast-iz* (*-iz* was a normal plural ending of Proto-Germanic). But at some stage before the earliest records of German in the eighth century AD, effort-saving mechanisms were set in motion and a few sound changes occurred. One was a type of assimilation (the 'Santa Siesta' principle from Chapter 3). In the word *gastiz*, there were two different vowels in close proximity, which required two very different configurations of the mouth. Moving the tongue quickly from a shape needed for an *a* {ah} to an *i* {ee} is really quite a bother, so to save effort, the first vowel *a* was 'coloured' by the *i*, and changed into something half-way between, namely to *e* {eh}. So *gastiz* became *gestiz*. Linguists call this process *i*-mutation, because the *i* caused the preceding vowel to change.

The final *z* of *gestiz* was also dropped at some stage, to give the plural form *gesti*, which is what we find in the first records of German in the eighth century. But the effort-saving spree did not come to an end right there. In the eleventh century, the final *-i* of *gesti* was weakened further to just a *schwa*, a reduced indistinct vowel (written ə in phonetic transcription) which can be heard in English words like *elephant* {eləfənt} or 'bother' {bothə}. And so *gesti* ended up as *gestə*, giving the pair *gast-gestə*. (In modern German orthography, *gestə* is spelled *Gäste*, but for simplicity, a phonetic spelling will be used here instead.) In other words, after the ending *iz* messed things up by changing *gastiz* to *gestiz*, this ending itself fell victim to the forces of erosion and disappeared, leaving behind a mere schwa.

So far, these two changes were entirely mechanical effort-saving devices. They had nothing to do with the *meaning* of the plural – in fact, they had nothing to do with any kind of meaning whatsoever. They were blind changes, influenced only by the phonetic environment. Nevertheless, the combination of these blind changes created the potential for a new meaningful pattern to emerge. The plural form *gestə* was stuck with an *e* in the middle (instead of the original *a*), but there was no longer anything to remind speakers of why this *e* had come to be there in the first place. The order-craving minds of a new generation of speakers could thus seize on the pattern *gast-gestə*, and assume that the change of vowel from *a* to *e* must be there for some purpose, and that purpose must be to indicate plurality.

And once the mutation from *a* to *e* was perceived to be a meaningful pattern, speakers could also extend it by analogy to other nouns, even those which from a historical perspective were not likely candidates. For example, the noun *hals* ('neck') originally had a different plural ending *-az*, so its plural form was originally **halsaz*, not *halsiz* – no reason for *i*-mutation there. If it were only down to effort-saving changes, then, the plural *halsaz* should have ended up as *halsə*. But the new generation of German speakers couldn't give a sausage about the 'historical perspective', so on the analogy of nouns like *gast-gestə*, they coined the pair *hals-helsə*:

gast *gestə*

hals *h?lsə*

hals *helsə*

Even newly borrowed nouns were subjected to this analogy. For example, the nouns *kardinal* and *general* entered German only in the thirteenth century, long after the original culprit for *i*-mutation (the ending *-iz*) had disappeared. But if the plural of *gast* is *gestə*, and the plural of *hals* has now come to be *helsə*, then what should be the plural of the newcomers *kardin**a**l* and *gener**a**l*, if not *kardin**e**lə*, and *gener**e**lə*? (In modern orthography, these are spelled *Kardinäle* and *Generäle*.)

To summarize, then, what created the pattern of vowel mutation (*a* → *e*) as a marker of plurality was a cycle of erosion and analogy. A sequence of effort-saving changes created the conditions for the appearance of this pattern (first, the ending *-iz* coloured the previous vowel *a* to *e*, to give *gestiz*, and then this ending itself was eroded out of all recognition, to leave just *gestə*). But it was not erosion on its own that turned these blind changes into a *meaningful* distinction. The grammatical function of the pattern was the brain-child of the order-craving mind.

In English, incidentally, the development initially ran along similar lines, except that it started a few centuries earlier than German. The noun *man* (originally *mann*) must have started with a regular plural form **mann-iz*, but then the effects of the vowel *i* changed the preceding *a* to *e*, giving *menn-iz*. Later, the final *-iz* was reduced, and was then lopped off altogether, leaving our present plural *men*. From this point onwards, however, English and German took rather different courses. In English, the pattern of vowel mutation never really took off, and was not extended and regularized to other nouns. It might be tempting to conclude from the comparison that the English mind was not quite as order-craving as the German, but in actual fact, the real reason for the difference was more mundane. In English, the mutation pattern was overwhelmed by a much more common plural pattern: the ending *-s*. So the mutation persisted only in a few very common 'exceptions', like *men*, and a small bunch of other erratic nouns.

Now I promised earlier that the Germanic nouns will land us exactly where we want to be. And just as a reminder of where that is: our ultimate aim is to understand how the architecture of the Semitic verb, with its abstract design of purely consonantal roots and vowel templates, could ever have evolved of its own accord. The first clue revealed that the ancestor of the Semitic languages must have had a fairly 'normal' verbal system, with pronounceable stems like *ktum*, *ptil* or *mūt* which had both consonants and vowels. I then suggested that the whole imposing edifice of the Semitic verb may have arisen from rather modest beginnings: the emergence of just one vowel alteration, which I called *a*-mutation. The vowel *u* or *i* of the ancient stem changed to *a* in the future tense, thus giving rise to pairs like *akt**u**m-akt**a**m* 'I covered-I will cover', *am**ū**t-am**ā**t* 'I died-I will die', and so on. The reason why we then got involved with the Germanic nouns was to find out how such a mutation could have developed in the first place, and how it could have assumed a grammatical function (in the Semitic case, of a future tense).

By now, it should be clear that we have arrived exactly where we wanted to be. The *a*-mutation in Semitic verbs must have developed along similar lines to the *i*-mutation in Germanic nouns. Of course, the details would have been quite different. For one thing, the *a*-mutation in Semitic could never have arisen from an ending like *-iz*, for the simple reason that an *i* cannot colour the vowel *u* (of *akt**u**m*) into an *a* (*akt**a**m*). Nevertheless, the principle must have been just the same: a cycle of erosion and analogy. Some culprit or other must have caused the vowel to change in the future tense, and must later have vanished as a result of further effort-saving changes. Speakers then came to perceive the vowel alteration as a meaningful pattern, and so extended it by analogy to other verbs. So what had started off as a series of blind effort-saving changes assumed a grammatical role – marking the future tense.

We will never know exactly what the culprit looked like in the ancestor of the Semitic languages. The *a*-mutation is simply too old for that. Nevertheless, one educated guess would be that the culprit in question may not have been a vowel, but rather some consonants, none other, in fact, than the 'laryngeals' which we met in Chapter 3 in relation to Saussure's celebrated hypothesis about the vowel system of Proto-Indo-European. In Indo-European, a laryngeal sound caused the vowel *e* in its vicinity to change to *a*, and then disappeared from the scene. In Semitic, laryngeal sounds are still around, and it may well be that they were responsible for the effort-saving change that kicked off the *a*-mutation. (Appendix B: Laryngeals Again? on page 286 suggests one scenario for how this might have happened.) But for now, since the general principles are clear, we can move on to find out how the idea of the consonantal root could have taken off from there.

CLUE 4: REVOLVING, REVOLUTIONS AND REVOLUTIONIZING

From what we have gathered so far, the first step towards the notion of a purely consonantal root may have been the rise of just one vowel mutation, which changed the vowel of the stem to *a* in the future tense. Of course, the pattern of one vowel mutation is still quite simple, but it is nevertheless a crucial cornerstone for the new concept of a purely consonantal root. The mutation inside the stem rocks the foundations of the old idea that the stem vowel is a permanent fixture, and presents this vowel not as an immutable constant, but rather as a variable whose alterations can mark a grammatical function. The vowel mutation acquaints speakers with an innovative scheme whereby a change of grammatical nuance may be marked not only by adding a prefix or a suffix to the verb, but also by changing the vowel inside it. Clearly, then, the *a*-mutation is a move in the right direction towards the notion of the purely consonantal root.

There are now just two more steps needed to bring us from this simple *a*-mutation to the design of the root-and-template system. The first of these is understanding how a verbal landscape dominated by roots with exactly three consonants could have arisen. There is no reason to assume that three-consonant roots had always held sway in Semitic. In fact, as we have seen, there still are verbs with only two consonants around even in the historical era: those hollow verbs like *mūt* and *ṣīḥ*. Of course, by the time we can start observing them, these hollow verbs have become just a small minority of exceptions, but there are grounds for suspecting that in prehistoric times, there were more of these hollow verbs around. (There is no need to go into all the reasons here, except for mentioning that they are based on both internal considerations and on parallels from other Afro-Asiatic languages, which have more verbs with two consonants than with three.) So we cannot take it for granted that three-consonant verbs were the rule from the very beginning. And we first need to explain how three-consonant verbs could have come to dominate the verbal scene in the ancestor of the Semitic languages.

But why does it matter whether or not the verbal system is dominated by three-consonant verbs? The reason is simply that the mature Semitic templates all require a full set of three consonants to function properly. Whereas the ancient *a*-mutation is unaffected by how many consonants there are in the root (it works equally well with two, *amūt-amāt*, or with three, *aptil-aptal*), all the elaborate templates of the mature system have precisely three slots for the three consonants. Roots with only two consonants simply cannot fit into templates like ⓢ*a*ⓝ*i*ⓖ or *u*ⓢ*a*ⓝⓝ*a*ⓖ, as there just aren't enough consonants to go around. It seems unlikely, therefore, that these templates could ever have developed in the ancestor of the Semitic languages, before the verbal landscape came to be dominated by roots with three consonants.

So how could three-consonant verbs succeed in taking over the system, if there were originally at least as many verbs with two consonants as with three? Once again, parallels from more familiar languages can set us on the right track. One method by which longer verbs can enter the language is through the 'swelling' of older shorter verbs, a phenomenon which can be seen even in English today. Look at how the verbs below start out lean and fit on the left, but then put on more and more weight as they move rightwards:

VERB →	NOUN →	(ADJECTIVE) →	VERB
(to) tail ('cut')	(a) tailor		(to) tailor
(to) compute	(a) computer		(to) computerize
(to) revolve	(a) revolution		(to) revolutionize
(to) profess	(a) profession	professional	(to) professionalize

What is going on here is a sort of cycle, from verb to noun and then back to verb again. An ending is used to turn a verb into a noun, and then another ending can turn this noun back into a verb, by which time the word has swollen with endings. Similar cycles can be seen in the Semitic languages, but there, the swelling tends to come from prefixes instead. And there are good reasons to think that many such cycles also took place in prehistoric times, so that verbs which started out with only two consonants swelled to three. One such cycle may have looked something like this:

VERB →	ADJECTIVE →	VERB
pil?	*ša-pil*	*a-šapil*
lie?	low-lying, lowly	I became low, I humbled myself

Let's assume that a prehistoric verb such as *pil*, perhaps meaning 'lie', was turned with the aid of a prefix *ša-* into an adjective *šapil*, meaning 'low-lying', and then the adjective was itself converted into a new verb *a-šapil*, 'I became low'. (Incidentally, in real life, adjectives in Semitic generally appear with case endings, so the adjective *šapil* would actually look something like *šapil-um*. We needn't bother with this case ending just for the moment, but it should not be forgotten altogether, since it will become relevant later.)

Of course, this is not the only way that new swollen verbs could have entered the language, but there is no need to get swamped by the details. What really matters for us is only that three-consonant verbs could have increased and multiplied with time, while some of the older hollow verbs gradually sank into oblivion, as old words often do. And so at some stage the sheer numbers tipped over the balance, and three-consonant verbs began to dominate the scene. They came to be perceived as the norm, while the old hollow verbs remained only as exceptions.*

CLUE 5: ON SYNCOPE AND THE LIBERATION OF CONSONANTS

We have already gained significant ground in our foray on the stronghold of the Semitic verb. Behind us is the knowledge of how one vowel mutation could have assumed the grammatical function of marking the future tense, and how a landscape dominated by three-consonant verbs could have developed. And yet, although we have now reached the final stage, the architecture of the Semitic verb still seems alarmingly distant. In particular, our one simple vowel mutation is still a long way from the mature system with its multitude of templates and nuances.

Nevertheless, we are much closer than may first appear, at least to the fundamental design of the Semitic verb, the purely consonantal root. We are in fact just a stone's throw away, for in order to understand how the idea of the consonantal root was conceived, we don't really need all those dozens of fancy templates like 'I will cause to snog' (*ušaⓢⓝaⓖ*) or 'she keeps on snogging intensely' (*uⓢtanaⓝⓝaⓖ*). To capture the essence of the root-and-template system, all that is required are a handful of the simplest templates, like the three below:

aⓢⓝiⓖ	PAST	'I snogged'
aⓢⓝaⓖ	FUTURE	'I will snog'
ⓢaⓝⓖum	VERBAL ADJECTIVE	'(a) snogged (person)'

*Incidentally, in modern Hebrew the process of swelling seems to be entering a new stage, since today, many verbs with four consonants are emerging in the language, through a similar process. For example, a verb ḥašev 'compute' is made into a noun *ma*-ḥšev 'comput-er', and this in turn is made into a verb again *e*-ma-ḥšev '(I will) comput-er-ize'. The original verb had three consonants ḥ-š-v, but the new one has four: m-ḥ-š-v. Many other new verbs are appearing in this way, and the number of four-consonant roots is now growing.

I suggest that if we can explain how just these three templates arose, the notion of a purely consonantal root will fall out for free. And there is even better news in store, since the first two templates have already been derived. We have hypothesized that some cycles of erosion and analogy must have created the *a*-mutation as a marker of the future tense, and that this *a*-mutation originally applied not only to the hollow verbs, but to three-consonantal verbs as well, producing pairs like *aptil* ('I twisted') and *aptal* ('I will twist'). But the templates *a*ⓢⓝ*i*ⓖ and *a*ⓢⓝ*a*ⓖ are really just a different way of showing exactly the same pattern of *a*-mutation more generally. So in fact, we are now really only one template away from the target. If we can only manage to explain the origin of the third template above, the verbal adjective ⓢ*a*ⓝⓖ*um*, then the consonantal root will be within spitting distance.

But what is so special about ⓢ*a*ⓝⓖ*um* anyway, and what makes it so different from *a*ⓢⓝ*i*ⓖ or *a*ⓢⓝ*a*ⓖ? The real novelty about ⓢ*a*ⓝⓖ*um* is the vowel *a* between its first two consonants. The verbal adjective deviates from the pair *a*ⓢⓝ*i*ⓖ and *a*ⓢⓝ*a*ⓖ, because in these the first two consonants behave as an inseparable cluster, much like in the English verbs *spin*, *drink* or *spring*:

[sp]-i-n	[sp]-a-n
[spr]-i-ng	[spr]-a-ng
a[ⓢⓝ]-i-ⓖ	a[ⓢⓝ]-a-ⓖ

The English verbs have three (or even more) consonants, but these always stick together in two groups. The vowel between the clusters may change, to give forms like *spin*, *span* or even *spun*, but one never gets forms like *sapin*, *supun* or *sapnum*. In ⓢ*a*ⓝⓖ*um*, however, a vowel has somehow slipped into the first cluster, so that its two consonants have been 'liberated' from each other. What remains to be explained, then, is how the vowel *a* could have made its way into the cluster ⓢⓝ of ⓢ*a*ⓝⓖ*um*.

What type of process could inject a vowel into a cluster of consonants? Of course, it would be much easier to understand a change in the other direction, and explain how a vowel was *dropped* from between two consonants – after all, erosion can do that sort of thing blindfolded before breakfast. But the opposite is a different matter, as it is far less easy to find a process that can take a vowel, insert it between two consonants, and even lend it a grammatical function. The only thing that can pull off that type of change is – once again – a cycle of erosion and analogy, the interplay of blind changes with the mind's craving for order.

The effort-saving change that was needed to start this cycle was actually quite straightforward. It is what linguists call 'syncope': the dropping of a vowel in the middle of a word. The effects of syncope are evident in English words like *ever-every* or *radical-radically*. The orthography may still represent the vowels in the second element of the pairs, but spoken language has long since dropped them, and they are simply pronounced {evry} and {radicly}. When there are too many short vowels in a row, there is just a great temptation to dispense with one of them.

To see what syncope can get up to in our case, let's go back to where we left off with the prehistoric ancestor of the Semitic languages. There are now two kinds of three-consonant verbs around. On the one hand there are those old verbs, scions like *a-ptil* ('I twisted'), which always had three consonants. But on the other hand there are those newly swollen upstarts like *a-šapil* ('I became lowly'), which acquired their third consonant only more recently, from the prefix *ša-*. Now imagine that syncope is unleashed on the language, and that it eliminates the middle vowel whenever there are three short vowels in a row. (This kind of syncope has actually occurred very often in the history of Semitic.) What effects does the syncope have on the two classes of stems? The old class of verbs remains unaffected, since *a-ptil* only has two vowels. But for the upstarts, the situation looks rather different: *a-šapil* has three short vowels in a row, and is thus a candidate for syncope. So the middle vowel is dropped, to give just *ašpil*.

What's more, the syncope doesn't even stop there. We saw that *a-šapil* was born from an adjective *šapil* 'low'. But as I mentioned earlier on, in real life the adjectives take case endings such as *-um*, and together with the case ending, the adjective *šapil-um* is itself a candidate for syncope, because it has three short vowels in a row. So the middle vowel is dropped, to give *šaplum*. The effects of syncope on the adjective and the verb that emerged from it are summarized in the diagram:

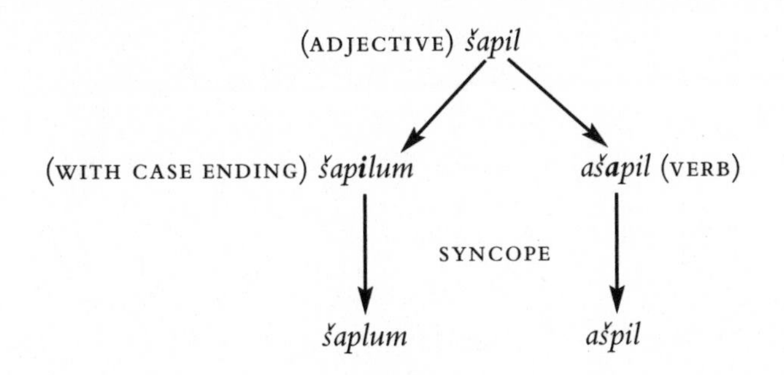

So far, this was simply a blind effort-saving spree, an instance of syncope that eliminated the middle vowel from a series of three vowels in a row. But now it's the turn of the order-craving mind. The system that new generations of speakers are faced with is quite different from the earlier stratified society, because the syncope has levelled out some of the old 'class distinctions'. For the upwardly-mobile verb *a-špil*, the change has really been quite a boon. Once syncope has removed from *a-šapil* the give-away vowel of the original prefix *ša*, the verb *a-špil* has become almost indistinguishable from the older verbs, scions such as *a-ptil*. So once the syncope has been and gone, and after any memory of the earlier distinctions has all but faded, the former upstarts display a peculiar pattern: the adjective from which they were derived retains the give-away *a*, but in the past tense, this *a* has been forgotten. So the following pattern comes to be established in speakers' minds:

ADJECTIVE	→	PAST TENSE
šaplum 'low'		*a-špil* 'I became low'

We, as linguists, may recognize that this pattern is the result of an intricate series of historical developments. We know that the vowel *a* in the adjective *šaplum* originally came from a prefix *ša-*, and that blind syncope did away with this ***a*** in the past tense of the upstarts. But the new generation of speakers have no idea about any of this. They simply discern a pattern where an adjective has a vowel *a* between the first two consonants whereas the past tense does not have it. And once speakers recognize this pattern, what could be more natural than to try to extend it to other verbs?

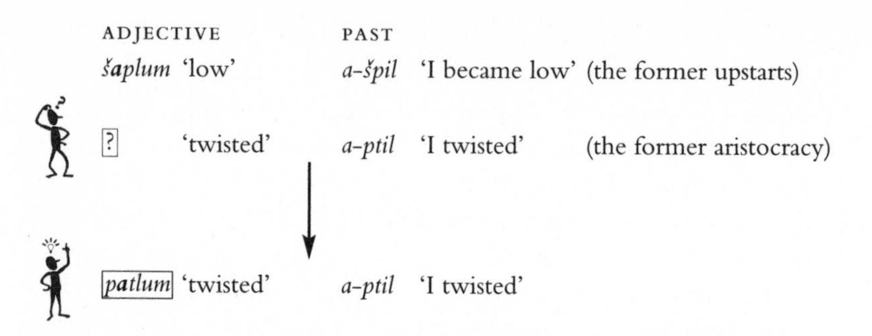

And so the scene is set for back formation. The new generations have no idea about the old distinctions of the past. They don't know that from a historical perspective, this pattern (ADJECTIVE: ◯*a*◯◯*um* → PAST TENSE: *a*-◯◯*i*◯) should apply *only* to those upwardly-mobile verbs that had sprung from adjectives. The new speakers simply extend the pattern (in reverse) to anything else that seems to fit: if the adjective corresponding to *ašpil* is *šaplum*, then what should be the adjective corresponding to *a-ptil*? It must be *patlum*, of course.

The back formation that created *patlum* does not seem anything out of the ordinary. But in extending and regularizing the pattern, speakers have introduced two major innovations. First, they have created a 'verbal adjective' – an adjective derived from a verb, rather than vice versa. And second, the speakers have liberated the two initial consonants of the old class of three-consonantal verbs, and inserted an *a* in between the two consonants of the initial cluster *pt* of *ptil*. What is more, this new vowel is not there simply for decoration – it has a meaningful grammatical purpose, to mark the verbal adjective. And so, all three consonants have achieved independence.

We are nearly there. At the stage we have arrived at (still somewhere in prehistory), there are now three different forms for each verb, as shown below. (The three dots in the past and future tenses stand for the person markers, the prefixes *a*- 'I', *ni*- 'we', and so on.)

(ANCIENT STEM)	PAST	FUTURE	VERBAL ADJECTIVE
(*ptil*) 'twist'	. . .-***ptil***	. . .-***ptal***	*patlum* 'twisted'
(*šapil*) 'become low'	. . .-***špil***	. . .-***špal***	*šaplum* 'low'

The only thing still missing is the idea of the purely consonantal root. But in fact, this idea is already inherent in the system we have reached. In the table above, I still included the ancient stem with its original vowels, but in some sense, this is already an anachronism. For when one examines the three different forms of the verb that are now in use (past, future and verbal adjective), it transpires that the only thing left in common to all three are the consonants. None of the stem's original vowels appears in all three forms any longer. The vowel *i* of *ptil* and *šapil* has only survived in the past tense, and the vowel *a* between the first two consonants of the former upstart *šapil* has only survived in the verbal adjective.

Now the bare stem never crops up in speech on its own – the forms that speakers actually use are the past, the future, and the verbal adjective. Since new generations of speakers can no longer even recognize the stem from the verbal forms they do use, and since they can no longer discern the vowels of the original stem as a common denominator, all that has remained in their perception as a uniting factor between the different verbal forms are the three consonants. For new speakers faced with this set-up, what bears the core sense 'twist' is no longer a pronounceable chunk *ptil*, but only the three consonants `p-t-l`. And at this point, it really makes sense to start talking about 'consonantal roots' such as `p-t-l` or `š-p-l`. So it would actually be more appropriate to present the table above in a different way, with consonantal roots and vowel templates:

CONSONANTAL ROOT	PAST	FUTURE	VERBAL ADJECTIVE
p-t-l	...-pt*i*l	...-pt*a*l	p*a*tl*um*
š-p-l	...-šp*i*l	...-šp*a*l	š*a*pl*um*
ⓢ-ⓝ-ⓖ	...-ⓢⓝ*i*ⓖ	...-ⓢⓝ*a*ⓖ	ⓢ*a*ⓝⓖ*um*

So we have finally extracted the essence of the Semitic verbal system! The system we have now arrived at is still quite simple, and does not fully correspond to the situation in the attested period in Akkadian (when the future tense of regular verbs was formed by the more complex template *a*ⓢ*a*ⓝⓝ*a*ⓖ). But what we do have now is the notion of a purely consonantal root and the basis for the vowel templates. The root-and-template design is really just a way of representing the pattern which has now emerged, whereby the vowels are determined by the grammatical nuance, and not by the whim of the stem. The three verbal forms we have derived are thus sufficient to kindle in speakers' perception the idea behind the root-and-template system. They show that the notion of a purely consonantal root need not have been sparked by any celestial flash of inspiration. All that was required to create this remarkable design was a fairly down-to-earth, albeit rather uncommon set-up: the emergence of a few verbal nuances which all share the same consonants, but no longer share any vowels. The vowels of the original stem must have lost their place in speakers' perception as a distinguishing feature for the core meaning of the verb (such as 'twist' or 'die'), and so they came to be viewed only as marking the grammatical nuance (past, future, and soon). And thus the idea of a purely consonantal root was born.

I want to know God's thoughts.
The rest are details . . .
(Albert Einstein)

At the beginning of the chapter, the structure of the Semitic verb seemed way beyond anything that the haphazard forces of change could have created by their own devices. It almost defied belief that such an algebraic design could have come about unless it was invented in some state-of-the-art language-planning laboratory. But after ransacking the rubble of ancient forms, we have now managed to understand, at least in principle, how such a scheme could have emerged through various cycles of erosion and analogy. In working out how, it is fair to say that we have cracked one of the toughest nuts that language has to offer.

Of course, it would be foolish to pretend that with the three simple templates above, everything has been accounted for. Far from it – there are dozens of templates which I have not even mentioned, and even those examples we did touch upon were simplified to a degree that would make many philologists cringe. But all along, the watchword was 'in principle' – and in principle, we now know how something as unlikely as the root-and-template system could have come into being. The rest are details . . .

If you want to find out more about those details, you can turn to Appendix C: The Devil in the Detail (page 289), which sketches how some of the fancier templates could have evolved. But if you are happy to stick with the principles, then there is only one further point that should be made here, and this has to do with how the template system could have burgeoned in complexity. I mentioned that there are many dozens of templates in the mature Semitic system, but only a handful were considered above, and each of these few had its own story to tell, as it arose through its own cycle of erosion and analogy. From this description, one could easily fall under the impression that every single template of the many dozens in the mature system had to emerge autonomously, through its own personal cycle of erosion and analogy, and without any interference from the other templates. So it would have to be by some spectacular fluke that all those dozens of cycles somehow coincided in one and the same language, and thus yielded the elaborate system with its many scores of templates.

But that would be quite the wrong way to look at it. The point is that once a few templates begin to emerge, speakers can start forming 'higher-level' analogies, by superimposing existing templates on one another. So when one nuance emerges in one tense, for example, new templates for the same nuance can be formed by analogy in all other tenses. Moreover, different nuances can also interlock. So, for instance, Appendix C explains how modern Hebrew has recently coined a rather recherché template, the passive of the reflexive ('he was made to snog himself'), by superimposing a passive template on a reflexive one. Similar processes could have occurred in prehistory, so that when one new nuance emerged, it could have interacted with all the others in a grid-like way, and have set off a whole row of new templates. The increase in the complexity of the system is thus a self-amplifying process, and once a critical mass of templates had developed, there could have been an explosion in the number of new templates, leading to the dozens around in the attested languages.

Finally, it is time to draw breath and reflect on what has been achieved so far. This chapter has shown that in the course of language's evolution, the effects of erosion often interact with the mind's craving for order. Language needs to be learned afresh by each new generation of speakers, and with each new generation the system is subjected to speakers' constant search for regular patterns. The vagaries of erosion can randomly give words a myriad of new shapes, some of which may by sheer coincidence contain elements that can be seized upon by the order-craving mind. And when speakers spot such patterns, they misconstrue these randomly produced elements as meaningful and can thus extend them by analogy to anything else that seems to fit. So, for instance, a haphazard sequence of effort-saving changes (which had nothing whatsoever to do with meaning) turned the German plural noun *gastiz* to *gestə*. But later generations of order-craving minds thought they spotted a pattern in pairs like *gast-gestə*, and presumed that this pattern must be there for some purpose – marking plurality. In consequence, they extended this model to other nouns, creating a more regular pattern.

If there is any element of invention in language, then this is surely it. But this invention is not the design of any one architect, nor does it follow the dictates of any master plan. It is the result of thousands of small-scale spontaneous analogical innovations, introduced by order-craving minds across the ages. So while language may never have been invented, it was nonetheless shaped by the attempts of generations of speakers to make sense of the mass of details they have to absorb. And as this chapter has revealed, the power of analogy can raise grand structures, even those which at first seemed most defiantly to bear the hallmark of a conscious designer.

By exploring the power of analogy, this chapter has rounded off the survey of the central mechanisms of linguistic creation. We have met the main motives behind the changes, and the major processes through which new grammatical structures arise in language: the compressing cycles of erosion and expressiveness, and the creative cycles of erosion and analogy. The last three chapters have also gathered a sizeable assortment of grammatical specimens, and have uncovered the origin of diverse types of linguistic structure in the recent and less recent past, from the Latin case system to the tense and person markers on the French verb, from Ewe prepositions to English auxiliaries, and from constructions of possession to anaphoric reference (pointing in the space of conversation). And so we are finally ready to piece together all these findings into a coherent whole, project them on to the remote past, and conjecture how, from very modest beginnings, the full complexity of language could have evolved.

7

The Unfolding of Language

girl fruit pick   turn   mammoth see
girl run   tree reach   climb   mammoth tree shake
girl yell yell   father run   spear throw
mammoth roar   fall
father stone take   meat cut   girl give
girl eat   finish   sleep.

This story may not scale the highest peaks of eloquence, but you should have had little difficulty following it. Even if its expressive scope is rather narrow, it nevertheless manages to convey quite a detailed sequence of events. What is more, its style has one striking advantage over a story in ordinary English: speakers of any language would be able to follow it without any problem, as long as they understood the meaning of each word. To make the story comprehensible, all you need to do is look up the corresponding words in any given language and, blithely ignoring the niceties of grammar (tenses, particles, cases, prepositions, conjunctions and the like), place the words in exactly the same order as they appear here.

The reason for this universal transparency is that the way this tale was articulated (in the literal sense of 'joined') does not rely on any rules peculiar to English, or to the grammar of any other particular language. Instead, the words are strung together according to a few natural principles, which are rooted in the deepest levels of our cognition. And as such, a story much like this one could have been told by our remote ancestors in the distant past, in what I have referred to loosely as the 'me Tarzan' stage of language evolution.

Of course, compared to this pared-down story-telling style, modern languages allow their speakers to relate even the same simple events with a remarkable wealth of detail and nuance. The paraphrase below may hardly be a torrent of eloquence either, but it nevertheless conveys the events on an entirely different level of sophistication:

A girl who was picking fruit one day suddenly heard some movement behind her. She turned around and saw a huge mammoth charging straight at her. She ran to the nearest tree and climbed up it, but the mammoth shook the tree so roughly that the terrified girl started yelling hysterically. Her father, who heard loud screams coming from the forest, realized that his daughter must be in danger, so he grabbed his spear and ran towards her. He threw his spear straight at the mammoth, which let out a blood-curdling roar and fell to the ground. With a sharp stone he cut some pieces of meat for the girl, who ate them up before falling fast asleep.

On the face of it, the gulf between these two versions of the story appears so wide that getting from the first one to the second may seem a hopeless undertaking. And yet I want to suggest that by now, we are very nearly there. The processes of creation explored in the previous chapters make it possible to sketch, at least in broad brush-strokes, how the elaborate features of the modern version could have arisen. To make the case for this claim, this chapter will embark on an imaginary fast-forward tour through the unfolding of language, starting from the 'me Tarzan' stage and proceeding all the way to the sophistication of modern languages.

Before setting off, however, the starting point I have chosen needs some justifying. One might well wonder why we have to start so late in the evolution of language, when there were already words for 'girl', 'tree', 'climb' and so on, as in the mammoth story above. Why not begin at the very beginning, when our hominid ancestors were coming out with their first meaningful grunts, and claim, for instance, that the earliest words were vocal accompaniments to hand gestures, or dream up another such plausible-sounding story? The problem with scenarios like these is that they don't really have a leg to stand on, as I argued in the introduction. Bones, shards and tools can tell us nothing about how the first words emerged, and they don't even say very much about when it happened. Moreover, there is no system of communication today (either among humans or among animals) that is in the process of developing its first articulate words, so there are no parallels from the present to go on.

Failing the discovery of a camcorder left behind by careless aliens on a previous visit, it is thus difficult to see how the first emergence of speech in hominids can ever be much more than the stuff of fantasy.

The evidence relied on in this book did not come from fossils or artefacts, but from the behaviour of language itself, as observed in the present and the attested period. As we have seen, this use of the present to recreate remote prehistory relies on the fundamental assumption that 'the present is the key to the past'. In other words, the underlying thesis is that the principles and processes of linguistic change in the distant past must have been similar to those that can be observed in action over the last 5,000 years or so. The method of reconstruction, therefore, is to project the present back on to the distant past and to assume, for instance, that the first grammatical elements emerged in distant prehistory through the same processes that have given rise to new grammatical elements in more recent times. This method is extremely powerful, of course, but it is also necessarily restricted in scope, since in applying it, we are confined to that portion of the past which the present really can unlock: the time when language already bore sufficient similarity to the present. So if we are to make the parallels plausible, we can start only when a few of the fundamental 'design features' of language were already in place.

Perhaps the most important characteristic of language which we must take as given is its symbolic nature: the use of arbitrary signs, which mean something only by agreed convention, not because they really sound like the object they refer to. We also have to assume that these arbitrary signs were conveyed vocally, using vowels and consonants which do not bear any meaning in themselves, but which derive their sense from being joined up into 'words'. (This method of combining meaningless sound-units into meaningful words is what linguists call 'duality of patterning' or 'double articulation'). And finally, we have to take it as given that these words were used essentially for the same purposes that motivate us today, not only to request things (water!), but also to convey information by making statements about the world ('mammoth fall'). All these features may appear self-evident and hardly even worth mentioning. But they are only so blindingly obvious because we are so blinded by familiarity. One only has to look at the communication systems of other animals to see that each one of these features was by itself already a huge achievement.

The 'me Tarzan' stage is the simplest level of language in which all these essential features are already present, and it is thus the earliest stage for which the present is still a key. Unfortunately, no one has any idea (or more accurately, too many people have too many ideas) about when exactly this point should be located in time: 40,000 years ago, 100,000 years, or even much earlier than that? For the purposes of our high-speed evolutionary tour, however, 'real time' doesn't really matter too much, because the point here is not to establish an exact chronology, but only to understand the general direction of development. So instead, this chapter will move in some sort of idealized 'linguistic time', in which the 'me Tarzan' stage will be taken as the zero-point: the earliest stage to which our method of reconstruction can be stretched, using the evidence that language itself provides.

Now it is all very well to say that the starting point should already have *some* words to go on – but which? I suggest that just three groups are sufficient as the initial raw materials: words for physical things (such as body parts, animals, objects, kinship terms like 'father'), words for simple actions (like 'throw', 'run', 'eat', 'fall'), and a third small group consisting of the pointing words 'this' and 'that'. We do not need to include at the starting point words for any abstract concepts, nor do we require any grammatical words and elements (prepositions, conjunctions, articles, endings, prefixes and the like). All these can subsequently develop from the raw materials in the three groups above.

Another point about this initial set-up with which one might want to take issue is the division of words into things and actions. Why should such a distinction be built into the system at the starting point? Shouldn't our evolutionary scenario actually account for it in some way? But it would be unreasonable to require our scenario to explain the emergence of the distinction between things and actions, since the conceptual basis for this distinction runs much deeper than language, and must have crystallized long before language was around. In order to have a 'mental representation' of who is doing what to whom, a clear distinction is required between objects and actions, and since this mental representation is a part of social intelligence that is well developed in non-human primates (and even in other animals), it must have been a fixture of our distant ancestors' cognition millions of years before language was even dreamt of. So in having separate words for actions and for things, language simply reflects a conceptual distinction that was already there.

(Incidentally, for reasons that will become clear later on, I will not use the syntactic labels 'noun' and 'verb' when describing our primitive language, and for the time being, I will only make a division based on meaning, between 'thing-words' and 'action-words'.)

A much more serious objection that can be raised against the proposed starting point of the mammoth story might run along these lines: it is all very well to begin with words, and even with separate words for things and for actions, but why start when our ancestors could already string these words together? How could the mammoth story combine words into a coherent whole, if it does not already rely on some grammatical principles? Doesn't the story rather beg the question, by presupposing the very rules of grammar that we are meant to explain? My rejoinder to these claims would be that the mammoth story was indeed put together according to some principles, but that these are not the principles of grammar as we understand them in modern languages. In particular, the story does not use any grammatical words or any other grammatical elements, and to achieve coherence it relies solely on one single strategy: the ordering of its words. Moreover, the choice of word order in the story is not based on the rules of English or of any other particular language, but rather stems directly from natural and transparent principles of coherence, which are deeply entrenched in the way humans perceive the world.

Terms such as 'natural' and 'transparent' principles of coherence may at first seem rather abstract, but what I have in mind is thoroughly down-to-earth. So before setting off on the main part of our tour, let us take a quick look at these natural principles, and assess how much of the mammoth story they can account for.

Monsieur Jourdain's Principle

The most important of the natural ordering principles seems so obvious that it's difficult not to take it completely for granted. The idea is simply that things which belong together in reality ought to appear side by side in language. It was no coincidence, for instance, that the following passage from the mammoth story read:

	(father. . .) *spear throw*	mammoth roar
Rather than, for example:	(father. . .) mammoth *throw*	*spear* roar
Or even:	(father. . .) *spear* mammoth	roar *throw*

In reality, the action of throwing involved the spear, and so the words *throw* and *spear* stick close together in language. And more generally, it is only natural that the word describing an action would appear close to the words referring to the 'participants' in that action. In fact, the combination of an action-word together with the central participants in the action is quite simply the core of the sentence in all languages. Some actions, such as 'roar', involve just one central participant, while others, such as 'throw', involve two: an ACTOR and a PATIENT (which is the linguistic term for the participant on which the action is performed, literally the one that 'suffers' the action).

Linguists call any reflection of reality in language 'iconicity', but this particular type of iconicity can be termed 'Monsieur Jourdain's Principle', because it is perfectly illustrated by that gentleman's natural flair for prose composition. When we last met him in Chapter 4, Monsieur Jourdain had just found out that he had been speaking prose for forty years without ever knowing it. Buoyed up by this discovery, he decides to write a short prose love-note to a 'lady of great quality', and asks his philosophy teacher for help with the composition. But he soon discovers that the help is not needed, because of his own natural eloquence:

M. JOURDAIN: I would like then to put into a note to her: 'Beautiful marchioness, your lovely eyes make me die of love,' but I want it put in a gallant manner and be nicely turned.

PHILOSOPHY MASTER: Put it that the fires of her eyes reduce your heart to cinders; that you suffer night and day for her the torments of a . . .

M. JOURDAIN: No, no, no. I want none of that; I only want you to say 'Beautiful marchioness, your lovely eyes make me die of love.'

PHILOSOPHY MASTER: The thing requires a little lengthening.

M. JOURDAIN: No, I tell you, I want only those words in the note, but turned stylishly, well arranged, as is necessary. Please tell me, just to see, the diverse ways they could be put.

PHILOSOPHY MASTER: One could put them first of all as you said them:
Beautiful marchioness, your lovely eyes make me die of love. Or else:
Of love to die make me, beautiful marchioness, your lovely eyes. Or else:
Your lovely eyes, of love make me, beautiful marchioness, die. Or else:
Die, your lovely eyes, beautiful marchioness, of love make me. Or else:
Me make your lovely eyes die, beautiful marchioness, of love.

M. JOURDAIN: But of all those ways, which is the best?
PHILOSOPHY MASTER: The way you said it:
Beautiful marchioness, your lovely eyes make me die of love.
M. JOURDAIN: I never studied, and yet I made the whole thing up at the first go . . .

Monsieur Jourdain's original formulation is the best, because what belongs together in reality also appears close together in the sentence. Take, for instance, the two pairs: *die-of love*, and **eyes-make**. Each pair groups together concepts that belong closely together in reality. In the original formulation, they also appear close to one another:

Beautiful marchioness, your lovely **eyes make** me *die of love.*

But in the philosophy master's versions, they become separated:

Of love to *die* **make** me, beautiful marchioness, your lovely **eyes**.
Your lovely **eyes**, *of love* **make** me, beautiful marchioness, *die.*
Die, your lovely **eyes**, beautiful marchioness, *of love* **make** me.
Me **make** your lovely **eyes** *die*, beautiful marchioness, *of love.*

Monsieur Jourdain's Principle seems so utterly obvious that you might be wondering why it needs so much attention. But the self-evidence of this principle only underlies how deeply entrenched it is in our cognition, and thus how crucial it is for making sense. It would not be an exaggeration to say that this is *the* single most crucial principle on which the whole structure of language is based. Take this principle away, and the whole towering edifice of language would immediately come tumbling down like a stack of cards.

Caesar's Principle

The second natural principle of ordering is also difficult not to take entirely for granted. The idea here is that the order in which events are expressed in language mirrors the order in which they occur in reality. This can be called 'Caesar's principle', because it is illustrated by that famous boast after his victory over King Pharnaces of Bosporus: *veni vidi vici*, 'I came, I saw, I conquered'. Why did Caesar use this order, rather than say *vidi vici veni*, for instance? Simply because in reality, he *first* came, *then* saw, and *then* conquered. (Linguists sometimes joke that he may on another occasion indeed have said *vidi vici veni*, but after a rather different type of conquest.) For the same reason, the mammoth story has the sequence 'girl fruit pick, turn, mammoth see . . .' because the girl *first* picked fruit, *then* turned around, and *then* saw the mammoth. Once again, this is a natural and transparent mapping from reality to language.

'Don't be a bore'

The third natural principle is concerned with which words need to be included in the narrative in the first place. The idea here is a variation on the familiar economy theme: what is either less important, or easily understood from the context, need not be (re-)stated. Suppose I had begun the mammoth story like this:

> . . . girl fruit pick girl turn girl mammoth see girl run girl tree reach girl tree climb

Even our distant forebears would surely have shouted me down for this repetition of entirely obvious information. There is no need to restate each time that it was the *girl* who turned round, the *girl* who saw the mammoth, and so on, because the listener can supply the 'missing' participants from the context. So it was enough simply to say:

> . . . girl fruit pick turn mammoth see girl run tree reach climb

Of course, speakers cannot always assume that the identity of the participants will be obvious to the listener. For example, had I not put 'girl run' in this sequence, it wouldn't be clear whether it was the girl who was running or the mammoth. As we shall shortly see, modern languages have devised effective means of keeping track of the participants without having to name them in full each time they are mentioned, by using pronouns like 'she' or 'it'. Still, even in modern languages, speakers rely to a considerable extent on the principle that whatever the hearer can pick up from the context may be left out of the sentence.

(And those speakers who neglect this principle often find that they only have themselves to talk to.)

'Me first' and 'actor first'

The three natural principles above already go a long way towards accounting for how the words in the mammoth story were strung together. But an important issue which they have not addressed is the order of words within each of the primitive clauses. Monsieur Jourdain's principle explains why the participants 'man' and 'spear', for instance, would naturally appear right next to the action 'throw'. But why 'man spear throw' rather than, say, 'throw spear man'? In the mammoth story, I used an order that accords with what seems to be a strong natural preference: mentioning the actor first, before both the action and the patient. One reason for this preference may simply be explained by Caesar's principle. Even if, strictly speaking, it makes no sense to say that 'man' comes before either 'spear' or 'throw' in reality (after all, these three describe one simultaneous event), there is still some sense in which the man, the instigator of the action, is perceived as prior to both the action and to the object that is merely affected by it.

The 'actor first' preference seems to be reinforced by natural tendencies of information flow, or in other words, preferences for how to convey information effectively. Earlier, I characterized simple sentences like 'father spear throw' as consisting of an action-word together with the words for the two participants. While this description was logically correct, it disregarded an important aspect of communication in real life, namely that the two participants are rarely of equal importance to the speaker. In the mammoth story, for instance, the sentence 'father spear throw' was uttered in order to extol the deeds of the father, not to describe the destiny of the spear. In general, speakers do not relay an event out of context as a clinical exercise in detached description. Rather, they usually describe an event in order to say something about one of the participants, the 'topic' of the whole utterance. And there seems to be a very strong natural preference for mentioning the topic first, and only then adding all the new information about it: what it does, what happens to it, and so on.

Of course, this raises an obvious question: which participants are most likely to be chosen as the topic of conversation? Clearly, the answer must be that the topic is the participant that is deemed worthy to be talked about, the one speakers consider the most important. And who is to say what is important? Well, cutting-edge linguistic research has established beyond all reasonable doubt that the most important thing in the whole wide world is . . . 'me'. And from this apex of importance, there is a clear pecking order all the way down to inanimate objects: 'me' → 'you' → 'woman'/'man' → 'snake'/'dog' → 'spear'/'stone'.

To see just how deeply rooted this hierarchy is in our perception, think about how hard it is for children to learn not to say things like 'me, John and Sarah', but 'John, Sarah and me (or I)' instead. The reason why it is so difficult to remember the polite formula is that this particular type of politeness imposes a highly unnatural order. And when one is not bound by the dictates of politeness or the conventions of written style to *pretend* otherwise, there is no question what should come first. Even the most pedantic of pedagogues is unlikely to complain about something like 'me and my goldfish (were watching telly together)' and correct it to 'my goldfish and I . . .'

The important point about all of this is that the 'me first' preference (by which I really mean 'more important first') often coincides with 'actor first'. In our world view, people tend to be both the actors and the important participants, whereas spears and goldfish tend to be neither actors nor topics, and feature only as the additional information passing through the story-line. The two preferences, 'actor first' and 'me first', thus reinforce one another, and so it's not surprising that among the world's languages, all but a handful prefer to mention the actor before the patient in the basic sentence, and a great majority also choose to mention the actor before both action and patient. (Only about ten per cent of languages put the action before the actor, as in '*throw* man spear', among them Welsh, biblical Hebrew and Maori.) It thus seems reasonable to assume that the same 'actor first' preference would have guided our ancestors in the 'me Tarzan' stage (if they were not speaking biblical Hebrew, that is).

But even if the actor comes first, there are still two choices for ordering the other two elements, action and patient: 'man spear *throw*' and 'man *throw* spear'. As a matter of fact, both orders seem to be equally natural, and they are equally common among the world's languages. 'Man spear *throw*' is the basic order in Japanese, Turkish, Korean, Basque and Hindi, to name but a few examples, whereas 'man *throw* spear' is the basic order in Chinese, English, Finnish, Swahili and Thai. In the mammoth story, I chose to use the first option, 'man spear *throw*', mainly in order to stress that the tale could be easily understood even though there was absolutely nothing particular to English grammar in the way it was articulated. But I could just as well have used the second option – the one which sounds more familiar to English ears. The story would not be any less natural if it ran like this:

girl pick fruit   turn   see mammoth   girl run   reach tree   climb
mammoth shake tree   girl yell yell   father run   throw spear
mammoth   roar   fall   father take stone   cut meat   give girl
girl eat finish   sleep.

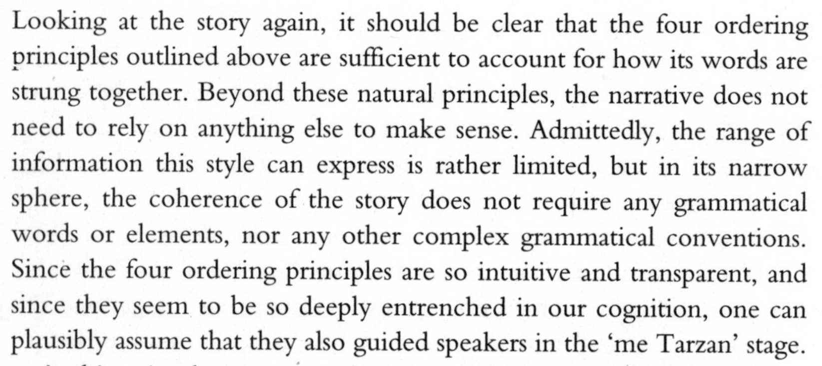

Looking at the story again, it should be clear that the four ordering principles outlined above are sufficient to account for how its words are strung together. Beyond these natural principles, the narrative does not need to rely on anything else to make sense. Admittedly, the range of information this style can express is rather limited, but in its narrow sphere, the coherence of the story does not require any grammatical words or elements, nor any other complex grammatical conventions. Since the four ordering principles are so intuitive and transparent, and since they seem to be so deeply entrenched in our cognition, one can plausibly assume that they also guided speakers in the 'me Tarzan' stage.

At this point, however, an objection could be made along the following lines: if these four principles are indeed so natural and universal, then one could expect that even modern languages would always abide by them without fail. And yet this is plainly not the case, since in modern languages it is not terribly difficult to come up with sentences which overrule many of these principles, apparently without the slightest difficulty. Here is one example, where most of the ordering principles are disobeyed in one way or another:

> Before being defeated by Caesar, King Pharnaces witnessed the arrival of the proud and well-armed Roman troops.

Caesar's principle is clearly violated, since 'defeated' is mentioned first, and 'arrival' only later, although in reality the order of events was the other way round. Monsieur Jourdain's principle also seems to be disobeyed, as things that belong together in reality, such as 'arrival' and 'troops', are quite far apart from one another. 'King Pharnaces' and 'defeated' even appear in different clauses. And to cap it all, the actor in the whole drama is not even mentioned at the beginning.

So if these ordering principles are so natural, then why is it that modern languages overrule them with impunity? The reason lies precisely in our object of enquiry: the emergence of complex grammatical structures. Over time, languages have evolved a system of more and more elaborate conventions, and those natural principles have undergone an impressive series of *-ations*: habituation, conventionalization, routinization, automatization, fossilization, sedimentation. The original simple principles have developed into increasingly more sophisticated rules, which sometimes appear quite detached from the transparent motives that had set them off in the first place. And through these complex conventions of grammar, modern languages have outgrown the slavish subservience to the natural ordering principles, and have thus gained a flexibility that gives them a much wider range of expression. Just as one example, speakers can now take the liberty of mentioning 'the arrival of the troops' only *after* 'defeated', because they have at their disposal a conjunction like 'before', which indicates that the order in reality was the other way round. This flexibility makes it possible to convey a lot of additional information over and above the temporal order of events. Take this sentence, for instance:

> King Pharnaces looked at his troops, and capitulated (. . . realizing he was outnumbered)

With the conjunction 'before', one can reverse the order of the clauses (that is, contradict Caesar's principle), still convey the correct sequence of events in reality, but nevertheless give the sentence an entirely different twist:

> Before capitulating, King Pharnaces looked at his troops (. . . and shouted 'I love you all!')

Incidentally, the use of subordinating conjunctions such as 'before', 'after', 'because of' and so on may be one of the few areas in the structure of language which developed fully only in the relatively recent past. At the opening of the book, I said that the available written records of any language extend at most 5,000 years into the past, and that the languages around by that time already have pretty much the full repertoire of complex features found in today's languages. The use of subordination seems to be one of the only exceptions to this claim, since the earliest attested stages of many languages do show a significant difference in this respect from what we are used to in modern written styles. The use of subordinating conjunctions in the earliest stages of ancient languages such as Sumerian, Akkadian, Hittite or Greek seems to have been much less developed, and in consequence, Caesar's principle had to be relied upon much more consistently. This is why the style of some ancient texts can seem so monotonous to us. Consider, for instance, this report by the Hittite King Murshili II (fourteenth century BC), which describes how he came to be afflicted by a severe illness (perhaps aphasia?) that impaired his ability to speak. To modern ears, the dramatic substance of the report contrasts starkly with the monotonous staccato of the style:

Seal of Murshili II, 'Great King, King of the Land of Hatti'

This is what 'my Sun', Murshili, the Great King, said:

Kunnuwa nannaḫḫun	I drove (in a chariot) to Kunnu
nu *ḫaršiḫarši udaš*	***and*** a thunderstorm came
namma *Tarḫunnaš ḫatuga tetḫiškit*	***then*** the Storm-God kept thundering terribly
nu *nāḫun*	***and*** I feared
nu*-mu-kan memiaš išši anda tepawešta*	***and*** the speech in my mouth became small
nu*-mu-kan memiaš tepu kuitki šarā iyattat*	***and*** the speech came up a little bit
nu*-kan aši memian arḫapat paškuwānun*	***and*** I forgot this matter completely
maḫḫan-ma *uēr wittuš appanda pāir*	***but afterwards*** the years came and went
nu*-mu wit aši memiaš tešḫaniškiuwān tiyat*	***and*** this matter came to appear repeatedly in my dreams
nu*-mu-kan zazḫia anda keššar šiunaš araš*	***and*** God's hand seized me in my dreams
*aišš-****a****-mu-kan tapuša pait*	***and then*** my mouth went sideways
nu . . .	***and*** . . .

Today, we would tend to use various conjunctions such as 'when', 'so', 'but', and thus would not need to follow the order of events so punctiliously in order to achieve coherence. For example, we might say: 'There was once a terrible thunderstorm when I was driving to Kunnu. I was so terrified of the Storm-God's thundering that I lost my speech, and my voice came up only a little. For a while, I forgot about the matter completely, but as the years went by, this episode began to appear in my dreams, and while dreaming, I was struck by God's hand (i.e. a disease), and my mouth went sideways.'

Modern languages have thus developed a sophisticated system of grammatical conventions, which enable them to make the relations between words and clauses more explicit, and thus to ensure coherence even when the natural principles are overruled. What they gained in consequence was a much wider and more intricate range of expression. But how could all this have developed? In the following pages, I will argue that grammatical structures evolved through precisely those processes which the previous chapters tried to illuminate: the metaphorical flow from concrete to abstract, the erosion in meaning and sounds, and the craving for order. So by now, we really have all the necessary tools at hand to construct the full-blown grammar of modern language, working with only the raw materials of the 'me Tarzan' stage.

The small print

Before proceeding, however, readers are required to acquaint themselves with the following disclaimer of warranty for the content of this chapter, and to agree to the terms and conditions of use appended herewith. Failure to comply with these terms may limit the author's liability of any kind, either express, implied or statutory, for any misunderstanding or misrepresentation direct or otherwise and howsoever caused, which may arise in relation thereto.

1. It cannot be over-stressed that the presentation of the 'me Tarzan' stage here is in almost all respects an extreme idealization. To take just one example, it may well be that at the time when humans already had as many distinct words as in the mammoth story, grammatical elements had already begun to develop. The point here, however, is not to give an exact chronology of which words developed before which rules. The aim is only to suggest that it is possible, in principle, to understand how the whole edifice of complex grammar could have developed from a much simpler set of principles.

2. Clearly, the presentation here must be highly selective, since it is impossible within one chapter to consider every single feature of even one language, let alone of all languages. So by claiming that one can reach the complexity of modern languages, I only mean that it's possible to sketch enough to make the case that the missing details could follow on much the same lines. In choosing which areas to include, I will focus mostly on basic features that are common to all languages. Nevertheless, as this book is written in English, the details are often presented with disproportionate emphasis on the structure of English. It is paramount, however, that this choice of convenience should not be taken to mean that there is an inevitable progression from the 'me Tarzan' stage to the niceties of English grammar, rather than to those of Swahili. If the book had been written in Swahili, the details would have looked somewhat different. But the principles would have been the same.

3. The order in which the different features will be presented is significant in that it aims to present a well-founded system, in which only grammatical elements that have already been derived may be used in the derivation of new elements. I am not trying to claim, however, that the order of presentation here is the only possible sequence in which structural features could have emerged. In fact, various grammatical elements could have developed simultaneously on different axes (so, for instance, the following three sections could easily have been ordered differently). The choice of which elements to present first must thus remain arbitrary to some extent, but this in no way detracts from the purpose of this exercise, for – once again – the aim is not to give an exact chronology, but only to argue that it is *possible* to derive complex grammar from the materials of the starting stage.

4. Perhaps the most important caveat that should be mentioned at the outset concerns the issue of innateness. The introduction forewarned that although this book is by no means about the innateness controversy, the question would inevitably be lurking somewhere in the background. Nowhere is this more obvious than in the present chapter, since behind the scenario which will be presented here lie profound questions about the workings of the brain. All the developments explored below presuppose speakers with a modern human brain, able to learn and handle complex linguistic structures. This presupposition will perhaps become most clear in the last section of this chapter, which describes the emergence of 'subordination', the mechanisms for combining clauses on different levels into complex hierarchical structures (some examples were mentioned in Chapter 1, page 31). Of course, if speakers' brains were not capable of handling hierarchically organized information, then none of the steps which will be presented below as 'natural' would be at all natural, or indeed possible. So much is uncontroversial, but what is less clear is how the ability to deal with complex hierarchical structures is actually coded in the brain. Are the specific linguistic mechanisms themselves part of our innate genetic inheritance? Or is the aptitude of the brain to learn and handle hierarchical linguistic structures just a consequence of a more general cognitive capacity, manifested also in the way we process visual information, for instance? The answer is that no one really knows, and this provides endless opportunities for debate (see note on page 310 for suggested further reading). There is one assumption, however, which

should not be too controversial, and which forms the basis for the following discussion, namely, that even a brain pre-equipped to learn and handle complex structures doesn't just invent the mechanisms for communicating them out of thin air. The scenario presented below is thus intended as an illustration for how the actual conventions of communicating complex information could have evolved.

If you agree with the terms and conditions above, then we can get on with the real business of 'growing' our grammar, and a good place to start is with the 'me' of 'me Tarzan'. So far, I have used 'me Tarzan' as a convenient loose term for our starting stage. But there are various reasons why one shouldn't take this nick-name too literally. For one thing, the immortal 'me Tarzan, you Jane' episode of Tarzan never really was – at least not in Edgar Rice Burroughs's original novel *Tarzan of the Apes* (1914). In the book, a somewhat different account is given for the course of Tarzan's language learning. The apes that Tarzan grows up with already speak quite a sophisticated language, and Tarzan, with the superior intelligence of an English Lord, is practically an intellectual even before he ever claps eyes on Jane. As a child, he had taught himself to read English, using the children's books left behind in the hut where his parents had died. So in fact, Tarzan's first missive to Jane is not 'me Tarzan, you Jane', but a touching love letter, displaying a mastery of the niceties of English grammar, ranging from verbal agreement to subordinate clauses: 'I am Tarzan of the Apes. I want you. I am yours. You are mine. We will live here together in my house. I will bring you the best fruits, the tenderest deer, the finest meats that roam the jungle . . . I will fight for you. I am the mightiest of the jungle fighters . . . When you see this you will know it is for you, and that Tarzan of the Apes loves you.'

But there is a rather more serious reason why referring to the 'me Tarzan' label should not be taken too literally. Doing so would imply that pronouns like 'me' are among the raw materials that should be taken as given at the starting point of our evolutionary tour. The thing is that pronouns such as 'me', 'you' or 'she' actually involve quite sophisticated grammatical machinery. Pronouns may be so pervasive in modern languages that one hardly gives them a moment's thought, but in fact these little words conceal some advanced technology: a mechanism of shifting reference.

SHIFTY WORDS, OR ON BEING A 'FOREIGNER'

There is a story of an Englishman sitting in a restaurant in northern France, struggling with some of the finer points of the menu. The attentive waiter spots his difficulty, and asks politely: 'Monsieur est étranger?' The Englishman looks shocked, and replies, with some dignity: 'Étranger? Mais non, je suis Anglais!'

When taking offence at being called a 'foreigner', what the Englishman failed to realize, of course, is that some words shift their reference according to who utters them and where. 'Foreigner' (or *étranger*, *Ausländer*, and so on) may be a rather marginal representative of the group of shifting words, but the prime examples of the class are those little pronouns like 'me' and 'you'. As opposed to words with stable meaning (like 'tree' or 'kick'), pronouns change their meaning according to who utters them: your 'me' is my 'you'. In fact, it's not only our Englishman who finds this shifting mechanism rather a strain. Young children usually have real difficulty with shifting reference, and find the pronouns 'me' and 'you' hard to master. When one is just starting out in life, it is far from obvious that 'you' refers to yourself when Mummy says it, but to Mummy when you do.

Far from being trivial, then, the mechanism of shifting is quite a sophisticated device, which builds our own system of coordinates into the reference, and signals to the listeners that they have to translate the reference into their own coordinates. The gain from all this shiftiness is that pronouns allow us to refer to people and things in a succinct and efficient way. But how could this effective mechanism ever develop? The clue may be found in one particular type of shifting words:

'This' and 'that' are clearly shifting words, because their reference depends on *where* they are uttered: in the picture on the previous page, for example, Jane's 'this' is Tarzan's 'that'. (Incidentally, British travellers sometimes forget this fact and refer to Britain as 'this country', even when they happen to be in Timbuktu.)

Now at the beginning of this chapter I included 'this' and 'that' among the list of raw materials for our starting stage, the primary concepts that must be taken as given. In view of the above, however, their inclusion might appear unjustified, since 'this' and 'that' already embody the mechanism of shifting. Nevertheless, 'this' and 'that' are not just any old shifting words. They are special, because they are so intimately linked to the act of physical pointing – they are pointing words *par excellence*. This intimate link between 'this-that' and physical pointing is perhaps most evident in the behaviour of young children, who initially seem to use the pointing words only as an accompaniment to an actual pointing gesture. Only later do the pointing words become 'emancipated' from the hand gesture and come to be used on their own.

The most compelling reason for taking the pointing words as primary concepts, however, does not come from children, but rather from observing the history of language itself. No matter how hard one tries to trace their historical origin, the pointing words in any language never seem to emerge from anything that was not a pointing word to start with. Unlike grammatical words, which over and over again can be seen to develop from nouns and verbs, pointing words appear to have been pointing words all along.

Pointing words can themselves be the source of many new grammatical elements (as we shall soon see), but when one tries to trace their own origin, the only observable developments seem to be changes between different types of pointing words, for example, changes between two equivalent pairs: 'this/that' and 'here/there'. The shifting principle behind the two pairs is identical, and the only difference between them is that 'this' and 'that' are used to point to an object, whereas 'here' and 'there' are used to point to a place. Some languages don't even make a consistent distinction between the pairs (in Latin, for instance, *hic* can mean both 'here' and 'this'). And even in languages where the two pairs are distinct, one pair often turns out to be the source for the other. (Very roughly, something like 'this (place)' can be the source of 'here', but the derivation can also go the other way, so that something like '(thing) here' can be the source of 'this'.) So for our purposes it does not matter so much which pair developed first, and I'll simply treat them as variations on the same theme. What is crucial, however, is that these pointing pairs do not seem to develop from anything that does not already contain a pointing element.

All this suggests that pointing words must have emerged directly as vocal accompaniment to an actual pointing gesture. And it is also likely that the pointing words could have acted as a bridge between the visual processing system and language. When Tarzan wants to determine where exactly Jane is pointing, he has to 'shift' or 'translate' the direction of her hand into his own visual system of coordinates – an act which requires a considerable amount of computation, but which our brain's powerful visual processing system does so instinctively that we never even notice the complexity involved. The words 'this' and 'that' could have imported the visual shifting mechanism into language when they became emancipated from the physical gesture and came to embody the shift of meaning in their own right.

And once the basic shifting mechanism behind 'this'-'that' (or 'here'-'there') is in place, it is possible to derive from it the whole gamut of other shifting words, and in particular, pronouns like 'me', 'you', or 'him'. The link between the pointing words and pronouns may not seem immediately obvious, but it may become more transparent when one takes into account that many languages don't just have a two-way distinction between 'this' and 'that', but rather a three-way one: 'this' (pointing to something near the speaker); 'that' (pointing to something further away from the speaker, nearer the addressee); and 'that yonder' (pointing to something far away from both speaker and addressee). Classical Latin is one example, with the triad *hic-iste-ille*, and Japanese has a similar distinction with *koko* 'here'- *soko* 'there (near addressee)'- *asoko* 'yonder'. From this three-way system, it is much easier to imagine how the triangle 'me-you-him' could have evolved, and some languages even illustrate the link quite transparently. In Vietnamese, for instance, it's not uncommon for speakers to use 'here' to refer to themselves, and 'there' to refer to the addressee:

Vietnamese

đó	*có chởi*	*vởi*	***đây***	*không?*
there	play	with	here	not?

'doesn't "there" want to play with "here"?'
(that is, 'don't you want to play with me?')

Something similar is found in the colloquial language of the early Latin comedies. In Terence's *Andria*, for instance, a slave urges his master to relinquish his love for a woman he will never be allowed to marry. The master responds philosophically that it's easy to give advice, but:

Latin

tu	*si*	***hic***	*sis*	*aliter*	*sentias*
You,	if	this/here	you.were	differently	you.would.feel

'If you were "this/here", you would feel differently'
(that is, 'if you were me . . .')

Third person pronouns (like 'he' and 'she') are generally nothing other than pointing words for distant objects ('that yonder'), which have been divested of their emphatic force. A well-known example is Latin *ille* 'that one (yonder)'. In earlier stages of Latin, *ille* was used only for 'real' physical pointing, that is, for pointing at objects in the distance. This physical pointing was then extended metaphorically to the 'space of conversation' (see Chapter 4, page 137), and *ille* thus came to 'point' at a previous mention of a person or thing in the discourse, meaning 'that one (which I mentioned a moment ago)'. But with time, both the emphatic force of *ille* and its form were eroded, and it eventually ended up in French simply as *il* 'he'.

Needless to say, there is quite a lot more to pronouns than that. Modern languages make a variety of distinctions on pronouns, such as case (*he-him-his*), gender (*he-she-it*), number (*he-they*), all of which help to fine-tune the task of pointing in the 'space of conversation' and reduce ambiguity in identifying previous referents. Modern languages have also developed various specialized types of pronouns, such as reflexives like 'himself' or 'herself', which are used in particular contexts for high-precision tasks of identifying referents unambiguously. (Appendix D: The Cook's Counterpoint (page 296) describes how such reflexive pronouns have developed in English.) But for the moment, since the basic pronouns are already at hand, we can get on with the business of 'growing' more sophisticated grammatical structures. And the most obvious place to start is with the number of participants in the clause.

GROWING THE CLAUSE

Consider the following sentences of the mammoth story, which are printed here with all the action-words highlighted:

father . . . ***take*** stone ***cut*** meat ***give*** girl girl ***eat finish***.

And compare this to normal English:

With a sharp stone, the father ***cut*** some meat for the girl, who ***ate*** it up.

There are, of course, many differences between the two versions, but perhaps the most striking one is how many participants cluster around each action-word. In the minimalist style of the 'me Tarzan' narrative, each action-word can only cope with at most two participants: the actor, and one other. In the English sentence, however, one verb 'cut' manages to handle no fewer than four participants ('with a sharp stone, the father ***cut*** some meat for the girl'). So all the information that is expressed in three consecutive 'me Tarzan' clauses is compressed into just one English clause. The key to this increased capacity is the emergence of prepositions like 'with' and 'for', which introduce the extra participants and specify their precise role in the action: 'instrument' (*with* a stone), 'beneficiary' (*for* the girl), and so on.

What could have created these more condensed clauses, with many different participants gathered around the action-word? By now, the general idea should not come as any great surprise. Just as longer words can emerge from the collapse and fusion of shorter words, one clause can grow heavier and acquire more participants when two simpler clauses collapse and coalesce into one. And as it happens, there is no need to resort to speculation about far-flung prehistoric periods to see how such a change can be set in motion, because developments of this kind are observable in many languages today and in the recent past.

The perambulations of the verb 'give' in various languages can provide a good illustration of this process. The literal sense of 'give' implies the transfer of an object from one person to another, but quite often, 'give' also gains an abstract metaphoric sense, and is used even when no physical transfer is involved. In English, for instance, you can 'give consideration' to a proposal, you can 'give someone the idea' that you like them, you can even 'give your soul' to them. In other languages, the metaphoric use of 'give' has proceeded even further. For instance, in Akan, a language spoken by around 7 million people in Ghana, you can give someone not only the fruits of your labour, but the labour itself:

Akan (Niger-Congo family)

o-yɛ	*adwuma*	*ma*	*ne*	*nua barima*	*no*
he-does	work	gives	his	brother	the

As with many other metaphors we have come across, the image here is clearly based in experience. In a physical act of giving something, the receiver is usually the beneficiary of the whole action. So in Akan, the verb *ma* 'give' is extended to mark more generally any type of beneficiary, even when no physical object changes hands. When such constructions are used repeatedly, they can undergo the types of changes that are by now familiar. What had started as a metaphoric sense becomes established as normal usage, the original meaning of physical action is worn away, and so the erstwhile action-word 'give' just comes to stand for the abstract notion of beneficiary. So to all intents and purposes, the 'verb' *ma* in this Akan construction can simply be translated as the preposition 'for', since it no longer evokes any sense of independent action. What started off as two separate clauses with two separate action-words ('he does work, gives his brother') has come to be condensed into just one clause ('he does work **for** his brother'), with only one action but with one more participant ('his brother').

The fate of the verb *ma* in Akan is far from unusual. Time and time again, and in language after language, 'give' verbs turn into prepositions meaning 'for' or 'to'. In the history of Chinese, for instance, such changes occurred more than once. In medieval Chinese, the verb *yǔ*, which originally meant 'give', lost its sense as an independent physical action, and around the eighth century AD came to mark the role of beneficiary or target, as in the example below:

Medieval Chinese (Sino-Tibetan family)
shuō yǔ ta dao
speak **give** him Dao
'speak **to** him (about) Dao'

In modern Chinese, another 'giving' verb, *gěi*, has undergone a similar process in recent centuries. But 'give' is not even the only verb that can undergo such a transformation. Below are a few more examples of other verbs, which have come to mark other roles in the action, such as direction ('from' or 'to') or instrument ('with'). In all these examples, what had started as two separate clauses collapsed into one heavier clause.

Thai (Tai-Kadai family)
Thân cà bin càak krungthêep
he will fly **leave** Bangkok
'he will fly **from** Bangkok'

Thai
Thân cà bin maa krungthêep
he will fly **come** Bangkok
'he will fly **to(wards)** Bangkok'

Efik (Niger-Congo family, spoken in Nigeria)
dá èkuri sìbé éto
take axe cut tree
'cut the tree **with** an axe!'

Chinese (Sino-Tibetan family)
shōushi le dōngxi gēn wǒ lái
prepare things **follow** me come
'prepare (your) things and come **with** me'

At first sight, the emergence of prepositions from verbs may seem rather strange, especially since in previous chapters, only nouns were discussed as a source of prepositions (for example 'back of' → 'behind'). But across the world's languages, changes from verb to preposition and from noun to preposition are both very common, and as it happens, even some English prepositions can boast verbs as their origin. Take the preposition 'past' in phrases such as 'he is past retirement age'. Few would suspect it today, but 'past' started out as an entirely normal verb, none other than the past tense of 'pass', as in Chaucer's phrase 'The day is short and it is *passed* pryme.'

Of course, all the examples quoted here come from the recent past, not from tens of thousands of years ago. Nevertheless, it is likely that very similar processes were responsible for the first appearance of heavier clauses after the 'me Tarzan' stage, and for the emergence of the first group of grammatical words: 'prepositions', those erstwhile action-words, which were drained of their original physical sense, and came to mark various types of relations. And once the prepositions for simple spatial relations had emerged ('to', 'from', etc.), they could have spawned the whole range of prepositions for temporal relations and other abstract notions (cause, reason, and so on), through the natural paths of metaphoric abstraction that were explored in Chapter 4.

Finally, as an added bonus, when the accompaniment preposition 'with' has developed from the verb 'follow', as in the Chinese example above, the preposition can give rise to the coordinating word 'and'. In Chinese (as well as in Turkish, Swahili, and many other languages), constructions such as 'bring X *with* Y' have come to be used more generally to mean 'bring X *and* Y'. And from coordinating two things, the word is often extended further to coordinate two sentences: 'do X *and* do Y'.

Incidentally, although I have only mentioned the emergence of *pre*positions so far, exactly the same principles apply to *post*positions as well. Whether a verb will turn into a preposition or a postposition depends on the basic choice in the arrangement of the action and the patient. In a language with the order '*take* stone, cut meat', the verb 'take' would develop into a preposition: '*with* stone cut meat'. But in a language with the order 'stone *take*, meat cut', the same verb would turn into a postposition: 'stone-*with* meat cut'. In fact, the seeds of a much wider phenomenon are buried here: the inverse word order between languages like English and Turkish.

We saw in Chapter 1 that from an English perspective, Turkish seems to arrange its words quite consistently back to front, whereas from a Turkish perspective, it is of course English that has got it entirely the wrong way round. What is beginning to emerge here is how this mirror-image effect ultimately goes back to just one basic choice that languages make at some stage during their history, about the arrangement of the action-word and the patient ('take stone' or 'stone take'). This preference can influence not just whether *pre*positions will emerge (as in English) or *post*positions (as in Turkish), but can ripple through the structure of a language, and have far-reaching repercussions on the order of many other elements. To appreciate the full chain of consequences that this basic choice can set off, we still need to develop various other grammatical structures. So if by the end of the chapter, you feel like peering behind the looking-glass of word order, Appendix E: The Turkish Mirror (page 301), will illuminate some of the details. But for now, let's draw breath and take stock of all the grammatical elements which have already been derived. With our newly acquired pronouns, prepositions and the coordinating word 'and', the mammoth story might now look something like this (new features are emboldened):

girl pick fruit turn see mammoth **she** run **to** tree **and** climb **it**
mammoth shake tree girl yell yell father run **towards her**
he throw spear **at** mammoth **it** roar **and** fall
with stone father cut meat **for** girl **she** eat finish **and she** sleep.

THE DOUBLE LIFE OF PROPERTY-WORDS

The mammoth story is beginning to look a lot less 'minimalist' than the version from the opening of the chapter. Nevertheless, there are still key features of modern languages that are missing from it. But before we go on to examine them more closely, a cautionary note should be sounded. The features which we still need to derive are fairly abstract and thus more complex than anything we have looked at so far. But in tracking them, we can gain an understanding of how some of the fundamental design-features of language could have emerged, such as the hierarchical structure of sentences. So make yourself a strong cup of coffee, and read on.

Perhaps the most important of the features that are still missing from our language is the shape of the participants themselves. So far, each participant was represented by a single thing-word, such as 'stone', 'tree' or 'daughter'. But in modern languages, each participant can be represented by a whole phrase, in which the thing-word is surrounded by an entourage of appendages with additional information about it: a sharp stone, the nearest tree, his terrified daughter, some pieces of the meat. To our ears, this set-up sounds so utterly obvious that it is hard to imagine how things could ever be otherwise, let alone recognize that there is something remarkable going on here. But when one does stop to think about it, the capacity of sentences to be composed of building-blocks which are themselves elaborate phrases soon emerges in its true light, as a real feat of engineering. This ability allows us to do in language what not even the most capable of architects can achieve: to stuff into each building-block an almost limitless amount of substance, but without distorting in any way the contours of its shape, or in other words, to pile appendages into the description of one participant, but without having any effect on the function of this participant in the sentence. The capacity of each participant to develop into a complex phrase will turn out to be a key to no less a principle than the hierarchical organization of the sentence. But how could this scheme ever have evolved? Instead of taking on the whole gang of appendages in one go, we can start with just one illustrative example, perhaps the archetypal appendage: property-words like 'sharp' or 'red'.

To start with, where do the names for properties actually come from? Property-words did not feature among the primary terms which were taken as given at our starting point, because they can be derived from the raw materials that are already at our disposal: words for physical objects and for simple actions. To get a sense of the process involved, one need only call to mind a few colour-words, such as *orange, olive, violet, silver, claret, burgundy*. All of these are commonly used as normal property-words nowadays ('her dress is orange', 'ultra-violet light', and so on) but their origin is still transparent. Initially, they referred to particular objects (fruit, flowers, metals, wines) which happened to have a striking property, namely their colour, and so the original thing-word came to be used more generally to denote the colour itself. While these examples may all refer to colours that are rather fancy, the origin of more basic colour-words is often the same. ‘Red’, for instance, sometimes comes from ‘blood’, as in the Semitic languages, where *dam* ‘blood’ is the source of *adam* ‘red’ (and hence, incidentally, via the Hebrew word for ‘red dust’, the name of *Adam*, ‘man’). In a similar vein, the word for ‘green’ often comes from something to do with ‘leaf’, or (as in English) from something to do with ‘grow’. Nor are such methods for deriving property-words limited to colours. Suppose you hear a politician complaining that the government has created a ‘mammoth deficit’ – you wouldn’t imagine she was admonishing the government for allowing the population of mammoths to dwindle to dangerously low levels. The word ‘mammoth’ here has simply been drafted to refer to one property of this species more generally, namely gigantic size. And if you go scavenging among the languages of the world, you’ll find similar sources for plenty of other property-words: ‘small’ often derives from ‘child’ or ‘baby’ (think for instance of ‘baby grand piano’), ‘strong’ can come from ‘a youth’, ‘sharp’ can come from ‘tooth’ or ‘shard’. So it is likely that in remote prehistory, similar processes were responsible for bringing property-words into existence.

But by imagining how property-words came to life we are only halfway to understanding their nature, since in modern languages property-words lead not one, but two quite separate lives. On the one hand, they exist as proud and independent members of the sentence: in a phrase like ‘the stone is sharp’, ‘sharp’ makes the main assertion about the stone, and is thus at the core of the sentence, fulfilling a function rather similar to that of an action-word (as in ‘the stone fell’). But on the other hand, property-words also lead a different, and less glamorous existence. In ‘the sharp stone fell’, ‘sharp’ is not an independent member of the sentence, but only lives under the stone’s shadow, and exists merely as an appendage to ‘stone’. What we have to explain, therefore, is how property-words developed this schizophrenic existence, and in particular, how their second role, their low life of appendagehood, could have emerged.

If we are to have any chance of tackling this question, it is crucial first to pin down the real difference in function between these two roles, and establish what exactly property-words achieve in their two lives. Now, for philosophers who view language as an object of clinical inquiry, and reduce the meaning of sentences to their bare logical content, the distinction between the two roles might seem clear enough. Philosophers have characterized the difference between 'the stone is sharp' and 'the sharp stone' as reflecting the difference between 'truth' and 'reference'. Propositions (anything from 'the stone is sharp' to 'my dog Rex does not believe in pre-nuptial agreements') have a 'truth value' – they make assertions about the world which may be either true or false. But words like 'stone' or 'fire' on their own do not make any assertion (or so it is claimed), since we cannot ask, for example, whether 'stone' is true or false. Such words only 'refer', they merely draw attention to things in the world. So philosophically speaking, the high life of property-words ('the stone is sharp') creates a truth-value, since it produces an assertion which may be true or false. But in their low-life role, property-words do not create a truth-value, since one cannot ask whether '$_{\text{the sharp}}$stone' is true, any more than one can ask whether 'stone' or 'fire' are true or false.

While all this may seem reasonable on paper, the reality of language is rather less neat. One shouldn't take the 'truth value' argument without a pinch of salt, since otherwise one might end up the way of those two distinguished professors, who over a glass of port late one evening were deeply engaged in an intense discussion about the nature of truth. As they were in the middle of debating the difference between 'truth' and 'reference', the housekeeper burst in, yelling 'Fire! Fire!' One of the professors patiently explained to her that 'fire' is only a referring expression, and as such cannot have any truth value . . . and those were his famous last words.

In real life, then, the mere act of reference (pointing or drawing attention to something such as 'fire') can be quite enough to make a crucial assertion ('run for your life – the house is on fire. . .') and can thus have as much truth value as any proper statement. So for all practical purposes, the difference between the two roles of property-words should be sought not in their ability or inability to create a truth-value, but rather in something more down-to-earth: the pragmatic function that they fulfil in different contexts. In 'the stone is sharp', 'sharp' makes an assertion about an object that has already been clearly identified. This construction would be used in a context where the listener already knows perfectly well which stone the speaker has in mind, and the purpose of 'sharp' is thus to make a new assertion about this stone. But in its low-life role ('$_{\text{the sharp}}$stone') 'sharp' is used in contexts where the speaker needs to clarify *which* stone he had in mind. The property-word here is a part of the pointing action itself – it is an extension or refinement of the act of reference.

When one thinks about the difference between the two roles in terms of this pragmatic context, it also becomes easier to imagine how property-words could have diverged into their two separate lives. The high life does not pose any particular problems, since here property-words could simply have been formed on the model of action-words: one can easily imagine that a sentence like 'stone sharp' (meaning 'the stone is sharp') was naturally formed on the model of 'stone fall'. True, English happens to use a 'copula' (the linguistic term for a connector like 'is') between 'stone' and 'sharp', and so its two constructions 'stone falls' and 'stone is sharp' don't look so alike. But many languages, such as Russian, don't need such a copula, and simply say the equivalent of 'stone sharp'. (In fact, copulas like 'is' are usually of a secondary origin, and often ultimately come from some marker of emphasis which with time and frequent repetition loses its force and becomes obligatory.)

The origin of the low life of property-words, however, is more shadowy. How did property-words assume their ancillary position as part of the act of reference itself, and what could have been their role models for this function? As it happens, there are already some words in our emerging language whose main purpose is to help the act of pointing. These are of course the pointing words 'this' and 'that'. Suppose, for instance, that one day Tarzan wants to draw Jane's attention to a certain stone, and says 'stone!' (meaning 'my dear, could you possibly pass me the stone please?'). Then he realizes that Jane has no idea which stone he means, so he might point at it and say 'that'. The next time, Tarzan wouldn't even wait for Jane's inquisitive look, and would say 'stone, that', meaning '(bring me) the stone, that one I am now pointing at'. In such a juxtaposition, the role of 'that' is unmistakable. It's not there to make any assertion about an object that has already been identified, but simply serves to identify *which* stone Tarzan had in mind. So 'stone' and 'that' join together into a single act of reference.

Incidentally, you might ask why it has to be 'stone that' rather than 'that stone', which would be more familiar from English. But there is no pressing reason. I could just as well have told the story differently, and said that Tarzan wants a stone, so he first points at it and says 'that', but then realizes that there are various other objects in the direction in which he is pointing, and Jane doesn't know which one he means. So by way of clarification, he would add 'stone'. And the next time, he would simply say 'that stone' to start with. Both orders are equally natural, and perhaps initially both would have been improvised depending on the context. But with frequent repetition, what might have started as just a preference for one order over the other can turn into a habit, which can fossilize into a rule, thus creating a fixed phrase, a complex 'referring expression' with a rigid order: either 'that stone' or 'stone that'. (The languages of the world today seem equally divided on which order they have chosen.)

Property-words could have taken the pointing words as their role-models for their low life incarnation ('sharp stone'), because the role they perform in this life is very similar to that of the pointing words. Of course, property-words do not really point, but they do help to refine the act of reference by narrowing down the range of objects in question. If, for example, there are many stones around, but only one of them is sharp, then saying 'sharp stone' achieves the same restricting effect as saying 'that stone' while pointing. And so one can imagine that 'sharp stone' might have been formed on the basis of 'that stone' (or 'stone sharp' on the basis of 'stone that').

To summarize, then, the two roles of property-words can be seen as the habituation-through-repetition of two different pragmatic tasks. In some contexts, speakers want to make an assertion about an object that has already been clearly identified. The conventionalization of this context is the high life of property-words, and ends up as the construction '(the) stone (is) sharp'. In other contexts, speakers need to refine the act of pointing itself, in order to identify *which* object they are talking about. It is this usage that has solidified as the low-life role of property-words, and ended up in English as the phrase '(the) sharp stone'.

This scenario for how property-words could have come to live the low life may seem all too simple. If there is any difficulty here, it is only to understand why there is even any need to explain something that appears so obvious. But the low life of property-words is in fact a parable for something much more fundamental, as it is the basis for the whole hierarchical structure of the sentence. The principle at stake here is the ability of a participant like [stone] to be represented by a whole phrase, which nevertheless behaves as if it were a single word as far as the rest of the sentence is concerned. The point is that when a phrase like [sharp stone] has established itself as one 'referring expression', it can be plonked anywhere in the sentence where [stone] could appear on its own: 'bring me [sharp stone]', '[sharp stone] fall', 'father throw [sharp stone] at mammoth'. What is more, all this happens without in any way affecting the primary level of the sentence, the basic 'who is doing what to whom' frame. So what we have just created here is a tiered structure, since 'sharp' in such sentences is really just an appendage that dances attendance on 'stone', and doesn't have a direct relation with any other element in the sentence.

Of course, the two-word phrase [$_{\text{sharp}}$stone] may not in itself look like much of a revolutionary 'tiered-structure', but once the foundations have been laid, a whole new edifice can rise and rest upon them. To begin with, once the appendage role has set into a solid construction [$_{\text{sharp}}$stone], this construction can be loaded with a much heavier cargo of meaning than its original *raison d'être* in merely identifying the referent. For instance, a mother might say to a child 'don't put that sharp stone next to the baby' even if there is just one stone around, so there is no need to identify *which* stone she has in mind. The actual meaning here would be more like 'don't put that stone next to the baby, because it's so sharp'. So the scaffoldings which arose to support one simple pragmatic distinction (helping to identify the referent) can now carry much heavier meaning-loads. The appendage can come to be used not only as an aid in identification, but as a means of cramming additional bits of information about the participant into one concise expression, without interfering with the main level of the sentence.

Even more importantly, once the principle of appendagehood has been established with one type of appendage, the flood-gates have been opened, and a stream of other types can gush in: plural markers (spear$_{\text{s}}$), quantifiers ($_{\text{any}}$spear), articles ($_{\text{the}}$spear), possessives ('spear$_{\text{of the father}}$') and so on. The list that follows suggests some common sources from which such appendages can develop.

- **Possessives.** Chapter 4 described how constructions for possession can develop from terms for 'seizing' or for physical proximity. In all the examples mentioned there, possession was expressed as an independent assertion (as in 'the child has toothache'), in a way parallel to the high life of property-words ('the child is ill'). But the notion of possession can also be expressed with one thing-word functioning as an appendage of another. The possessive (the thing-word that functions as the appendage) then helps to identify which object is being referred to: 'the $_{\text{neighbour's}}$child' performs a similar role to 'the $_{\text{ill}}$child'. Sometimes, languages do not even need any particular grammatical elements to mark the possessive as appendage, and just plonk it next to its 'head': $_{\text{door}}$handle, $_{\text{street}}$child, $_{\text{wine}}$bottle, $_{\text{church}}$property. Nevertheless, most languages also employ more explicit means to mark possessives, as in the English constructions '$_{\text{neighbour}\textbf{'s}}$child' or 'piece$_{\textbf{of}\text{ meat}}$'. The *-'s* possessive is much too old to betray its ultimate origin, but the construction with 'of' developed more recently. Initially, 'of' denoted a simple physical relation, a direction 'from' or 'out of' something (as in 'Joan of Arc'), so a 'piece of meat' originally meant a piece *from* the meat. The whole phrase 'of meat' then came to be used as an appendage, and in a metaphoric process of abstraction, the physical aspect of being 'from' something came to describe possession more generally, as in 'king$_{\text{of the castle}}$', 'houses$_{\text{of parliament}}$', and so on.

- **Quantifiers** like 'any', 'every', 'all', which in modern languages are used to perform complex logical operations, often develop from much simpler property-words. 'All', for instance, frequently derives from the property-word 'whole', as shown by the French *tout* and Italian *tutti*, which both derive from the Latin *totus* 'whole'. The conceptual link between 'whole' and 'all' probably passes through collective entities such as 'group', 'herd', and so on. When the 'whole group' is there, it implies that *all* people in the group are there, and through this association the property 'whole' can be extended to the more complex notion of inclusion.

- **Plural markers** often develop from the quantifier 'all', or from intrinsically plural terms such as 'people'. One example can be seen in southern dialects of American English, where a plural form of the pronoun 'you' has emerged, *y'all*, obviously from the fusion of 'you all'. The Dutch second person plural pronoun *jullie* has a similar origin, as it is a contraction of *jou lui* 'you people'.

- **Articles.** Definite articles invariably come from pointing-words like 'that'. English 'the' is in fact just an eroded form of 'that'. French *le* has a similar origin, the Latin *ille* 'that'. (I mentioned earlier that *ille* was also the source of the French pronoun *il* 'he'. The reason for the divergence in form is different paths of erosion: when *ille* was used together with a noun, as in *ille liber* 'that book', the stress pattern was such that erosion hacked at it mostly from the front, and so it ended up as *le livre* 'the book'. But when it was used on its own, *ille* 'that (one)' was eroded from the other end, and so turned into French *il* 'he'.) Indefinite articles generally come from the word 'one'. English 'a' is just a shortened version of 'an' which in turn is a shortened version of 'one'. Both German *ein* 'one' and French *un* 'one' have also come to be used as indefinite articles, and the same path can be seen in countless other languages.

Once the principle of appendagehood has been established, the thing-word can attract an increasingly longer and more elaborate entourage of appendages, for if one appendage can be added without interfering with the main level of the sentence, then why stop there? Appendages can thus be piled up: $_{\text{the sharp}}\text{stone}_{\text{s}}\ _{\text{of the father}}$, and furthermore, each appendage itself can grow more complex, by acquiring appendages of its own. For example, a thing-word serving as an appendage may pick up its own appendages, as in $_{\text{the}}\text{stone}_{\text{of the }_{\text{old}}\text{ father}}$. And even property-words can acquire their own appendages, in the form of comparative and superlative forms, such as sharp$_{\text{er}}$ or near$_{\text{est}}$. Superlatives, for example, often derive from the quantifier 'all', in expressions such as 'near$_{\text{of all}}$'.

With some of the examples mentioned above, we have even reached a mechanism that can be repeated again and again:

$$\text{the handbag}_{\text{of the aunt}_{\text{of the wife}_{\text{of her lover}}}}$$

The last section will describe how this principle can ultimately be extended to yoke an entire clause into a state of appendagehood, and thus create subordinate clauses. There are still a few more steps to be taken before we can get there, but it is worth stressing that the foundations for subordination have already been laid here.

Now, decked out with all the different types of appendages, the mammoth story could look something like this:

a girl pick fruit turn see **a huge** mammoth
she run to **the nearest** tree and climb it
the mammoth shake **the** tree **the** girl yell yell
her father hear **loud** noise**s from the forest** and run towards her
he throw **the** spear at **the** mammoth and it roar and fall
with a **sharp** stone **the** father cut **some pieces of the** meat for **the** girl
she eat finish and she sleep.

FROM NOUN TO VERB, AND BACK

So far, I have avoided the labels 'noun' and 'verb' when describing our emerging language, and divided words purely on the basis of their meaning, into thing-words and action-words. You may have been wondering why – and if you weren't, you may now be wondering why it even makes any difference whether we call something a 'thing-word' or a 'noun' anyway. There are various reasons why it matters, however, and matters quite a lot. The point is that the thing-versus-action distinction and the noun-versus-verb distinction are altogether different. As I argued at the beginning of the chapter, the distinction in meaning between things and actions goes much deeper than language – it is a fundamental feature of human cognition that precedes language by millions of years. As far as language is concerned, therefore, the thing-versus-action distinction is an axiom. Language did not draw the dividing-line between the two types of concepts, it simply mirrored a division that was already there, if not in the world itself, then at least in the way evolution has programmed our neurons to interpret the world.

The syntactic categories noun and verb, however, have an entirely different status, and represent a purely language-internal division of labour, which is determined not by meaning, but by the roles words assume in the sentence. As Appendix A: Flipping Categories (page 277) illustrates, the syntactic categories noun and verb are based on distribution, that is, on the particular slots in which words appear in the sentence. Nouns, for instance, are words that fit into slots such as X in 'the long X-s'. And while it may be true that all thing-words (words for objects, people, animals) behave as nouns, the opposite certainly doesn't hold. In modern languages, there are plenty of nouns that are not physical things: a 'day', for instance, is not an object but a period of time, and 'movement' is most certainly not a thing – it is a description of an action. Still, both 'day' and 'movement' are perfectly respectable nouns, because they have the same distribution as other nouns, and appear in characteristic noun-slots, such as 'the long X-s'. So one can say 'the long *day*-s' just as naturally as 'the long *leg*-s'.

In modern languages, therefore, the distribution of a word cannot be predicted purely on the basis of its meaning, and this is why a syntactic category like 'noun' is so important for understanding the workings of language. 'Explode' and 'explosion' both refer to the very same violent action, but they have completely different roles in the sentence: the former behaves like 'go' and 'sleep', whereas the latter behaves like 'table' or 'tennis-ball'. So if you want to predict how these two words will interact with other words in the sentence, you have to know that one is a verb, and the other is a noun.

But if the syntactic categories 'noun' and 'verb' are so important, then why did I ignore them so far, and rely only on the thing/action distinction? The reason is that I do not believe we have to take 'noun' and 'verb' as primary God-given concepts. As crucial as these syntactic categories are to the structure of modern language, they probably crystallized only later on in the course of language's evolution.

In the 'me Tarzan' stage there were no words around for abstract concepts, and the vocabulary consisted only of words for physical things and actions. Any differences in distribution between these two groups were a direct consequence of the meaning distinction, so crucially, the behaviour of each word in the primitive sentences at our starting stage could be predicted directly from its meaning. (For example, thing-words clustered as participants around an action-word, but not vice versa.) In this set-up, there really was no need to rely on a separate syntactic distinction, since meaning and distribution coincided exactly.

Furthermore, most of the typical slots that we use to define syntactic categories were not relevant at the 'me Tarzan' stage. To define slots for nouns in modern languages we rely mostly on the characteristic entourage of appendages, so for instance, the slot X in 'the long X-s' is defined by the appendages that surround it: an article, an adjective and a plural marker. But since none of these trappings existed at our starting point, and since the differences in distribution were based directly on the difference in meaning between things and actions, it simply did not make sense to impose a noun-verb distinction on the language at that stage and pretend that a syntactic (that is, distribution-based) distinction already existed independently of the distinction in meaning.

With the developments sketched in the last sections, however, the situation has begun to change. For one thing, the entourage of appendages has given thing-words visibly distinctive slots. But far more importantly, the emergence of terms for abstract concepts has undermined the validity of meaning as an accurate indicator for distribution. The flow from concrete to abstract has created many words for concepts that are no longer physical objects, but nevertheless behave like thing-words in the sentence. For example, the thing-word 'sun' could come to be used for 'day'; 'throat' could be the source of 'voice' or 'sound' or 'life' or 'soul'; 'way' could give rise to 'manner'; 'person' to 'status' or 'condition' – dozens of such examples were mentioned in Chapter 4. The resulting abstract concepts are no longer thing-words, but they inherit their distribution from the thing-words that gave rise to them. A new category of words has thus emerged, which includes not only real thing-words, but also other concepts that behave like thing-words in the sentence. This category, which we can now call 'noun', has now broken away from its *raison d'être* in physical objects. Or looking at it the other way round, language has developed the means for manipulating abstract concepts by presenting them *as* things, and treating them as if they were thing-words.

Languages have even developed specialized grammatical machinery for producing terms for abstract nouns on demand. Think of an English ending like *-hood*, which can take a flesh-and-blood thing-word like 'maiden' and turn it into an abstract concept 'maidenhood', meaning the condition of being a maiden. The development of such off-the-peg abstraction markers can follow the by now familiar paths of erosion in meaning and sound. The following example from a thirteenth-century homily illustrates the origin of English *-hood*:

Of þeos	*þre*	***had**,*				
Of these	three	states,				
*meiden**had***	*and*	*widewe**had***	*and*	*te*	*þridde*	*wedlac**had***
maidenhood,	and	widowhood,	and	the	third	wedlockhood

(. . . maidenhood is by far the best)

The ending *-hood* started out in life as a noun in its own right, *had* (nothing to do with the past tense of 'have', incidentally), which initially meant just 'person', but then acquired the abstract meaning 'state' or 'condition'. The first *had* in the example above represents its original status as an independent word. But *had* also came to be combined with nouns in possessive constructions like *meiden had* 'maiden state', and with frequent use, the two nouns coalesced to become one word, thus producing an abstraction ending *-had* (which later on underwent sound change to *-hood*). Similar developments are found in countless other languages, and so we can safely assume that they must have taken place in much the same way in remote prehistory, thus opening up a whole host of possibilities for creating abstract concepts on demand.

The most striking aspect of the uncoupling of the syntactic noun-verb distinction from the distinction in meaning between things and actions is the ability of modern languages to convert thing-words into verbs ('to cage', 'to chair', 'to water'), and to turn action-words into nouns ('move*ment*', 'explos*ion*', 'beginn*ing*'). When trying to discover how the machinery for achieving such syntactic acrobatics could have developed, one soon finds that there is a marked asymmetry between the two directions, since the conversion of nouns into verbs is much the easier way round. Many languages can simply take a noun, and without any further ado stick it into a verb slot, to express an action that is somehow related to the thing in question. 'To cage' is to put into a cage, 'to skin' is to remove the skin, 'to water' is to supply with water. There is little conceptual difficulty about this operation, since no element of abstraction is involved ('to water', for instance, is just as physical an activity as 'to pour' or 'to flow'). Moreover, when a noun is 'verbed', the meaning of the action in question is usually obvious from the context. As long as you are familiar with the name Google, for instance, you won't need to rush to a dictionary in order to work out what 'to Google someone' might mean. Since this process seems so easy and natural, one can assume that the same trick also occurred naturally to our remote ancestors, so that when they wanted to express an action for which there was no convenient label, say to remove the skin from a hunted animal, an obvious choice would have been to take the characteristic thing-word involved in that action ('skin') and use it in a verb-slot, to denote the action in question.

But the transformation in the other direction is an entirely different matter. Turning an action into a noun (a process which linguists call 'nominalization') seems to be a much more involved affair, which in many languages calls for heavy grammatical guns, such as various types of endings: *-ment* (movement), *-ion* (explosion, promotion), *-ing* (feeling), *-age* (usage) and so on. There also seems to be a fundamental asymmetry in the conceptual status of the conversions in the two directions. I have just said that 'to skin' is a simple physical action, which need not involve any abstraction: it is just a convenient label for a particular activity that has something to do with a 'skin'. But an 'explosion' is not just some particular object that is somehow involved in the action 'explode' – it's not a bomb, or a fuse, or a shard. 'Explosion' is the action itself, somehow conceptualized as a thing. It is thus a concept at a higher level of abstraction.

How could the ability to present actions as nouns have developed? This question poses a much more difficult challenge than understanding the conversions in the other direction, but for some reason, linguists have so far neglected to take up this challenge, and thus the evolution of the grammatical mechanisms of nominalization still remains largely uncharted territory. One reason why little attention has been paid to the origin of nominalization markers is that in the last few decades, linguists have fixed their gaze intently on the main thoroughfares through which content words, solid nouns and verbs, are transformed into grammatical elements (like *-hood*, *gonna*, and so on). The strange thing about nominalization markers, however, is that they never seem to take these main routes of change from 'content' to 'grammar' – they don't reach verbs in broad daylight and on the king's highway. Instead, it appears that they steal their way on to verbs through circuitous byways. They first have to be thoroughly transformed into grammatical elements somewhere else (on nouns or adjectives), and only then are they extended to verbs, resorting to manoeuvres such as analogical 'back formation' to get there.

The French nominalization ending *-age* provides one example of how such manoeuvres can be achieved. In modern French, the ending *-age* can be stuck on verbs of all colours and persuasions to turn them into nouns: *arrivage* 'arrival' (from *arriver* 'arrive'); *arrosage* 'watering' (from *arroser* 'to water'); *chauffage* 'heating' (from *chauffer* 'to heat'). But *-age* started out in Old French in a rather different role, and could originally only be added to *nouns*, in order to turn them into more abstract nouns, rather like English *-hood*. One of the earliest examples of *-age* is in the word *courage* (in Old French spelled *corage*), from the noun *cœur* 'heart'. And there were many other such abstract noun formations in Old French, such as *orphelin-age* 'orphan-hood', which did not survive in the modern language.

The ending *-age* stole its way on to verbs only later on, through an analogical innovation similar to the 'back formations' we met in the previous chapter (those which produced 'greed' and 'grot' from 'greedy' and 'grotty', as well as the Semitic verbal adjective ⓢaⓝⓖum '(a) snogged (thing)' from the verb aⓢⓝiⓖ 'I snogged'.) The suffix *-age* was invested with the power to turn a verb into a noun when speakers applied a pattern for turning nouns into verbs 'in reverse', that is, in a direction which from the historical perspective was the wrong way around. The French noun *mari-age* 'marriage' can provide a convenient canvas for sketching how this analogy could have proceeded.

In Old French, there was a noun *mari* 'husband', to which the ending *-age* seems to have been added directly, giving *mari-age*, which meant something like 'spousehood'. But since nouns in French could easily be transformed into verbs simply by being placed in verb slots (as I mentioned earlier, the NOUN→VERB direction of change is much the easier way round), the noun *mari* also begat the verb *marier* 'to marry'. There were thus two different words in the language which both derived from the original noun *mari*: the abstract noun *mariage* and the verb *marier*. As these two are so close in meaning (after all, 'spousehood' can naturally be understood as the abstract state resulting from the action of 'spousing' someone), it was only natural that an intimate link would emerge in speakers' perception between the verb and the abstract noun. The role of the noun *mari* as the original intermediary between the two could easily be forgotten, and speakers could assume that *mari-age* was directly derived from the verb *marier*. From the historical perspective this assumption was quite wrong, for *-age* originally had no power to turn a verb into a noun – all it could do was turn one noun (*mari*) into another (*mariage*). The only reason why the abstract noun *mari-age* seemed to express the action resulting from the verb *marier* was that the verb itself had originally derived from a noun (*mari*).

But as usual, speakers had no idea about the historical perspective, and by assuming a direct link between *marier* and *mariage*, speakers invested *-age* with entirely new powers to take an action and turn it into an abstract noun, or in other words, to nominalize a verb. And having recognized the pattern, it seemed only natural to extend it to other verbs: *nettoyer* 'to clean' → *nettoyage* 'cleaning', *assembler* → *assemblage*, *arriver* → *arrivage*, and countless others.

I have chosen *-age* as an example, since its extension from nouns to verbs occurred in relatively recent times. But the circuitous route which *-age* had to take to get to the verb seems to represent nominalization markers more generally. For example, a similar analogy appears to have invested the English ending *-ing* with the powers of nominalization (as in 'to feel' → 'a feeling', 'to meet' → 'a meeting'), and in general, whenever the origin of nominalization markers can be traced back far enough, they turn out to have once been grammatical markers on nouns or adjectives which were later extended to verbs through some analogical process. Of course, as there has been so little research into this area, all the claims above should be taken as tentative and preliminary. Nevertheless, it seems plausible that the grammatical machinery for nominalizing verbs first developed in prehistory in much the same way. Once words for abstract concepts had emerged and could be manipulated as if they were things, and once 'noun' and 'verb' had crystallized as distinct syntactic categories, then markers of nominalization could have emerged from analogical innovations similar to the one which invested *-age* with the power to turn a verb into a noun. The resulting ability to nominalize verbs may not seem such a revolutionary step in itself, but it has far-reaching consequences. Not only does it cement the separation between the meaning-based distinction (thing/action) and the syntactic distinction (noun/verb), but as we shall soon see, nominalization serves as one of the two main pillars on which rests the whole edifice of subordination.

THE NUANCES OF THE ACTION

One whole area of grammar that is still entirely missing from our unfolding language is the various nuances of the action: 'he yells', 'she yelled', 'was yelling', 'will yell', 'must have yelled', 'was made to yell', and so on. But in fact, much of this ground has already been covered in previous chapters. Chapter 5, for instance, demonstrated with the English 'going to' and French 'have to' how future tense markers can develop. And Appendix C: The Devil in the Detail describes how some elaborate nuances, such as causatives and passives, emerged in the Semitic languages.

Markers for other nuances can emerge along much the same lines. Past tense markers, for instance, can develop from 'come from' (as in French *il vient d'arriver* 'he has just arrived'). Markers for continuous action, as in 'she *was* rid*ing*', often originate from constructions like 'be *on* something'. The Dutch phrase *zij was aan het rijden* (literally 'she was on the riding') still betrays this origin transparently, but in fact, the English equivalent comes from exactly the same source: what started out as 'she was on riding' eroded first to 'she was a-riding' and finally to just 'she was riding'. Markers for completed actions, as 'she has eaten' or 'she ate up' often derive from the verb 'finish', in juxtapositions such as 'eat finish'. The ancient Chinese verb *liǎo*, for instance, started out as an independent action meaning 'finish', but in the modern language, has eroded in meaning and form into the grammatical element *-le*, which denotes completed action:

tā *shuì-***le** *sānge* *zhōngtóu*
she sleep-**le** three hour
'she has slept three hours'

One further axis of variation that has not been mentioned so far is 'modality': the expression of what speakers think about an action ('should happen', 'ought not to happen') or know about it ('couldn't have happened', 'must have happened'). Nuances of obligation often originate from verbs of possession – our old acquaintances from Chapter 4. The close link between possession and obligation can clearly be seen in English expressions such as 'I *have* to do it', 'I've *got* to do it', and even 'I *ought* to do it' ('ought' goes back to a verb meaning 'possess', and has exactly the same origin as the verb 'own'). Similar developments from possession to obligation can be observed in languages all over the world, and the image behind them seems to be that one is responsible for the things in one's possession, so if an action 'belongs' to you, it belongs to your sphere of responsibility, and so it is your duty to do it.

Markers of obligation can then flow further into even subtler domains, and become indicators of likelihood. The intimate relation between obligation and likelihood is nicely illustrated by an anecdote from the Soviet era. The story goes that during his state visit to Moscow, Fidel Castro is shown around the capital by Leonid Brezhnev. First of all, Castro is invited for a beer, which he downs in one go, and praises heartily. 'Yes,' says Brezhnev, 'it was provided by our good friends from Czechoslovakia.' Then Castro is chauffeured around the city, and is rather taken by the limo. 'Yes,' says Brezhnev, 'these cars are provided by our good friends from Czechoslovakia.' Later on, they visit an exhibition of fine crystal, and Castro duly waxes lyrical. 'Yes,' says Brezhnev, 'the crystal is provided by our good friends from Czechoslovakia.' 'They must be very good friends,' says Castro. 'Yes,' says Brezhnev, 'they must.'

Castro's 'must' is a statement about likelihood, whereas Brezhnev's is of course a diktat of obligation. In this anecdote, it is Brezhnev's heavy-handed 'must' which shifts the meaning unexpectedly, but from a historical perspective, Brezhnev's 'must' actually represents the original meaning, whereas Castro's is only a derivative. In fact, the extension of obligation markers to the domain of likelihood is an extremely well-trodden path. In English, practically all the original markers of obligation and permission have acquired a meaning of likelihood: 'they *must* be very good friends', 'they *should* be getting their results next week', 'he *may* have met her', 'it *can't* have happened'. The logic behind the common shift from obligation to likelihood is simply that in real life, the weight of obligation on you to do something closely correlates with the likelihood that you will do it.

In fact, the development of likelihood markers is a perfect example of one of those long paths of metaphor, which lead from the simplest of physical activities all the way through to the subtlest of grammatical nuances. Markers of likelihood can develop from markers of obligation, which can themselves develop from markers of possession, which in turn originate from the simple physical activity of 'seizing' or 'getting':

SEIZING →	POSSESSION →	OBLIGATION →	LIKELIHOOD
('get me a beer')	('he's got a car')	('I've gotta go')	('she's gotta be there by now')

Finally, in addition to the standard when-how-and-what-you-think-about-it nuances, modern languages have also developed means for imparting more specific information about the manner in which an action occurs, by using 'adverbs' such as *loudly*, *sharply*, and so on. In terms of their role in the sentence, such adverbs can be regarded as appendages of the verb, just as adjectives like 'loud' are appendages of the noun. In fact, many languages do not even make a consistent distinction between the two, and simply use adjectives also as verb-appendages, as in 'speak loud and clear' or 'love me tender, love me sweet'. Nevertheless, in some languages particular grammatical markers have developed for adapting property-words into adverbs. The origin of such elements is often an independent noun meaning something like 'manner', 'way', or 'frame of mind'. The English ending *-ly*, for instance, goes back to a Proto-Germanic noun **līka*, which originally meant 'body' or 'appearance', but also came to express 'manner'.

All the examples above represent common and recurring paths along which markers of verbal nuances develop in language after language. And so it is likely that very similar paths led to the first emergence of grammatical markers for verbal nuances in remote prehistory. With these new elements in place (nuances of the action, adverbs, and nominalized verbs such as 'movement' or 'scream') our story might now look something like this:

A girl **was** pick**ing** fruit **one day**. **Suddenly** she hear**d** some **movement** behind her. She turn**ed around** and **saw** a huge mammoth. She **ran** to the nearest tree and climb**ed** it. The mammoth **shook** the tree **roughly**. The terrified girl yell**ed hysterically**. Her father hear**d** loud **screams** from the forest. He **thought**: my daughter **must be** in danger. He grabb**ed** his spear and **ran** towards her. He **threw** his spear straight at the mammoth, and the mammoth **let** out a roar and **fell** to the ground. With a sharp stone the father **cut** some pieces of meat for the girl. She **ate** them **up** and **fell fast** asleep.

SUBORDINATION

Our language now has nuanced actions, it has pronouns, it has heavier clauses with many different participants, and it has participants that can themselves be surrounded by an entourage of appendages. There is only one last major feature that is still missing, a property that is often touted as the jewel in the crown of language, and the best example for the ingenuity of its design: the ability to subsume a whole clause within another, and thus to produce expressions of infinite variety, as in the increasingly convoluted descriptions of the seal from Chapter 1:

- The seal
- The seal that was eyeing a fish
- The seal that was eyeing a fish that kept jumping in and out of the icy water

And there is no need to stop there, because in theory, the mechanisms of subordination allow the sentence to go on and on for as long as there is breath to spare:

> I must have already told you about that quarrelsome seal that was eyeing a disenchanted but rather attractive fish that kept jumping in and out of the icy water without paying the least attention to the heated debate being

conducted by a phlegmatic walrus and two young octopuses who had recently been tipped off by a whale with connections in high places that the government was about to introduce speed limits on swimming in the reef area due to the overcrowding caused by the recent influx of new tuna immigrants from the Indian Ocean where temperatures rose so much last year that . . .

Subordination allows us to convey highly complex information in a coherent way, by weaving different assertions on multiple levels into one intricate whole, while keeping the complexity of each of these levels under control. The paragraph above, for instance, has just one simple sentence at its primary level: 'I must have already told you about that seal.' But from the 'seal' downwards, more and more information is interlaced using subordinate clauses of different types: 'a seal *that was* . . .', 'had been tipped off *that* . . .', 'introduce speed limits *due to* . . .'

To understand how this whole range of knots could have evolved to tie clauses together, let us consider one showcase example, the archetypal (and probably also the oldest) type of subordinate clause, the relative clause. The defining feature of relative clauses is that they function as appendages of a noun, as in 'a seal$_{\text{that was . . .}}$', 'an argument$_{\text{being conducted}}$', or 'the Indian Ocean$_{\text{where temperatures rose}}$'. As these examples illustrate, there is a variety of different markers used to turn a clause into an appendage of a noun. But as far as the basic principles are concerned, it would be fair to say that the whole elaborate contraption of relative clauses is really just a spin-off from one fundamental feature of linguistic design: the ability to take any verb and turn it into an appendage of a noun, as in 'the $_{\text{running}}$lion' or 'fear$_{\text{of swimming}}$'. And what is more, this ability is in fact already present in our developing language, because it is really just a combination of two mechanisms that have already been derived: appendagehood and the nominalization of verbs.

Earlier on in this chapter we saw how the notion of appendagehood could have developed, allowing the noun to attract hangers-on (adjectives, as in '$_{\text{tall}}$child', or other nouns in a possessive construction, as in 'fear$_{\text{of heights}}$'), which supply additional information about it, but do not interfere with its role on the main level of the sentence. The grammatical mechanisms for nominalizing verbs, that is, for turning verbs into nouns (or adjectives), have also already been derived. The section 'from noun to verb, and back' showed how an analogical process invested the abstract-noun ending *-age* with the power to turn a verb into a noun. And in the previous chapter (page 204), I suggested that a similar process could have created verbal adjectives in Semitic, that is, adjectives like 'running' or 'twisted' which are derived from verbs. Now, putting the ability to nominalize a verb together with the ability to turn a noun or adjective into an appendage, it becomes clear that our language already has the ability to take any verb and squeeze it into the role of an appendage to any noun: 'the $_{\text{running}}$lion', 'a $_{\text{twisted}}$mind', or 'fear$_{\text{of swimming}}$'. But in compressing a verb – the nucleus of a whole clause – into the role of a mere appendage, we have in fact got subordination in all but name. The basic machinery is already in place, and the rest is only a matter of natural expansion of this squeezed appendage-verb.

Real adjectives like 'tall' or 'sharp' are quite content in their role as appendages (as in '$_{\text{tall}}$child'), because by their very nature, they are designed for this subservient role. Even nouns seem fairly content in the humble role of an appendage ('fear$_{\text{of heights}}$'), and have no pressing need to expand. But with verbs, the situation is entirely different. Verbs are by their very nature the hub of an entire clause, and are used to being at the centre of the action, with numerous participants crowding around them. And as we have seen, it has taken some pressure to squeeze those bundles of energy into the role of mere appendages. (For example, some heavy conceptual machinery, the analogical process of 'back formation', was needed to press the verb into the role of an adjective or a noun.) It is hardly surprising, then, that straitjacketed into the role of an appendage, a verb would feel rather repressed, and would wish to expand, in order to be surrounded by the cohorts of participants it is accustomed to. So once constructions like 'the $_{\text{running}}$lion' are already a staple feature of the language, then it is only a small step for speakers to extend them to something like 'the $_{\text{running after the fox}}$lion' (or 'the lion$_{\text{running after the fox}}$'), in which the verbal adjective 'running', while still subordinate to the noun, nevertheless acquires some participants of its own. This modest expansion looks obvious and natural, but just consider what it has created: we now have an entire clause, with action, participants and all, subsumed as an appendage of a noun. In other words, we have now arrived at a relative clause.

Of course, one may object that 'the lion$_{\text{running after the fox}}$' is only a 'participial clause', and doesn't really look like a 'proper' English relative clause such as 'the lion$_{\text{that ran after the fox}}$'. Nevertheless, some languages, such as Turkish, conduct practically all their business of subordination with precisely such participial relative clauses, and in fact, all the fundamental principles of subordination are already present in this construction. In particular, the possibility of recursion (the ability to go on inserting one clause within another) is already contained in the mechanisms that we have derived. The relative clause appended to the noun 'lion', 'running after the fox', itself includes a noun 'fox'. So if it's possible to do the trick once, and subsume a clause under the noun 'lion', what prevents us from doing it all over again, and subsuming another clause under 'fox': the lion$_{\text{running after the fox}_{\text{chasing the rabbit}}}$? And again, and again – in theory, it is possible to go on and on:

the lion$_{\text{running after the fox}_{\text{chasing the rabbit}_{\text{sniffing the dandelion}_{\text{blowing in the wind}_{\text{coming from the east}}}}}}$

Still, what about the origin of those relative clauses such as 'the lion$_{\text{that ran after the fox}}$', which we have all been schooled to regard as the 'proper' representative of this class in English? There are two main features that distinguish such clauses from the participial ones above: the presence of a relative marker such as 'that' (a grammatical word which introduces the subordinate clause and marks its boundary), and the replacement of a verbal adjective 'running' by a 'finite' form of the verb 'ran' (a form with tense and person markings, which looks just like a normal verb in an independent clause). Unfortunately, the exact details of how these two features developed in the history of English are beyond our reach, because the process occurred before the attested period, and the traces it left in the earliest records are highly inconclusive. Nevertheless, clues from other languages suggest that the emergence of both features can be understood as a natural consequence of the appendage-verb's drive towards expansion.

The motivation for using a grammatical word like 'that' to introduce the relative clauses must stem from the increasing length and complexity of these clauses. Once relative clauses grow more elaborate and laden with participants (each of which may come with its own personal relative clause), listeners may start finding the precise boundaries between the clauses difficult to determine. Trick examples such as 'fat people eat accumulates', or 'I saw the horse cantering past the barn fall' illustrate some of the pitfalls of relative clauses without a special marker to introduce them. The boundaries become apparent, of course, when the relative marker 'that' is added: 'fat that people eat accumulates', or 'I saw the horse that was cantering round the barn fall'. In some languages, the use of a pointing word like 'that' to introduce relative clauses can be traced to an emphatic construction, probably employed to increase transparency. Instead of just saying something like 'the lion$_{\text{running after the fox}}$', speakers can add both emphasis and clarity by dangling the relative clause not from the 'lion' itself, but from a pointing-word in apposition to it: 'the lion, that (one)$_{\text{running after the fox}}$'. With time and frequent repetition, however, the pointing-word can lose its emphatic force, and come to be perceived as simply the marker that introduces the relative clause: 'the lion$_{\text{that running after the fox}}$'.

Finally, it is not too difficult to imagine the motivation for using a finite verb like 'ran' in the relative clause, instead of a verbal adjective. A form like 'running' cannot specify nuances such as tense, and so it is only natural for speakers to try to expand their range of expression by replacing 'running' with a finite verb, and thus gain the ability to distinguish between 'the lion$_{\text{that ran after the fox}}$', 'the lion$_{\text{that will run after the fox}}$', 'the lion$_{\text{that should have run after the fox}}$' and so on.

Stripped to its bare essentials, therefore, the development of the relative clause, that prized instrument of linguistic sophistication that allows us to subsume unrestricted amounts of information under one participant, may be understood as a very natural sequel to a somewhat forced operation. Once a verb, normally the core of a whole clause, has been forced into the subservient role of a mere appendage, it is natural for speakers to let it expand back to its original dimensions as the centre of a clause, while still maintaining its subordinate status as an appendage. The result is a whole clause which functions as an appendage to a noun.

With subordination, we have finally reached the end of our whistle-stop tour through the evolution of complex language. The mammoth story could now look something like this:

A girl **who was** picking fruit one day suddenly heard some movement behind her. She turned around and saw a huge mammoth charg**ing** straight at her. She ran to the nearest tree and climbed up it, but the mammoth shook the tree **so roughly that** the terrified girl started yell**ing** hysterically. Her father, **who** heard loud screams **coming** from the forest, realized **that** his daughter must be in danger, **so** he grabbed his spear and ran towards her. He threw his spear straight at the mammoth, **which** let out a **blood-curdling** roar and fell to the ground. With a sharp stone he cut some pieces of meat for the girl, **who** ate them up **before** falling fast asleep.

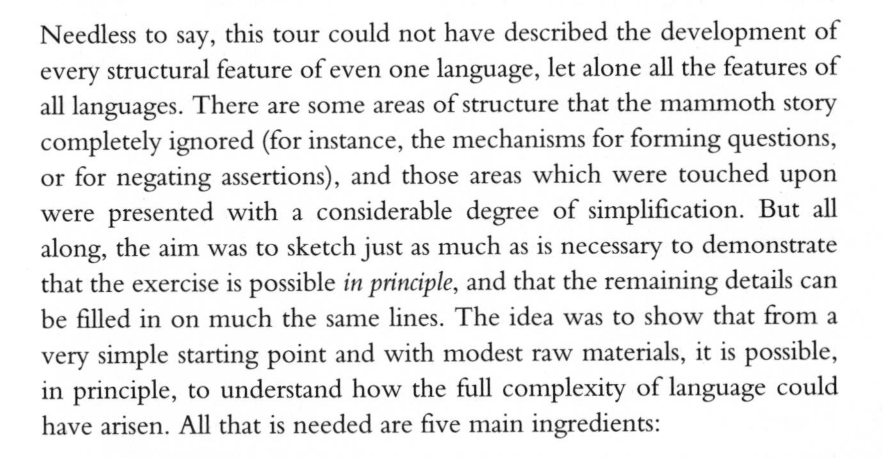

Needless to say, this tour could not have described the development of every structural feature of even one language, let alone all the features of all languages. There are some areas of structure that the mammoth story completely ignored (for instance, the mechanisms for forming questions, or for negating assertions), and those areas which were touched upon were presented with a considerable degree of simplification. But all along, the aim was to sketch just as much as is necessary to demonstrate that the exercise is possible *in principle*, and that the remaining details can be filled in on much the same lines. The idea was to show that from a very simple starting point and with modest raw materials, it is possible, in principle, to understand how the full complexity of language could have arisen. All that is needed are five main ingredients:

(i) A human brain (capable of learning a language, drawing analogies, thinking in terms of metaphor, and so on).
(ii) Human beings who wish to communicate with each other for essentially the same purposes as those that motivate us today.
(iii) Words for some simple physical objects and simple actions.
(iv) A few natural principles of ordering, which stem from somewhere very deep in our cognition.
(v) A bit of time.

EPILOGUE

This book began with a paradox. Language seems so skilfully crafted that it appears to be the work of a master architect – and yet its complex structure must somehow have arisen of its own accord. This initial paradox led to a series of other puzzles. Why is it that even the most imposing linguistic edifices are always marred by irregularities? Why do earlier stages of languages seem so much better behaved than the unruly present? And most worrying of all, why do linguistic structures only seem to disintegrate when one follows them over the course of time? These problems also raised wider questions about directionality. Are the forces of change really steering language in one particular direction, or are they driving it round and round in circles? A lot of ink has flowed since these questions were first posed, so if we briefly return to them by way of recapitulation, we can gauge how far we have come.

The previous chapters revealed that complex linguistic structures can arise through the natural forces that are changing language all the time, even today. The elaborate conventions of language needed no gifted inventor to conceive them, no prehistoric assembly of elders to decree their shape, nor even an overseer to guide their construction. Of course, saying that language changes 'of its own accord' does not mean that it evolved independently of people's actions. Behind the forces of change there are always people – the speakers of a language. Nevertheless, language change joins a long list of phenomena, from traffic jams to the appearance of beaten tracks through fields, which are brought about through people's actions, but are not wilfully intended by them. The transformations in language do not arise from anyone's preoccupation with large-scale landscape design, but emerge from much more spontaneous and immediate concerns, such as saving effort in pronunciation (economy) or the desire to heighten the effect of an utterance (expressiveness).

The accumulated pressure of such spontaneous actions nonetheless creates powerful and untiring forces of change: the flow towards abstraction, and erosion in meaning and sounds. The combination of these forces operates on language like a relentless bleaching and compressing machine. To increase expressive range, solid nouns and verbs are drafted as metaphors for abstract concepts, but with frequent use their original vitality fades and they turn into pale grammatical elements bleached of independent meaning. And to heighten the effect, words are piled up into new constructions, but through the grind of repetition the piles are gradually worn down, and can be compressed into a single word again. The more often a construction is used, the stronger the pressures of erosion, and so the more likely it is to be condensed. The grammar of a language thus comes to code most compactly and efficiently those constructions that are used most frequently. In other words, grammar codes best what it does most often. All this lends language the appearance of a skilfully crafted instrument, but what forged this instrument was not the workshop of any wordsmith, it was the constant pressures of effective communication and of transmission over the generations. Language is a tool that has been worn into shape by continual use.

If there is any element of 'invention' in language, it is surely the mind's craving for order – the instinctive difficulty to accept that so much is just random, arbitrary and coincidental. The forces of change occasionally produce forms with ear-catching features, quite by chance. And as a language is transmitted from generation to generation, such features pass through the filter of new speakers' order-craving minds. The deep-seated assumption that patterns can't be random makes speakers seize even on accidental features and invest them with meaning. The element of invention thus consists of spotting a coincidental pattern such as 'fork' (which happens to sound like 'four+k') or 'grotty' (which sounds like 'grot+y'), presuming it must be there for some good reason, and accordingly creating new forms such as 'threek' and 'grot'. And as we have seen, the cumulative effect of such small-scale inventions can sometimes create the most spectacular results.

Nevertheless, even such innovations do not create new materials out of thin air. Innovations are always based on some recycling principle, and employ old means for new ends: existing words are drafted to convey novel senses, existing patterns are filled with novel functions. The users of language have thus perfected the art of making the most of what's already there. And it is for this reason that in the previous chapter, only very modest raw materials were needed to start us off on the tour through the unfolding of complex language. All that was required at the 'me Tarzan' stage were words for physical objects and actions (as well as two pointing words), and a few natural principles for ordering them. From these basic materials, the natural forces of change could have fashioned the structure of language in all its prolix splendour.

Another way of measuring how far we have come is to descend for a moment from the high plane of principles and recall some of the actual linguistic structures which were on display at the very beginning of the book, and which originally seemed so unlikely to have arisen through anything other than a meticulous plan. In the previous chapters, we revisited most of these structures, from the Latin case system to the Semitic verb, and gained a 'hands-on' familiarity with how they could have evolved. There is one example, however, which appeared right at the opening, but which has not featured since then: the Sumerian word *munintuma'a* 'when he had made it suitable for her'. This sentence-word comes from a dedication written some 4,500 years ago by Enannatum, a ruler of the Sumerian city Lagash (which lay not far from today's Basra in southern Iraq). In his inscription, Enannatum boasts of a temple he has dedicated to the Goddess Inanna, saying that 'he made the Eanna temple for her higher than all the mountains, and decorated it for her with silver and gold'. And then comes *munintuma'a*: 'when he had made it suitable for her . . .'

In the introduction, I mentioned the compact structure of Sumerian words, whose verbs are made up of fixed slots, which allow a single sound to carry a specific portion of meaning:

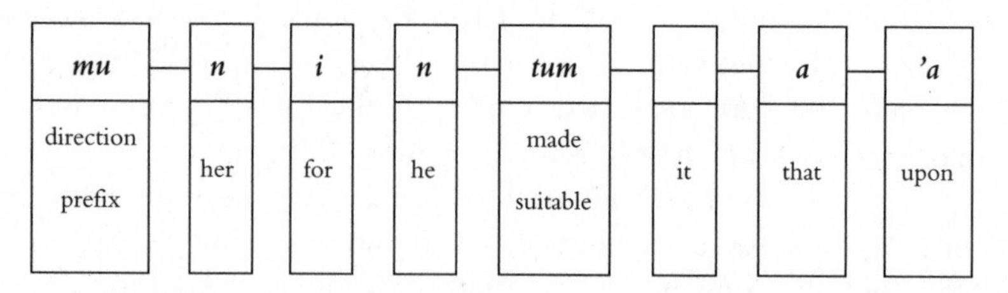

Reading roughly back to front: 'upon that he made it suitable for her'.

Inanna, the Sumerian Venus

Enannatum, ruler of Lagash (~2500 BC)

In fact, even the absence of a sound in one of the slots can convey specific information, as can be seen from the empty slot immediately after the root *tum*. This slot stands for the direct object, and when empty, it signals that the direct object is an 'it'. (Just for comparison, if the meaning were 'when he had made *you* suitable for her', then this slot would be filled by *en*.)

But how could such a design have emerged? Although the actual details can never be known (the development which brought about this structure took place more than 5,000 years ago), the principles should no longer seem too mysterious. The different slots around the stem *tum* 'made suitable' must have developed through the compacting effect of erosion, when wave after wave of once independent words (pronouns, prepositions, postpositions) crashed on to the verb and fused with it on both sides. The inner slots, the ones closest to the stem, represent the earlier waves, and the outer slots represent later ones. Even the empty slot in the middle must have been a natural result of this process of compression. One can assume that initially, certain pronouns, like 'it', could be omitted in some contexts. Once the first wave of pronouns had fused with the stem, an 'empty ending' could have come to stand for a particular direct object 'it'. But with time, the 'empty ending' was pushed inwards by the fusion of new elements, thus creating an empty slot in the middle of the word. So in fact, even a nifty design such as the Sumerian slot-structure need not have been consciously invented, and could have arisen through the natural forces of change.

SEXED TURNIPS AND EDIBLE AEROPLANES

The question of regularity and irregularity in language – the strange symbiosis of the orderly and the haphazard – has accompanied us in various guises throughout the book. Initially, it might have seemed baffling that alongside all the grand structures of language there should be so much that is untidy: erratic English past-tenses, irregular Latin flowers, not to mention sexed German turnips. What was even more worrying was that much of this irregularity appeared to be of fairly recent origin. The utterly irregular Latin pair *flos-floris*, for instance, can be traced back to a perfectly regular ancestor, *flos-flosis*. The conclusion that was initially drawn from such examples was that the further back in time one digs, the more perfect the language, and if one could only reach far enough into prehistory, one would discover a Golden Age of perfection. But this Golden Age turned out to be an optical illusion, created by one critical oversight. While present irregularities may indeed go back to past regularities, the processes of change can also level out old irregularities and create new regular forms. The changes towards regularity, however, leave behind much less evidence. For instance, if there didn't happen to be any records of Old English and related languages, there would be no way of telling today that there was ever an *s-r* irregularity in the past tense of the verb 'choose': *ceas-curon* ('I chose–they chose'). So languages were no more perfect in prehistoric times than they are now, it's just that scores of irregularities have been swept away by the breezes of change and have vanished without trace, like yesterday's footprints on a sand-dune.

Nevertheless, the realization that prehistoric languages must have been as badly behaved as modern ones only sharpens the fundamental question about the role of irregularity in language: why is there so much of it? Or to echo Mark Twain, why are German turnips female (*die Rübe*) and German maidens neuter (*das Mädchen*)? Alas, the origins of the German gender system lie so deep in the past that it is impossible to reconstruct all the actual developments that led to its many idiosyncrasies. But even if the details are beyond reach, the principles responsible should no longer be so mysterious. Genders can start out as logical and transparent classification systems. The markers for the female gender, for instance, could have developed simply from the word 'woman' or 'girl', and initially the female gender would have included just what one would expect: people of the feminine sex. But a series of simple changes could quickly have confused the picture beyond all recognition. Since the German details cannot be recovered, here is an example which can answer Twain's question indirectly, by showing how an entirely different language has managed to include aeroplanes in the 'vegetable gender'.

One might well wonder what a 'vegetable gender' is in the first place. In linguistic jargon, however, 'gender' has nothing to do with sex, and can refer to any kind of classification that a language imposes on nouns. While sex-based gender is an extremely common type of classification, some languages have special genders not only for 'male' and 'female', but also for classes of nouns such as 'long objects', 'dangerous things', or 'edible parts of plants'. Many aboriginal languages of Australia, for example, have a special gender for 'edible vegetables', and the grammatical element that marks this gender seems to have originated, unsurprisingly, from the word 'vegetable' itself. So far so good – in theory, all this sounds quite reasonable. But what may seem rather less obvious is why one aboriginal language, Gurr-goni (spoken in Arnhem Land in northern Australia), should include in this vegetable gender the noun 'aeroplane'.

The explanation is in fact fairly straightforward. As a first step, the gender of 'edible vegetables' must have been extended to other plants, and hence to all kinds of wooden things more generally. Then comes an equally plausible move: canoes are made of wood, and so by a very natural extension, they came to be included in this class as well. Since canoes also happened to be the main means of transport for the speakers of Gurr-goni, the class was then widened to include means of transportation more generally. And so, when the borrowed word *erriplen* first entered the language, it was naturally assigned to the 'edible vegetable' gender. Each extension in this chain of changes was in itself quite natural, and made perfect sense in its own local domain. The end-result, however, puts even Twain's turnips in the shade.

Of course, genders are just one example of the mischief that languages can get up to. But the reasons why gender systems so often misbehave are symptomatic of the causes for irregularity elsewhere. It is precisely because language was never created according to a master plan that order and chaos are so hopelessly entangled. One would be hard-pressed to find any change in language which is irrational or irregular when considered in its own local environment. The only problem is that the motives for change rarely take heed of anything outside their local environment, and can thus produce inconsistencies across language as a whole. To take just one example, in American English, 'dove' is now emerging as the past tense of 'dive', clearly by analogy on the very common verb 'drive-drove'. In this local domain, the change makes perfect sense, because 'dive-dove' becomes more similar to 'drive-drove'. But in the wider domain of the verbal system, the change has created another irregular past tense. Similarly, the effort-saving change that created the pair *flos-floris* made perfect sense on the local level of sounds: it changed *s* to *r* only in those phonetic environments where an *r* required less effort to pronounce. But when one moves away from the local sound-environment and looks at the wider picture of word-structure, it transpires that the change has created chaos, leaving *flos* with *s* in one case, but *r* in all the other cases. Innovations thus arise from local small-scale concerns, such as saving effort or extending one pattern on the model of another. And while a series of such innovations can sometimes accumulate to produce structures on a grand scale, no overseer guides the construction, and so linguistic structures rarely rise without some irregularities cropping up in almost every corner.

TIME'S ARROW AND TIME'S CYCLE

Perhaps the most difficult puzzle which has teased us throughout the book is the question of directionality: where is language heading? Are changes just a matter of 'decay', or do they amount to 'progress'? Is time spear-heading language in one particular direction, or is language just whirling round and round in circles?

The previous chapters have shown that each of the recurrent paths of change mostly goes just one way. Metaphors flow from concrete to abstract, not the other way around; erosion makes words shorter and weaker, not longer and stronger. Indeed, it was this intrinsic directionality that enabled us to gaze into the distant past and imagine what a much more primitive stage in language's evolution might have looked like. The logic was quite simple: if words for abstract concepts always develop from more concrete terms, then there must have been a period before there were words around for abstract concepts. And if grammatical elements always originate from content words like nouns and verbs, then there must have been a stage (which I nick-named 'me Tarzan') before language had any grammatical elements.

Nevertheless, even if all these individual paths of change go just one way, does it necessarily mean that language *as a whole* is moving in one particular direction? If this question concerns the initial period of growth just after the 'me Tarzan' stage, then the answer must surely be 'yes'. The developments which followed that stage made language qualitatively different: abstract concepts and grammatical elements appeared for the first time, and language thus became a more powerful tool of communication. But if the question of directionality refers to later periods, after that initial spurt of growth, then matters become much less straightforward. Have languages been moving in a clear direction more recently?

The previous chapters illustrated that even if individual paths of change lead in only one direction, the different forces of change can nevertheless combine to create a cyclic effect, thus leaving language as a whole in a rough state of equilibrium. For example, erosion can make longer words shorter, but expressiveness can motivate speakers to pile up shorter words, and erosion can then condense the pile into one longer word again. On average, then, words need not get either much shorter or much longer over the centuries. The same logic applies to grammatical structures such as case systems: they emerge when independent postpositions fuse with nouns, but erosion can then wear the endings away altogether, only to make way for another round of fusions. So in the past few tens of millennia, languages could have been moving in cycles, happily ever after.

The only problem with this idyllic cyclical scenario is that it doesn't square with what can actually be observed in the last few millennia. The Indo-European languages, for example, have seen a marked drift towards shorter words and simpler word-structure (or 'morphology', in linguistic jargon). The ancient ancestor, Proto-Indo-European, had as many as eight different cases for nouns, most of which had distinct forms for singular, plural and dual, thus giving a mesh of almost twenty distinct endings for each noun. But over the last 5,000 years or so, this complex array of endings has largely eroded away. In Modern English, for example, only two distinct forms of the noun remain: *boy* and *boy+s* (the latter standing for *boys*, *boy's*, and *boys'*). The information that the ancestor language conveyed through case endings is expressed in modern English with the combinations of independent words: 'with the boy', 'to the boy', 'of the boy', 'by the boy', and so on. As one moves forwards in time, then, morphology seems to have become simpler and simpler. Moreover, this drift towards ending-less words is by no means restricted to English, and can be seen in all the daughter languages of Proto-Indo-European, even if not exactly to the same degree. So is there something untoward here?

In itself, the wearing away of all those ancient endings is anything but mysterious. As we have seen, erosion is a mighty and merciless force, and given sufficient time, no endings can withstand it. So the disappearance of the original Proto-Indo-European endings could simply be one phase of these cycles: old endings die away, but new ones re-emerge from the ashes. The only problem with this explanation is that in the last five millennia, few significant new waves of fusion seem to have begun. The drift towards simpler word-structure came about because old endings were worn away (just as we would expect), but perhaps contrary to expectation, new fusions have generally failed to materialize, and so few new endings were created.

Linguists in the nineteenth century felt that this drift towards simpler word-structure was a debasement, and a source of shame. Moulded by the precepts of German Romanticism, linguists like Schleicher and von Humboldt convinced themselves that the structure of words embodied the 'soul of a language', and that languages with a complex system of endings were at the 'highest form of perfection', while languages with shorter words were either primitive or corrupted. That, of course, was pure prejudice, because prepositions (such as 'to', 'with', 'by') and auxiliaries (such as 'will', 'must', 'can') convey exactly the same information as the revered case and verbal endings, and no less well. Neither system is inherently 'better' than the other, and each has its advantages and disadvantages. Elaborate systems of endings may be more compact, but prepositions and auxiliaries are more user-friendly, since they maintain a more transparent relation between meaning and form.

So while it is true that most of the old endings have indeed decayed (that is, eroded almost entirely out of existence), it is absurd to call the drift the 'decay of the language'. In fact, had nineteenth-century linguists been less dazzled by all things old and classical, they might have observed that the drift was not even entirely without exceptions. As we saw in Chapter 5, the French verb acquired a new set of endings for the future tense, and in modern spoken French, new person prefixes are emerging from the fusion of pronouns with the verb. There are also other scattered examples for new endings and prefixes emerging in other Indo-European languages. Furthermore, nineteenth-century linguists did themselves a disservice by concentrating so much on one area in language, morphology, to the detriment of all others. For while European languages may have lost in the complexity of their word-structure over the last few millennia, they have undoubtedly become more complex in other areas, for instance in the variety of subordinate clauses they employ, or in their inventory of distinct sounds.

Nevertheless, even if the nineteenth-century interpretation of the drift towards simpler word-structure can be dismissed as so much Romantic prejudice, the actual existence of this drift cannot be written off so lightly. Word-structure *has* become much simpler in the Indo-European languages, and although this is neither 'good' nor 'bad', it is still a fact, and one that begs explanation. Why have European languages moved *en masse* towards simpler morphology? And why have new fusions generally failed to materialize?

The first explanation that comes to mind is that the last few millennia just happen to constitute one phase of a very long cycle. According to this line of argument, the languages have simply gone through the phase of shedding their old endings, but have not started acquiring new complex morphology just yet. So maybe it's simply a coincidence that we happen to be around in this stage right now, and if we could observe the Indo-European languages in a thousand years or so, they might all be picking up case endings once again. Of course, it is rather difficult to disprove such an argument with hard evidence, for obvious reasons. (But watch this space for the second edition in 3005.) Still, the idea that the last few millennia simply happened to be a 'shedding phase' seems rather unlikely, for by anyone's standards, 4,000 years is a long time. New case endings can arise within a much shorter period than just one millennium, and sometimes, several complete cycles can be observed over the course of such a time-span. So if it were all entirely a matter of chance, then over the historical period, one would expect to observe not only the disintegration of old case systems but also the emergence of many new ones. And as this has not really happened, the argument that we just happen to be in a shedding phase doesn't have a case ending to rest on.

But if the drift is not just a coincidence of observation, what else could it be? Is there any plausible reason why endings eroded away during the historical period, but were generally not replaced by new fusions? When trying to address this question, one must venture off the beaten track of established scholarship, and step out into more dangerous and speculative terrain. The following remarks, therefore, should be seen as no more than tentative and provisional, a reconnaissance mission to a territory that linguists have yet to chart.

SCHLEICHER'S REVENGE?

August Schleicher, as we have seen, came up with a remarkable theory to explain the drift towards simpler word-structure in the Indo-European languages. Like any other living organism, he argued, languages have a period of growth followed by a period of decay. And the pivotal moment between these two stages is none other than the 'dawn of history'. In prehistoric times, according to Schleicher, nations were busy perfecting the structure of their language (by which he actually meant word-structure). But once history dawned, they started spending their energies elsewhere, and so their languages began to decay. As other linguists later pointed out, however, language is *not* a living organism which must first grow and then decay, but a system of conventions used for communication between people. The changes in these conventions result from the pressures of everyday communication,

August Schleicher (1821–1868)

and since people must have communicated with one another in roughly the same way before and after history began, the motives for change in language must have been the same in prehistory as today. So there should really be no reason why a such an about-turn from language-building to decay should have occurred right at the 'dawn of history'.

But hang on a moment. What does it actually mean to say that people communicated in 'roughly the same way' before and after the dawn of history? Clearly, people 10,000 years ago did not communicate in precisely the same way as we communicate today. They did not write letters or emails, did not read books and newspapers, did not speak on the telephone, did not listen to the radio, and so on. More importantly, they lived in much smaller communities than ours, and had contact with a much narrower circle of people. Communication was thus almost exclusively among intimates, in stark contrast to these days, when a significant proportion of our communication is with strangers. But do such differences in communication patterns really matter, and could they somehow be involved in the drift towards simpler word-forms?

One thing is certain: these differences in the patterns of communication cannot affect the fundamentals of language change. Speakers can't have been any less lazy 10,000 years ago, and must have taken just as many short cuts in pronunciation as we do now. Like us, they must have been motivated by the need for greater expressiveness, and their order-craving minds must also have worked in much the same way as ours. Nevertheless, it is also evident that the course of language change is determined by a fine balance between different forces, so is it possible that even a slight upset to the balance could have made a significant difference? There appear to be good reasons to think so. In today's world, the languages with the most complex word-structure tend to be the 'exotic' tongues of simple tribal societies, typically spoken by at most a few hundred people. (As I mentioned in the introduction, this is in stark contrast to popular prejudice that 'primitive peoples' speak 'primitive languages'.) Of course, this does not mean that complex word-structure is found only in small societies – just think of Arabic, spoken by hundreds of millions. But on the whole, the correlation between simpler societies and more complex word-structures seems much too strong to be discounted as pure coincidence.

But if it's not just a coincidence, then there must be something in the nature of the communication patterns in smaller societies which makes elaborate word-structure more likely to develop and less likely to be levelled out. Again, I should stress that we are very much on terra incognita here, but at least two possible reasons have been suggested. One factor which may contribute to more complex word-structures in smaller societies may be the lack of pressure for simplification that results from contact with strangers who speak different languages or dialects. Complex morphology, such as elaborate systems of endings, seems to be the most difficult thing to learn in a language other than one's mother-tongue. Even people whose own language has complex morphology generally find learning fiddly endings in another language very tricky. And so, when there is a lot of contact between speakers of different languages, or even different varieties of the same language, complex word-structure is one of the first areas to undergo simplification. (The England of around a millennium ago is a good example, since it is often argued that the intense contact between English, French and Danish was a major factor in the rapid disintegration of the English case and verbal endings.) In larger and more complex societies, there is generally much more contact between speakers of different dialects and even different languages. And so it seems likely that in such societies, the pressures for simplification are greater than in smaller societies that are less exposed to contact with different varieties of speech.

Another factor that may contribute to more complex word-structure is the absence of literacy. In fluent speech, there are no real 'spaces' between words, and so when two words frequently appear together they can easily fuse into one. In the written language, however, there are visible gaps between words, and this reinforces our perception of the border between them, and can thus hamper new fusions. This does not mean that in literate societies words can never fuse (just think of 'gonna', 'won't', 'let's', or 'o'clock'). But it is likely that without literacy, such fusions would have been much more widespread and would have proceeded much more rapidly. So literacy may well be a counter-force that hinders the fusion of words, and thus slows down the emergence of more complex word-structure. And even if factors such as contact and literacy only slightly tip the balance against fusions and in favour of simplification, over time, their effect on the course of change could become significant.

Seen from this angle, Schleicher's fantastical theory, when stripped of its coating of Romantic prejudice, may still turn out to be not so fantastical after all. For all we know, the languages of small preliterate societies before the historical period may have been more likely to develop elaborate word-structure than the languages of the civilizations that emerged after the 'dawn of history'. With the rise of more complex literate societies, the pressures for simplification in word-structure could have mounted, and the likelihood of words fusing could have declined, thus creating the drift towards simpler morphology that so distressed Schleicher and many others. Since there has been hardly any serious research into the possible relation between the structure of society and the structure of language, all this is very much on the level of perhaps and maybe. Nevertheless, there may still be a chance to move beyond mere speculation, if linguists set about studying the languages and cultures of the indigenous tribes that still survive in remote corners of the globe, from the Amazonian rainforests to the highlands of Papua New Guinea. But this opportunity is fast slipping away. For just like the rainforests and the coral reefs, the languages of the world are vanishing. At an estimated death-rate of one language every two weeks, it seems that before this century is out, between half and three-quarters of the world's six thousand or so languages will have disappeared, and among them almost all the languages of small preliterate societies. At present, only a dedicated minority of linguists is engaged in documenting those 'exotic' languages. So there will have to be a radical shift in attitude if the languages and their rich oral tradition, as well as the chance to learn about the relationship between language and culture, are not to be lost forever.

APPENDIX A

Flipping Categories

A few minutes after his talk, de Troy is in the cafeteria, sipping an espresso. The RSPEL *member comes in from the conference room and takes a seat next to him.*

RSPEL MEMBER: Dr de Troy, a word, if I may . . . Look, it's not that I think your presentation wasn't persuasive. And I'm rather loath to admit it, but I see now that destruction is somehow behind the emergence of even very elaborate structures in language. Still, I have to say that I feel rather cheated, since you never really answered my question about what it is that transforms something from a noun to a preposition, or from a verb to an auxiliary. You talked very generally about 'content words' and 'grammatical words', and you argued that the change from one camp to another was a gradual process, because it was the outcome of gradual erosion in meaning. But you see, what I really wanted to know was not so much the change from 'content' to 'grammar', but the actual transformation between syntactic categories. Surely, the switch from verb to auxiliary or from noun to preposition can't just be a matter of gradual changes in meaning. After all, it's not as if a word can be a noun and a preposition at the same time, is it? So there must have been something that actually transformed 'back' from a noun to a preposition, and there must also have been something that changed 'go' from a verb to an auxiliary. And what I would really like to know is when exactly these metamorphoses from one category to another took place, and what exactly sparked them. So please don't just fob me off with stories about gentle changes in meaning again . . .

DE TROY: Well, I'm afraid that these mysterious metamorphoses are much less momentous than you might imagine . . . But you know what, instead of just theorizing about it all, why don't I throw the question back at you? If you expect me to explain how something flipped from one syntactic category to another, isn't it fair enough to ask first what the difference between these two categories is supposed to be?

RSPEL MEMBER: But that's completely obvious, isn't it? Anyone who's had an elementary education knows full well that 'go' is a verb, 'will' is an auxiliary, 'back' is a noun, 'under' is a preposition.

DE TROY: But I wasn't really asking about your elementary education. What if I were to claim that the flip from one category to the other only seems so mysterious because your schooling has inculcated these categories into you as absolute God-given entities? I said earlier that in actual language, words don't walk around with designer T-shirts labelled 'content' or 'grammatical element'. But you see, the same applies to the labels 'noun' and 'verb'. So why don't we just forget for a moment that 'go' is a verb simply because that's what we've always been told, and try to agree on why we give it that label?

RSPEL MEMBER: Well, surely you hardly need reminding that verbs are words that refer to actions, nouns are words that refer to things, prepositions refer to relations, and auxiliaries mark tense and the like . . .

DE TROY: Hmm . . . But if this is all so simple, then don't you think your accusation that my theory fell short in some way was rather uncalled for? Look, first you ask me not to feed you any more 'stories about gentle changes in meaning', and demand to know what the magic ingredient was that transformed a verb into an auxiliary. But then, when I ask you what the difference between a verb and an auxiliary actually is, what do you tell me? A nice story about . . . meaning! According to your explanation, once 'going to' was no longer used to express the action of movement, and came to mark tense, it should automatically be relabelled an auxiliary. And once 'back of' came to express the relation 'behind', it should automatically be termed a preposition.

RSPEL MEMBER: But you know as well as I do that there is more to it than that. I didn't want to imply that meaning is the only difference between categories, and I realize of course that the match between meaning and syntactic categories isn't perfect: 'movement' is a noun, not a verb, although it refers to an action. 'Future' is also a noun, not an auxiliary, although it refers to time. So besides meaning, there are also structural properties that set the categories apart.

DE TROY: And what exactly are these 'structural properties'?

RSPEL MEMBER: Well, for one thing, auxiliaries appear before infinitive verbs: 'I *will* wash', 'they *could* see' – whereas normal verbs don't appear before infinitives: you don't say 'I *wash* see', or 'I *bring* see'. On the other hand, verbs can appear before an object, as in 'I *see* a cow', but auxiliaries can never take an object. You can't say 'I *could* a cow'.

DE TROY: Great. So what you are saying, really, is that a syntactic category is a group of words which appear in similar positions in the sentence. And if I may generalize from all of this, the implication is that the reliable method for defining a syntactic category is not by searching for a common meaning, but for a common distribution: the particular slots in which a group of words appears. It's true that things like 'tree' and 'bucket' are always nouns, but as you rightly point out, there are also nouns like 'movement' or 'future', which are certainly not physical things. The reason why we call them nouns is that they appear in the same slots as other nouns. For example, nouns typically appear in the slot X in 'a great X' – you can replace X here with 'bucket' or 'tree', but also with 'movement' and 'future'. Auxiliaries typically appear in different slots, for instance 'he Y see' – you can replace Y here with 'will', 'should', 'must', 'can', and so on. And verbs appear in slots like 'he Z-s the bucket' – you can replace Z with 'see' or 'kick'. And in general, a syntactic category is a group of words which we perceive to be similar, because they have a similar distribution – they appear in the same slots in the sentence.

RSPEL MEMBER: There is nothing to disagree with here. But all this still doesn't answer my original question about how something *switched* from one category to another.

DE TROY: No, it doesn't tell us that quite yet, but it does allow us to formulate the question in a more sensible way – which is more than half-way towards answering it . . .

RSPEL MEMBER: Fine then, so I should rather ask how it was that a verb like 'go' suddenly started appearing not in slots that are typical of verbs, but in slots characteristic of auxiliaries.

DE TROY: But don't you see, now the whole question appears in a very different light. The point is that the verb 'go' *as such* never started appearing in slots characteristic of auxiliaries. What changed into an auxiliary was not 'go', but only a particular phrase, which had appeared in auxiliary slots all along.

RSPEL MEMBER: What? Now you are saying that 'go' never changed into an auxiliary?

DE TROY: No, I'm simply formulating things more carefully. Look, you'd agree, wouldn't you, that it's not any old 'go' that turned into an auxiliary. In a phrase like 'I'm going to the cinema', for instance, 'going' is an entirely normal verb.

RSPEL MEMBER: Of course it is, since you can replace it with other verbs: 'I'm driving to the cinema', and so on. But what I meant was 'go' in the construction 'be going to *do* something'.

DE TROY: But that's exactly it. What turned into an auxiliary was not just any 'go'. It was the phrase 'is going to' in one very specific construction – when it appeared before an infinitive verb. And just think about it this way: forget for a moment that 'is going to' has three different components, and take it as one unit X = 'is-going-to'. If you look at it this way, you see that 'is-going-to' appeared in the same slots as auxiliaries all along. Just like *will* or *must*, it fits into slots like 'he X do something'.

RSPEL MEMBER: So are you trying to say that nothing happened at all? We started off with something that appeared in auxiliary slots, and we ended up with something that appeared in auxiliary slots . . .

DE TROY: But what has changed is that the *internal* structure of the phrase has collapsed. 'Going to' began life as a combination of different elements, a shorthand for 'going (somewhere, in order) to' do something. This phrase contained two independent parts: the verb 'go' denoted movement, and the preposition 'to' marked the purpose of this movement. Speakers didn't perceive the similarity of this phrase to auxiliaries, because they didn't think of it as a unit. If you want to get a feel of how 'going to' must have sounded originally, then think of a phrase like 'working to' in the sentence 'he is working to earn money'. In theory, one could say that 'is working to', as one unit, appears in the auxiliary slot X: 'he X earn money' – after all, you can replace this X with *will*, *must*, and so on.

RSPEL MEMBER: So why don't we analyse 'is working to' as an auxiliary?

DE TROY: Because we don't perceive these words as one unit. They still feel like a combination of different components: a verb 'working', and a preposition 'to', denoting the purpose of the work. So while it's true that 'is working to' would fit into auxiliary slots if it were a unit, this fact remains pretty irrelevant as long as the phrase does *not* really feel like one unit. Now, I suppose that for speakers in the fifteenth century, the structure of the phrase 'is going to' felt just like that of 'is working to' today. But with time, 'is going to' lost its independent meaning and came to denote the future, so in the perception of speakers, the individual components lost their distinctive roles. The whole 'is going to' thus came to be perceived as one unit, and was reduced to just *'s gonna*. And in this new role as a unit, the similarity between *'s gonna* and auxiliaries became apparent: here was a phrase that appeared in auxiliary slots and had a similar meaning to other auxiliaries: marking tense.

Actually, in some varieties of English, especially in the States, the *'s* of *'s gonna* has already been ditched, and many speakers simply say things like 'he *gonna* come'. I know you might view this change as the worst of vulgarities, but it's really very natural and even logical, because the *'s* no longer has any obvious function. Originally, the 'is' was there to introduce the *-ing* form on the verb 'going'. But since not much is left of that original verb, the *'s* nowadays just feels like excess luggage, and so speakers simply ditch it. And in the varieties of English where this change has already happened, *gonna* now appears on its own in exactly the same slot as auxiliaries like *will*: 'he X come'. But you see, all this happened without any magic leap from one slot to another. What really made *gonna* similar to auxiliaries was nothing other than gradual erosion in meaning and sounds.

RSPEL MEMBER: And what about the changes between other syntactic categories, for instance when a noun like 'back' turns into a preposition meaning 'behind'?

DE TROY: It's the same story all over again. It wasn't just the noun 'back' that turned into a preposition, but a particular phrase, '(at the) back of'. And when you think about this phrase as one unit, you see that it had been in preposition slots all along. 'At-the-back-of' had always fitted into the slot X in 'the pool X the house', which never accommodated nouns like 'table' or 'knife', but rather prepositions like 'behind' or 'around'. So what brought 'back of' into the preposition camp was no gymnastic leap between slots, but just the collapse of its internal structure. Once 'back of' started being used metaphorically to denote a spatial relation, the individual components lost their relevance, and the phrase came to be perceived as a unit. In fact, it's quite likely that 'back of' has already began to fuse into something like *backa*. But just like *gonna*, *backa* never had to somersault into its present slot, it had been there all along. What turned 'at the back of' into a preposition was the erosion of the original meaning, and resulting collapse of its internal structure.

RSPEL MEMBER: But can't one at least pinpoint a definite time when the change took place? Can't one say, for instance, that the point when 'going to' turned into an auxiliary was when it became one word, *gonna*, which appears in auxiliary slots?

DE TROY: Well, it's not quite as simple as all that, because things can be more gradual than we have so far allowed, even in terms of distribution. I said before that auxiliaries are words that typically appear in characteristic auxiliary slots. This definition rather took it for granted that if a word fits into *one* characteristic auxiliary slot, it would also fit into all the others.

RSPEL MEMBER: And isn't that the case?

DE TROY: Well, you can easily check this out with 'gonna'. I've just mentioned that 'gonna' fits exactly into the auxiliary slot 'he X come' – at least in some varieties of English. But let's just check for a moment whether 'gonna' fits into all other auxiliary slots. Take questions, for instance. When there is an auxiliary in a sentence like 'he will come', then you form a question simply by moving this auxiliary to the front, as in 'will he come?' In other words, the auxiliaries 'will', 'shall', 'must', and so on fit into the slot X in 'X he come?' But just try saying 'gonna he come?' – it doesn't really work, does it? Even speakers who drop the 'is' in 'he gonna come' would never dream of saying 'gonna he come?' Instead, they shove the 'is' back in again, and move that to the front: 'is he gonna come?' So in questions, 'gonna' still behaves more like 'working to': the question 'is he *gonna* come?' is formed in the same way as 'is he *working to* earn money?'

RSPEL MEMBER: So what exactly are you getting at? Would you now define 'gonna' as an auxiliary, or do you think it's still a verb?

DE TROY: Well, I would simply say that 'gonna' is a word which fits into *some* auxiliary slots, but not into others. In some constructions it behaves like the auxiliaries 'will' et al., but in others it still behaves more like a normal verb. Not that 'gonna' has anything to be ashamed of, mind you. 'Gonna' may not have an identical distribution to the more established auxiliaries, but this doesn't mean that it performs its function as a future marker any less well than 'will' or 'shall'. It simply means that 'gonna' has a somewhat different distribution from the established auxiliaries – for complex historical reasons I don't want to get into here. 'Gonna' just doesn't fall neatly into either the group of verbs or of established auxiliaries.

RSPEL MEMBER: But doesn't it cause huge problems if a word like 'gonna' is half-way in between, and doesn't know whether it's this, that, or the other?

DE TROY: Problems for whom, exactly? It might cause a rumpus in school's neatly packaged world, or for anyone who believes in perfect platonic forms. But well – most of us have never had the privilege of attending Plato's academy. You see, we don't actually speak in 'verbs' and 'auxiliaries' – we just speak in words. And as far as the word 'gonna' is concerned, we simply remember in which particular slots it appears. Why should that be problematic?

RSPEL MEMBER: For one thing, don't problems arise from the fact that speakers need to memorize individually all the particular slots in which 'gonna' appears? I thought that the point about syntactic categories is that they group together words of a feather, so that speakers don't have to memorize individually all the different slots in which every member of the group can appear. It's enough, for example, to memorize in which slots one noun like 'table' appears, and then you already know that 'chair', 'sausage' and thousands of other words would appear in just the same slots.

DE TROY: I agree in general, but you see, 'gonna' is such a basic and common grammatical marker that remembering the few peculiarities in its distribution is really just a drop in the ocean of details that speakers have to contend with. Don't you think speakers would react with amazement if you suggested to them that they might have problems with handling 'gonna', because it appears in some auxiliary slots but not in others?

RSPEL MEMBER: Well, maybe. But surely, this indecisive state of affairs can't go on forever? At some stage 'gonna' is gonna have to make up its mind and turn into a real auxiliary . . . Or are you saying that it will just remain stuck where it is indefinitely?

DE TROY: Of course it's always possible that 'gonna''s circumstances might change at some stage – it would be rash to rule it out. So it's quite possible, in theory, that a new generation of speakers might extend 'gonna' by analogy on 'will' to all auxiliary slots, and start saying things like 'gonna he come?' for instance. But while this is all imaginable, frankly, I don't think it's a terribly likely scenario. I don't want to bore you with all the details, but I think that gonna is more likely to stay put where it is right now, 'stuck', so to speak, somewhere between verbs and established auxiliaries. It's certainly not causing much grief to anyone . . .

RSPEL MEMBER: Gosh, I must say this rather flies in the face of everything I have always thought about syntactic categories. I had always assumed that a word must be one thing or the other, either a verb or an auxiliary, either a noun or a preposition. And now you are telling me that 'gonna' can be both, or perhaps neither. But if words don't always fit neatly into one syntactic category or the other, then why bother with these syntactic categories in the first place? Aren't these classifications pretty useless?

DE TROY: No, I wouldn't go as far as that. I would only say that these syntactic categories are not watertight. As the linguist Edward Sapir once put it, 'all grammars leak'. The main syntactic categories can be very helpful in capturing broad similarities between words. What's more, a label like 'verb' must also reflect some psychological reality: the perception in people's minds that words like 'kick', 'bite', and a great many others, behave in a very similar way and appear in similar slots. So syntactic categories can be very helpful, especially when you take a bird's-eye view of language. But when you focus on the details, you often find that words don't always fall conveniently under one of the main labels. A word can start acquiring the distribution of another category only gradually, and sometimes it can even remain stuck between categories. When one tries to describe a language, this should not pose serious problems, as long as one remembers that syntactic categories are only meant to be descriptive labels – they are supposed to serve us, not rule us. So when you ask a question such as 'when did a word move from category A to category B?', you should remember that the word never had to perform any complicated acrobatics. What you are really asking is: 'when do I decide to stop using the label A for a word, and start using the label B?' So if you discover that a word like 'gonna' won't oblige, and won't fit neatly under either of your labels, then you should remember that what's problematic is not the word itself, but your labels. This doesn't make your labels completely useless, it just means that they are not perfect in catching every aspect of language.

RSPEL MEMBER: Well, I will certainly have to ponder all of this. But . . . I'm terribly sorry, I have to dash off now – I really don't want to miss the talk on 'between you and I' . . .

APPENDIX B

Laryngeals Again?

In Chapter 6 I suggested that the *a*-mutation may have been the first step taken by the prehistoric forebear of the Semitic languages towards the root-and-template system. The *a*-mutation was the change of vowels in the ancient stem from *u* or *i* to *a*, giving rise to pairs such as *aktum-aktam* 'I covered-I will cover', *aptil-aptal* 'I twisted-I will twist', *amūt-amāt* 'I died-I will die'. I argued that this mutation must have emerged on similar lines to the cycle of effort-saving changes and analogy that brought about the *i*-mutation pattern in German nouns such as *gast-gestə* and *hals-helsə*'. In Germanic, the original culprit for the effort-saving changes was an ending *-iz*, which coloured the previous vowel from *a* to *e*.

The origin of the Semitic *a*-mutation lies so far back that it is impossible to know what precise phonetic environment was responsible for bringing it about. Still, even if only out of sheer curiosity, it is tempting to speculate what the culprits for the *a*-mutation in Semitic *might* have looked like. One educated guess would be that the culprit in question may not have been a vowel at all, but rather a group of consonants: the 'laryngeals' which have already featured in Chapter 3, in connection with Saussure's theory about the vowel system of Proto-Indo-European. Saussure postulated that the prehistoric ancestor of the Indo-European languages had some long-lost sounds which had coloured the vowels in their vicinity, but which then disappeared from all the daughter languages. After his death his theory was proved, when one of these rogue sounds was found in the newly discovered but very ancient Indo-European language Hittite.

Now, in the Semitic languages, one does not need visionary powers to hypothesize the existence of laryngeals, for they are very much around even today. What is more, there is even historical evidence to show that these laryngeal consonants forced vowels in their vicinity to change to *a*. The reason for this colouring is that the laryngeals are produced so far down the throat that in order to utter them, the tongue has to take a position very similar to an *a* anyway. In Hebrew, for example, the word for 'apple' was originally *tapūḥ*, but the laryngeal sound *ḥ* caused the word to change to *tapūaḥ*. A helping-vowel *a* was inserted before the *ḥ*, in order to enable the mouth to move more easily into the shape needed for it. Crucially, however, this change only happened when the laryngeal was at the end of a word. When there was another vowel following *ḥ*, there seems to have been no time for this leisurely helping-vowel *a* to creep in, so the plural 'apples' remained *tapūḥ-im*, and was not modified to *tapūaḥ-im*.

It is quite possible that the culprits behind the prehistoric *a*-mutation were also laryngeal consonants. We can never hope to reconstruct the actual set-up in which they caused the vowel to change, but here is one way it *could* have happened. Suppose that once upon a time, the past tense was not bare-ended, as I presented it in Chapter 6, but was marked by an ending. It doesn't really matter what the ending was, so let's say for the sake of argument that it was *-u*. Let's also suppose that the future tense (which may have started out in life as just a more indefinite present tense) was a form without any ending at all:

ANCIENT STEM		ANCIENT PAST		ANCIENT PRESENT/FUTURE	
ptil	'twist'	*aptil-u*	('I twisted')	*aptil*	('I twist')
mūt	'die'	*amūt-u*	('I died')	*amūt*	('I die')
ṣīḥ	'laugh'	*aṣīḥ-u*	('I laughed')	*aṣīḥ*	('I laugh')

Now imagine for a moment that an effort-saving change was set in motion, similar to the one which modified the Hebrew 'apple': speakers inserted a helping-vowel *a* before the laryngeal *ḥ*, but only when it was at the end of the word. How would such a change affect the forms above? The present tense *aṣīḥ* would become *aṣīaḥ*, because the *ḥ* is at the end of the word. But in the past tense *aṣīḥ-u*, where the *ḥ* was not at the end, no change would have occurred. In other words, the ending *-u* could have 'protected' the past tense from the change. After the change has taken its course, the situation would look like this:

ANCIENT STEM		ANCIENT PAST		ANCIENT PRESENT/FUTURE	
ṣīḥ	'laugh'	*aṣīḥ-u*	('I laughed')	*aṣī**a**ḥ*	('I laugh')

Now suppose that some generations later, the ending *-u* of the past tense is eroded away and eventually disappears altogether. So forms like *a-ṣīḥ-u* end up as just *a-ṣīḥ*. The only distinguishing feature now left between the past and the present/future tense would be the gliding-vowel *a* inside the stem:

ṣīḥ	'laugh'	*aṣīḥ*	('I laughed')	*aṣī**a**ḥ*	('I laugh')

Speakers in subsequent generations would have no idea that the *a* in *a-ṣī**a**ḥ* was originally inserted purely as an effort-saving device. They would simply observe a pattern, whereby the only differentiating feature between past and present tenses is the gliding-vowel *a* inside the stem. So their order-craving mind could interpret this helping-vowel *a* as a *meaningful* pattern, and assume that the reason why it was there was to indicate the present/future. And once this pattern is recognized, it could be extended by analogy to other verbs like *mūt*, *ptil*, and so on, which never had a laryngeal to their name in the first place:

mūt	'die'	*amūt*	('I died')	*amū**a**t*	('I die')

As it happens, the forms above are very similar to the forms of the hollow verbs found in the earliest stages of Akkadian. But later on in the history of the language, the vowel sequences *ia* and *ua* were ground down and reduced to just *a*, producing the *a*-mutation in its pure form: a change from *i* or *u* in the past to *a* in the future:

ṣīḥ	'laugh'	*aṣīḥ*	('I laughed')	*aṣ**ā**ḥ*	('I laugh')
mūt	'die'	*amūt*	('I died')	*am**ā**t*	('I die')

Of course, as I stressed above, the scenario presented here is no more than an educated guess, whose only purpose is to illustrate *one* way in which the *a*-mutation could have emerged. My only claim is that the development could in general have proceeded along such lines.

APPENDIX C

The Devil in the Detail

Between the three simple vowel templates derived in Chapter 6 and the full complexity of the mature Semitic verbal system lies a mind-boggling amount of detail, much of which can never be recovered. Nevertheless, there are enough clues to give us an idea about how at least some of the more elaborate templates could have evolved, and the following pages will briefly survey the possible origins of the 'reflexive', 'intensive', 'causative' and 'passive' templates. Finally, the last section will look at the origin of a rather fancy template in modern Hebrew, in order to give some idea of the sort of processes that could have made the root-and-template system burgeon in complexity.

1. Reflexive

The reflexive nuance 'snog oneself' is expressed in the Semitic languages by templates that insert a *t* between the first two root-consonants. In Arabic, for instance, *i*ⓢ*ta*ⓝ*i*ⓖ is the template for 'snog yourself!' The obvious question about this reflexive *t* is where it could have sprung from, and how it managed to find its way in between the consonants of the root. As with most other details, the ultimate origin of the *t* lies well beyond historical reach, but the most likely explanation is that *t* started out as a full 'reflexive pronoun', an independent word like 'himself'. This pronoun (perhaps originally *ta*) would have appeared before the verb, so that something like '*ta* snog' would simply have meant 'snog himself'. Then, through the familiar processes of erosion, *ta* could have fused with the verb to become a prefix: . . . *t(a)*-snog.

But what could have pushed this prefix in between the root consonants? The culprit must have been a fairly common type of effort-saving change, called *metathesis*, in which a pair of consonants swap places, to make uttering them in sequence easier. Examples of metathesis can be seen with the Old English verb *aksian*, in which the pair *ks* was jiggled around to give the modern English as 'ask'. Similarly, Old English *hros* became 'horse', *brid* changed to 'bird', *thrid* to 'third', and *waps* to 'wasp'.

There are very good reasons to suspect that a metathesis must have been responsible for making the reflexive *t* swap places with the first root consonant (. . . ***t***ⓢ. . . → . . . ⓢ***t*** . . .). In fact, in some of the Semitic languages, such as Hebrew, the metathesis did not occur in all verbs, but only when the first root-consonant was difficult to pronounce immediately after a *t*. So it is likely that the other Semitic languages also started out with a more haphazard metathesis, but that at some later stage, the metathesis was extended by analogy, and regularized to all verbs.

2. *Intensive*

The intensive templates in Semitic are characterized by the doubling of the second root consonant. In Akkadian, for instance, the intensive future template is *u*ⓢ*a*ⓝⓝ*a*ⓖ ('I will snog intensely'), and in Hebrew, the past intensive is ⓢ*i*ⓝⓝ*e*ⓖ ('he snogged intensely'). It is possible that this consonant doubling is a remnant of what started out as the reduplication (repetition) of the whole stem. Reduplication is in fact an extremely common strategy among the world's languages. Forms such as *runrun*, *cutcut*, or *redred* are used in many languages to express meanings such as 'run a lot', 'cut repeatedly', 'very red'. But often, erosion hacks away at the repeated forms, so that only 'partial reduplication' remains. The Latin word *memento*, for instance, is a relic of a reduplication of the Proto-Indo-European root **men* 'think', presumably through an erosion of *menmen* to *memen*. Sometimes, erosion or assimilation of reduplicated forms can create doubled middle consonants. In the Micronesian (Malayo-Polynesian) language Trukese, for instance, the adjective *cön* 'black' has an intensive form *cöccön*, which clearly comes from an original duplication *cöncön (cöncön* → *cöccön*). In this way, a doubled middle consonant may come to be associated in speakers' minds with an intensive meaning, and the pattern may thus be extended and regularized. In Semitic, duplication also seems to have reached verbs from intensive adjectives, but the details of the process are beyond our reach.

3. Causative templates

The causative templates are characterized by a prefix *ša-* (or a weakened form *ha-* or even just *a-*), as in Akkadian *u-ša*ⓢⓝ*i*ⓖ 'he caused to snog'. The simplest explanation for the origin of the prefix *ša* would be that it started out in life as an independent word, a verb meaning 'make', 'cause', or 'do'. According to this theory, something like '*ša* snog' would literally have meant 'make snog', and then, through erosion, the *ša* must have fused with the verb to become a prefix. This scenario would certainly accord with evidence from other languages, where verbs like 'cause' or 'do' are often the source of causative constructions. In the Germanic languages, for instance, something that comes close to a causative template has arisen from a verb meaning 'make', through the familiar *i*-mutation. In English, there are a few verbs (and adjectives) that change their vowel to mark a causative:

BASIC VERB	CAUSATIVE
to fall	to fell ('make fall')
to sit	to set ('make sit')
to drink	to drench (originally: 'make drink')
to rise	to raise
to lie	to lay

The pattern began, millennia ago, with the Proto-Indo-European verb **yo* 'make'. By the time of Proto-Germanic, a form of this verb, *-*ian*, must have fused with the preceding verb to give a causative ending. So a Proto-Germanic verb like **fall-ian* was just the combination 'fall-make'. Then, the *i* of the ending *-ian* caused an *i*-mutation in the preceding vowel, and so the *a* of *fall* changed to *e*, to give **fell-ian*. Later on, the ending was entirely eroded, and so **fell-ian* ended up as '(to) fell'.

It would appear, then, that the most tempting origin for *ša-* in Semitic is simply a verb meaning 'make' or 'cause'. But there are various reasons to believe that the actual development in Semitic was less straightforward. Earlier on, I mentioned that the prefix *ša-* served to derive nouns or adjectives from verbs (and was thus involved in the cycles of swelling of new verbs from old ones). And it may be that the origin of the causative prefix *ša-* should also be sought in such cycles of swelling from verb to noun to verb. When a verb is derived from a noun or adjective, one of the most common resulting meanings is 'to make (into) X', as, for example, in English 'to ice', 'to compact', to 'cool (something)', and so on. Now consider a cycle like this:

VERB	→	ADJECTIVE/NOUN	→	VERB
kūn		*ša-kun*		*šakun*
to be firm		(a) firm (thing)		to make (into a) firm (thing)

The second stage of this process creates the causative meaning 'make into an X' as a natural result of the transformation of a noun/adjective into a verb (just as in 'to ice'). But if we now ignore the middle stage, and only look at the two verbs on either side, the following relation has emerged:

VERB	→	VERB
kūn		*šakun*
to be firm		to make firm

From the historical perspective, the link between 'be firm' and 'make firm' is not direct, but goes through an adjective or noun. But new speakers who spot the relation between the two verbs may no longer be aware of the original link between them, and simply (mis)interpret *ša-* as a prefix that turns a verb 'to X' into another verb 'to make X' (or 'to cause to X'). And once they recognize the pattern, they can extend it by analogy and generalize it to other verbs, thus making it into a regular causative prefix. It seems likely that a process of this nature was responsible for creating the causative prefix *ša-*.

4. Passive template

The passive template ('to be snogged') is characterized by the doubling of the first root consonant, as in Akkadian *a-ⓢⓢaⓝiⓖ* ('I was snogged'). What lies behind this doubling is the ('Santa Siesta') principle of assimilation. Originally, the passive was formed with a prefix *n*: *a-nⓢaⓝiⓖ*, and in fact, in Arabic the *n* is still mostly audible. But in the other Semitic languages, the *n* assimilated to the first consonant of the root, so that *a-nⓢaⓝiⓖ* became *a-ⓢⓢaⓝiⓖ*.

But what could have been the origin of passive prefix *n-*? In light of the latest research, it seems probable that the *n*-prefix in Semitic started out as an independent verb (perhaps *na*), meaning 'be' or 'become'. This verb would have been placed before the verbal adjective ⓢ*a*ⓝ*i*ⓖ '(a) snogged (thing)' to produce verbal constructions with a passive meaning: *a-na* ⓢ*a*ⓝ*i*ⓖ 'I was/became snogged'. Later, the verb *na* must have eroded and fused with the adjective, so that *a-na+*ⓢ*a*ⓝ*i*ⓖ merged into *an*ⓢ*a*ⓝ*i*ⓖ 'I became snogged' (and later *a*ⓢⓢ*a*ⓝ*i*ⓖ).

5. Passive of reflexive, or how one is 'made to snog oneself'

Various other templates could have developed along similar lines to the four examples mentioned so far. But it would be misleading to imagine that each of the many dozens of the templates in Semitic emerged in isolation, and without any input from the rest of the system. In fact, as I mentioned in the end of Chapter 6, when the system grows in complexity, there is also a growing scope for speakers to recognize regular patterns and correspondences between existing templates, and to produce innovations by analogy on a higher level. To see what such higher-level analogical innovations can involve, we can leave prehistory behind and jump all the way to the 1940s, to see how an entirely new template was created in modern Hebrew, *hit*ⓢ*u*ⓝⓝ*a*ⓖ 'he was made to snog himself'.

Hebrew has an intensive and a causative template, each of which also has a passive counterpart:

		PASSIVE COUNTERPART
INTENSIVE:	ⓢ*i*ⓝⓝ*e*ⓖ 'he snogged intensely'	ⓢ***u***ⓝⓝ***a***ⓖ 'he was snogged intensely'
CAUSATIVE:	*hi*ⓢⓝ*i*ⓖ 'he caused to snog'	***hu***ⓢⓝ***a***ⓖ 'he was made to snog'

In both cases, the passive counterpart is formed by taking the two vowels of the original template (*i–e* or *i–i*) and changing them into the sequence ***u–a***. So in speakers' perception, the vowel sequence ***u–a*** has come to be associated with a passive meaning.

Hebrew also has a reflexive template, *hit*ⓢ*a*ⓝⓝ*e*ⓖ 'he snogged himself'. Until the 1940s the reflexive template didn't have any passive counterpart – after all, it is rather unusual that one would have cause to speak about someone who was 'made to do something to himself'. But in modern political life, all kinds of unlikely things can happen. Take the root p-t-r ('set free'), for instance, which in the reflexive template yields *hit*patter 'he set himself free', or more specifically, 'he resigned'. It is not unheard of in politics that people are 'made to set themselves free', so to speak. And in 1948, a politician vented his frustration at having been forced to resign by coining a new form. Recognizing the ***u–a*** sequence as the mark of the passive counterpart from the intensive and causative templates, he extended this sequence by analogy to the reflexive form:

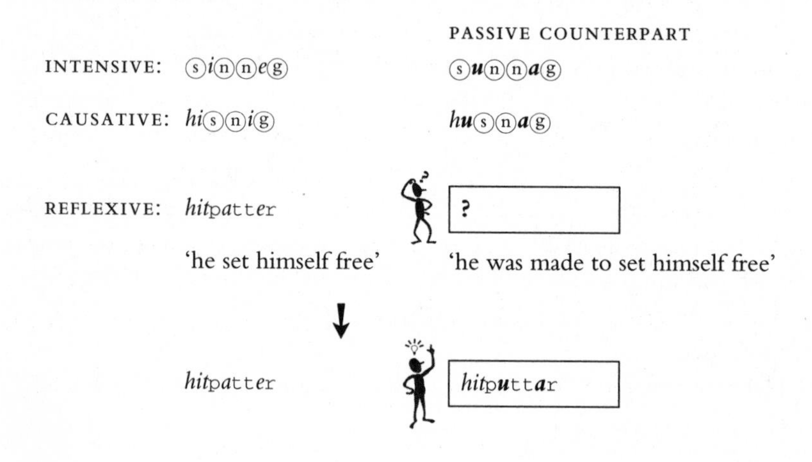

And thus the form *hit*p***u***tt***a***r was born, meaning 'he was made to set himself free', that is, 'he was forced to resign'. This form soon caught on, and was then extended to other verbs as well, such as 'he was made to volunteer' or 'he was made to wash himself'. And so a new template emerged: *hit*(s)***u***(n)(n)***a***(g), with the nuance 'he was made to snog himself'.

Of course, in itself, this example may seem rather insignificant. Nevertheless, it does demonstrate the principle by which many of the dozens of templates in Semitic could have emerged. As the system grew more complex, more and more higher-level analogies could be formed. For instance, when a template with a new nuance emerges, say the 'iterative' ('he kept on snogging'), this new nuance can interact with existing distinctions, and so by high-level analogies, new templates can be formed for things like 'causative iterative' ('he kept causing to snog'), 'passive iterative' ('he kept being snogged'), and so on. So once a critical mass of templates (perhaps only ten or so) had emerged, there could have been an 'explosion' in the number of new templates formed, leading to the dozens attested in the historical languages.

APPENDIX D

The Cook's Counterpoint

G. F. Handel C. W. Gluck The cook

The composer George Friedrich Handel was never renowned for the high esteem in which he held his colleagues. According to a well-known anecdote, when he was once asked what he thought of the composition skills of his compatriot Christoph Willibald Gluck, Handel retorted that Gluck was no better at counterpoint than his cook. When I first heard this story, I was struck by a grave existential question: *whose* cook? Was Handel referring to Gluck's cook, or to his own?

I was only to settle the question when I eventually came across the original source of the anecdote, in the memoirs of the music historian Charles Burney. There, Handel is quoted verbatim:

> I remember when Mrs Cibber, in my hearing, asked Handel what sort of a composer [Gluck] was; his answer, prefaced by an oath . . . was 'he knows no more of contrapunto as mein cook, Waltz'.

So the mystery was solved. (In fact, Gustavus Waltz was not only Handel's cook, but also a professional musician, a singer and an actor, so the insult was not as indiscriminate as it first appears.) The moral of the story, in any case, is that the pronoun 'his' can sometimes fail to point at referents unambiguously. 'His' refers to any male in the singular, and since both Handel and Gluck answer this description, the sentence 'Handel thought that Gluck was no better ... than *his* cook' is ambiguous, because 'his cook' can mean either Gluck's cook, or Handel's cook. In this case, then, the grammar of English falls short in the task of disambiguating the two participants.

As was mentioned in Chapter 7 (page 230), however, in some other contexts English has developed a clever mechanism, a particular category of pronouns called 'reflexives', which help in the task of fine-tuning the reference, and manage to eliminate precisely such ambiguities. Consider this example:

Gluck thought Handel admired him.

The pronoun 'him' also refers to any male in the singular, so in theory, 'him' should have been just as unclear as 'his' was in the first example. The sentence should have had two possible meanings: 'Gluck thought Handel admired Gluck' or 'Gluck thought Handel admired Handel'. But in fact, any English speaker knows without a second's thought that only the first of these two interpretations is possible, and that 'him' can *only* refer to Gluck. Why? The reason is that when English speakers want to express the other option, and say that Handel actually admired Handel, they always use a special type of pronoun, the reflexive 'himself'. Reflexive pronouns are used to indicate that the two participants in the same action are one and the same. So in the example above, the possibility that 'him' refers to Handel is eliminated, because we know that if it were Handel, the sentence would have to be 'Gluck thought Handel admired himself'. Quite an effective mechanism, then, for producing an unambiguous reference. Reflexive pronouns manage to eliminate the ambiguity not only by their presence, but also by their absence.

How can such a handy device develop? The clue to the origin of reflexives (in English, as in many other languages) is found in another group of pronouns, which share the same form as reflexives, but which are used for a different purpose: adding emphasis. Think of sentences like 'guess who didn't turn up to the launch party? The author *himself*', or 'the chess-computer Deep Blue defeated Kasparov *himself*', or 'the minister *himself* was spotted on the tube this morning', and so on. In such examples, the pronoun *himself* is not used to disambiguate between two male participants (there is only one human participant in each sentence anyway). *Himself* here just serves to emphasize that it was the author 'of all people' (who didn't turn up to his own launch party), it was the world-champion Kasparov 'and none other' who was beaten by a computer. In other words, a speaker would use *himself* when the identity of the participant is surprising or unexpected in the context (for example, when a minister takes the tube), in order to convey something like: 'yes, I know it may come as rather a surprise, but I really do mean the person I have just named'.

So the same 'himself' seems to be serving two rather different functions: it can be used as an emphatic pronoun ('the author himself never turned up'), and it can be used in the non-emphatic grammatical function of a reflexive ('Handel admired himself'). Given all we know about the direction of change in meaning, it is not too difficult to work out what the historical relation between these two usages must be. Since meanings tend to erode over time, it must be the emphatic sense of 'himself' which was there first, and the reflexive function must have developed from it. Indeed, the records show that the emphatic use of 'self' goes back to the earliest attestations of English, but that the reflexive use is younger, and had not yet developed in the Old English period (roughly before 1066). The absence of a special reflexive pronoun in Old English can be surmised from sentences in which an ordinary pronoun is found where modern English would have to use a 'self' form instead. Here is an example from *Beowulf*, where the hero dresses him*self* for battle, but the actual form used is *hine* 'him'.

syðþan	*he*	***hine***	*to guðe*	*gegyred*	*hæfde*
once	he	**him**	to battle	dressed	had

'once he had dressed him (i.e. himself) for battle'

The word 'self' did exist in Old English, but at that time it was still emphatic in nature, and its reflexive function had yet to emerge. And how could this reflexive function actually develop from an emphatic sense? The change must be considered in the context of the common actions of life, which one generally directs towards others, rather than towards oneself. On the whole, one tends to 'admire', 'liberate', 'hurt', 'love', 'resent', 'talk to', 'listen to', 'send things to' others, not oneself. So when, for a change, one does direct an action towards oneself, this is often more surprising and less expected in the context. And here is the link between emphatics and reflexives, for as I have just mentioned, emphatic pronouns tend to be used exactly when a participant is unexpected in the context. The following example from Old English may help to clarify the nature of the link:

þæs þe	*he*	*hine*	***sylfne***	*us*	*sendan*	*wolde.*
because	he	him	**self**	us	send	wanted

'because he (God) wanted to send to us him himself'

In this line from a religious poem, the word *sylfne* 'self' serves to emphasize that, contrary to what one might expect, God wanted to send us none other than God personally. So here, 'self' still carries special emphasis, and functions as a proper emphatic pronoun. Nevertheless, since emphatic 'self' forms came to appear more and more frequently in contexts where the two participants of an action are (surprisingly) one and the same, they gradually lost their emphatic force in these contexts, and speakers simply started expecting a 'self' form whenever the two participants in the action were the same. What had started as a mere inclination to add a 'self' form for extra emphasis became a trend, which then fossilized into a rigid rule: the 'self' forms became obligatory whenever the actor was doing something to 'himself'.

The cleverest thing about all this is that once 'self' forms were no longer just an optional extra, but had come to be expected whenever the two participants were the same, then the *absence* of a 'self' form, as in 'Gluck though that Handel admired him', could be taken as a definite statement that the action was *not* performed on oneself, that is, that Handel admired Gluck. And this is how the 'self' forms came to play a useful grammatical function even through their absence.

Unfortunately, English never got round to developing the same distinctions on the pronoun 'his' (otherwise I would have been spared years of uncertainty as to the object of Handel's derogatory remark that Gluck was no better at counterpoint than *his* cook). But some languages have extended the reflexive versus non-reflexive distinction to possessive pronouns as well. In Norwegian, for instance, the pronoun *hans* means 'his', and *sin* means 'his-self', so that the following sentence:

Händel	*svarte*	*at*	*Gluck*	*ikke*	*var*	*noe*	*bedre*	*i*	*kontrapunkt*	*enn*	***hans***	***kokk***
Handel	answered	that	Gluck	not	was	any	better	in	counterpoint	than	his	cook

would be unambiguous, since *hans kokk* can only refer to Handel's cook, whereas *sin kokk* can only be Gluck's cook.

APPENDIX E

The Turkish Mirror

In Chapter 7 I mentioned the mirror-image effects in the order of words between English and Turkish, which is well illustrated by the Turkish sentence-word *şehirlileştiremediklerimizdensiniz,* literally 'you are one of those whom we can't cause to become someone from town'. From an English perspective, Turkish arranges the elements almost exactly back to front (the only element that is slightly out of synch is the 'we'):

şehir- li- leş- tir- eme- dik- ler- imiz- den- siniz
town-someone.from-become-cause.to-can't-whom-those-we- one.of-you.are

From the Turkish point of view, however, it is of course the English that is completely the wrong way round. If this reversal in word order were peculiar to English and Turkish, one could perhaps just dismiss it as the result of some bizarre coincidence, which made the ordering principles in one of the languages go completely haywire. But it turns out that neither English nor Turkish are at all unusual in their ways. They are in fact representatives of two vast opposing camps, into which the world's languages seem to be divided roughly half and half. Arabic, Thai and Mixtec (an American-Indian language spoken in Mexico), just to take a handful of examples, arrange their elements more or less like English, whereas Japanese, Greenlandic Inuktitut (spoken by the 40,000 Inuit in Greenland) and Kannada (a Dravidian language spoken by 40 million people in southern India) arrange the elements roughly as in Turkish. This means that English tongues and minds can easily get into a terrible twist when trying to learn Turkish, but the Japanese, who have a reputation for struggling with English, often astound teachers of Turkish by the ease and speed with which they learn that language, even though there is no family relation between Turkish and Japanese whatsoever –

Turkish and Japanese are as far removed from each other as either of them is from English.

But why is it that languages from all over the world, and even without any family affiliation, seem to converge into two opposing word-order camps, and gravitate towards two diametrical poles? I hinted at the beginning of the book that the mirror-image effect in the ordering of elements is largely a consequence of just one basic choice that languages make at some stage during their history, between two equally natural alternatives. And in Chapter 7 we started to get a glimpse of what it is that stands behind this mirror, when the basic choice in the positioning of one particular couple, the verb and the object, was shown to determine whether prepositions or postpositions will emerge in a language. In a language with the order verb-object (or VO for short), as in 'take stone, cut meat', the verb 'take' can develop into a *pre*position, standing before its noun: '*with* stone cut meat'. But in a language with the order object-verb (OV) 'stone take, meat cut', the same verb will turn into a *post*position instead: 'stone *with* meat cut'. In short, when prepositions or postpositions develop from verbs, they inherit their alignment with respect to their noun from the alignment of the verb with respect to its object.

But this is only the beginning. In the 1960s, the linguist Joseph Greenberg made the rather startling discovery that the basic choice in the alignment of the verb and the object correlates across languages not just with the appearance of prepositions (as in English) or postpositions (as in Turkish), but with the order of a whole series of other elements. It seems that the choice between VO and OV can ripple throughout the structure of language, and have far-reaching repercussions on the order of many other linguistic pairs. But why?

For some grammatical elements, such as auxiliaries like 'will' or 'must', the reason for the correlation is not too hard to fathom, as it has to do with direct inheritance, just as in the case of prepositions and postpositions. We have seen that auxiliaries originate from normal verbs: 'will', for instance, started out in life as an independent verb meaning 'want'. Now, in a language like English, where the basic order is VO (as in 'want coffee'), it is only natural to say also 'want (to) drink'. But in a language which has the OV word order ('coffee want'), it would also be natural to say 'drink want (to)'. So when a verb like 'will' loses its original sense ('want to') and becomes a future auxiliary, in a VO language like English the auxiliary would naturally end up *before* the verb ('will drink'), but in a language like Turkish with OV word order, the auxiliary would end up *after* the verb: 'drink will'. Indeed, in the Turkish monstrosity above, the auxiliaries *leş* ← *tir* ← *eme* 'become ← cause to ← can't' appear in precisely the opposite order from English 'can't→cause to→become'. So it is not only prepositions and postpositions, but also auxiliaries (and a range of other elements) which can inherit their alignment directly from the position of the verb in the couple verb-object.

But even that is not the end of the story, since the basic choice between OV and VO also seems to correlate across languages with the alignment of other pairs in the sentence, such as the head-noun and the appendage noun in a possessive construction ('$\text{son}_{\text{of the ruler}}$'), which couldn't possibly have inherited their order directly from the alignment of the verb and object. In theory, there are two ways in which the head noun ('son') and the appendage ('ruler') can appear: one option is to have the head noun first, as in the English construction '$\text{son}_{\text{of the ruler}}$', and the other option is to have the appendage before the head, as in the English construction '$_{\text{ruler's}}\text{son}$'. Greenberg discovered that languages which have VO order ('take stone') strongly prefer the order HEAD-APPENDAGE ($\text{son}_{\text{of the ruler}}$), whereas languages which have OV order ('stone take') tend to have a strong preference for the order APPENDAGE-HEAD ($_{\text{ruler's}}\text{son}$).

Of course, English itself immediately shows that even if this correlation is very strong, it is not without exceptions, since English is a VO language, but it has two constructions: $\text{son}_{\text{of the ruler}}$ but also $_{\text{ruler's}}\text{son}$, which strictly speaking should belong to the other camp. Now, the complex historical reasons for how English ended up with two constructions are much too muddy to get into here. But recklessly bulldozing over the details, one can say that the $_{\text{ruler's}}\text{son}$ construction is a very old relic, and developed at a prehistoric period when the language was actually OV and not VO. (Remember, for instance, that the OV order was still used in the English of Ælfric's day, around AD 1000, in *ic hi worhte* 'I them made' rather than 'I made them'.) During the historical period, however, English changed its word order from OV to VO, and the '$\text{son}_{\text{of the ruler}}$' construction is much younger, and dates from a time after the language had already changed. So in some sense, even if English seems at first to flout the rule that VO should go (only with) with HEAD-APPENDAGE, it appears that even English is not such as flagrant exception to the correlation after all, because its two constructions are a testimony to a rather messy process of changing over from OV to VO.

But why should there be such a correlation in the first place, between VO and HEAD-APPENDAGE, and vice versa? Why should the alignment of the verb and object have any bearing on the choice between head noun and the appendage noun, when (as opposed to prepositions and auxiliaries) the possessive construction could not have developed directly from the verb-object couple?

It turns out that even though some pairs do not inherit their position directly from the verb and object, they nevertheless tend to be placed in a compliant alignment in the dance of the sentence, in order to prevent them from tripping up on the feet of either the leading couple, verb and object, or one of its toeing-the-line acolytes. In particular, the two nouns in the possessive construction arrange themselves so as to keep in step with prepositions or postpositions, and thus avoid constructions that are difficult to process. We have seen that possessive markers like 'of' can originate from prepositions (or postpositions) meaning 'from'. And to get an idea of what difficulties can ensue from an 'inconsistent' order, let's consider first what a possessive construction would look like when the possessive marker is a preposition (say 'of') stuck before the appendage noun 'ruler'. The HEAD-APPENDAGE and APPENDAGE-HEAD constructions would look like this:

The possessive marker is a preposition

NOUN-APPENDAGE:	son	of-ruler
APPENDAGE-HEAD NOUN:	of-ruler	son

Notice that in the first order (HEAD-APPENDAGE), the possessive marker 'of' is nestled safely in between the two nouns, whereas the second order (APPENDAGE-HEAD) has the possessive marker rather perilously dangling at the edge. Are both constructions as good as each other? It seems that they are not, and that the second order is more problematic, because it can lead to cumbersome constructions that are difficult to process. To see why, consider what happens when we add another noun to the construction, an appendage to the appendage 'ruler', so that instead of just 'son of the ruler' we want to say 'son of the ruler of Ruritania'. The two orders will yield:

NOUN-APPENDAGE:	son	of-ruler	of-Ruritania
APPENDAGE-HEAD NOUN:	of-of-Ruritania	ruler	son

The first order causes no problems, since the marker of possession comes between the head noun and the appendage, and so one can easily add more and more appendages without much difficulty for comprehension. But in the second order, things quickly get rather convoluted. According to the rules, the appendage 'Ruritania' should stand before its head noun 'ruler', to produce the phrase [of-Ruritania ruler]. But this whole phrase is the appendage of the head noun 'son', so one gets the tortuous 'of-[of-Ruritania ruler] son'. It's no wonder, then, that in a language where the possessive marker is a *pre*position, there is a strong motivation for speakers to prefer the first order, HEAD-APPENDAGE, and thus make sure that the possessive marker is nestled safely between the two nouns.

But now let's look at what happens in a language where the possessive marker is a *post*position, say *-s*, just for the sake of argument. What would the two orders look like in this case?

The possessive marker is a postposition

HEAD NOUN-APPENDAGE:	son	ruler-s
APPENDAGE-HEAD NOUN:	ruler-s	son

Here, we get exactly the mirror-image, since it is the first order (HEAD-APPENDAGE) which puts the *-s* at the edge, whereas the second order (APPENDAGE-HEAD) places the *-s* safely in between the two nouns. And so this time, it is the second order which can easily be extended, while the first quickly gets gummed up:

HEAD NOUN-APPENDAGE:	son	ruler	Ruritania-s-s
APPENDAGE-HEAD NOUN:	Ruritania-s	ruler-s	son

So it's hardly surprising that speakers in languages where the possessive marker is a postposition tend to opt for the APPENDAGE-HEAD order

(${}_{\text{ruler's}}$son), in order to avoid such pile-ups. This is not to say, of course, that there are never any exceptions – there always are, to everything. Some languages do actually use the problematic order, and Sumerian is a good example. While there is no need to get into the historical nitty-gritty of why and how Sumerian ended up with such an awkward state of affairs, Sumerian provides a perfect illustration for why an inconsistent order can be clumsy and problematic. The possessive marker in Sumerian is a postposition *-ak*, stuck on the appendage noun:

ensi	*Lagash-**ak***
ruler	Lagash-**s**

'ruler of Lagash'

As long as there is just one appendage, this construction hardly causes any problems. Even with two appendages, the Sumerians still managed somehow, and stuck two *-ak*'s at the end:

dumu	*ensi*	*Lagash-**ak-ak***
son	ruler	Lagash-**s-s**

'son of ruler of Lagash'

But when it came to a chain of three appendages, even the Sumerians themselves couldn't quite cope. They seem to have got into a twist and lost count, as they never remembered to stick on the third *-ak*:

dam	*dumu*	*ensi*	*Lagash-**ak-ak***
wife	son	ruler	Lagash-**s-s**

'wife of son of ruler of Lagash'

Sumerian, then, is an exception which very much proves the rule: when the possessive marker is a postposition, it is natural for speakers to prefer the order ${}_{\text{ruler's}}$son (otherwise they would get cumbersome constructions as in Sumerian), and when the possessive marker is a preposition, it is natural to prefer the order 'son$_{\text{of ruler}}$'. But since prepositions, as we have seen, tend to appear in VO languages while postpositions develop in OV languages, we now already have a third pair that tends to correlate with the basic choice between VO and OV. VO (as in English) correlates with prepositions, auxiliary-verb order, and HEAD-APPENDAGE order, whereas OV (as in Turkish) correlates with postpositions, verb-auxiliary and APPENDAGE-HEAD.

And in a domino effect, the alignment of various other elements can take the lead from the pairs that have already been mentioned. Additional elements inherit their alignment directly from the verb-object couple, or from descendants of that couple, or from pairs which have aligned themselves according to that couple in order not to trip up in the dance, and so on and so forth. Just as one final example, take the position of relative clauses. The last section of Chapter 7 showed that relative clauses are modelled on, and can develop historically from, the possessive construction, when the appendage noun in a possessive construction is gradually extended into a whole clause. The relative clause thus inherits its alignment from the position of the appendage noun in the possessive construction, so the order HEAD-APPENDAGE would naturally result in relative clauses *following* the head noun ('those$_{\text{whom}}$. . .') as in English, but the order APPENDAGE-HEAD would result in relative clauses *preceding* the noun ('. . . $_{\text{whom}}$those') as in Turkish.

And on it goes, with various other elements joining in the fray, ultimately accumulating to create the startling mirror-image effect between English and Turkish. The reason why, from an English perspective, Turkish sentences have to be processed exactly 'back to front' is that Turkish consistently chooses to align its pairs the opposite way round from what an English speaker finds natural. Behind this effect is one basic choice which English and Turkish made about the ordering of the verb and object. Turkish chose OV ('stone take'), whereas English chose VO ('take stone'). In making the choice English gravitated towards one pole, whereas Turkish moved towards the other, with more and more pairs aligning themselves with the verb-object couple or with one of its already lined-up acolytes. And this is why to English ears the Turks seem to 'talk backwards', whereas for the Turks or Japanese it is of course the English language that is consistently the wrong way round.

Notes

INTRODUCTION: 'THIS MARVELLOUS INVENTION'

Page 1 'this marvellous invention': Arnauld and Lancelot, *Grammaire générale et raisonnée* (1660), 27: 'Cette invention merveilleuse de composer de vingt-cinq ou trente sons cette infinie variété de mots qui n'ayant rien de semblable en eux-mêmes à ce qui se passe dans notre esprit, ne laissent pas d'en découvrir aux autres tout le secret, et de faire entendre à ceux qui n'y peuvent pénétrer, tout ce que nous concevons, et tous les divers mouvements de notre âme.' (All translations, unless otherwise stated, are by Guy Deutscher.)

Page 2 'every body perseveres': Newton's First Law of Motion (in the English translation of Andrew Motte, 1729), from his *Principia Mathematica* (1687): 'Corpus omne perseverare in statu suo quiescendi vel movendi uniformiter in directum nisi quatenus a viribus impressis cogitur statum illum mutare.'

Page 2 **The Sumerians: Suggestions for further reading**: S. N. Kramer, *History Begins at Sumer: Thirty-nine Firsts in Man's Recorded History* (1989), and *The Sumerians: Their History, Culture and Character* (1967). See also various articles about the language, culture and history of the Sumerians in J. M. Sasson, *Civilizations of the Ancient Near East* (2000).

Page 3 Sumerian *munintuma'a*: from an inscription of Enannatum, ruler of Lagash in the twenty-fifth century BC, ed. Steible (1982), 185. I am grateful to Bram Jagersma for this example.

Page 9 Uniformitarianism: On the history of this idea in linguistics, see Christy (1983).

Page 12 No systems of communication today are evolving their first words: Some readers may wonder why I have not mentioned pidgin and creole languages in this context. The reason is that pidgins are by no means systems of communication that are in the process of developing their first words. While they are indeed simplified languages, crucially, they incorporate all the fundamental 'design features' of language, and they are spoken by people who already have command of a fully complex human language (their mother tongue) and who are thus aware of the range of expression that a normal language affords. It is thus far from obvious that the linguistic behaviour of such speakers, even under conditions of extreme simplification, would reflect exactly a stage in the evolution of language when people had yet to discover the unbounded possibilities of expression that a complex language provides. In general, I will not rely on evidence from pidgins and creoles in this book, since our understanding of their nature and especially of their genesis is still highly uncertain. In particular, an increasing body of evidence seems to suggest that much more of pidgin and creole structure may be accounted for by the influence of substrate languages than has traditionally been assumed (see, e.g. Lefebvre (2004)), and this undermines attempts to present pidgins and creoles as accurate reflections of earlier stages in the evolution of language.

Page 12 Arguments for early emergence of language in *Homo erectus*: Bickerton and Calvin (2000), 104, Bickerton (1990), 138. For evidence for the control of fire from at least 700,000 years ago, see Goren-Inbar et al. (2004), 725.

Page 13 Chimpanzee tool use as a culturally transmitted activity: Boesch (1993), McGrew (1993).

Page 13 'Hand axes' produced by imitation: Davidson and Noble (1993), who also stress that these tools require much less planning than might at first appear.

Page 13 Discrepancy between cognitive potential and realization: Renfrew (1996).

Page 13 Earlier hominids could not produce the vowel *i*: Lieberman (1984), Lieberman (1991).

Page 13 'Explosion' in arts and technology: Klein and Edgar (2002).

Page 14 Symbolic artefacts as evidence of language: Davidson and Noble (1993).

Page 14 Perforated shell-beads in South Africa: Henshilwood et al. (2004). These finds support the view held by archaeologists such as Davidson that the 'microliths' (little stone tools shaped into distinct geometric forms) from the Kassies River Mouth in South Africa, which date from around the same time, should also be seen as evidence of the use of symbols. See Davidson and Noble (1993).

Page 14 'When it comes to linguistic form, Plato. . .': Sapir (1921), 219.

Page 15 Brisset's 'coac coac': Brisset (2001), 717, 'Un jour que nous observions ces jolies petites bêtes, en répétant nous-même ce cri: *coac*, l'une d'elles nous répondit, les yeux interrogateurs et brillants, par deux ou trois fois: *Coac*. Il nous était clair qu'elle disait : quoi que tu dis?'

Page 15 **Scenarios for the first emergence of language: Suggestions for further reading:** An excellent introduction is J. Aitchison's *The Seeds of*

Speech (1996). Selections of articles representing different theories on the emergence of language can be found in M. Christiansen and S. Kirby, *Language Evolution* (2003); A. Wray, *The Transition to Language* (2002); T. Givón and B. F. Malle, *The Evolution of Language out of Pre-language* (2002). A collection of fascinating articles on the relation between tools and language, and the use of tools by hominids and primates is K. Gibson and T. Ingold, *Tools, Language, and Cognition in Human Evolution* (1993). Web-links to other resources and online articles can be found on *www.unfoldingoflanguage.com.*

Page 16 **Kanzi: Suggestions for further reading:** For an engaging biography of Kanzi by his trainer, Sue Savage-Rumbaugh, and an account of his learning process and linguistic abilities, see Savage-Rumbaugh et al., *Apes, Language, and the Human Mind* (1998). See also Savage-Rumbaugh and Rumbaugh (1993), and the webpage of the Language Research Center of the Georgia State University *www.gsu.edu/~wwwlrc/biographies/kanzi.html*, where it is also reported that Panbanisha, Kanzi's younger sister, has developed language comprehension and production skills even more advanced than those of Kanzi. For a critical evaluation, see e.g. Steven Pinker's *The Language Instinct* (1994).

Page 19 **The innateness controversy: Suggestions for further reading:** For proponents of the 'innatist' view, see S. Pinker's *The Language Instinct* (1994) and *The Blank Slate* (2002), or R. Jackendoff's *Foundations of Language* (2002). For advocates of the opposite view, see G. Sampson's *Educating Eve: The 'Language Instinct' Debate* (1997), T. Deacon's *The Symbolic Species* (1997), or M. Tomasello's *Constructing a Language* (2003). A recent issue of the journal *The Linguistic Review* (no. 19, from 2002) is devoted entirely to debating (in characteristically polemical tones) the 'poverty of stimulus' argument. Recently, Chomsky himself has offered a very different take on the question of what needs to be pre-wired in the brain. A co-authored article in the journal *Science* (Hauser, Chomsky and Fitch (2002)) argues that the only specific pre-wired linguistic mechanism is 'recursion' (the ability to re-apply an operation to a construction, in theory indefinitely, to create increasingly complex hierarchical structures, as in 'this is the farmer that . . . that . . . that lay in the house that Jack built'). The article also suggests that recursion did not evolve specifically for language but for other cognitive abilities such as navigation. For a critical discussion see Pinker and Jackendoff (forthcoming).

Page 19 Cultural evolution: Cavalli-Sforza and Feldman (1981).

CHAPTER 1: A CASTLE IN THE AIR

Page 21 'Basque is really a strange language': *Scaligerana*, or the collection of Scaliger's aphorisms: Scaliger (1695), 48-9 (s.v. *Basque*). On Scaliger's linguistic skills see the Funeral Oration by Daniel Heinius (Heinius 1927 [1609]).

Page 21 Aardvark: From Dutch *aard-vark*,'earth-pig', this is the name of the 'ant-bear', an ant-eating mammal found in South Africa, famous mostly for its prominent position at the head of English dictionaries.

Page 24 Turkish word 'you are one of . . .': Some of the glosses are only approximations. In particular, *dik* is a non-future participle marker that nominalizes the clause 'can't cause to . . .' *Ler* is a morpheme which pluralizes the whole clause nominalized by *dik*. And *imiz* is a possessive pronoun 'our' (rather than 'we'). In connection with the participle *dik*, however, *imiz* marks the subject in the participle clause. So more literally, the Turkish word should be translated 'you are one of those of our not being able to turn into someone from town.' On the structure of such participle constructions in Turkish see Haig (1998), 50-70.

Page 29 Sensitivity to hierarchical structure: Chomsky (1971), 29, who uses a hungry dog as an example, rather than a seal. But the structure of the example is the same.

Page 34 Neo-Aramaic example (Alqosh dialect): E. Coghill (p.c.).

Page 41 Gender systems: Corbett (1991), 8-12. Among the languages of the world which have gender distinctions, there seem to be only a few which have a consistent or nearly consistent logical classification. Tamil is an example of an almost entirely consistent system, and in some sense, English is another example, although a fairly marginal one, since gender in English is only manifested by the pronouns *he*, *she*, *it*, and is not formally marked on nouns themselves.

Page 43 Jemez number ending *-sh*: Mithun (1999), 81, 443.

CHAPTER 2: PERPETUAL MOTION

Page 45 '*Eppur si muove!*': Galileo is reputed to have made this defiant statement in 1632, after he was forced by the Inquisition to recant his claim that the earth moves around the sun.

Page 46 *Polychronicon*: Rawson Lumby (1876), 297.

Page 48 Translations of Wycliffe and Ælfric: Both translated not from the original Hebrew, but from the Latin Vulgate, where *Noah* is called *Noe*.

Page 52 Seventeenth-century pronunciation of *all* as {owl}: Lass (1999), 94ff.

Page 52 'Men of mature age': Eastlake (1902), 992. The *h*-less pronunciation of words such as *'ospital* should not be taken to mean that the speakers Eastlake describes dropped all their *h*'s, since the words that Eastlake mentions are all of French origin. The process by which *h* reappeared in pronunciation, because of the influence of spelling, can be seen more recently with the adjective 'historic', which was originally pronounced without an *h*, hence the still current phrase 'an historic moment'.

Page 53 'I take it you already know': This poem appeared in the *Manchester Guardian* on 21 June 1954, in the Miscellany section on page 3, with the title 'Brush up your English: Hints on pronunciation for visiting foreigners'. It is signed T. S. W. Taylor and Taylor (1983), 99 attribute it to T. S. Watt (and change the word 'lough' in the original on line 4 to 'laugh').

Page 54 German biblical translations: AD 1000: translation of Notker, from Tax (1981), 333 and Tschirch (1955), 122; Modern German: Elberfelder translation. French biblical translations: AD 400: Vulgate; AD 1200, from Michel (1860), 131; Modern French: Darby translation.

Page 55 Languages multiply happily of their own accord: The account given here for divergence due to geographical separation is of course highly simplified. For discussions of the different patterns of change and divergence resulting from geographical dispersal, see Dixon (1997), Nettle (1999).

Page 56 'Give us this day': Indo-European data from Lockwood (1972).

Page 59 **Mbabaram: Suggestions for further reading:** for a fascinating account of the search for Mbabaram and other aboriginal languages, see R. M. W. Dixon, *Searching for Aboriginal Languages: Memoirs of a Field Worker* (1989). On the change from *gudaga*, which is still the word for 'dog' in the neighbouring language Yidin, to *dog*, see ibid., pp. 126ff., Dixon (1972), 347–52, Dixon (1991).

Page 60 Role of contact in language change: Labov (2001).

Page 61 Change emerging from the accumulated behaviour of individuals: Keller (1994). For a general discussion of the reasons for language change, see also Aitchison (2001).

Page 64 'This is my loved son that liketh me': *Oxford English Dictionary*, s.v. *like*, v.[1] 1.a. (*The pylgremage of the sowle*; from the French of G. de Guilleville *c.* 1400) with spelling normalized from 'This is my loued sone that lyketh me'.

Page 65 'Should we not be monstrously ingratefull': *Oxford English Dictionary*, s.v. *resent*, v. II.9 (Isaac Barrow, *Sermons*).

Page 65 'I was sure that this instance of his friendship': *Oxford English Dictionary*, s.v. *resent*, v. II.9 (Bishop William Warburton, *Letters from a late eminent prelate to one of his friends*).

Page 67 'the process of linguistic change has never been directly observed': Bloomfield (1933), 347.

Page 68 The role of variation in sound change: I do not wish to imply that the realization that change proceeds through synchronic variation has settled all questions regarding sound change. One area that is still controversial is to what extent sound change proceeds across all words at the same time, or progresses word by word ('lexical diffusion'). For a review of the state of the art, see Labov (1994), Part D.

Page 71 Charles I quotes: *Oxford English Dictionary*, s.v. *resent* v. II.9, and *resent* v. I.2.

CHAPTER 3: THE FORCES OF DESTRUCTION

Page 73 'Beloved men, know that this is the truth': From the opening of Wulfstan's *Sermo Lupi ad Anglos*.

Page 73 'Tongues, like governments': Samuel Johnson: *Dictionary of the English Language*, 1755. Reprinted in Bolton (1966), 154.

Page 73 'a mistake was a mistake': Clive James, 'The unmysterious suicide', *Times Literary Supplement*, 21 June 2002.

Page 74 'most people who bother with the matter': George Orwell, 'Politics and the English Language', reprinted in Bolton and Crystal (1969), 217.

Page 74 Schleicher quotes: Schleicher (1850), 11, 231.

Page 74 'The greatest improprieties . . .': Thomas Sheridan's *General Dictionary of the English language* (1780), quoted from MacMahon (1998), 383.

Page 74 'I do here, in the Name of all the Learned': Jonathan Swift's *Proposal for Correcting, Improving and Ascertaining the English Tongue*, reprinted in Bolton (1966), 108.

Page 75 'six hundred years ago . . .': Grimm (1819), x.

Page 75 Koster quotes: Koster (2001), 29, 31. French 'altération' is not a neutral term, so the more accurate meaning of 'altération qui se mue en altérité' is 'debasement which turns into otherness'.

Page 75 Discussion between Hugo and Cousin: Victor Hugo, *Choses vues 1830–1846*, Séance du 23 Novembre 1843 (Hugo (1972), 273).

Page 76 'gradually lost the proper and instinctive sense': Paris (1862), 3–4.

Page 76 'practically everyone. . . in those days': Cicero, *Brutus* 258 (ed. Kytzler (1977), 194): 'sed omnes tum fere . . . recte loquebantur. sed hanc certe rem deteriorem vetustas fecit.'

Page 76 'every age claims': Weigel (1974), 7.

Page 78 'With the Third Declension . . .': Sayers (1963), 180.

Page 79 Date of Latin change from *s* to *r*: Touratier (1975).

Page 83 Grimm's law: The formulation of the sound shifts appeared in the second edition of Grimm's *Deutsche Grammatik* (1822), three years after the first edition (1919).

Page 86 Table of 'home grown' and 'borrowed later' cognates: The reconstructions are based on Kluge (1995) and Watkins (2000). Only the roots are given here, in order to facilitate the comparison with the modern languages. The symbols *r̥, m̥* stand for long *r* and *m* sounds which behave like vowels, somewhat like in the English word *bottom*. The *k* of roots like *kerd* and *kwon* was originally palatalized (that is, pronounced {ky}, as in the English word 'cube'), so the Indo-European roots should properly be written *k̂erd* and *k̂won*. But in the so-called 'centum' branches of Indo-European, which include all the ones mentioned in the table, the palatal velar *k̂* merged with the plain velar *k* (and likewise *ĝ* merged with the plain *g*, and *ĝh* with the plain *gh*), so I will not specifically mark the palatalization in any of the etymologies here or elsewhere in the book.

Page 87 A system where 'everything holds together' (*tout se tient*): This is often attributed to Saussure, but apparently was articulated first by Antoine Meillet (1903), 407.

Page 87 'The Germans' mighty progress and urge for freedom': Grimm (1848), 417: '. . . mit dem gewaltigen das mittelalter eröfnenden vorschritt und freiheitsdrang der Deutschen zusammenhängt, von welchen Europas umgestaltung ausgehn sollte.'

Page 87 Japanese *para-kiri*: Martin (1987), 10–12, 399.

Page 89 'By leaving out a Vowel to save a Syllable': Jonathan Swift's *A Proposal for Correcting, Improving and Ascertaining the English Tongue* (1712). Reprinted in Bolton (1966), 113–15.

Page 90 Danish song: 'Fo' ajle di små blomster' (Opvåvni), by Mads Hansen (1870).

Page 91 'Clinton Sends Vowels': This piece originally appeared in the American satirical magazine *The Onion* (December 1995), but was then widely circulated unattributed on the internet.

Page 91 Czech phrase 'stick finger down throat': Strictly speaking, it is inaccurate to say that the Czech phrase does not contain vowels, since the sound *r* in words like *strč*, *prst*, is long and builds the core of a syllable as vowels do.

Page 96 *The Complaints of Khakheperre-seneb*: Lichtheim (1973), 146, Parkinson (1996), Parkinson (1997).

Page 98 French intensifiers: In modern French, see Koster (2001), 32. In Old French, see Gamillscheg (1957), 753.

Page 99 Middle English emphatic combination *ne . . . nawt*: Fischer (1992), 280, Jack (1978), 29–39. Notice, incidentally, that the use of 'double negation', which would be frowned upon by purists today, was entirely normal then.

Page 99 'At all' as an intensifier: Originally, 'at all' was used to add emphasis also to 'normal' affirmative sentences, as in 'They were careless at all, they thought all things were cock-sure' meaning 'they were very careless', or 'careless in every way'. *Oxford English Dictionary*, s.v. *all* A.9.b (H. Latimer, Sermons and remains *c.*1555).

Page 101 'one may truthfully say that . . .': Quoted in Olender (1997), 51-9.

Page 101 'What a dreadful pity . . .': Voltaire's Letter to Catherine the Great, 26 May 1767, ed. Besterman (1974): 'Je ne suis pas comme une dame de la cour de Versailles, qui disait: c'est bien dommage que l'aventure de la tour de Babel ait produit la confusion des langues; sans cela tout le monde aurait toujours parlé français.'

Page 103 Saussure's theory: His *Mémoire sur le système primitif des voyelles dans les langues indo-européennes* is dated 1879, but appeared in 1878. Saussure's term for what I have called 'rogue sounds' was *coefficients sonantiques* ('sonant coefficients').

Page 105 The root *pā*(*s*) 'protect': This root has a short form *pā* and an extended form *pās*. The example used by Saussure (1879,129-30) is the short form *pā* (as in Sanskrit *pā-tár* 'protector'), but for ease of comparison I use the extended form *pās* here.

Page 105 Critical acclaim of Saussure's theory: Mayrhofer (1988).

Page 105 Contribution of Hermann Möller: Szemerényi (1973), 7. Möller also made significant improvements to Saussure's system, increasing the number of the *coefficients sonantiques*. He didn't use the term 'laryngeals' initially (in 1879 he called them 'glottal', a year later 'guttural', and it was only in 1911 that the term 'laryngeal' appeared) but he made the connection with the Semitic sounds from the beginning.

Page 106 **The Hittites and the discovery of Hittite: Suggestions for further reading:** C.W. Ceram, *Secret of the Hittites: The Discovery of an Ancient Empire* (1973), O. R. Gurney, *The Hittites* (1981), J. G. Macqueen, *The Hittites and Their Contemporaries in Asia Minor* (1986). For an introduction to the cuneiform script, see C. B. F. Walker, *Cuneiform* (1987).

Page 108 The Hittite phrase NINDA-*an ettsa-tteni. . .*: Hrozný's report on his decipherment appeared in December 1915, in the *Mitteilungen der Deutschen Orient-Gesellschaft*. It is often claimed that 'now you will eat bread and drink water' was the very first Hittite phrase that Hrozný managed to decipher, but in his own report, he only mentions it as one of the first. The actual transcription of the Hittite sentence is: *nu* NINDA-*an e-iz-za-at-te-ni wa-a-tar-ma e-ku-ut-te-ni*. Since the Babylonians themselves borrowed the cuneiform script from the Sumerians, the word-signs that they used, and which were then adopted by the Hittites, were based on Sumerian words. NINDA is Sumerian for bread. The Old High German cognate which I spell *ettsan* for transparency was actually spelled *ezzan*. Hrozný also thought that *eku* looked rather like Latin *aqua*, which strengthened his conviction that it meant 'drink'. But this *was* just a coincidence. Linguists today think that *eku* came from the Indo-European root **eg^wh^*-'drink', which in Latin (after some sound changes) ended up in the word *ēbrius* 'drunk', from which we have English *inebriated*.

Page 109 An 'almost unbelievable accident': Kuryłowicz (1927), 101: 'Cette question serait insoluble dans l'état actuel de la grammaire comparée si, par suite d'un accident presque invraisemblable, le hittite ne semblait pas avoir conservé le caractère consonantique de $ə_2$.'

Page 111 Schleicher quotes: 'at first sight we observe precisely the opposite', 'precisely the fact that we find language already fully constructed', 'Only when a nation has perfected its language', all from Schleicher (1850), 11-12; 'Languages are natural organisms': Schleicher (1863), 6; 'history, that enemy of language': Schleicher (1850), 134.

Page 112 'languages are historical creations, not vegetables': Bonfante (1946), 295. His criticism of Schleicher is aimed mainly at the details of the family-tree model. Similar criticism was expressed much earlier, most forcefully by the founders of the Neo-Grammarian movement, H. Osthoff and K. Brugmann (1878), iii-xx. For a history of nineteenth-century linguistics, see Morpurgo Davis (1998).

Page 113 The *s-r* irregularity in Old English 'choose': As it happens, there are also cognate forms in closely related languages, such Dutch *kiezen* 'choose' and German *auserkoren* 'chosen', which could have suggested even without records from older stages that there was something untoward with *s* and *r* in the Germanic languages. Still, without the historical records, we would never have any cause to reconstruct all the idiosyncrasies of 'choose' in Old English.

CHAPTER 4: A REEF OF DEAD METAPHORS

Page 115 The definition of metaphor: Linguists have debated whether, and to what extent, two types of metaphoric processes should be distinguished in language: 'metaphor' and 'metonymy' (see e.g. Kövecses (2002), Ch. 11). Metaphor is meant to involve a transfer of a concept to a distant domain, whereas metonymy is the transfer to an adjacent domain (as, for example, in referring to the monarchy as 'the crown', or to someone with a drink problem as 'on the bottle'). Since the metaphors in this chapter generally have a 'basis in experience', some may prefer to call them metonymies.

But for our purposes, the niceties of the distinction are of no particular concern, since the crucial aspect of the process is the movement from concrete to abstract domains, not whether the abstract domain is 'adjacent' or 'distant'.

Page 115 'Metaphors, I said!': Skármeta (1988), 16 (translation: K. Silver).

Page 121 Conceptual metaphors: Lakoff and Johnson (1980), *Metaphors We Live By*.

Page 123 Molière quote: *Le Bourgeois Gentilhomme* ('The Middle Class Gentleman'), Act II, scene IV. Translation: Project Gutenberg.

Page 125 'if the house be discovered by tempest': *Oxford English Dictionary*, s.v. *discover* v. 1. (Edward Coke, *The institutes of the lawes of England*, 1628.)

Page 126 'decide' from 'cut': Basque example from Larry Trask (p.c.), Indonesian example from A. Gianto (p.c.), Endo example from J. Zwarts (p.c.), Mandarin Chinese *jué* (more commonly *jué dìng*) ('cut/breach', 'decide') from G. Sampson (p.c.). Compare also French *trancher* ('cut/slice', but also 'settle a matter once and for all').

Page 127 Transfer from concrete to abstract: Metaphors in the other direction are much rarer, but travelling is one area where such metaphors are found. For example, we can say that 'Cambridge is at *an hour's* distance from London'. Here we measure the distance (space) by the time it takes to traverse it.

Page 128 Metaphor as an analogical process: Gentner et al. (2001).

Page 129 Most languages don't have a 'have' verb: Heine (1997a), 75 reports that from a sample of 110 languages, about 14 per cent expressed possession with a transitive verb.

Page 130–132 Examples of possession: Russian, So, Mupun, Quechua, Breton, Nama, from Heine (1997a), 92–5. Turkish, Irish, Tamil, Dullay, from Heine (1997b), 48–59. Waata from Heine et al. (1991), 37. In Turkish, this is not the most common construction for expressing possession, and is used only in specific circumstances. Akkadian example: from an Old Babylonian letter: Frankena (1974), no. 57.

Page 133 'dictionary of faded metaphors': 'Wörterbuch erblasseter Metaphern', literally 'turned-pale metaphors'. From *Vorschule der Aesthetik*, §50 (Paul (1967), 184).

Page 136 '*Outside* . . . is used in a sense not known to the language': Elwyn (1859), 82, quoted from the *Oxford English Dictionary*, s.v. outside D. II. 4. b.

Page 138 Ewe *megbé*: Heine et al. (1991), 65. *Megbé* itself seems to be a compound, as according to Westermann (1954), *me* itself can mean 'back'.

Page 139 Hebrew 'face': The sound *p* has weakened to *f* in some environments, but for transparency, I use *p* throughout.

Page 140 Body-part examples: Anttila (1972), 149 (Hungarian); Heine and Kuteva (2002) (all the rest except Hebrew). While parts of the body are the most common source of spatial terms, other objects can also serve in this function. One example is the French preposition *chez*, meaning 'at' or 'by', whose origin is the Latin word *casa* 'house' (Gamillscheg (1928), 309). The Scandinavian preposition *hos* ('by', 'at') has the same origin, the word *hus* 'house'. The Akkadian *bīt* ('house') also developed into a preposition meaning 'at' in later stages of the language.

CHAPTER 5: THE FORCES OF CREATION

Page 144 'Let us put our trust in the eternal spirit': The ending paragraph of Bakunin's first publication, 'Die Reaktion in Deutschland' (Bakunin (1842), 1002).

Page 147 The history of 'going to': Scheffer (1975), 270, Danchev and Kytö (1994) (but note their error on p. 63: the alleged early example from 1567 is actually from 1657: the Parliamentary Diary of Thomas Burton, entry of 12 January 1657: 'Especially when you are going to lay a tax upon the people, it is fit you should be unanimous' (Rutt (1828), 339). See also Traugott and Dasher (2002), Hopper and Traugott (2003), 1-3, 93.

Page 148 'as they were goynge to bringe hym there': Rolls of Parliament (*Rotuli Parliamentorum*) 1278-1503, ed. Strachey (1767), Vol. 5, 16.

Page 148 'was goyng to be broughte into helle': From *The Revelation to the monk of Evesham* (Aber (1869), 43). This was a translation of a Latin work composed much earlier, around 1196, called *Visio Monachi de Eynsham.* The Latin source has 'infelix. . . agitur in gehennam' ('the unhappy one is driven into hell').

Page 150 Fletcher quote: *Women Pleased,* act III, scene ii.

Page 150 'To be short, You see that My Magazine . . .': Speech of Charles I to the Gentry of Yorkshire on 12 May 1642, Fulman and Perrinchief (1662), 401.

Page 150 '"going to" is the signe of the Participle of the future': Poole (1646), 26.

Page 151 'Going to' more restricted in use before nineteenth century: Traugott and Dasher (2002), 84. For example, 'raising' phrases with inanimate subjects, such as 'it is going to rain' only seem to appear in the latter half of the nineteenth century.

Page 151 'Now Willie lad, I'm ganna gie You': Alexander Douglas (of Strathmiglo), *Poems, Chiefly in the Scottish Dialect* (1806), Cupar-Fife, p. 70, quoted from Wright (1900), 659, s.v. *go* 4.

Page 154 Basque, Tamil, Zulu examples of 'going to': Heine and Kuteva (2002), 161–3.

Page 158 Report of the Inquisition: Schiaparelli (1929), 74 (no. 19, AD 715, giugno 20, Siena. Breve de Inqiositione): 'Uuarnefrit gastaldius mihi dicebat: Ecce missus uenit inquirere causa ista, et tu, si interrogatus fueris, quomodo dicere habes? Ego respondi ei: Caue ut non interroget, nam si interrogatus fuero, ueritatem dicere habeo.'.

Page 159 Fredegar's account of Daras: Wolfram (1982), 70 (book II, par. 62). The historical reality behind this story is a bit more complex. Fredegar does not mention Kavadh by name (and refers to him only as the Persian king), and he also seems to have conflated two Byzantine emperors into one story. Dara(s) was founded (or at least fortified) in AD 507, by the Byzantine emperor Anastasius, a predecessor of Justinian, after he had made a temporary peace with Kavadh. Twenty-three years later, the same Kavadh was again engaged in war with the Byzantines, this time with emperor Justinian. Justinian's legendary general Belisar routed Kavadh in a famous battle near Daras, and two years and a few military reverses later, Justinian again negotiated a peace (with Kavadh's son), ending the war. In Fredegar's story, all three events seem to have been conflated. Today the ruins of Daras lie in the small village of Oğuz near the town of Mardin in eastern Turkey, not far from the Syrian border. (*Encyclopædia Iranica*, Vol. VI, 1993, s.v. *dārā*.)

Page 160 Contraction of *dare habes* to *daras*: the modern French for 'you will give' is not *daras* but *donneras*, because at some later stage, the verb *dare* dropped out of use and was replaced by *donare*.

Page 161 Table of Late Latin to Modern French: Based on Valesio (1968), 159.

Page 162 Table with 'mwa jem': based on Lambrecht (1981), 15, Schwegler (1990), 112, Klausenburger (2000), 25, 83. The original pronouns now form a phonological unit with the verb, they cannot be stressed, they never appear in isolation.

Page 164 Origin of case ending *-ibus*: Szemerényi (1996), 165.

Page 165 Latin 'wolf': The Latin *lupo* actually started out in Indo-European as *$*wlk^{w}o$*, and has the same origin as English *wolf*.

Page 167 'I knew I had to say thank you': Mann (1986), 185.

Page 168 *Au jour d'aujourd'hui*: the phrase has in fact quite a long pedigree, and is even attested in literary genres, for instance in Alphonse de Lamartine's *Méditations poétiques* (1820): '[Dieu] le sait, il suffit: l'univers est à lui / Et nous n'avons à nous que le jour d'aujourd'hui!'

Page 169 Cycles of auxiliaries fusing with the verb: In the era separating Indo-European from modern French, three such cycles took place. The Latin future endings (as in *canta-bo* 'I will sing') must have originated from the fusion of an auxiliary 'be' with the verb (or as an analogical formation on the fusion of 'be' in another construction). By the time of Late Latin, these future endings had been weakened, but then a cycle started again when another auxiliary, 'have', merged with the verb to give a new set of endings in early French (*chanter-ai* 'I will sing'). In modern colloquial French, a new cycle is underway, with constructions such as *je vais chanter* 'I'm go(ing to) sing'.

Page 169 'That which one calls construction comes': Paul (1880), 351: 'Das, was man Aufbau nennt, kommt ja . . . nur durch einen Verfall zu Stande, und das, was man Verfall nennt, ist nur die weitere Fortsetzung dieses Prozesses.'

Page 170 'Merging of two words into one is excessively rare': Bloomfield (1933), 415.

CHAPTER 6: CRAVING FOR ORDER

Page 174 Role of analogy in cognition and intelligence: Holyoak and Thagard (1995), Gentner et al. (2001).

Page 176 Grotty and grotesque: 'grotesque' itself came from a noun 'grotto'. The *Oxford English Dictionary*, s.v. *grotesque* speculates that 'the etymological sense of grottesca would be "painting appropriate to grottos". The special sense is commonly explained by the statement that grotte, "grottoes", was the popular name in Rome for the chambers of ancient buildings which had been revealed by excavations, and which contained those mural paintings that were the typical examples of "grotesque"'.

Page 177 One 'Weetabick' and 'a chee': Burridge (2004), 10.

Page 178 **The Semitic languages: Suggestions for further reading**: On the language, culture, and history of the Akkadians (Babylonians and Assyrians), see A. L. Oppenheim, *Ancient Mesopotamia: Portrait of a Dead Civilization* (1964); J. Oates, *Babylon* (1986), and for the legacy of this culture S. Dalley, *The Legacy of Mesopotamia* (1998). For a collection of articles on the language, culture, writing, and history of the Ancient Near East, see J. M. Sasson, *Civilizations of the Ancient Near East* (2000). On the history of Hebrew, see A. Sáenz-Badillos, *A History of the Hebrew Language* (1993). On the culture and history of the Phoenicians, see S. Moscati, *The World of the Phoenicians* (1999). On Aramaic and the Aramaeans, see E. Lipinski, *The Aramaeans: Their Ancient History, Culture, Religion* (2000). For an introduction to Arabic and its history, see K. Versteegh, *The Arabic Language* (1997). A linguistic survey of the Semitic languages can be found in R. Hetzron, *The Semitic Languages* (1997).

Page 181 'This is what Babi says to Shartum': The text of this Old Akkadian letter was published by Veenhof (1975) (see also Kienast and Volk (1995), 153). The tablet is currently kept in the Vrije Universiteit, Amsterdam. The photograph was taken by Guy Deutscher.

Page 183 Semitic is family with longest history: the only serious contestant to the length of attested history is ancient Egyptian, whose written records start around 3000 BC, and whose later descendant, Coptic, was spoken until around AD 1500.

Page 185 Template variants *a*ⓢⓝ*u*ⓖ and *a*ⓢⓝ*i*ⓖ: In fact, there is also a third alternative, *a*ⓢⓝ*a*ⓖ, but for simplicity this will be ignored here.

Page 187 Arabic verbs *aktum*, *aftil*: The form given here is the short form, called the 'jussive'. The normal form has an ending *-u*. Note, moreover, that due to a secondary development in the history of the West-Semitic languages (including Arabic, see tree on p. 179), the Arabic forms in question have come to denote the non-past rather than past tense. But the transformation in the tense-aspect system of the West-Semitic languages is a later (and very complex) development which need not concern us here.

Page 188 The emergence of the simple past-*aktum*: Forms like *aktum* may not originally have had a past-tense meaning, but could have been non-differentiated for tense. The past nuance may have developed later, when a new form emerged with a specific present/future meaning, thus displacing the original to the territory of proper past.

Page 189 Quirk vowel as an indication for the original stem vowel: In some Semitic languages (such as Hebrew), the root vowels of the original verb have undergone thorough transformation, and have been regularized and standardized, so as to make them quite unreliable for determining the identity of the vowel in the ancient stem.

Page 190 *a-ṣāḥ* ('I will laugh'): In the earlier stages of Akkadian, the future appears as *a-ṣiāḥ*, which later contracts to *a-ṣāḥ*. See Appendix B: Laryngeals Again?

Page 191 Antiquity of the *a*-mutation: On the reconstruction of *a*-mutation to Proto-Cushitic, see Zaborski (1975), 163-5. Diakonoff (1988), 86 postulates the same for Proto-Berber. There is also evidence from within the Semitic languages themselves to suggest that the pattern is very old. One reason is that when records begin in the third millennium BC, the *a*-mutation pattern seems already to be receding. In Akkadian itself, and even more so in the later attested Semitic languages, speakers used different means to bring more and more of the hollow verbs into the fold of the regular three-consonant system (for example, by repeating the second consonant of the root twice). A further indication for the antiquity of the *a*-

mutation comes from some of the most common verbs in Akkadian, such as 'go' and 'give'. These verbs do not misbehave in exactly the same way as the hollow verbs, but they do show the *a*-mutation in the future tense: *a-ddin* ('I gave') *a-ddan* ('I will give'), *a-llik* ('I went') *a-llak* ('I will go'). Since the simplest and most common words often cling on to ancient patterns that have been abandoned by the rest of the language, the *a*-mutation in verbs like 'give' and 'go' is a strong reason to suspect that we are dealing with a very old relic. There are also indications that the *a*-mutation in Semitic originally applied to three-consonant verbs as well, see Knudsen (1984).

Page 193 Origin of the vowel mutation (ablaut) in Germanic verbs: Szemerényi (1996), 87, 121.

Page 198 Grounds for suspecting that there were more two-consonant verbs in prehistory: First, the decline in the ranks of the hollow verbs during the historical period itself suggests that the further back in time one goes, the more numerous they were. This suspicion is strengthened when one looks at other branches of the Afro-Asiatic family, which even today have more verbs with two consonants than with three. It is thus possible that they reflect the more ancient state of affairs, in which two-consonant verbs were the majority. For a critical assessment, see Zaborski (1991).

Page 199 Swelling cycles: In a few cases, the old and the new verbs still coexist in the attested period. One example is the verb *kūn* ('to be firm, upright'), and *ša-kun* ('to make firm', 'install') – it seems clear that the latter is a swollen version of the former. In other cases, such as with **pil* (or perhaps *pal* or *pul*), the original verb is no longer attested, but we can suspect it was once there, because it has swollen in two different direction, both with the prefix *ša-*, to give the root `š-p-l` ('become lowly'), and with the prefix *na-* to give the root `n-p-l` ('fall').

Page 205 The psychological reality of consonantal roots: Prunet et al. (2000).

CHAPTER 7: THE UNFOLDING OF LANGUAGE

Page 213 Conceptual distinction between 'things' and 'actions': On possible neurological precursors and correspondences to the thing-action distinction, see Hurford (2003), and Givón (2002b), 17.

Page 215 M. Jourdain's skills: See also Hawkins (1994), 440-41.

Page 218 Choice between 'man spear *throw*' and 'man *throw* spear': Givón (1979), 275ff. has suggested, in fact, that the order 'man spear *throw*' was the dominant order in earlier periods. His reasoning is based partly on the observation that in historical time, changes in word order from 'man spear *throw*' to 'man *throw* spear' are very common, but changes in the opposite direction, from 'man *throw* spear' to 'man spear *throw*' are exceedingly rare.

Page 222 The reliance of ancient languages on time iconicity (Caesar's principle): Deutscher (2000), 175ff.

Page 223 Murshili's aphasia text: R. Lebrun (1985), 103-37, Farber et al. (1987), 289. The Hittite conjunction *nu* is cognate with the English 'now', but its use corresponds more closely to English 'and'. In Hittite, sentences always have to start with some linking particle (except for the first sentence in the 'paragraph'). *Nu* is the most common of these sentence initial particles, and in this sense, 'and' is the closest translation. The place name Kunnu is preceded by the logogram DU6 which means 'ruin mound', so some scholars have normalized it as Tell-Kunnu.

Page 226 'I am Tarzan of the Apes. I want you . . .': Burroughs (1914), 195. In fact, the proverbial 'me Tarzan, you Jane' line does not even appear in this precise form in the 1930s Tarzan film. The origin of the line is apparently much less glamorous, and seems to have been a quip made in a Hollywood car-park by Johnny Weissmuller (Tarzan) to Maureen O'Sullivan (Jane). Seeing her struggling to lift a heavy suitcase, Weissmuller effortlessly swooped it up and tossed it into her car, muttering, 'Me Tarzan, you Jane.'

Page 227 'Monsieur est étranger? . . .': 'You are a foreigner, Sir?' . . . 'Foreigner? Certainly not. I'm English!'

Page 228 Pointing words (demonstratives): On children's use of demonstratives, see Clark (1976), Diessel (1999), 111, Tanz (1980). For the primitive status of demonstratives, which are not known to develop from any construction that does not already include a pointing (deictic) element, see Diessel (1999). There have been some suggestions in the literature (Heine and Kuteva (2000), 159) for a development from the verb 'go' to a demonstrative, but these seem quite speculative.

Page 228 Equivalence of 'this' and 'here', 'that' and 'there': Diessel (1999), 14, Heine and Kuteva (2002), 172. In English, both 'there' and 'that' derive from the same Indo-European root **to-*. In Korean, *ieki* 'here' comes from *i-eki* 'this place', and *keki* 'there', from *ke-eki* 'that-place' (Diessel (1999), 21), but derivation in the opposite direction is also found, where 'this' comes from something like 'thing here', and 'that' from 'thing there'. Very common is a development in which an element from one pair is reinforced by elements from the other pair. This can be seen, for instance, in French *ceci* 'this' and *cela* 'that', which come from a combination of *ce* 'that' with *ici* 'here' and *là* 'there'. Similarly, Swedish *den här* (literally 'that here') is used for 'this', and *den där* (literally 'that there') is used for 'that'.

Page 230 Origin of pronouns: For Vietnamese, see Nguyên (1992), 181 (*có* is an affirmative particle which I left untranslated). Another example is the Akkadian ending *-am*, which originally meant 'towards here', but has developed into a pronominal ending 'to me', and in fact became the usual way of expressing first person indirect object, see Kouwenberg (2002). But pointing words are not the only source from which pronouns can develop. First person pronouns are known to derive from various designations for 'man', 'person, 'people', e.g. Latin *homo* 'man' > colloquial French *on* 'we'.

Page 230 Latin *ille*: Harris (1978), 100-101.

Page 232 Akan 'give': Lord et al. (2002).

Page 233 Chinese 'give': Peyraube (1988), 207, Peyraube (1996), 178-82.

Page 233 Collapse of two actions into one: Thai examples from Blake (2001), 161-2, see also Matisoff (1991), 439 for similar use of the Thai verb *paj* 'go'. Efik example from Heine and Kuteva (2002), 289, Chinese from Peyraube (1996), 191. On the perception of the two original actions as one event, see Givón (1991).

Page 234 'The day is short and it is *passed* pryme': Chaucer's 'The Friar's Tale'. In modern times, a similar process can be observed with the verb 'following', see Olofsson (1990). In a phrase such as 'the people following us', 'following' is still a verb denoting movement, and one can replace it by other verbs, such as 'chasing'/'trailing'/'leading', or by 'who follow': 'the people who follow us'. But today, 'following' is used more widely, in phrases such as 'she dumped him *following* their row', where 'following' is no longer in a verb slot (one cannot say 'she dumped him *who follow* their row') and must be understood as a preposition. The more established preposition 'during' started out just like 'following', as a participle of the verb 'to dure' (which has since gone out of use).

Page 234 'With' as a source of 'and': For Chinese *gēn*, see Peyraube (1996), 191; for Turkish and Swahili, see Heine and Kuteva (2002), 80-83; for African languages, see Lord (1993), Ch. 4.

Page 237 'Red' and 'Adam': The connection between 'red' and 'Adam' was probably the word *adama* '(red) soil'. The Book of Genesis related *Adam* to *adama* by claiming that God 'formed man of the dust of the ground, and breathed into his nostrils the breath of life'. This scenario for the origin of human beings may not seem very likely, but modern linguists believe that the *etymology* is in fact quite plausible. A similar etymological relation is found in Latin *humanus* ('human') and *humus* ('soil').

Page 240 Combination of demonstrative and noun into a complex referring expression: Himmelmann (1997), Diessel (1999), 69. For looser status of 'that' in Old English, see Traugott (1992), 173. It is interesting that among the two-sign combinations that the bonobo Kanzi produces, by far the most common ones involve using a symbol for an object (say 'peanut') followed by a physical pointing gesture 'that', see Savage-Rumbaugh and Rumbaugh (1993), 101.

Page 242 Origin of articles, quantifiers, plural markers: Haspelmath (1995), 363-82, Heine (1997a), 71ff. Note that unlike property-words, elements such as plural markers and articles are not purely subordinate 'modifiers', since they do interact with other elements on the main level of the sentence. For example, the verb changes according to whether the subject noun is singular (the duck swim-*s*) or plural (the ducks swim). So as opposed to a modifier (such as 'old' in 'the old duck swims'), which has no direct relation with any other element in the sentence except the noun it modifies, the relation between the noun and the plural marker *-s* is a symbiosis in which each of the elements determines part of the phrase's profile towards the rest of the sentence. (On how such a symbiosis develops historically, see Himmelmann (1997).) Nevertheless, for simplicity of presentation, I subsume here under the general term 'appendage' not only pure modifiers, but also all the other elements in the noun phrase except for the head noun, including determiners (such as the definite article) and quantifiers (such as 'all', 'each'). Concerning the development of 'all' from 'whole', note that the terms for the property 'whole' itself often develop from even simpler physical properties such as 'healthy' or 'undamaged'. The English word 'whole' has the same origin as 'health', and its close synonym 'entire' is borrowed from Latin *in-teger*, literally 'un-touched'.

Page 247 'Of these three states': from the homily *Hali meidenhad* (*c.*1230), ed. Furnivall (1922), 23.

Page 247 Asymmetry between nominalization and verbalization: Hopper and Thompson (1985), 176, Woodworth (1991), 62ff. It is true that English can turn a verb into a noun without any ending: 'take a walk', 'have a go', and so on, but many languages cannot.

Page 249 Development of French *-age*. The ultimate origin of *-age* is the Latin ending *-(a)ticus*, which already in Latin had long been established as a thoroughly grammatical marker, whose function was to turn a noun or adjective X into 'someone/something of or belonging to X' (as in the Late Latin *silva* 'forest' and *silvaticus* 'someone/something belonging to the forest', which ended up in modern French as *sauvage* 'savage'). On the history of *-age* in French, see Meyer-Lübke (1966), 61-3. It is not known with which noun(s) exactly the passage of *-age* to verbs started. I chose *mariage* because it is a familiar word, but Meyer-Lübke uses a different example, the measure 'aune' (English 'ell', the measure of an outstretched arm), to which *-age* was added to give *aunage* (like English 'mileage'). Since *aune* was also turned into a verb *auner* 'to measure by the aune', speakers could have associatied the abstract noun *aunage* directly with the verb *auner*.

Page 250 Origins of nominalization markers: Various types of nominal markers are extended to verbs, for instance case markers (Blake (1999), for

European and Australian examples), nominal classifiers (Aikhenvald (2000), 332), and various abstract-noun markers. The latter themselves often originate from collectives or designations of time and place, such as the Germanic *-ing/ung* (which must originally have been denominal, see Jespersen (1948), 205 and Kluge (1995), s.v. *-ung*: 'Letztlich liegen ig. *k*-Erweiterungen zu n-Stämmen vor, so daß das Suffix ursprünglich denominal gewesen sein muß'), German *ge-* (as in *Ge-spräch*), or the Basque suffixes *-te*, *-tze*, and *-keta* (Trask 1995). Even zero-nominalization (as in English 'a walk', 'a run') could have originated ultimately from an equivalent process of analogical back formation: a noun 'an X' can be turned into a verb 'to X', but if the verb at a later stage is perceived to be the basic element in the pair, speakers can assume that the derivation went in the other direction, and so by analogy extend the pattern to other verbs.

Page 251 'she was on the riding': Strictly speaking, the presentation of such developments should have waited until the next section, because they involve embryonic subordination, where one verb functions as a dependent of another. But as the next section will argue, the ability to present a verb as a dependent of another has in fact already been achieved in the previous section, with the ability to nominalize verbs.

Page 251 'Finish' developing into a markers of completed action: Chinese example from Li and Thompson (1981), 186. For the verb 'finish' as the source of tense and aspect markers in other East Asian languages, see Matisoff (1991), 436. Markers of completed action often themselves turn into more general indicators of past tense, as in modern German and French, where what had originally been the markers of a completed action 'I have eaten' (*Ich habe gegessen, j'ai mangé*) has come to be used as a past tense more generally. On the sources of other tense, mood, and aspect markers across languages, see Bybee, Perkins and Pagliuca (1994).

Page 252 Shift from possession to obligation: Further examples in Matisoff (1991), 427.

Page 252 Fidel Castro on a state visit to Moscow: Based on Lukes and Galnoor (1987), cited in Smith and Tsimpli (1995), 77.

Page 258 Demonstratives (pointing words) in apposition as the source of relative markers: Deutscher (2001).

Page 258 Expansion of nominalized verbal forms to relative clauses: Matisoff (1972), DeLancey (1986), Genetti (1991), Harris and Campbell (1995), 291-3, 310-13, Noonan (1997), Blake (1999).

Page 259 Origin of question words and negation words: Since interrogatives (question words) did not feature in the mammoth story, their origin was not discussed in the chapter. But in fact, it seems that like demonstratives (see note for p. 228), they also have a primitive status, since they are not known to develop from nouns and verbs, or from anything else that does not have an interrogative element to start with (Diessel (2003)). This means that in addition to the demonstratives 'this' and 'that', one interrogative element (such as 'what') should also be assumed as part of our 'raw materials'. The whole range of question words could then develop from this interrogative element, on the lines of 'what-place' > 'where', 'what-person' > 'who', and so on. Negation words are known to develop from more specific (intrinsically negative) verbs such as 'leave', 'abandon', 'lose', 'fail' (see Heine and Kuteva (2002), 188, 192).

EPILOGUE

Page 262 Sumerian *munintuma'a*: From an inscription of Enannatum, ruler of Lagash, *c.*2450 BC (Steible (1982), 185). On the structure of such forms in Sumerian, see Attinger (1993), 192ff., Edzard (2003), 87ff. The actual developments which created the structure of the Sumerian verb must have been extremely complex. An attempt at reconstructing a few of the details is offered in Coghill and Deutscher (2002). For a general discussion of the investment of zero-morphemes with specific meaning, see Bybee (1994).

Page 265 *Erriplen* in Gurr-goni in the 'vegetable gender': Aikhenvald (2002), 408.

Page 268 Drift towards simpler word structure as 'debasement': Towards the end of the nineteenth century, some linguists tried to swing the pendulum to the other extreme and claim that the drift was actually 'progress'. Most prominent was the Danish scholar Otto Jespersen (1894).

Page 269 Examples for new endings and prefixes emerging in Indo-European languages: Persian, for instance, has acquired a new dative (and later accusative) case ending from an erstwhile postposition, and in Czech, prepositions have merged with the noun to give case prefixes, although this is not reflected in the spelling.

Page 269 The variety of subordinate clauses has increased in modern European languages: Kortmann (1997) for adverbial subordination, Deutscher (2000), Chs.10–11 for complementation.

Page 271 Patterns of communication in small societies: Givón (2002a), Ch.9.

Page 272 Correlation between simple societies and complex morphology: Dixon (1997), Kusters (2003), Perkins (1992), Trudgill (1992). On contact as a factor that encourages simplification, see Trudgill (1992), 195-212, who takes as one example Norwegian and Faroese (a very small and until recently very isolated community), which have both developed from a common ancestor fairly recently. But whereas Faroese has kept much more of the endings of the ancestor language, Norwegian has lost almost all of them.

Page 273 Factors that may contribute to the drift towards simpler morphology: Another factor which has been advanced to explain the slower rate of new fusions in the historical period is the change in word order from OV to VO (see Appendix E: The Turkish Mirror) that many Indo-European languages have undergone during the historical period. There seems to be a marked asymmetry between the rate of suffixation and prefixation, with postpositions, for instance, tending to fuse more easily than prepositions (see Cutler et al. (1985), Hall (1988), Bybee et al. (1990)). As OV languages tend to have postpositions and post-verbal auxiliaries, whereas VO languages prepositions and pre-verbal auxiliaries, the change from OV to VO could have decreased the rate of new fusions.

Page 273 Languages of the world are vanishing: For estimations of the rate of language loss, see Crystal (2002), 19, and Dixon (1997), 116.

APPENDIX A: FLIPPING CATEGORIES

Page 281 Use of 'gonna' in American English: In African American English, *gonna* has been further shortened to *gon*, and the auxiliary 'is' is no longer present in constructions such as 'you gon come'. But in questions and negative sentences, an auxiliary is inserted, as in 'you ain't gon(na) come' (Green (2002), 36, 40).

Page 284 'All grammars leak': Sapir (1921), 38.

APPENDIX B: LARYNGEALS AGAIN?

Page 287 Effect of laryngeals in changing vowels to *a* in Semitic languages: Lipinski (2001), 45.10,14, Mosacti et al. (1964), 16.110.

Page 288 The pattern *aṣīḥ* - *aṣīaḥ* extended to verbs without a laryngeal: For reasons of presentation, I use a hollow verb as an example. But this is not meant to imply that the *a*-mutation had its source specifically with hollow verbs. I could just as well have used a three-consonant verb with a final laryngeal as an illustration.

APPENDIX C: THE DEVIL IN THE DETAIL

Page 289 Reflexive template: Lieberman (1986), 610ff. offers a survey of the *t*-stems in Semitic and Afro-Asiatic languages.

Page 290 Intensive template: for a comprehensive discussion of gemination (doubling of the middle consonant) in Semitic, see Kouwenberg (1997), and especially pp. 445ff. for a historical scenario. Trukese data from Goodenough (1963). For Indo-European, see Niepokuj (1997).

Page 291 Causative template: For the view that *ša* comes from a verb 'make', see Hodge (1971), 41. Heine and Reh (1984), 276 reconstruct a verb **iss/*ass* 'make' for Proto-Cushitic, and think it is the origin of the Somali causative suffix *-is*. For discussion see Tropper (1990), 8ff. Some scholars have argued that *ša* is pronominal in origin, but cross-linguistic evidence makes this unlikely.

Page 292 Passive template: Testen (1998), Kouwenberg (2004). Zaborski (2001), 595 suggests as etymology the Bedja verb n/nV 'to be'.

APPENDIX D: THE COOK'S COUNTERPOINT

Page 296 'I remember when Mrs Cibber': Burney (1785) ('Sketch of the Life of Handel'), 33.

Page 298–9 'once he had dressed . . .': *Beowulf*, line 1472; 'because he wanted to send to us him himself': *Christ I*, line 129. We know that *sylfne* is emphasized, since it alliterates with *sendan*.

Page 300 Norwegian *hans kokk* and *sin kokk*: It is much more usual in Norwegian to say 'kokk-en hans' (cook-the his) than 'hans kokk' (his cook), but for ease of comprehension, I chose the more formal (ultimately Danish influenced) version.

APPENDIX E: THE TURKISH MIRROR

Page 302 Greenberg's discovery of word-order correlations: The original publication detailing these discoveries appeared in Greenberg (1963). For a modern assessment and revision, see Dryer (1992), Croft (2003), Ch.3. For diachronic explanations for these correlations, see Aristar (1991), Givón (2001), Ch.5, and for a general discussion of the role of diachrony in linguistic universals see Givón (2002a), Ch.6.

Page 303 Two possessive constructions in English as relics of a change from OV to VO: The actual picture is much more tangled than presented here. For a history of the two constructions and their use, see Rosenbach (2002), Ch.7, who shows, among others, that even in the Old English period there was already some flexibility in the placement of the head-noun and the genitive, and that in later stages of English, the status of the *'s* possessive marker changes from a case marker to a marker with a phrasal scope. For a discussion of how and why languages change from OV to VO, see e.g. Harris and Campbell (1995), Ch.8.

Page 304 Correlation between HEAD-APPENDAGE and prepositions: The picture presented here is highly simplified. For example, cumbersome constructions such as 'of-of-Ruritania ruler son' and 'son ruler Ruritania-s-s' only refer to a situation where: (a) the marker of possession appears on the appendage rather than on the head noun, (b) this marker is a preposition or postposition that has a whole phrase as its scope, rather than a case marker that applies only to just one word. When either of these conditions is not met, different constructions arise. But the examples here are only meant to demonstrate the type of processing difficulties that may arise with 'inconsistent' ordering of certain pairs. For the most thorough examination of processing issues relating to word order, see Hawkins (1994), Hawkins (2004).

Bibliography

Aikhenvald, A. (2002), *Classifiers: A Typology of Noun Categorization Devices*. Oxford University Press.

Aitchison, J. (1996), *The Seeds of Speech: Language Origin and Evolution*. Cambridge University Press.

Aitchison, J. (2001), *Language Change: Progress or Decay?* (3rd edn). Cambridge University Press.

Anttila, R. (1972), *Introduction to Historical and Comparative Linguistics*. Macmillan.

Arber, E. (ed.) (1869), *The Revelation to the Monk of Evesham 1196. Carefully edited from the unique copy, now in the British Museum, of the edition printed by William de Machlinia about 1482.* (English Reprints 18.) Southgate, London (unnamed).

Aristar, A. R. (1991), 'On diachronic sources and synchronic pattern: an investigation into the origin of linguistic universals'. *Language*, 67:1–33.

Arnauld, A., and Lancelot, C. (1660), *Grammaire générale et raisonnée, ou la grammaire de Port-Royal. Réimpression des éditions de Paris*, 1660 et 1662. Genève: Slatkinem, 1972.

Attinger, P. (1993), *Eléments de linguistique sumérienne: la construction de* du_{11}*/e/di 'dire'*. Fribourg: Editions Universitaires Fribourg Suisse.

Bakunin, M. A. (under the pseudonym Jules Elysard) (1842), 'Die Reaktion in Deutschland'. *Deutsche Jahrbücher für Wissenschaft und Kunst* 5.247–251:985–1002.

Besterman, T. D. N. (ed.) (1974), *The Complete Works of Voltaire: Correspondence and Related Documents, Vol. 32: April–December* 1767. Banbury: Voltaire Foundation.

Bickerton, D. (1981), *Roots of Language*. Ann Arbor: Karoma.

Bickerton, D. (1990), *Language and Species*. University of Chicago Press.

Bickerton, D., and Calvin, W. H. (2000), *Lingua ex Machine*. MIT Press.

Blake, B. J. (1999), 'Nominal marking on verbs: some Australian cases'. *Word*, 50: 299–317.

Blake, B. J. (2001), *Case* (2nd edn). Cambridge University Press.

Bloomfield, L. (1933), *Language*. New York: H. Holt and Company.

Boesch, C. (1993), 'Aspects of transmission of tool-use in wild chimpanzees', in

Gibson and Ingold (1993).

Bolton, W. F. (1966), *The English Language. Essays by English and American Men of Letters 1490–1839*. Cambridge University Press.

Bolton, W. F., and Crystal, D. (eds.) (1969), *The English Language*, Vol. 2. Cambridge University Press.

Bonfante, G. (1946), '"Indo-Hittite" and areal linguistics'. *American Journal of Philology*, 67: 289–310.

Brisset, J. P. (2001), *La Science de Dieu ou la création de l'homme*, in *Œuvres Complètes de Jean-Pierre Brisset*. Les Presses du Reel.

Burney, C. (1785), 'Sketch of the life of Handel', in *An Account of the Musical Performances in Westminster-Abbey and the Pantheon . . . 1784, in Commemoration of Handel*. London, printed for the benefit of the Musical Fund. (Reprinted by Frits A. M. Knuf, Amsterdam: 1961.)

Burridge, K. (2004), *Blooming English*. Cambridge University Press.

Burroughs, E. R. (1914), *Tarzan of the Apes*. Leipzig: Bernhard Tauchnitz.

Bybee, J. L. (1994), 'The grammaticization of zero: asymmetries in tense and aspect systems', in W. Pagliuca (ed.), *Perspectives on Grammaticalization*. John Benjamins, 235–54.

Bybee, J. L., Pagliuca, W., and Perkins, R. D. (1990), 'On the asymmetries in the affixation of grammatical material', in W. Croft, K. Denning and S. Kemmer (eds.), *Studies in Typology and Diachrony: Papers Presented to Joseph H. Greenberg on His 75th Birthday*. John Benjamins.

Bybee, J. L., Perkins, R. D., and Pagliuca, W. (1994). *The Evolution of Grammar: Tense, Aspect and Modality in the Languages of the World*. University of Chicago Press.

Cavalli-Sforza, L. L., and Feldman, M. W. (1981), *Cultural Transmission and Evolution: A Quantitative Approach*. Princeton University Press.

Ceram, C.W. (1973), *Secret of the Hittites: The Discovery of an Ancient Empire*. Schocken Books.

Chomsky, N. (1971), *Problems of Knowledge and Freedom*. Fontana.

Christiansen, M. H., and Kirby, S. (eds.) (2003), *Language Evolution*. Oxford University Press.

Christy, T. (1983), *Uniformitarianism in Linguistics*. John Benjamins.

Clark, E. V. (1976), 'From gesture to word: on the natural history of deixis in language acquisition', in J. S. Bruner and A. Garton (eds.), *Human Growth and Development*. Oxford University Press.

Coghill, E., and Deutscher, G. (2002), 'The origin of ergativity in Sumerian, and the "inversion" in pronominal agreement: a historical explanation based on Neo-Aramaic parallels'. *Orientalia*, 71: 267–90.

Corbett, G. C. (1991), *Gender*. Cambridge University Press.

Croft, W. (2003), *Typology and Universals* (2nd edn). Cambridge University Press.

Crystal, D. (2002), *Language Death*. Cambridge University Press.

Cutler, A., Hawkins, J.A., and Gilligan, G. (1985), 'The suffixing preference: a processing explanation'. *Linguistics*, 23:723–58.

Dalley, S. (ed.) (1998), *The Legacy of Mesopotamia*. Oxford University Press.

Danchev, A., and Kytö, M. (1994), 'The construction be going to + infinitive in Early Modern English', in D. Kastovsky (ed.), *Studies in Early Modern English*. Mouton de Gruyter, 59-79.

Davidson I., and Noble, W. (1993), 'Tools and language in human evolution', in Gibson and Ingold (1993).

Deacon, T. (1997), *The Symbolic Species: The Co-evolution of Language and the Human Brain*. Penguin.

DeLancey, S. (1986), 'Relativization as nominalization in Tibetan and Newari'. Presented at the 19th International Conference on Sino-Tibetan Languages and Linguistics, 1986. (http://www.uoregon.edu/~delancey/papers/relnom.html).

Deutscher, G. (2000), *Syntactic Change in Akkadian: The Evolution of Sentential Complementation*. Oxford University Press.

Deutscher, G. (2001), 'The rise and fall of a rogue relative construction'. *Studies in Language*, 25:405–22.

Diakonoff, I.M. (1988), *Afrasian Languages*. NAUKA.

Diessel, H. (1999), *Demonstratives: Form, Function, and Grammaticalization*. John Benjamins.

Diessel, H. (2003), 'The relationship between demonstratives and interrogatives'. *Studies in Language*, 27:635–55.

Dixon, R. M. W. (1972), *The Dyirbal Language of North Queensland*. Cambridge University Press.

Dixon, R. M. W. (1989), *Searching for Aboriginal Languages: Memoirs of a Field Worker*. University of Chicago Press.

Dixon, R. M. W. (1991), 'Mbabaram', in R. M. W. Dixon and B. J. Blake (eds.), *Handbook of Australian Languages*, Vol. 4, 349–402.

Dixon, R. M. W. (1997), *The Rise and Fall of Languages*. Cambridge University Press.

Dryer, M. (1992), 'The Greenbergian word-order correlations'. *Language*, 68:81–138.

Eastlake, C. L. (1902), 'Changes in the pronunciation of English'. *The Nineteenth Century*, 52: 992–5.

Edzard, D. O. (2003), *Sumerian Grammar*. Leiden: Brill.

Elwyn, A. L. (1859), *Glossary of Supposed Americanisms*. Philadelphia: J. B. Lippincott.

Farber, W., Kümmel, H. M., and Römer, W. H. Ph. (1987), *Texte aus der Umwelt des alten Testaments* (Band II). *Religiöse Texte: Rituale und Beschwörungen I.* Gütersloh: Gerd Mohn.

Fischer, O. C. M. (1992), 'Syntax', in N. F. Blake (ed.), *Cambridge History of the English Language, Vol. II: 1066–1476*. Cambridge University Press, 207-408.

Frankena, R. (1974), *Briefe aus dem Berliner Museum* (*Altbabylonische Briefe in Umschrift und Übersetzung*, 6). Leiden: Brill.

Fulman, W., and Perrinchief, R. (eds.) (1662), *Basilika: the workes of King Charles the martyr: with a collection of declarations, treaties, and other papers concerning the differences betwixt His said Majesty and his two houses of Parliament*. Vol. I. London: James Flesher for R. Royston.

Furnivall, F. J. (ed.) (1922), *Hali Meidenhad: An Alliterative Homily of the Thirteenth Century, from Ms. Bodley 34, Oxford, and Cotton Ms. Titus D. 18, British Museum*. (Early English Text Society. Original series: 18.) Oxford University Press.

Gamillscheg, E. (1957), *Historische französische Syntax*. Tübingen: Niemeyer.

Genetti, C. (1991), 'From postposition to subordinator in Newari', in Traugott and Heine (1991), 227-56.

Gentner, D., Holyoak, K. J., and Kokinov, B. N. (eds.) (2001), *The Analogical Mind: Perspectives from Cognitive Science*. MIT Press.

Gibson, K., and Ingold, T. (1993), *Tools, Language and Cognition in Human Evolution*. Cambridge University Press.

Givón, T. (1979), *On Understanding Grammar*. Academic Press.

Givón, T. (1991), 'Serial verbs and the mental reality of 'event': grammatical vs. cognitive packaging', in Traugott and Heine (1991), 81-127.

Givón, T. (2001), *Syntax: An Introduction*, Vol. I. John Benjamins.

Givón, T. (2002a), *Bio-Linguistics: The Santa Barbara Lectures*. John Benjamins.

Givón, T. (2002b), 'The visual information-processing system as an evolutionary precursor of human language', in T. Givón and B. F. Malle (eds.), *The Evolution of Language out of Pre-language*. John Benjamins.

Goodenough, W. (1963), 'The long or double consonants of Trukese'. *Proceedings of the Ninth Pacific Science Congress*, Bangkok, 77-80.

Goren-Inbar, N., Alperson, N., Kislev, M. E., Simchoni, O., Melamed, Y., Ben-Nun, A., and Werker, E. (2004), 'Evidence of hominin control of fire at Gesher Benot Ya'aqov, Israel'. *Science*, 304 (30 April 2004).

Green, L. J. (2002), *African American English, a Linguistic Introduction*. Cambridge University Press.

Greenberg, J. H. (1963), 'Some universals of grammar with particular reference to the order of meaningful elements', in J. H. Greenberg (ed.), *Universals of Language: Report of a conference held at Dobbs Ferry, New York, April 13–15, 1961*. MIT Press, 73-113.

Grimm, J. (1819), *Deutsche Grammatik*. Part I. Göttingen: Dieterichsche Buchhandlung.

Grimm, J. (1822), *Deutsche Grammatik* (2nd edn). Part I. Göttingen: Dieterichsche Buchhandlung.

Grimm, J. (1848), *Geschichte der deutschen Sprache*. Leipzig: Weidmannsche Buchhandlung.

Gurney, O. R. (1981), *The Hittites*. Penguin.

Haig, G. (1988), *Relative Constructions in Turkish*. Wiesbaden: Harrassowitz.

Hall, C. J. (1988), 'Integrating diachronic and processing principles in explaining suffixing preference', in J. A. Hawkins (ed.), *Explaining Language Universals*. Blackwell, 321-49.

Harris, A. C., and Campbell, L. (1995), *Historical Syntax in Cross-Linguistic Perspective*. Cambridge University Press.

Harris, M. (1978), *The Evolution of French Syntax: A Comparative Approach*. Longman.

Haspelmath, M. (1995), 'Diachronic sources of *all* and *every*', in E. Bach et al. (eds.), *Quantification in Natural Languages*. Dordrecht: Kluwer, 363-82.

Hauser, M. D., Chomsky, N., and Fitch, W. T. (2002), 'The faculty of language: What is it, who has it, and how did it evolve?' *Science*, 298: 1569-79.

Hawkins, J. A. (1994), *A Performance Theory of Order and Constituency*. Cambridge University Press.

Hawkins, J. A. (2004), *Efficiency and Complexity in Grammars*. Oxford University Press.

Heine, B. (1997a), *Cognitive Foundations of Grammar*. Oxford University Press.

Heine, B. (1997b), *Possession. Cognitive Sources, Forces, and Grammaticalization*. Cambridge University Press.

Heine, B., and Reh, M. (1984), *Grammaticalization and Reanalysis in African Languages*. Hamburg: Helmut Buske.

Heine, B., and Kuteva, T. (2002), *World Lexicon of Grammaticalization*. Cambridge University Press.

Heine, B., Claudi, U. and Hünnemeyer, F. (1991), *Grammaticalization: A Conceptual Framework*. University of Chicago Press.

Heinius, D. (1927) [1609], 'Funeral Oration for J. Scaliger', in *Autobiography of Joseph Scaliger*. Harvard University Press.

Henshilwood, C., d'Errico, F., Vanhaeren, M., van Niekerk, K., and Jacobs, Z. (2004), 'Middle Stone Age shell beads from South Africa'. *Science*, 304: 404.

Hetzron, R. (ed.) (1997), *The Semitic Languages*. Routledge.

Himmelmann, N. P. (1997), *Deiktikon, Artikel, Nominalphrase: zur Emergenz syntaktischer Struktur*. Tübingen: Niemeyer.

Hodge, C. T. (1971), 'Afroasiatic s-causative'. *Language Sciences*, 15: 41-3.

Holyoak, K. J., and Thagard, P. (1995), *Mental Leaps: Analogy in Creative Thought*. MIT Press.

Hopper, P. J., and Traugott, E. C. (2003), *Grammaticalization* (2nd edn).

Cambridge University Press.

Hopper, P. J., and Thompson, S. A. (1985), 'The iconicity of the universal categories 'noun' and 'verb'', in J. Haiman (ed.), *Iconicity in Syntax*. John Benjamins.

Hrozný, B. (1915), 'Die Lösung des hethitischen Problems'. *Mitteilungen der Deutschen Orient-Gesellschaft* 56:17-50.

Hugo, V. (1972), *Choses vues: souvenirs, journaux, cahiers, 1830–46;* édition établie, présentée, et annotée par Hubert Juin. Gallimard.

Hurford, J. R. (2003), 'The neural basis of predicate-argument structure'. *Behavioral and Brain Sciences*, 26: 261-316.

Jack, G. B. (1978), 'Negative concord in early Middle English'. *Studia Neophilologica*, 50: 29-39.

Jackendoff, R. (2002), *Foundations of Language: Brain, Meaning, Grammar, Evolution*. Oxford University Press.

Jespersen, O. (1894), *Progress in Language with Special Reference to English*. Macmillan.

Jespersen, O. (1948), *Growth and Structure of the English Language* (9th edn). Doubleday Anchor Books.

Keller, R. (1994), *On Language Change: The Invisible Hand in Language*. Routledge.

Kienast, B., and Volk, K. (1995), *Die sumerischen und akkadischen Briefe des III. Jahrtausends aus der Zeit vor der III. Dynastie von Ur.* (Freiburger altorientalische Studien 19). Stuttgart: Steiner.

Klausenburger, J. (2000), *Grammaticalization: Studies in Latin and Romance Morphosyntax*. John Benjamins.

Klein, R. G., and Edgar, B. (2002), *The Dawn of Human Culture*. Wiley & Sons.

Kluge, F. (1995), *Etymologisches Wörterbuch der deutschen Sprache*, 23. Auflage, bearbeitet von E. Seebold. De Gruyter.

Knudsen, E. E. (1984), 'Innovation in the Akkadian present'. *Orientalia Suecana*, 32-5:231-40.

Kortmann, B. (1997), *Adverbial Subordination : A Typology and History of Adverbial Subordinators Based on European Languages*. Mouton de Gruyter.

Koster, S. (2001), *Adieu grammaire*. Presses Universitaires de France.

Kouwenberg, N. J. C. (1997), *Gemination in the Akkadian Verb* (Studia Semitica Neerlandica). Assen: Van Gorcum.

Kouwenberg, N. J. C. (2002), 'Ventive, dative and allative in Old Babylonian'. *Zeitschrift für Assyriologie*, 92: 200-240.

Kouwenberg, N. J. C. (2004), 'Assyrian light on the history of the N-Stem', in J. G. Dercksen (ed.), *Assyria and Beyond: Studies Presented to Mogens Trolle Larsen*. Leiden: Nederlands Instituut voor het Nabije Oosten, 333-52.

Kövecses, Z. (2002), *Metaphor, A Practical Introduction*. Oxford University Press.

Kramer, S. N. (1967), *The Sumerians: Their History, Culture and Character*. University of Chicago Press.

Kramer, S. N. (1989), *History Begins at Sumer: Thirty-nine Firsts in Man's Recorded History*. University of Pennsylvania Press.

Kuryłowicz, J. (1927), 'ə indo-européen et ḫ hittite', in *Symbolae Grammaticae in Honorem Ioannis Rozwadowski*. Kraków: Uniwersytetu Jagiellonskiego.

Kusters, C. W. (2003), *Linguistic Complexity. The Influence of Social Change on Verbal Inflection*. Utrecht: LOT.

Kytzler, B. (ed.) (1977), *M. T. Cicero: Brutus*. Lateinisch-Deutsch. München: Heimermann.

Labov, W. (1994), *Principles of Linguistic Change*. Vol. 1: *Internal Factors*. Blackwell.

Labov, W. (2001), *Principles of Linguistic Change*. Vol. 2: *Social Factors*. Blackwell.

Lakoff, G., and Johnson, M. (1980), *Metaphors We Live By*. University of Chicago Press.

Lambrecht, K. (1981), *Topic, Antitopic and Verb Agreement in Non-standard French*. John Benjamins.

Lass, R. (1999), 'Phonology and morphology', in R. Lass (ed.), *Cambridge History of the English Language, Vol. III: 1476–1776*. Cambridge University Press.

Lebrun, R. (1985), 'L'aphasie de Mursili II'. *Hethitica*, 6:103-37.

Lefebvre, C. (2004), *Issues in the Study of Pidgin and Creole Languages*. John Benjamins.

Li, C., and Thompson, S. A. (1981), *Mandarin Chinese: A Functional Reference Grammar*. University of California Press.

Lichtheim, M. (1973), *Ancient Egyptian Literature, a Book of Readings*, Vol. I. University of California Press.

Lieberman, P. (1984), *Biology and the Evolution of Language*. Harvard University Press.

Lieberman, P. (1991), *Uniquely Human: The Evolution of Speech, Thought, and Selfless Behaviour*. Harvard University Press.

Lieberman, S. J. (1986), 'The Afro-Asiatic background of the Semitic N-Stem'. *Bibliotheca Orientalis*, 42:577-628.

Lipinski, E. (2000), *The Aramaeans : Their Ancient History, Culture, Religion*. Leuven: Peeters.

Lipinski, E. (2001), *Semitic Languages. Outline of a Comparative Grammar*. 2nd edn. Leuven: Peeters.

Lockwood, W. B. (1972), *A Panorama of Indo-European Languages*. Hutchinson.

Lord, C. (1993), *Historical Change in Serial Verb Constructions*. John Benjamins.

Lord, C., Yap, H., and Iwasaki, S. (2002), 'Grammaticalization of "give": African and Asian perspectives', in I.Wischer and G. Diewald (eds.), *New Reflections on Grammaticalization*, John Benjamins, 217-35.

Lukes, S., and Galnoor, I. (1987), *No Laughing Matter: A Collection of Political*

Jokes. Penguin.

Lumby, J. R. (ed.) (1876), *Polychronicon Ranulphi Higden monachi Cestrensis: together with the English translations of John Trevisa (c.1390) and of an unknown writer of the fifteenth century*. Vol. 6 (containing Vol. 5 of the *Polychronicon*). (Chronicles and memorials of Great Britain and Ireland during the Middle Ages, 41.) London: Longman.

MacMahon, M. K. C. (1998), 'Phonology', in S. Romaine (ed.), *Cambridge History of the English Language, Vol. IV: 1776–1997*. Cambridge University Press, 373-535.

Macqueen, J. G. (1986), *The Hittites and Their Contemporaries in Asia Minor*. Thames & Hudson.

Mann, G. (1986), *Errinerungen und Gedanken: Eine Jugend in Deutschland*. Fischer Verlag.

Martin, S. E. (1987), *The Japanese Language Through Time*. Yale University Press.

Matisoff, J. (1972), 'Lahu nominalization, relativization, and genitivization', in J. Kimball (ed.), *Syntax and Semantics*, Vol. 1. Seminar Press, 237-58.

Matisoff, J. (1991), 'Areal and universal dimensions of grammatization in Lahu', in Traugott and Heine (1991), Vol. 2, 383-453.

Matthews, P. H. (1997), *The Concise Oxford Dictionary of Linguistics*. Oxford University Press.

Mayrhofer, M. (1988), 'Zum Weiterwirken von Saussures *Mémoire*'. *Kratylos*, 33: 1-15.

McGrew, W. (1993), 'The intelligent use of tools: twenty propositions', in Gibson and Ingold (1993).

Meillet, A. (1903), *Introduction à l'étude comparative des langues indo-européennes*. Hachette.

Meyer-Lübke, W. (1966), *Historische Grammatik der französischen Sprache. Zweiter Teil: Wortbildungslehre*. Carl Winter Universitätsverlag.

Michel, F. (1860), *Libri Psalmorum versio antiqua Gallica e cod. ms. in Bibl. Bodleiana asservato: una cum versione metrica aliisque monumentis pervetustis*. Oxonii: E typographeo academico.

Mithun, M. (1999), *The Languages of Native North America*. Cambridge University Press.

Morpurgo Davies, A. (1998), *Nineteenth Century Linguistics* (G. Lepschy (ed.), *History of Linguistics*, Vol. 4). Longman.

Moscati, S. (1999), *The World of the Phoenicians*. Phoenix Giant.

Moscati, S., Spitaler, A., Ullendorff, E., and von Soden, W. (1964), *An Introduction to the Comparative Grammar of the Semitic Languages*. Wiesbaden: Harrassowitz.

Nettle, D. (1999), *Linguistic Diversity*. Oxford University Press.

Nguyên, P. P (1992), 'La deixis en Vietnamien', in M. A. Morel (ed.), *La deixis*.

Presses Universitaires de France.
Niepokuj, M. (1997), *The Development of Verbal Reduplication in Indo-European.* Washington: Institute for the Study of Man.
Noonan, M. (1997), 'Versatile nominalizations,' in J. Bybee, J. Haiman and S. Thompson (eds.), *Essays on Language Function and Language Type. In Honor of T. Givón.* John Benjamins.
Oates, J. (1986), *Babylon* (revised edn). Thames & Hudson.
Olender, M. (1997), 'From the language of Adam to the pluralism of Babel'. *Mediterranean Historical Review,* 12: 51-9.
Olofsson, A. (1990), 'A participle caught in the act. On the prepositional use of *following*'. *Studia Neophilologica,* 62: 23-35.
Oppenheim, A. L. (1964), *Ancient Mesopotamia: Portrait of a Dead Civilization.* University of Chicago Press.
Orwell, G. (1946), 'Politics and the English Language', *Horizon,* Vol. 13, reprinted in Bolton and Crystal (1969).
Osthoff, H., and Brugmann, K. (1878), *Morphologische Untersuchungen auf dem Gebiete der indogermanischen Sprachen* I. Leipzig: S. Hirzel.
Paris, G. (1862), *Étude sur le rôle de l'accent Latin dans la langue Français.* Paris: A. Franck.
Parkinson, R. B. (1996), 'Khakheperreseneb and Traditional Belles Lettres', in P. Manuelian (ed.), *Studies in Honor of William Kelly Simpson.* Boston: Museum of Fine Arts, 647-54.
Parkinson, R. B. (1997), 'The Text of Khakheperreseneb; New Readings of EA 5645, and an unpublished Ostracon'. *Journal of Egyptian Archaeology,* 83:55-68.
Paul, H. (1880), *Principien der Sprachgeschichte.* Halle: Niemeyer.
Paul, J. (1967), *Jean Pauls Werke* (1763-1825) (ed. N. Miller). 5. Bd. *Vorschule der Ästhetik. Levana oder Erziehlehre. Politische Schriften.* München: C. Hanser.
Perkins, R. D. (1992), *Deixis, Grammar and Culture.* John Benjamins.
Peyraube, A. (1988), *Syntaxe diachronique du chinois: Evolution des constructions dative du XIVe siècle av. J.-C. au XVIIIe siècle.* Paris: Institut des Haute Etudes Chinoises, Collège de France.
Peyraube, A. (1996), 'Recent issues in Chinese historical syntax', in C. T. J. Huang and Y. H. A. Li (eds.), *New Horizons in Chinese Linguistics.* Kluwer, 161-213.
Pinker, S. (1984), *The Language Instinct.* Penguin.
Pinker, S. (2002), *The Blank Slate: The Modern Denial of Human Nature.* Viking.
Pinker, S., and Jackendoff, R. (forthcoming), 'The faculty of language: what's special about it?' *Cognition.*
Poole, J. (1646), *The English Accidence or, A short plaine, and easie way, for the more speedy attaining to the Latine tongue, by the help of the English.* Reprinted 1974, as *English Linguistics* 1500-1800, Vol. 5. Scolar Press.
Prunet, J. F., Béland, R., and Idrissi, A. (2000), 'The mental representation of

Semitic Words'. *Linguistic Inquiry*, 31:609–48.

Renfrew, C. (1996), 'The sapient behaviour paradox: how to test for potential', in P. Mellars and K. Gibson (eds.), *Modelling the Early Human Mind*. Cambridge: McDonald Institute.

Rosenbach, A. (2002), *Genitive Variation in English: Conceptual Factors in Synchronic and Diachronic Studies*. Mouton de Gruyter.

Rutt, H. T. (ed.) (1828), *Diary of Thomas Burton, Esq. Member in the Parliaments of Oliver and Richard Cromwell, from 1656 to 1659*. London: Henry Colburn.

Sáenz-Badillos, A. (1993), *A History of the Hebrew Language* (translated from the Spanish by J. Elwolde). Cambridge University Press.

Sampson, G. (1997), *Educating Eve: The 'Language Instinct' Debate*. Cassell.

Sapir, E. (1921), *Language: An Introduction to the Study of Speech*. New York: Harcourt, Brace.

Sasson, J. M. (ed.) (2000), *Civilizations of the Ancient Near East* (4 vols). Hendrickson Publishers.

Saussure, F. de (1879), *Mémoire sur le système primitif des voyelles dans les langues indo-européennes*. Leipsick: Teubner.

Savage-Rumbaugh, S., and Rumbaugh, D. M. (1993), 'The emergence of language', in Gibson and Ingold (1993).

Savage-Rumbaugh, S., Shanker, S. G., and Taylor, T. J. (1998), *Apes, Language, and the Human Mind*. Oxford University Press.

Sayers, D. L. (1963), 'The teaching of Latin: a new approach', in *The Poetry of Search and the Poetry of Statement, and Other Posthumous Essays on Literature, Religion and Language, by Dorothy L. Sayers*. Victor Gollancz, 177–200.

Scaliger, J. (1695), *Scaligerana, ou Bons Mots, Rencontres Agréables, et Remarques Judicieuses et Sçavantes de J. Scaliger*. Avec des notes de Mr. le Fevre, et de Mr. de Colomiès; le tout disposé par ordre alphabétique en cette nouv. éd. A Cologne (Amsterdam?) M.DC.XCV.

Scheffer, J. (1975), *The Progressive in English*. North-Holland Publishing.

Schiaparelli, L. (1929), *Codice diplomatico Longobardo, a cura di Luigi Schiaparelli*, Vol I. Roma: Istituto Storico Italiano.

Schleicher, A. (1850), *Die Sprachen Europas in systematischer Übersicht*. Bonn: König.

Schleicher, A. (1863), *Die Darwinsche Theorie und die Sprachwissenschaft*. Weimar: Hermann Böhlau.

Schwegler, A. (1990), *Analyticity and Syntheticity. A Diachronic Perspective with Special Reference to Romance Languages*. Mouton de Gruyter.

Sheridan, T. (1780), *A General Dictionary of the English Language: One main object of which, is, to establish a plain and permanent standard pronunciation. To which is prefixed a rhetorical grammar*. London: J. Dodsley, C. Dilly and J. Wilkie.

Skármeta, A. (1988), *Ardiente Paciencia* (Burning Patience), translated from the

Spanish by Katherine Silver. Methuen.

Smith, N., and Tsimpli, I. M. (1995), *The Mind of a Savant. Language Learning and Modularity*. Blackwell.

Steible, H. (1982), *Die altsumerischen Bau- und Weihinschriften* (Freiburger altorientalische Studien 5). Wiesbaden: Steiner.

Strachey, J. (ed.) (1767), *Rotuli Parliamentorum: ut et petitiones et placita in Parliamento tempore Edwardi R. I. (Edwardi II., Edwardi III., Ricardi II., Henrici IV., V., VI., Edwardi IV., Ricardi III., Henrici VII.*, 1278-1503.)

Szemerényi, O. (1973), 'La théorie des laryngeals de Saussure à Kuryłowicz et à Benveniste'. *Bulletin de la Société de Linguistique de Paris*, 68:1-25.

Szemerényi, O. (1996), *Introduction to Indo-European Linguistics* (4th edn). Oxford University Press.

Tanz, C. (1980), *Studies in the Acquisition of Deictic Terms*. Cambridge University Press.

Tax, P. W. (1981), *Die Werke Notkers des Deutschen. Neue Ausgabe ; Bd. 9. Der Psalter: Psalm 51–100*. Tübingen: Niemeyer.

Taylor, I., and Taylor, M. M. (1983), *The Psychology of Reading*. New York: Academic Press.

Testen, D. (1998), 'The derivational role of the Semitic N-Stem'. *Zeitschrift für Assyriologie und vorderasiatische Archäologie*, 88:127-45.

Tomasello, M. (2003), *Constructing a Language: A Usage-based Theory of Language Acquisition*. Harvard University Press.

Touratier, C. (1975), 'Rhotacisme synchronique du latin classique et rhotacisme diachronique', *Glotta, Zeitschrift für griechische und lateinische Sprache*, 53:246-81.

Trask, R. L. (1995), 'On the history of the non-finite verb forms in Basque', in J. I. Hualde, J. A. Lakarra and R. L. Trask (eds.), *Towards a History of the Basque Language*. John Benjamins, 207-34.

Traugott, E. C. (1992), 'Syntax', in R. M. Hogg (ed.), *Cambridge History of the English Language, Vol. I: The beginning to 1066*. Cambridge University Press, 168-269.

Traugott, E. C., and Heine, B. (eds.) (1991), *Approaches to Grammaticalization* (2 vols). John Benjamins.

Traugott, E. C., and Dasher, R. B. (2002), *Regularity in Semantic Change*. Cambridge University Press.

Tropper, J. (1990), *Der ugaritische Kausativstamm und die Kausativbildungen des Semitischen*. Ugarit Verlag.

Trudgill, P. (1992), 'Dialect typology and social structure', in E. H. Jahr (ed.), *Language Contact: Theoretical and Empirical Studies*. Mouton de Gruyter, 195-212.

Tschirch, F. (1955), *1200 Jahre deutsche Sprache: die Entfaltung der deutschen*

Sprachgestalt in ausgewählten Stücken der Bibelübersetzung vom Ausgang des 8. Jahrhunderts bis in die Gegenwart. Berlin: de Gruyter.

Twain, M. (1880), *A Tramp Abroad*. Chatto & Windus.

Valesio, P. (1968), 'The Romance synthetic future pattern and its first attestations'. *Lingua*, 20:113-61.

Veenhof, K. (1975), 'An Old Akkadian private letter: with a note on *ṣiāḫum/ṣīḫtum*'. *Jaarbericht van het Vooraziatisch-Egyptisch Genootschap, Ex Oriente Lux*, 24:105-10.

Versteegh, K. (1997), *The Arabic Language*. Edinburgh University Press.

Walker, C. B. F. (1987), *Cuneiform*. British Museum Press.

Watkins, C. (2000), *The American Heritage Dictionary of Indo-European Roots* (2nd edn). Houghton Mifflin Company.

Weigel, H. (1974), *Die Leiden der jungen Wörter. Ein Antiwörterbuch*. Zürich: Artemis.

Westermann, D. H. (1954), *Wörterbuch der Ewe-Sprache*. Berlin: Akademie Verlag.

Wolfram, H. (ed.) (1982), *Quellen zur Geschichte des 7. und 8. Jahrhunderts (Fontes historiam saeculorum septimi et octavi illustrantes). Die vier Bücher der Chroniken des sogenannten Fredegar*. Darmstadt: Wissenschaftliche Buchgesellschaft.

Woodworth, N. L. (1991), *From Noun to Verb and Verb to Noun: A Cross-linguistic Study of Class-changing Morphology* (unpubl. Ph.D. diss., University of New York at Buffalo).

Wray, A. (ed.) (2002), *The Transition to Language*. Oxford University Press.

Wright, J. (1900), *The English Dialect Dictionary: being the complete Vocabulary of all dialect words still in use, or known to have been in use during the last 200*. Vol. II. London: Frowde.

Zaborski, A. (1975), *The Verb in Cushitic* (Studies in Hamito-Semitic I). Warszawa: PWN.

Zaborski, A. (1991), 'Biconsonantal roots and triconsonantal root variation in Semitic: solutions and prospects', in A. S. Kaye (ed.), *Semitic Studies in Honor of Wolf Leslau on the Occasion of His 85th Birthday*, Vol. 2, 1675-1703. Wiesbaden: Harrassowitz.

Zaborski, A. (2001), 'Verbale Flexion und Derivation mit T und M/N – ein etymologischer Versuch', in S. Wild and H. Schild (eds.), *Kultur, Recht und Politik in muslimischen Gesellschaften* (Akten des 27. Deutschen Orientalistentages). Vol. 1, 593-9.

Glossary

(The definitions of linguistic terms given here are often simplified, and refer exclusively to the way the terms are used in this book. For the definitive guide to linguistic terminology, see Matthews (1997), *The Concise Oxford Dictionary of Linguistics*.)

ACCUSATIVE: The case of a direct object of the verb. In English, only some pronouns show a distinction between 'nominative' (the subject case, as in '*he* bit the dog') and 'accusative' (the direct object case, as in 'the dog bit *him*'). In some languages, however, nouns show the same distinction. In Latin, for example, the noun 'consul' would appear as *consul* in the nominative case (for instance in saying 'the consul bit me'), but the form *consulem* would be used in the accusative case (for instance in saying 'I bit the consul').

ADJECTIVE: A syntactic category; a group of words that serve to modify a noun, and typically include properties (such as 'big' or 'old'). See discussion in Appendix A: Flipping Categories on the nature of syntactic categories.

ADVERB: A syntactic category; a group of words that serve to modify a verb, as in 'why are you going *slowly*?' See discussion in Appendix A: Flipping Categories on the nature of syntactic categories.

APPENDAGE: Used in this book for elements which accompany a noun, provide additional information about it, and together with it build a phrase. The typical appendage is what is traditionally known as 'modifier', an element which is not obligatory in the sentence, and does not have a direct relation with any other element in the sentence except with the noun it modifies, for example the adjective 'sharp' in '*sharp* stones'. Under the term 'appendage' I also include other elements that accompany the noun, such as 'determiners' (for instance the definite article 'the' in '*the* sharp stone') or quantifiers (for example 'all' in '*all* the sharp stones').

APPOSITION: The juxtaposition on the same level of two elements of the same syntactic role, as in 'my cousin' and 'the manager' in the sentence 'my cousin, the manager, hired me for the job'. Whole clauses can also be in apposition, as in 'the world is round, I heard about it yesterday'.

ARTICLE: A grammatical word which can mark a participant as definite ('*the* girl') or indefinite ('*a* girl').

ASSIMILATION: A type of effort-saving sound change by which one sound becomes more similar (or identical) to another sound in its environment. For example, the original *n* was assimilated to the following *r* in ***inr**elevant* → ***irr**elevant*.

AUXILIARY: A syntactic category of 'helping verbs', which can accompany the main verb in the sentence and indicate nuances of the action such as tense ('*will* go') or modality ('*may have* gone', '*must* go'). See discussion in Appendix A: Flipping Categories on the nature of syntactic categories.

CASE: In some languages, nouns and pronouns can have different forms depending on their role in the sentence. These different forms (usually different endings) are called 'cases'. Some English pronouns, for example, make a three-way distinction: *he, him, his*: 'he$_{\text{NOMINATIVE}}$ threw him$_{\text{ACCUSATIVE}}$ out of his$_{\text{GENITIVE}}$ house'. In languages such as Russian, Tamil or Latin, such differences can be seen on nouns, not just on pronouns.

CLAUSE: A syntactic unit that can be identical to a (simple) sentence, or a part of a (complex) sentence. In English, a clause consists of one main verb together with all its participants and modifiers. A simple sentence, such as 'this sentence is made up of just one clause', is made up of just one clause. But a complex sentence, such as 'this is a sentence which contains more than one clause', contains two clauses: a main clause 'this is a sentence', and a subordinate clause 'which contains more than one clause'.

CONJUNCTION: A word such as 'and', 'if', 'when', 'because', which introduces a coordinate or a subordinate clause.

CONSONANT: A sound (such as *p, v, d, k*) produced by obstructing the flow of air in some part of the mouth or throat.

COORDINATION: The juxtaposition of two clauses on the same level, usually with a conjunction such as 'and' between them ('I came in and saw her').

DATIVE: The 'giving case', or the case of the 'indirect object', typically used for the role of the recipient in the action of giving ('she gave it *to him*'), or for roles modelled on that of a recipient ('she showed it *to him*').

DEFINITE ARTICLE: A grammatical element, such as English 'the', which typically marks a participant as having been already mentioned or as previously known to the hearer.

DIACHRONIC VARIATION: Changes in a language over the course of time.

DIRECT OBJECT: The grammatical role of the second core participant in an action. Patients of simple physical actions are the prototypical direct objects (for instance 'the spear' in 'the man broke *the spear*'). But many other actions, such as 'love' or 'see' also take a direct object, although their second participant cannot strictly speaking be regarded as a 'patient'.

FRICATIVE: A consonant such as *f*, *v*, or *th* that is produced without a complete blockage of the air, but through the friction produced by the air's movement through some narrow passage, for example, between the lips (*f*, *v*), or between the tongue and the teeth (*th*).

GENDER: Any grammatical classification system of nouns. Gender can be based not only on sex (male vs. female), but also on other essential features, such as animacy (animate vs. inanimate).

GENITIVE: The case used for a noun or pronoun that modifies another noun, typically for the 'possessor'. In English, the genitive can be marked with a suffix *-s*, as in *George's* and *manager's* in '*George's* dog bit the *manager's* daughter'.

GRAMMAR: The structure of a language. In linguistics, 'grammar' is not a synonym for 'good grammar' or for 'speaking properly'. Studying the grammar of a language does not mean prescribing how people *should* speak it, but rather describing how they *do*.

GRAMMATICAL WORD: A word such as 'than', 'a', or 'of', which does not carry meaning on its own, but serves in a structural role of specifying the relations between content words. See discussion in Chapter 5 and Appendix A: Flipping Categories on the difference between content words and grammatical words.

ICONICITY: A reflection of reality in the organization of language. One example of iconicity is the principle by which the order of events in reality is mirrored in the order in which they are expressed in language.

INDEFINITE ARTICLE: A grammatical element, such as English 'a', which marks a noun as not definite. (See 'Definite article'.)

INDIRECT OBJECT: The grammatical role which typically includes the recipient of a giving action (for instance *George* in 'she gave the book to *George*') as well as participants in other actions modelled on a giving action ('she showed it to *George*'). (See also 'Dative'.)

INDO-EUROPEAN: A language family that includes most of the modern languages of Europe (except Basque, Hungarian, Finnish and Estonian), as well as many languages from Iran to India. The prehistoric ancestor language, from which all modern Indo-European languages developed, is called Proto-Indo-European.

INFINITIVE: A form of the verb, found among others after auxiliary verbs such as 'will' or 'can', which does not mark person. In English, for example, third person singular is marked on verbs with a suffix *-s*, as in 'she walk*s*'. But after an auxiliary, the infinitive form 'walk' is used instead: 'she can walk', not 'she can walk*s*'.

INTRANSITIVE VERB: A verb such as 'walk' or 'die', which has only one core participant (called the subject), and does not take a direct object (as opposed to a 'transitive verb').

MODALITY: The expression of what the speaker thinks about an action ('should happen', 'ought not to happen') or knows about it ('couldn't have happened', 'must have happened').

MORPHOLOGY: The internal structure of words.

NOMINALIZATION: The process of turning a verb into a noun. The nominalization endings *-ing* and *-ion*, for instance, turn verbs such as 'build' and 'legislate' into nouns: 'building', 'legislation'.

NOMINATIVE: The subject case. (See 'Case', 'Subject', 'Accusative'.)

NOUN: A syntactic category that typically includes all 'things' (people, animals, inanimate objects), and various other abstract concepts (such as 'day', or 'movement') that are represented in language *as* things. See discussion in Appendix A: Flipping Categories on the nature of syntactic categories.

OBJECT: Used in this book as a shorthand for 'direct object'.

PARTICIPANT: Someone or something that is involved in an action. A participant can be expressed either by just one word, for instance [Sarah] and [cats] are the two participants in the sentence '[Sarah] breeds [cats]'. But a participant can also be expressed by a whole phrase, for example '[the woman next door] breeds [small Siamese cats with yellow spots on their foreheads]'. (See 'Appendage'.)

PARTICIPIAL CLAUSE: A relative clause whose verb is a participle, or a 'verbal adjective'. In 'the lion running after the fox', 'running after the fox' is a participial clause.

PARTICIPLE: A verbal adjective, that is, a verb that is used to modify a noun, as in 'the *crying* girl' or 'my *bleeding* thumb'.

PASSIVE: A construction in which the direct object of a verb turns into the subject. The sentence 'a bullet killed the soldier' can be turned into a passive construction, by making the direct object 'soldier' the subject: 'the soldier was killed by a bullet'.

PATIENT: The participant on which an action is performed (literally, the one that 'suffers' the action), as for instance *the spear* in 'the man broke *the spear*', or 'the man threw *the spear*'.

PERSON: A distinction between forms referring to the speaker ('I/we'), which are called 'first person', forms referring to the addressee ('you'), which are called 'second person', and forms referring to people or objects that are neither the speakers nor the addressee ('he/she/it/they/George/the cat), which are called 'third person'.

POSTPOSITION: A grammatical word which performs the same function as a preposition but appears *after* a noun, rather than before it.

PREFIX: A grammatical element which is tagged on to the beginning of a word.

PREPOSITION: A syntactic category, a group of words which appear before a noun (or more accurately, before a 'noun phrase', that is, the noun together with its entourage of appendages), and specify various types of relations, such as spatial (*in* the house) or temporal (*from* January). Prepositions can also mark the precise role of a participant in an action, for instance 'beneficiary' ('I did it *for* George') or 'agent' ('he was murdered *by* the butler').

PRONOUN: Used in this book as a shorthand for 'personal pronoun', a category of words such as 'I', 'you', 'she', 'it', which are said to take the place of a noun in the sentence (or more accurately, the place of a 'noun phrase', that is, the noun together with its entourage of appendages). Traditionally, personal pronouns are divided into 'first person pronouns' ('I', 'we', 'us'), which refer to the speaker(s), 'second person pronouns' ('you', 'your'), which refer to the addressee(s), and 'third person pronouns' (such as 'she', 'it', 'them') which are used to refer succinctly to other people or objects that have already been mentioned, or whose precise identity is clear from the context.

PROTO: (As in 'Proto-Indo-European', or 'Proto-Semitic') A designation for a presumed prehistoric language from which various attested descendants have sprung.

REFLEXIVE: A construction used when the two participants in an action are one and the same, as, for example, with the English reflexive pronoun 'herself' in 'she hurt *herself*'.

RELATIVE CLAUSE: A subordinate clause that serves as an appendage to a noun. The clauses in subscript are relative clauses: 'here is a subordinate clause$_{\text{which serves as an appendage to a noun}}$', or 'a clause$_{\text{that serves as an appendage to a noun}}$ is called a relative clause'.

ROOT: Used in this book for the form of the verb which supplies its basic meaning, and to which other elements can be added to indicate various nuances. In Latin, the root *ed-* gives the basic meaning 'eat', and various endings are used to indicate the nuances: *edo* 'I eat', *edemur* 'we will be eaten', etc. In the Semitic languages, the root is not a pronounceable string of sounds, but a group of only consonants, such as Arabic `s-l-m` 'be at peace'.

SCHWA: A reduced vowel (transcribed ə) found in English words like *elephant*, pronounced {eləfənt}.

SEMITIC: A language family that includes among others Arabic, Hebrew and Aramaic, as well as extinct languages such as Akkadian and Phoenician.

STEM: Used in this book to refer to a root which is a continuous and pronounceable string of sounds (such as Latin *ed-* 'eat' or *dict-* 'say'), as opposed to the purely consonantal roots of Semitic (such as Arabic `s-l-m` 'be at peace').

SUBJECT: The grammatical role of the participant about which the main assertion is made, and in which the agent of simple actions such as 'kick' or 'come' typically appears, as in '*the horse* kicked a boy, or '*the boy* will go to hospital'.

SUBJUNCTIVE: In English, a form of the verb (by now almost extinct) used in some types of subordinate clauses. For example, 'I wouldn't do it if I *were* you', or 'lest it *be* thought that . . .'

SUBORDINATE CLAUSE: A clause which cannot stand on its own, and which functions as an element of another clause. A relative clause is one type of subordinate clause.

SUFFIX: An ending. A grammatical element attached to the end of a word.

SYNCHRONIC VARIATION: Variation in a language at any given point in time.

SYNTACTIC CATEGORY: A group of words which have a similar distribution in the sentence, and appear in the same 'slots'. For example, 'nouns' such as 'nose', 'shoes', or 'egocentricity' can all appear in the noun-slot X in 'your remarkable X'. See discussion in Appendix A: Flipping Categories on the nature and definition of syntactic categories.

SYNTAX: The part of the grammar (that is, the structure) of a language which comprises the relations between words in the sentence (rather than the internal structure of words 'morphology', or the sound system of a language 'phonology').

TEMPLATE: Used in this book for patterns of mostly vowels in the Semitic language, into which the consonantal root is inserted. For example, the Arabic template ◯*a*◯*i*◯*a* forms the past tense in the third person 'he', so inserting into it the root `s-l-m` 'be at peace' gives ⓢ*a*ⓛ*i*ⓜ*a* ('he was at peace').

TENSE: The expression of the time of an action.

TRANSITIVE VERB: A verb (such as 'kick', 'love', 'see') that refers to an action with two core participants, the second of which is a direct object (as opposed to an intransitive verb such as 'walk' or 'die', which has only one core participant).

VERB: A syntactic category; a group of words that make the main assertion about the subject, and which typically denote actions. See discussion in Appendix A: Flipping Categories on the nature and definition of syntactic categories.

VOICED: A sound produced with the vibration of the vocal cords. The consonants *d, b, v*, for instance, are voiced.

VOICELESS: A sound produced without vibrating the vocal cords. The consonants *t, p, f*, for instance, are voiceless.

VOWEL: A sound (such as *a, e, o*) that is produced with little obstruction to the flow of air (as opposed to a consonant).

Acknowledgments

This book has benefited to an exceptional degree from the insights and advice of colleagues, friends and family. Its shortcomings would have been tenfold were it not for their scrutiny of earlier drafts. For their generosity in sharing their time and knowledge, I am deeply indebted to Sasha Aikhenvald, Eleanor Coghill, Michal Deutscher, Bob Dixon, Avrahamit Edan, Olga Fischer, Jim Hurford, Tomas Klenke, Bert Kouwenberg, Peter Matthews, Ferdinand von Mengden, Reviel Netz, Nicholas Postgate, Uri Rom, Anette Rosenbach, Katharine Scarfe Beckett, Michael Steen, Peter Steen, Balázs Szendrői, Kriszta Szendrői, Ragnhild Tønnessen.

I am grateful to Caroline Dawnay, whose literary instincts helped to make the book publishable; to Ravi Mirchandani, for his deft editorial guiding hand; to Sara Bershtel, for her astute editing at the eleventh hour; and to Caroline Knight, Annie Lee, and especially Andrea Belloli, for seeing the book through production.

I also wish to thank the following for their help: Jan Gerrit Dercksen, Ben Haring, Paul Heggarty, Catherine Heyrendt, Bram Jagersma, Alwin Kloekhorst, Guus Kroonen, Bettelou Los, Robert Meekings, Hans Frede Nielsen, Ségolène Plyer, Sophie van Romburgh, Gerjan van Schaaik, Özlem Schmidt, Claudia di Sciacca, Christina Staffe, Rosemary Steen, Marten Stol, Klaas Veenhof, Jake Wilson.

Much of the research for the book was done during a fellowship at St John's College, Cambridge, and I owe a debt of gratitude to the Master and Fellows of St John's for the privilege of working in such a stimulating academic environment.

My chief thanks, however, go to those whose encouragement, judgement, and inspiration were indispensable from first to last: Jan Hendrik Schmidt and, above all, Janie Steen.

G. D.

Amsterdam, December 2004

Credits

P. 5: Cesare Maccari, *Cicero Denouncing Catiline*. Palazzo Madama, Rome. Photo: Scala, Florence; p. 83: Lazarus Sichling, *Jacob and Wilhelm Grimm*. Photo: Mary Evans Picture Library, London; p. 102: Sir William Jones. Photo: Mary Evans Picture Library, London; p. 104: Ferdinand de Saussure. Photo: Granger Collection, New York; p. 107 top: Aerial view of Hattusa today. Photo: © copyright Peter Neve, reproduced with permission of Peter Neve and the Deutsches Archäologisches Institut; p. 107 bottom: Gouta Nanami, Impression of Hattusa in its heyday. © copyright shirogumi.inc. www.nanami3d.com; p. 108: A copy of a Hittite cuneiform tablet (KUB 13.4, 65-72). Reproduced with permission of the Bildarchiv Preußischer Kulturbesitz; p. 117: Removal van in Athens. Author's photo; p. 159: Justinian and Kavadh. Author's photo; p. 180: A letter from the Old Akkadian period. Author's photo, with permission of Radboud University, Nijmegen; p. 182 clockwise from top left: Head of Sargon I. Iraq Museum. Photo: Giraudon; www.bridgeman.co.uk; Piero della Francesca, *Legend of the True Cross: Adoration of the Sacred Piece of Wood and Meeting between Solomon and the Queen of Sheba*, detail. San Francesco, Arezzo. Photo: Scala, Florence; Silver shekel of Carthage depicting Hannibal, from the Mogente Hoard, Valencia, Spain, *c.* 230 BC. Photo: © copyright The Trustees of The British Museum; Kahlil Gibran photographed in 1921. Photo: © E.O. Hoppe/ CORBIS; Haile Selassie, Emperor of Ethiopia. Photo: Mary Evans Picture Library, London; p. 222: Seal of Murshili II. Reproduced from *Ugaritica III*, p. 90, with permission of the Librairie Orientaliste Paul Geuthner; p. 263 left: The 'Queen of the Night' (Inanna, or Ishtar, Old Babylonian period). Photo: © copyright The Trustees of The British Museum; p. 263 right: Stone plaque depicting Enannatum. Photo: © copyright The Trustees of The British Museum; p. 271: August Schleicher. Photo: AKG Images, London; p. 296 left to right: Portrait of G. F. Handel by Hudson, *c.* 1748. Photo: © Lebrecht Music and Arts Photo Library; Portrait of C. W. Gluck. Photo: © Lebrecht Music and Arts Photo Library; The cook (Gustavus Waltz). Reproduced from William C.

Index